**The Social Life
of Financial Derivatives**

The
Social Life
of Financial
Derivatives

Markets, Risk, and Time

Edward LiPuma

DUKE UNIVERSITY PRESS

Durham and London

2017

Cataloging-in-Publication Data is available from the Library of Congress.
ISBN 9780822369561 (hardcover : alk. paper)
ISBN 9780822369561 (pbk. : alk. paper)
ISBN 9780822372837 (ebook)

Cover art: Design and illustration by Matthew Tauch

For my daughter, Laura; my wife, Susan;
and my friend and inspiration, Randy Martin

Contents

ACKNOWLEDGMENTS   ix

Prefacing a Theory of the Derivative   1

Chapter 1   Originating the Derivative   27

Chapter 2   Social Theory and the Market for
the Production of Financial Knowledge   81

Chapter 3   Outline of a Social Theory of Finance   116

Chapter 4   Temporality and the Financial Markets   144

Chapter 5   Theorizing the Financial Markets Socially   170

Chapter 6   Rituality and the Production of Financial Markets   199

Chapter 7   The Speculative Ethos   229

Chapter 8   The Social Habitus of Financial Work   267

Chapter 9   The Social Dimensions of Black-Scholes   304

Chapter 10   Derivatives and Wealth   336

NOTES   355

REFERENCES   389

INDEX   399

Acknowledgments

I am entirely responsible for the text but not for the ideas. What follows, both theoretically and thematically, is the ongoing result of my participation in the Cultures of Finance Group, which as I will relate was far more than what academics normally mean by a group. What defines and animates the finance group is an intellectual entwinement of the deepest order. Each idea is forged in and through its involvement with the ideas of the other members, such that every concept would have had a different and lesser shape if developed separately. Incorporated into the root of each new idea or theme are the vision and insights of the group. It is an assemblage that cannot be deconstructed or decomposed into its original elements because the process of incorporation centers on what can only be called a dialectical fusion. From Benjamin Lee, my collaborator and friend, I continue to learn the radiant value of thinking across the grain, more relationally than I would do on my own; from Randy Martin I learned the importance of ideas as a form of play and to never abandon the political uptake and power of social thought; from Robert Meister I learned a new way of thinking about finance some fifteen or so degrees removed from my usual reality; from Arjun Appadurai I learned the importance of keeping in contact with my anthropological roots; and from Robert Wosnitzer I learned that for theory to stay grounded it can't stray too far from practice. I would like to thank my wonderful friend Moishe Postone, whose theorization of production-centered capitalism was the ground I pushed against to create an exposition of circulatory capital. In the end as in the beginning, good theory is like the neutron of an atom, whose existence and value depends on its engagement with the protons of practice and the intellectual enlightenment from the encircling electrons. For collaborations at their highest constitute the most majestic form of plagiarism.

Prefacing a Theory of the Derivative

Crises seem to arrive from another dimension, somehow beyond what we know or can remember. At first, only fragments register, and then even when the crisis unfolds and destroys, its inner design can remain withheld for a long time. — EDWARD LIPUMA 2015

If nothing that has happened these past seven years or so [2008–2015] has shaken any of your long-held economic beliefs, either you haven't been paying attention or you haven't been honest with yourself. — PAUL KRUGMAN 2015

The financial crisis of 2008 inspired this book. It is thus, on that account, about derivatives. For derivatives not only motivated the 2008 crisis, they are instrumental in transforming the character of crisis itself. More in a moment about the dimensions of contemporary crises: for now simply note that the crisis speaks that finance is replacing production as the dynamic of capitalism. Not everyone thinks so, either that derivatives animated the crisis or that crisis itself represents something new owing to the ascension of circulatory capitalism. That is, capitalism with derivatives as ushering in a turning in the character of capital itself which, as it makes this truth our reality, tells us that we need to construct a better theory of financial capital. This project entails a more socially informed playbook—beginning with the construction of an articulate social theory—for grasping the derivative, its markets, and the agency of those who drive it. We need this heightened sociality as a condition of self-understanding the economy of the present and its politics. That is the message of the crisis; though most Marxisms and all of neoclassical economics disagree.[1] Even through a certain embarrassment, both feigned and genuine, about having no theoretically real account of the crisis, and, more importantly, no account of the derivative and the ascension of speculative capital. And thus the motivation for offering an approach that shades into an experimental practice of the present. Whatever one's views, the reality, our reality, is that derivatives matter greatly because they are constitutive of the economics that matter to the politics of the present and trajectory of our collective future. Especially the left needs to remember that a politics of condemnology, however warranted, however just, is not a substitute for a bone-deep theoretization of the derivative.

The book has a narrative arc. Though the results unfold cumulatively like a set of transparencies that, one laid over the other, produce a composite so that the succession of chapters throw light on one another and the themes and counterthemes weave a more encompassing composition. In this composite image, the derivative represents, and is the exemplar in the financial realm, of the emergence of a transformed form of the social. *The argument is that derivative-driven capitalism, as exemplified by the financial markets, is reproduced by the transformed form of the social that it is instrumental in producing.* A dynamic, historically specific and directional, has been set in train in which the social that engenders the derivative is transformed by it. A transformed dynamic to capital, to the production of culture and knowledge, to the institutions of finance, and to the design of subjectivity has now entered the house. On an even larger scale, derivative-driven capitalism introduces a transformed form of capital which is redesigning the formula for social reproduction. Social theory was not ready for this revolution and it is unprepared for its revelation. But then again, a revolution (be it industrial or derivative) takes on the appearance of clear, linear, ordained process only when, in the work of creating a retrospective narrative that will serve as a foundational fiction of their success, the winners remove the contingency, artifice, and violence. Then set in gear a re-history machine that recasts the revolution. In the revised storyline, which naturalizes all that is social, the derivative materializes as the natural destiny of an economy in which the market is the arbiter of our reproduction.

But no matter the ideology, there is the crisis that years later won't let go of our economic reality. Luckily, such crises have a peculiar quality: they illuminate the hidden sociality of a market, which moves the participants to apprehend the crisis by reference to the sociality they've worked so hard to repress. Crisis can also allow the discovery of a social unknown: herein, the performativity of the market. That the social remains off-stage is itself social: it codes how the culture of capitalism presents the social in cameos so veiled and so misrecognized that they are invisible to the financial eye. In normal times that is. Normal meaning when volatility still has the bit in its mouth, the pricing models hum, and the participants have faith in one another and in the markets. In the throes of crisis, however, financial markets tend to resemble nothing so much as a medieval carnival in which, for a circumscribed time, the world's inverted, forcing the participants' reflections to probe like instruments into a wound they illuminate the more they fulminate. First of all for plausible answers as to why the markets imploded and then to reassure themselves that the state of emergency has passed. And finally, to summon the spirits of absolution and amnesia, and to announce that reason's resurrection has lifted the spell of recklessness and that, on closer inspection, it turns out that nothing that terrible ever really happened. Thus, the logic of the claim—what lawyers refer to as a theory of the case—that underwrites the suit filed by American International Group (October 2014) to recover money it paid the government for its bailout.

The reciprocal evolution of capitalism and science means that the production of knowledge about the economy has become inseparable from the science of how it works. Until the crisis the only official economic theory was that systemic failure is impossible (Friedman 2012), a prognostication made on the grounds that markets are efficient and self-correcting. Systemic failure is supposedly a seven, eight, nine sigma event (a sigma being a standard deviation), meaning that it is as improbable as winning nine or ten state lotteries consecutively (or having a Marxist like David Harvey recieve the Nobel Prize in Economics). Until the crisis, the official Marxist theory was that systemic crisis is all but inevitable, though only through the mechanics of production in that financial circulation is supposedly parasitic of the production of value and thus the contradictions inherent in its reproduction. But reality eventually has its say and the history of science reports that this assuredly is not the first time that "could-not-happen events" have undermined established paradigms, even as that history confirms that adherents never see, let alone anticipate, the gathering storm. This history also reveals that when the life of a theory—and with it the livelihood and self-esteem of its advocates—depends on the integrity of the theory's assumptions this generally leads to a suspension of critical judgment. In its place flowers a religious like fervor, disguised as scholastic commitment, to defend the assumptions against theoretical critique and deflect the insults instigated by damaging evidence. As Fyodor Dostoevsky observed, "it is difficult to change Gods" (*The Possessed*). Nevertheless, crises create openings; in this case at hand, an invitation to entertain an approach founded on circulation and the social. Because neoclassical economics and Marxism have traditionally marginalized the sphere of circulation, the question required by our present predicament is what would a social theory of the derivative look like?

The crisis head-slapped those still in doubt that the flow of capital is more than an assistant of production, more than a monetary bridge between what we produce and what we consume. The crisis illustrated that finance was now about more than allocating capital to enhance commodity production: increasingly, finance was fixated on speculation, the deployment of opportunistic and nomadic streams of capital, the creation of derivative instruments to game risk, and above all the violence of systemic collapse. Indeed, the crisis generated an extraordinary *violence*, in people's dispossession of their jobs, homes, life savings, retirements, and their hopeful vision of their future. Families were disfigured, communities dismembered, and thus our basic human security compromised. Sometimes the effects of violence are more violent than the original insult, exemplified by the financial crisis. Few images are more stark than row after row of abandoned houses in cities like Detroit or Cleveland, the bodies of the homeowners having moved on, the boarded up houses take on the appearance of so many decapitated heads, whose slow decay will poison the community for years to come.[2] From an economic and political standpoint, and again from the standpoint of a collective moral conscience or the creation of a desired society founded on emancipatory justice, it is thus important to try our best to grasp the character of the derivative markets that set off the destruction. And may do so again. No matter how remote from the ordinary they appear, no matter how distant from the conventional array of disciplinary concerns. The claim is a judgment: that social science has a moral obligation to hone its analytical weapons on the derivative markets. And that this obligation entails an investigation that drills down into the sociostructures of derivative finance. An investigation that cannot be reduced to clean linear narratives, the simplifying idea that an untimely release of our "animal spirits" derailed an efficient market, a morality play of good against bad, the solipsism of the moral hazard, or readily digestible oppositions such as the oft repeated one of "Wall Street versus Main Street." But above all, an analysis that cannot be reduced to a language that refuses to be socially analytical to the point of demanding our full concentration.

This book is not easy. It asks for your sustained attention on the promise I'll do everything in my power to make the social ground and implications of the derivative more visible. This book contains a series of analyses of the derivative and its markets from the perspective of social theory. To gain this perspective there's no way to avoid the stilts of elevated language: notions like performativity, objectification, and, above all, sociality are critical to the work's conceptual architecture. For they allow us to treat ordinary actions as portals through which the investigation can access a social world that is free of binaries but bountiful of deeply configured relationships. I will seek to follow the advice of Wislawa Szymborska, the luminous Polish poet who, in writing about the political economy of her homeland, observed that it was first necessary to "borrow weighty words" and then labor mightily so that they become lighter and clearer.[3] And so I have borrowed, retooled, and sometimes invented new concepts to help us assemble and theorize a social theory of the derivative. The concept of a *social theory* is, above all, a currency that speaks a willingness to engage, to theorize, what is social about our collective life and our experiences as people.

The social theoretical approach advanced here differs from conventional economic analysis, but also from analyses emanating from Marxist, postmodern, and science studies perspectives. Given the distance that needs to be covered, I will stop and spell out the differences only when—as is the case for neoliberal economics—they help illuminate the derivative by illuminating the scientific ideology that underpins technical models and state governance. Even on this issue, my goal is less to critique neoliberal economics for blinding itself to the sociality of the market than to theorize and thematize the social grounding of the derivative. Each chapter speaks to the issues derivatives present to make sense of how derivatives are structured, how their markets work, and how and to what effect the logos of the derivative inflects the lives of households everywhere. I see the account as a theoretical montage, a process of constructing a composite perspective by suturing together elements of social theory wherever and whenever they prove useful. I see the approach as an enlightened materialism: by which I mean respecting objective sociostructures without adopting an objectivist theory of objectification (which elevates structure over agency and production over circulation). Correlatively, this entails an abiding respect for the work of the subject without succumbing to a love affair with agency (which cannot help but privilege interactions and networks over sociostructures). By this concept of montage, I point toward a theory of derivative-driven capitalism grounded in contemporary social reproduction. Such a theory would apprehend that the way we are producing culture, knowledge, and subjectivity is bound up with derivative-driven capitalism. Inexorably and intrinsically so. The centering view is that the derivative is the form of value production and derivative markets a machine of accumulation commensurate with circulatory capitalism. Especially for many working-class households—meaning those households who survive through the sale of their members' labor (be it physical and/or intellectual) rather than from a return on assets—these new forms of value and accumulation appears as a financialization of life.

History matters even if this account does not focus on the history of the derivative markets. The social conditions that led to the ascension of the derivative and cradled the financial crisis did not arrive full born. They evolved unevenly but cumulatively, like the intermittent and explosive lava flows from a volcano, until a new terrain took shape. They originate in the early 1970s with the demise of Bretton Woods, the extraordinary escalation in petroleum prices, and establishment of derivative markets. These markets gained their full momentum in the realization of the 1987 crash when it become clear that derivatives can engender the volatility that they trade. So there arose capital markets driven by derivatives, designed to disassemble and reassemble capital itself, leveragable beyond anything formerly imaginable, founded on the newly minted notion of abstract risk, animated by speculative, nomadic, opportunistic pools of capital whose ties with production had been severed, and inhabited by hedge funds, nonbank banks, and other speculative investment vehicles like proprietary trading desks.[4] Few things are more distinctive of derivative markets than the immediacy, rapidity, and creative impulse of their evolution. Most remarkably, a directional dynamic toward the fabrication of a regime of labor/work founded on employing risk driven capital assemblages, i.e. derivatives, to make speculative wagers on market volatility in a self-valorizing pursuit of monetary and symbolic profits. To do this, finance would be driven to innovate new ways to dissemble and reassemble capital, the impulse power of creative destruction, what capitalism said was its source of perpetual economic growth, all too easily becoming self-destructive creativity.

As noted, the overtext for the analysis is the 2008 crisis and its seemingly eternal aftermath, though the ultimate objective is to help fire a conversation on the creation of a sociotheoretical approach to finance capital and, more broadly, a capitalism whose driving dynamic is circulation. The crisis is central for four reasons: (1) it is continuing to cause enormous damage to working-class households as it denudes them of their wealth and simultaneously increases their risks and precarity; (2) the crisis exposes the sociality that the financial field renders invisible on condition of its reproduction; (3) the crisis opens the reinforced door that has sealed off finance as the exclusive dominion of neoclassical economics; and (4) the crisis begins to point the way towards an account of capitalism that links the financial crisis to the crisis of work.

Indeed, though the echoes are already fading, the seemingly impossible volatility of finance markets and their near death experience resonated across the spaces where the scienctization of the market and the market's use of science cohabit. A social reading is that beyond the manifest aspects of crisis and rescue what has happened to us has laid bare the underlying social foundations of the derivative and its markets, in the process calling into question the formal models that academics had canonized as settled science and most practitioners had taken as the only scientifically approved operational paradigm. But a social reading is neither orthodox nor does it have institutional uptake. The almost religious like orthodoxy (See Merton 1992; Fama 1991) was (and is) that free markets are so inherently efficient and self-correcting that theorizations that postulate the possibility of market failure (Minsky 2008) can be safely dismissed.[5] Going into the crisis this was the viewpoint of the academe, financial market-makers, and government regulators, these three statuses deeply intertwined as federal regulators are almost always recruited from orthodox economic departments and prominent investment banks. It is no accident that Goldman Sachs has contributed a slew of Treasury secretaries, who after their tenure in public office, returned immediately to the financial workplace. This regime of incestuous circulation of personnel became institutionalized in the 1970s when the primary axis for the global money markets became the Treasury, the Federal Reserve, and Wall Street. A culture and mechanism of circulation emerged in which individuals would rotate between economic positions at major universities, in government posts, and in financial institutions, in the process all but effacing the difference (in missions and dispositions) between those who regulate and those who are regulated. The outcome was a financial system manned by neoclassical economists and neoclassically trained MBAS[6] who were convinced that derivatives were the creative way to offset risk and that systemic failure is impossible.[7] But the real is that markets did fail systemically and the crisis that ensued continues to impoverish us economically and to diminish us politically. And so the matter of derivatives could not be more important to any discussion about wealth and power.[8]

Crisis and Wealth

The crisis points to a politics of wealth in which, for many, the only thing that is abundant is scarcity. Indeed, and here the indeed measures the deed not done: the politics of wealth we have refused to embrace defines us more than the one we have settled for. The accumulating crises underline the need for a theory that is sufficiently beyond economic convention that it must construct most of its own concepts, starting from circulation, the derivative, and the centrality of the social and including a kind of conversion machine that translates high-kiting scholastic treatises into practical accounts that live much closer to the ground. The analytical aim is not to sell or celebrate the derivative and its markets but to delineate them as analytical objects. Few things are ever more political or more secretively powerful than the (mis)construction of social objects. Though I couldn't help but put this scholastically, it does help to remember that this is why the financial sector works so hard to "public-relation" us into seeing it as a certain kind of object: one that in fairly rewarding individual achievements is beneficial to us all.

In the light of our compromised security, it is possible and necessary to locate and inventory the crises (in the plural) that confront us. The economic backdrop is that the production of an increasing array of commodities has been shifting to Brazil, India, and especially China. In the process, derivative markets specializing in the allocation of capital became capitalism's largest market. The derivative markets are the way in which capitalism assigns value to capital at risk when it evolves a new platform for self-expansion whose mainspring is the circuitry of capital itself. This ascent of derivative markets marking a remarkable transformation in the substance and politics of wealth: the proportion of EuroAmerican wealth held in financial as opposed to physical assets (e.g. real estate) is increasing dramatically. In significant part owing to the financialization of what were once physical assets. The financial implications of this shift is that from 1973 on the market for derivatives has grown from nearly nil to hundreds of trillions, as reported by the Bank for International Settlements (2013). More, the velocity of its growth at increasing levels of complexity are outrunning state and international regulatory regimes, the popular capacity to imagine such astronomical numbers and the force they portend, the medias wherewithal to portray the full character of the crisis, and the political power that increasing wealth has bequeathed to the financial sector.

There is, first of all, a crisis of everyday life. Its framework is the progressive "subsumption" of labor to the logos of the derivative in that the activities instrumental to the reproduction of the household have increasingly come under the "calculative imperatives of finance" (Bryan, Rafferty, and Jefferis 2015:318). This appears in what is referred to as financialization: of education, medical care, retirement, epitomized by the transformation of houses into assets. That finance will educate us to use our house as an ATM machine. Financialization has turned what was once sources of security—our homes, schooling, and retirement—into perilous investments, an education little more than a call option on future employment that may expire worthless, a retirement portfolio increasingly resembling a put option on not living too long. In addition to their day jobs, everyone needs to become an investor: knowledgeable about the ins and outs of a financial system founded on secrecy, complexity, and the power of large numbers. With some steel-cold irony, Dick Bryan (2014) refers to this as a hedge fund of your own life. The meaning is that to fund our lives, from educating ourselves and our children to retiring with security, depends on knowing how to speculate/invest in financial assets. This is coded as *financial literacy* as though fluency in finance and the mechanics of the market is equivalent to the skill of the enlightened life, whereby we learn to read so we can read to learn. But it turns out that for most people, financialization is an end posing as a means—and too often a dead end at that.

There is a crisis of financing production in that the basic mechanisms of capital accumulation and allocation—what underlies capitalism as a political economy—remain dysfunctional. Exemplified by the worldwide shortage of liquidity and collateral and the inability of the Federal Reserve and European Central Bank to right the problem despite interventions greater than were once fathomable (even by John Maynard Keynes). The commercial paper market, a generally unknown but core source of funding for the everyday operations of production, flipped over during the crisis year and then struggled mightily to right itself. Especially for smaller and medium-sized production companies, commercial loans have been difficult to obtain, which, among other things, impairs their expansion and thus new job formation. As late as March 2015, Gershon Distenfeld, a leading bond manager at Alliance Bernstein, told CNBC that the key problem in the bond market is the continuing absence of liquidity, which means that the only firms that can easily access the bond market are those (exemplified by Apple) that are sitting on a mountain of cash.[9] The drop-off point for this evaporation of liquidity, as indicated on a liquidity chart discussed by Distenfeld, was the bankruptcy of Lehman Brothers. On top of this, the US Federal Reserve and the European Central Bank (ECB) have been unwilling to forcefully stimulate bank lending.

This speaks to a crisis of governance. Specifically in respect to the economic responsibility of the government towards those who are governed. Until the ascent of the derivative markets, a principal of government was to provide all those goods and services deemed essential to our social reproduction but did not have a home in the private market economy. Chief among these were the provision of infrastructure, consumer protection, regulation of the currency and commerce, and the fostering of economic security (e.g. unemployment insurance and housing loans). Increasingly, however, the mission of the government has transformed from preserving our economic security to that of financial institutions and markets. So increasingly governance is about keeping the financial markets solvent and liquid. Note that both the original bailout, the Troubled Asset Relief Program (TARP), and the massive program of quantitative easing orchestrated by the Federal Reserve injected an extraordinary amount of liquidity (upward of $300 billion) into the financial system without including any provision to ensure that the financial system would use this additional liquidity to bolster the production based economy of working class households (as opposed to padding their own balance sheets). The US government has effectively become the debtor of last resort for the financial system.

In the political register, there is a crisis of peoplehood in that Americans seem to be abandoning their founding constitutive vision—a vision that said we, as a people, have an unbreakable and mutual obligation to stand by one another and to do what is good for the common good. Where the celebration of citizenship once trumped our divisions, nowadays these divisions are increasingly who we are and what we stoop to fight for. The wealthiest disowning their commitment to the common good and then turning around and portraying themselves as another oppressed minority. But even more, those possessing and possessed by power and wealth want to convince the working class majority that the abandonment of our founding covenant is who we really are. That covenant tells us that we should listen to the voices of those dispossessed, that its timbre resonates our present turmoil. It tells us that many working-class rural towns and urban neighborhoods are fast becoming posthumous places, where poverty, desperation, and joblessness have become so presupposed that the residents describe their future in the past tense ("Our son won't find work cause the bank [fore]-closed on the factory; took everything right down to the tiles on the floor"). And then there is the legion of demagogues who claim that immigrants searching for work and safety are the cause of our malaise, and that if we could only band together to exile them we would solve the crisis of work.

To these crises we added a crisis of scientific understanding. In the analysis of our predicament, the production centric models that scholars had relied on since the birth of capitalism can no longer get the job done by themselves. This is not because production is somehow becoming less important—the total quantity of commodities being produced and circulated continues to increase—but because the sociohistorical form of circulation now ascendant adds a radically new logic to capitalism that production based models cannot encompass. A new logic founded on a different mode of instrumentation (the derivative), a redefined directional dynamic (toward the amplification of risk), and a new mode of social mediation (through the abstraction of risk). So much so that in an article entitled *After Economy?*, Randy Martin (2013) proposes that "by abstracting capital from its own body, carving it up into more or less productive aspects that can be applied toward gain or loss, dispossessing any given capital of those attributes" (e.g. its interest bearing) which can be isolated into speculative bets, "derivatives do to capital what capital itself has been doing to concrete forms of money and productive conditions like labor, raw materials, and physical plants" (p. 89). The suggestion is that when a principal capitalist activity consists in the derivative disassembling and reassembling of capital itself, this turn requires a path of understanding that can apprehend that what was once *the economy* is becoming something increasingly different. Nothing signifies the difference more than a crisis originating in the systemic immobilization of the markets responsible for capital's circulation: that is, a crisis originating in the destruction of capital as opposed to a long history of economic crises originating in the character of the commodity markets: the destruction of demand or the contraction of supply. Analyses that see nothing unusual here—the present crisis simply a reincarnation of past financial lapses—are no longer contemporaneous with themselves. Regardless of their pedigree.

This book is also necessarily about what the financial field and its ally neoliberal economics are sure the crisis could not be about: namely, capitalism as a sociohistorically specific form, currently in a highly transformative phase owing to the ascension of circulation (illustrated by the collapse of the distinction between national monies and global capital); capitalism as created within, and constitutive of, a form of social life that is intrinsically laminated to a more encompassing social; a rising culture of financialization that broadens, deepens and valorizes a speculative ethos sequestered in our imagination since the birth of capitalism that in the name of securitization and financialization has taken flight; a space of derivative markets that is evolving and canonizing a new dimension of subjectivity (a monetization of the self and other); a disarticulated worldview that visualizes the world contradictorily as hyperconsistent yet subservient to sudden random misfirings of human behavior (as inscribed in the contradictory view that economically rational agents where so besotted by greed that they behaved irrationally to the point of mutual self-destruction); a derivative logos that is remaking the world (including that of productive labor) as temporary assemblages of deconstructed parts, exemplified by the decline of unions and the rise of the independent contractor who, instead, serially "swaps" a service for a sum (see Bryan and Rafferty 2013 for an analysis of the logic); and a realist account of economic reason able to discern the conjuncture of the imbricated and embodied logics of practice. To phrase this as transparently as possible: for analysis to say something real about the financial crisis, the analysis must be about the real as it is constituted. Now, here, in the midst of the practices which define our lives.

The financial of 2008 crisis has more to tell us then it can imagine. Though not if we concentrate on what the financial field says about itself. Its own powers of revelation are shallow, such that self-understandings that emanate wholly from within finance are of only derivative value. For they begin and end with the surface forms of circulatory capital, the derivative conflated with its appearance as though it moved and thought and behaved independently of the social world it must necessarily presuppose. On the financial view, the derivative is simply another new specie of commodity, imbued with thingly properties that endow it with an objective existence independent of social life. The propensity of finance economics and the field's own forms of technical analysis is to naturalize and individualize the markets and their participants. Naturalization and individualization are realized through analytical schemes that treat collectively-created relational objects (e.g. credit, liquidity, debt) as though they are simply singular concrete object types that have a life of their own in respect to economic individuals. From its perch, markets are preconstructed and thus so eminently natural that everything required to produce and reproduce them seems to require no work at all. This viewpoint wipes away the collective works of the participants, including the work of the scientists whose labors include their construction of the derivative, the market, and risk as an analytical object. Inside the walls of finance there's no way to imagine that these "objects" in crisis are not objects at all, the term a metaphor suggested by the design of English (Lee 1997:35), but rather relational constructs working within socially imaginary ones.[10] Missing literally in action is that agents' individual acts crystallize as a collective relation, which reproduces or endangers *a derivative market*. The financial view has no view of the crisis because by removing the sociostructural all that is left are wayward individuals and the inexplicable one-off event. And, of course, the pain and violence.

The rapid response is to reinstate the social that finance has redacted. The social is imagined here as the fugitive familiar whose return to the scene of the crisis will help us understand. Especially why bad things happen to good people as well as bad. This move is sometimes referred to as bringing the social back in—as though the social was waiting on the back porch for the invitation to enter the economic house. Rather than always already a constitutive dimension of finance's sociostructure. This solution is also its own problem if analysis does not consider that the social that is already there is socially transforming. This appears, first of all, in the reality that the financial crises inspired by derivatives are fundamentally different from those animated by the withdrawal of deposit capital from the "traditional" banking system. Epitomized and emblazoned historically as depositors' runs on standard banks. Or a collapse of exchange values, as when a national currency experiences hyperinflation (the Argentinean peso in the late 1990s) or the capital allocated to a class of things (e.g. tulip bulbs or internet stocks) evaporates and prices collapse. Crises authored by derivatives are animated by the way in which capital itself is dissembled and reassembled. Financial derivatives rip capital apart, apart from any reference to production. They then technically reassemble the dismembered attributes according to a very competitive, deeply inculcated, and treadmill like logic that serves to heighten the possibility of systemic destruction. To grasp the derivative and its capacity to destroy the economy requires an investigation of the sociospecific forms of structure and agency that define its markets and market-makers. An analysis of this order is, from my perspective, necessarily grounded and enframed by a concept of *the social*. The concept is critical because it moves us beyond approaches, that founded on reification of the economic, cannot begin to honor the complex socialities constitutive of finance.

The Concept of the Social

While this concept of the social is foreign to finance economics—at least in its contemporary incarnation—it has a history that traces back to the pioneering work of Emile Durkheim and Max Weber and several entwined lineages of successors who have materially refined the idea. A concept of the social is also an undercurrent in the economics of John Maynard Keynes and the entire generation of theorists who had suffered through the Great Depression.[11] The social has a specific reference. It constitutes the unmarked term that encompasses all of the ways in which concrete human actions enacted within sociospecific practices (such as executing a derivative trade) are the product of the organization (both objectively through the institutions of the financial field and subjectively in the dispositions inculcated in its participants)[12] of deeply imbricated community, economic, political, and moral/ethical dimensions of contemporary life. The concept of the social seeks to capture the reality that, at the level of concrete human actions, these dimensions of our contemporary existence are intrinsically interwoven. Such that foregrounding one dimension or another is inherently a kind of action on the social which, in turn, influences deeply the way we apprehend the world.[13] This notion of the social foregrounds the reality that human action is intrinsically collective. Concretely, this means that the buying and selling of a security, speculating on its forthcoming value based on the participants' willingness to assume an unknowable amount of abstract risk, is possible only for agents who have already acquired dispositions geared to the plural and entwined species of rationality that course through the financial field (i.e., maximizing profits, producing subjects' self-esteem, competitive dynamic, speculative ethos, and even a sense of nationalism). Concretely, this also means that the dispositions that motivate each and every trade serve to combine a past (history) and a forthcoming; they speak to the relationship between the organization of agents' dispositions constitutive of the financial habitus and the structure of possibilities (e.g., wagering on credit default swaps) constitutive of the financial field at a given point in time. Concretely, the structures of the financial field and the specific markets are built into the cognitive and generative schemes that the agents implement to apprehend the financial field and its markets. From this perspective, the real-world dynamic founded on the relation between the structure of agents' dispositions and that of the financial field and its markets is always the outcome of multiple competing determinations. The true point, which is beyond the ken of economistic accounts, is that financial actions have determinations but are never the result of purely rational cognitive decision making (even in the case of program trading) because they originate in the encounter between dispositions, schemes, and truths shaped by the financial history from which they spring and the potentialities of the financial field and markets going forward. That said, the genesis and ascension of the structures of circulation, in finance and beyond, always with a global orientation that imbricates spaces of difference (such as nations), require a revised social theory. The social theory that once did a good day's labor cannot be counted on to get to the heart of the crisis because the finance it references has moved on, finance after 1973 progressively becoming a transformed form of what it was in the prederivative days of production-directed capital. Accounting for this transformation requires that we read the crisis three turns removed from conventional approaches. While the uptake of these theoretical revisions will become fully apparent only in the context of the larger investigation, it is worth providing an overview to indicate the trajectory.

Three Theoretical Turns

Although their value (and judgment on that value) will become apparent only in the course of the analyses, I would like to preview the three theoretical turns that orient what follows. The first turn is ontological: that we grasp the financial crisis through a theory and thematic that annuls the privileging of production that has underpinned the entire spectrum of accounts from the most neoclassical to the most resolutely Marxist. This ontological equilibration of production and circulation will touch off a chain reaction, leading to other levelings of the theoretical (and methodological) field that, in turn, will lead to a reconceptualization of what a social theory of finance should look like. Perhaps equally a reconceptualization of what social theory confronting the transformed social of circulatory capitalism should embrace as its conceptual architecture. Note also that the centrality of production has been accompanied by a privileging of structure or totality at the expense of agents' practice and performance. What is more, neoclassical and Marxist theory both seem to visualize capitalism in territorial and systemic terms, such that "the economy" names the structure of production articulated by a national and/or class-based populace. But this too is a theoretical hindrance to the apprehension of modern derivative markets. Instead, an entirely different account for the reproduction of capital markets will emerge once we put the objectification of totality and the performativity of practice on equal footing.

The second turn is epistemological: that we transition from a theory founded on directional and oppositional categories to a theory founded on the notion that the categories unfold as *spread* phenomena. There is a powerful in other words here: namely that we will apprehend the realities of financial practice as spread phenomena on the grounds that this provides a more accurate analytic. The spread will allow us to understand the real as being intrinsically relational. Critical if the objective is to apprehend anything as relational and as animated as real-time trading. So spreads are relational spaces that allow for movement in multiple directions simultaneously. These movements across the space and in respect to the spread appear temporally as intervals, times of revaluing, defined by differences in velocity, volatility, and valorization. This "spread" approach replaces understandings of the social predicated on immobile configurations of points and positions, agents versus structure, or opposing spheres of social life. It replaces approaches that apprehend the social world as ensembles of preassembled systemic forms, forms that disciplines can then grasp in substantialist, linear, deterministic terms.

Thinking the world through the spread approach, there can be no opposition between production and circulation, material wealth and financial assets, pricing models and the real recalibration of prices, investing versus speculation, because they are all mutually imbricated dimensions of capital. What have so often appeared as conceptual oppositions reappear as historically generated spreads. And thus mutually implicated in the creation of the economic conjuncture. Indeed, a spread transcends the opposition that it stages as a condition of its resolution. So the real production of a derivative that circulates, replicated at a real price in wealth-creating money, speculating on the investment even as the participants invest in speculation, whose outcome inflects the real economy by inflecting the design and flow of capital and permeating our reproductive logos will necessarily fold the oppositions into one another. By the same token, the ascent of finance does not bespeak a directional shift from commodity production to financial circulation, but, alternatively, the circumstantial foregrounding of one aspect of the spread that runs from production through circulation to consumption or final demand. The question of the derivative has to do with the contemporary dynamic unfolding of this spread in respect to the deep structure of capital. And more specifically, the transformative effects of the ascension of the derivative markets on this structure.

The question of how derivatives work structurally is inseparable from the question of what kind of work is necessary to reproduce them practically. And to trade them on a global scale as a matter of institutionalized practice. This work and workplace are not an accidental occurrence, nor do they emerge as a determination of corporate rules and norms or from some inevitable exfoliation of the logic of capitalism. Rather, the work and workplace of finance unfolds as the dynamic creation and enactment of a sociostructure, that is, in respect to the encounter between a spectrum of possibilities delimited by the force of constraints and the agenda of the participants. The workplace opens a space that enframes the activity of trading, then provisionally closes this interval of space-time (or spread), only to animate it again repeatedly in what appears to be a mime of the dynamic and nonlinear replication that characterizes the derivatives markets. The flywheel of openings and closings is important because it compels agents to bring their other interests and logics into the workplace and to export the derivative logic into other spheres of social life. Conceptualizing the making and replication of markets as a spread phenomena is significant because, as we will see, the conventional logic that habitually opposes work with play and both with ritual impedes an understanding of how the workers who make and trade derivatives make derivatives work. We will eventually reach the concept that a spread is a specific instantiation of sociality that mobilizes ritual/play/work to resolve the certainty of uncertainty inherent in the real-life unfolding of financial practice.

The third turn is toward a more immanent understanding of science inasmuch as an analysis of the markets must attend to the scientific means and methods that agents use instrumentally to construct those markets. Critically by conceptualizing science (a science of finance in its disciplinary version as finance economics and also its secular forms) as a sociospecific vision that, having become part of the real relations of the production of the economic, is partially constitutive of the financial field, markets, and the present crisis, and simultaneously as the source of a more reflexively creative theory that can apprehend and reinsert the full and founding sociality that its own ideology exteriorizes. Note that modern derivative markets are unique in that they grew up in the house of science, nurtured by its analytical tools of evidence and argumentation, habituated to its use of numbers and mathematical calculation, its sources of renewable legitimacy deposited in science and the rationalist thinking that scholastic reasoning celebrates, and, most of all, to its tendency to conceptualize analysis as a physical science of natural types (a physics of finance). To understand derivative markets it is necessary to interrogate the embrace of science that these markets embrace as a condition of their existence—this use of science methods appearing in derivative-pricing models, product innovation, the divination of technical indicators, the development of trading platforms, the analytics of (quasi)historical patterns, and so on exponentially.

A Social Theory of Finance

One question sometimes asked of me is why should financial derivatives interest anthropologists? How did I come to see my intellectual calling to be an illumination of the derivative? One answer is that since the inception of the discipline, the calling of most anthropologists has been to illuminate the social practices of tribes living outside of EuroAmerica. But the world has transformed socially and economically, not least with the ascension of a culture of financial circulation, and thus the need to turned our attention to the tribes that occupy lower Manhattan and Canary Wharf. A kindred answer is that I do not visualize myself as an anthropologist in the conventional sense even if the investigation does incorporate its traditions such as ethnography and a concern for the social. Perhaps more important, I think of anthropology with a small a, meaning that the approach taken here is intellectually omnivorous in its willingness to appropriate whatever concepts and insights illuminate the material. Be these concepts and insights from sociology, economics, finance, linguistics, or anyplace else.

There is a reason for this. A remarkable fact about the world now unfolding, a reality seemingly magnified on a daily basis, is that our technology, culture, and economy are transforming faster than the institutions designed to understand and monitor them. They are transforming faster than our ability to render them strategically intelligible to citizens and policymakers. This lag is especially true with respect to the social sciences. The various disciplines have resisted coming to terms with the reality that their differences do not simply reflect differences in their objects of investigation. They more reflect a cultural politics of investigation that inculcates different concepts, desires, and dispositions in their respective academic communities. The propensity has been to translate academic boundaries into boundaries of knowledge production. Even more, this repressed politics tends to fabricate putative differences in their objects of investigation through the valorization of filtration processes that screen out much of what is critical to grasping the world (of finance) as it is currently evolving. It is for this very reason that Emanuel Derman, one of the founders of quantitative modeling and a former managing director at Goldman Sachs, observed that his practical experience of the "efficient market model" revealed that it is "driven as much by ideology as by the facts" (2011:109).

It is hard not to concur with Derman's view, which is ultimately rooted in this understanding of mathematics. And because few things are more social than ideology his observation points to the necessity of an alternative theorization that grasps finance as inherently social and transdisciplinary. The derivative and its markets are going to test our collective ability to play with others. Indeed, from our perspective, the gulf dividing the disciplines is much broader and deeper than the separation—if there is one—between the dimensions of social life. There seems to exist a reality-magnifying and very misrecognized complicity between the scientific fields and their analytical objects: the social practices, methodologies, and institutional structure of the disciplines all too easily suppressing the constructive character of their relationships to their analytical objects even on those rare occasions when it becomes visible as artifice. That these divisions have no epistemological foundation is nowhere more evident than in the study of finance, especially markets that are collapsing from an acknowledged crisis of faith. Disciplinary divisions, however seemingly natural, have only a social foundation; they exist and are reproduced only insofar as the contemporary history of the academe has canonized and institutionalized them. The main argument is that we can grasp globally enmeshed cultures of financial circulation only by dissolving or at least ignoring this authoritarian division of disciplines because it is no longer contemporaneous with itself. Whatever the merits of the EuroAmerican tradition of the institutional division of disciplines, it is an impediment in grasping the present structure of financial circulation. Either the divisions will dissolve or the financial world will not be understood.

The focus of the account seems simple enough: what kind of work do these tribes do? How, as the longstanding and rather quaint phrase goes, do they make a living? Hunting and gathering money is the answer, though there is, of course, more to this economy than any encapsulating description. Indeed, it turns out that we will need to draw upon all of the intellectual and theoretical resources at our disposal to explain how the financial field is constituted, what are the social practices of a species of work that centers on acquiring and allocating speculative capital to place risky bets on market volatility, what are the existential dimensions of a form of work that involves decision making under uncertainty? The intellectual and theoretical resources called on will include quite a bit about what we have distilled from studying tribes more remote than our own. Hopefully, I can construct a perspective that is able to apprehend the sociostructures and socialities that enframed and encouraged the derivative-driven financial crisis.

It is not only the public and its representatives who appear to possess very little understanding of modern finance. Academic scholarship has also failed to theorize and thematize the ascent of the derivatives markets and the culture of financial circulation. While a library of popular accounts is quickly taking shape, they center almost exclusively on the sequencing of events and the personalities involved not on the underlying structure. Nonetheless, it is clear that to apprehend the present and evolving structure of capitalism it is necessary to grasp the deep structure of financial circulation, which is EuroAmerican in genesis and arcane in its architecture, but global and pervasive in its implications. My view is that the character and a cause of the crisis is a financial field and markets whose social complexity is so deeply buried in their molecular structure that their appearance, and how the participants portray their own appearance not only publicly to the camera but also importantly to themselves in their practice of constructing their own subjectivities, tends to flatten out this complex terrain. This observation is important analytically. It reminds us why is necessary to break with participants' ordinary experience of the financial markets in order to account for their experience. This separation is necessary because everyday experiences invariably arise from specific positions within the financial field. Participants cannot help but to see and grasp the financial field from the particular positions that they occupy, resulting in a real but only partial picture of the encompassing structure of relations that generate their actions. To give an example that our analysis will return to: traders on the proprietary trading desk who are speculating daily with enormous sums of an investment bank's money have a different experience and vision of the financial field from the mathematically trained quants who reside on a different floor of the building, both of which are more often than not distant and segregated from the views and capacities of upper management. This reality means that an analysis that exposes the sociostructures that found the field will cut against the grain of both scholastic and insider understandings.

In essence, the view is that to be scientifically rigorous in the investigation of the financial crisis entails a methodology that grasps how the objects of finance are doubly constructed and dialectically so, through the mediated relationship between the field's participants and the scholars who analyze what they do. I have sought to harness all of the resources gained from studying both primitive and derivative economies and systems of circulation to put this methodology into practice. Let it equally be noted in the interests of honesty that there is never going to be a productive dialogue between the silence of abstractionism and the investigation of concrete social relations: for on the one side are unchanging natural laws and neural pathways, on the other the meanings and values that collectivities attach to themselves and the fields they create. Pierre Bourdieu tells us that this "deliberately selective apprehension of the real" necessarily consists in "bracketing off the economic and social conditions of rational dispositions (in particular those of the calculating dispositions applied to economic matters) and the economic and social structures that are the condition of their exercise . . ." (1998:94–95). It will thus require a new species of finance economists—a species who care enough about wealth and the power of the derivative to genuinely care about the social.

And thus the aim of the book in its entirety. The derivative is about wealth in motion, although differently from before in that the rapidity, global reach, and sum of the wealth circulating is ushering in a transformed form of capitalism. And with that, a transformed political economy. For these reasons, I want to introduce the you that is the reader to an alternative language for thinking about finance, and about thinking through the challenges financialization is now presenting. I want to do this in a way that pays no attention to the entrenched segregation of disciplines or the convention that what validates scholarship is discussions of the "inside-baseball" (or "inside-cricket" if you will) debates that fill the disciplinary journals. I want to inject a new ensemble of concepts, such as rituality, the performative objectification of totality, cultures of circulation, the dynamics of volatility and liquidity, how the spread of possibles (prices) across an interval (the time until a contract's expiration) creates a specific kind of agency, and the habitus of financial practice—into theorizations of the derivative. This social reading of the derivative is, and can only be, preliminary. That said, my hope is that by the book's end a new optic for visualizing the derivative begins to come into focus.

One nonconcluding observation. Like a swift river against soft rock, the financial industry has gradually but relentless eroded the safeguards (e.g., Dodd-Frank) put in place as a consequence of the crisis. Behinds the backs of the citizens, though with the complicity of politicians whose overriding concern is getting reelected, systemic risk is again on the rise. Omnivorous dark pools of speculative capital that circulate all sorts of derivatives on underground markets are getting larger and larger. Proprietary trading desks are back in principal, even if they operate under assumed names. And while few things in finance are guaranteed because the future is always up for grabs, a betting man or woman not afraid to speculate would lay odds on another financial crisis. This is not a prediction simply a real possibility. If some year in the future resembles 2008, we should be dismayed but not that surprised. For the real lesson of the crisis is that a desire for profit will trump politics, governance, and our mutual well-being.

Means and Methods

Analyses are judged by the logical coherence of the theory but also by their correspondence to the world. This second term of judgment means that a key question in evaluating an analysis that purports to be about the world (of, for example, finance) is how researchers know what they know, socially and scientifically. For finance, what is the methodology in the larger sense of the term, this expansion necessary because finance, in contrast to how it is mapped by neoliberal economics, actually references an open, uncertain, generative universe.

Anthropologists, especially as it constitutes a key element of their heritage, but other disciplines also, have a concept of ethnography. By ethnography is meant fieldwork whose objective is the extended on-the-ground study of a community and its way of life. In this investigation, I have drawn upon this methodology. And so what follows is based on direct observation, dozens of formal interviews, and innumerable other occasions, such as wine tastings, interacting with derivative traders who were interacting with each other. Without succumbing to the positivist fetishism of "data"—which cannot help but conflate data, information, and knowledge—I have used this field experience to help build a picture of derivatives, their markets, and their market-makers. This observational platform is necessarily interpretative: as the overt behavior of the participants rests on concepts, dispositions, embodied sensibilities, institutional contexts, and practices that are hardly visible the way a building or mountain is visible. What renders this task somewhat quixotic is that the analyst resides among those who, absorbed in their work and the machinations of the field, will habitually dismiss (as philosophical or worse metaphysical) any mention of that which is foundational. Nonetheless, this must be done and so I have sought to conscientiously shuttle between empirical data and interpretative frame.

I have also been shaped by my own trading experiences and have incorporated into the analysis. For the past two decades, I have traded derivatives for my own account, mostly exchange-traded derivatives but even there it is entirely possible to conjoin several "vanilla" instruments (e.g., simple options) into a more complex and more opaque position. Trading derivatives entails placing one's own money on the line which in turn imbues a sense of the market, of the game, and their affective pull. It is one thing for someone to tell you about speculation, volatility, and the double-edged sword of leverage. It is quite another to have a sickening feeling bubble up from the pit of your stomach as a position deteriorates by a substantial sum in just a few minutes, and you are now compelled to make a decision as to whether to further leverage the bet when (but also if) the volatility swing bottoms or whether to accept the price of failure and exit the losing position before the loss becomes catastrophic. On the more analytical side, there is the singular experience of making the calculation that this particular derivative at this price is worth speculating on. All the while aware that this decision-making under uncertainty could easily go south if unexpected or unimagined events occurred. Many of the insights about the feel of the trade derive from conversations with traders and my own experiences of trading. This is central because the phenomenology of trading arises from the carefully calculating body. The zone of practical practice is a place where mind, memory, and body are indistinguishable.

There is a politics that assists my method of understanding. My objective is not to condemn the derivative the way evangelicals condemn abortion: as an evil in and of itself so inherently malevolent that no good can ever come of it. Rather, my aim is to understand the derivative in order to harness its power and then turn that power toward the interests of the collective good. In this vein, I have been contemplating with Robert Wosnitzer (also a member of the financial group) on how we might design a derivative whose purpose is to assist finance education by shifting the tuition risk of investing in schooling from students to market speculators. Creating a derivative is one way of getting to know them.

In addition, I have recorded and then analyzed literally thousands of hours of broadcasting by the financial media. This includes the stories reported on CNBC and Bloomberg, their analyses of the internal and exogenous forces that shape domestic and foreign markets, and the interviews they conduct with hedge fund managers, corporate leaders, politicians, presidents of the Federal Reserve banks (e.g., the New York branch), institutional investors, buy-side analysts, economists, and, of course, money center banks and pivotal derivative mainstays such as JP Morgan, Goldman Sachs, and Morgan Stanley (e.g., their mandatory reports for the US Comptroller of the Currency). My analyses combine this dimension of practice fieldwork based information with a reading of journalist accounts in respect to the technical literature on strategies for trading derivatives and the mathematics of financial models.

Through no intention or merit of my own, I am in a very good position to assess the financial markets. Beginning in 1973, the foundational year in the genesis of derivatives markets, I began my study of economics at the University of Chicago. I studied substantivist economics formally and neoliberal economics informally but diligently, thus getting a handle on the mainstream theorization of noncapitalist and capitalist societies. Economics was just beginning to image itself as physics such that my penchant for math made this turn both interesting and puzzling. More, when I arrived in Chicago I roomed with my cousin who was one of the pioneering traders discovering their way on the fledgling Chicago Board Options Exchange (founded in 1973). My cousin and his fellow traders taught me about options, although I considered them little more than a curiosity at the time. Nonetheless, this experience alerted me to derivatives and as their markets expanded exponentially and thus also their importance to an increasingly globalized political economy, so too my interest. The point of convergence was that societies once driven by their own internal design were now being encompassed by the derivative markets. The initial expression of this interest was the collaboration with Benjamin Lee on several articles (LiPuma and Lee 2002) and a book *Financial Derivatives and the Globalization of*

Risk (2004). This book is an extension and development of its conclusion that to comprehend the present we need an adequate theorization of the social life of derivatives. This book is intended as a contribution to that project.

The Plan of the Book

Each of the chapters of the book is a self-contained analysis, and can thus be read independently. Nonetheless, they are intended to have a cumulative effect as each chapter develops a specific theme in pursuit of the social analysis. The opening chapter sets out the question of what a derivative is and how it works. Not just what a derivative names contractually, but what it says about speculation and the organization of time set against its historical origins. At issue is the way in which the logos of the derivative leads to markets predicated on innovation and the abstraction of risk. The second chapter focuses on the conditions of the crisis and how derivatives have an especially intricate relationship to the production of knowledge about them. If science has any mission it is to know. If Herman Melville were writing this chapter and his subject was the London whale and the derivative transactions that impaled the finances and reputation of JP Morgan he would probably put a banner under the chapter title that read: How Finance Thinks about Derivatives. Being a Meditation on the Production of Knowledge and Ignorance. For the life and power of the derivative is inseparable from the knowledge created and circulated on its behalf. The third chapter sets out the problems that confront a project whose objective is to apprehend the financial field socially. It explores the theoretical and thematic ground of these problems, underlying how the systemic crisis that rocked the markets in 2008 and beyond affords a privileged opportunity to map a social approach to finance. The fourth chapter examines the temporality of the financial field and derivative markets. Its primary concern is to trace the historical ascent of a culture of financial circulation, to reveal the operations of a "treadmill effect" that causes derivative markets to become increasingly unstable over time, and to illustrate how the derivative deals with the future's inherent uncertainty. Time is critical to the social approach developed here because the reintroduction of time foregrounds the social's constitutive power in the making and reproduction of derivative markets. The fifth chapter details the foundations of the social process by which derivative markets are produced and reproduced. It argues that there is a problematic that is hidden from our view by an economistic approach: namely that *a market enacted as a continuous set of transactions functions (i.e., remains liquid) because its agents presuppose the market as a(n imagined) totality, even as the very existence of that totality depends upon the continuity of those transactions.* The sixth chapter shows that the market-making process emanates from the concrete social relations of the agents who participate in and are invested objectively and subjectively in these markets. The analysis here focuses on the dynamic between the objectification of a market as an imagined totality that frames economic action and the performativity of these actions in objectifying a market (and also *the market*). This dynamic that is the basis for dynamic market replication derives from a progressive set of social mediations that need to be defined. The key to understanding this dynamic turns out to be a rituality, secular in character and anything but transparent, that underwrites the circulation of derivative contracts. The seventh chapter examines the speculative ethos that has come to simultaneously permeate the derivative markets, and through the culture and economy of financialization, the life of ordinary citizens. What is interesting and transformative about the speculative ethos is that, although the propensity to speculate is intrinsic to capitalism's motivating and cognitive structures, and has thus been present as a cultural form since its inception, the present ethos is new in its willingness to attach to objects formerly considered outside the sphere of speculation. Notably, housing and education but also an increasing ensemble of other objects. The eighth chapter treats the financial habitus by developing an account of the cognitive and motivating structures that underpin trading and the fabrication of investment vehicles. I develop the notion of the *monetized subjectivity* to take the analysis beyond the simplistic narrative of greed and hubris run amok in a permissive environment. The ninth chapter returns to the interplay of the naturalistic hypostasized model with the concrete sociality of real markets. It focuses on the multiple missions of the Black-Scholes equation, deconstructing its mathematics to reveal the underlying sociality that the equation itself must presuppose to generate the markets that the model attempts to model. The analysis focuses on the character of the interval and spread between the mathematical pricing model and what derivative traders, caught up in the swirl of socially generated risks, actually do. All of the chapters speak to the structural and abstract violence engendered by financial markets and circulatory capitalism. Not least its corrosive effect on the covenant of mutual cooperation and prosperity that once upon a time defined who we aspired to be.

This account, like all others, situates itself somewhere on the spectrum from life to learning, between the power to hone a lingua franca of finance and the irregular pockmarked reality out of which all finance, and all narratives about finance, arises. Capturing this reality requires a way of speaking that desires to include all of the determinations that shape the financial field and derivatives markets. The crisis of 2008 is a good place to start but the destination has to be an understanding somewhere up ahead of exactly what finance and the derivative are turning us into. The goal, in other words, is to analyze the spread between capitalism and capitalism with derivatives. Perhaps if analysts do their job then maybe the interpassivity that has descended like a veil across the electorate will be lifted. In its place hopefully a strategic intelligibility that allows for a narrowing of the breach between the beneficiaries of risk and those who shoulder it. This intelligibility would encourage our matriculation from an economy of innumerable meaningless choices to a politics of just optionality. It is one thing to be able to choose from among several hundred breakfast cereals, quite another to restore the covenant by which we can continually roll over the option to participate in the wealth of society.

I am dismayed by the fact that economic theorists are generally willing to settle for so little. In its stead should be a hunger, as deep as the social itself, to grasp the circulatory economy that contributes both the ink and the wording of the transformation we are now undergoing. The derivative shows us that when we encounter a transformative reality, understanding rests less on picking a new assortment of concepts then on picking a new intellectual self to inhabit that reality. In this choice, I am much guided by my friend and co-contributor, Randy Martin (1957–2015), who said that politics is not a fixed form we labor to know, but something that we know by continually tearing it down and rebuilding it to our collective good.

Chapter 1

Originating the Derivative

The duality of the concrete and the abstract characterizes the capitalist social formation. —MOISHE POSTONE 1993:152

Anyone who wants to understand the present political economy, but does not understand the derivative and its markets, can only by taken seriously by those equally in the
dark. Indeed, the longer one circles the financial crisis' aftermath the more the political
economy of the present comes into view. —EDWARD LIPUMA 2015

Of all the dodges of discourse, the science of allusion holds a special place. The writer
scientist depicts one reality by allusion to another. And so the derivative is said to be
like something else, in the process losing the fact that its power to impose a logic on
our lives derives from an existence that refuses to reference anything but itself. —A
memory paraphrase of RANDY MARTIN, 2013

What Is the Derivative?

If we are determined to understand finance we must engage the derivative. If
we are called on this account to unlock the derivative and its logos, it is necessary to begin at the foundation. To analyze the derivative socially, to theorize
its design and the agency that it commands, to produce knowledge that en-
hances our vision and illuminates what remains problematic and unknown,
begins with the simple, not so simple, question of what is the derivative. There
is a more pragmatic way to articulate this question: namely, why should derivatives trade and why trade derivatives? The foregone ideological answer is
money and profit, animated by the gods/demons of avarice. But the answer

is a kind of cultural self-deception, albeit a very necessary one, in that it substitutes a functional precondition (credit money), a contingent result (making a profit), and an animal spirit for an accountable explanation. And so our ideology, beloved for its earthly grit and simplicity, ends up presupposing what needs to be explained. For the real question has another more inherently social form: what is the derivative and its markets such that capitalism with derivatives is transforming who we are?

If I start at the conclusion this is my answer. The derivative is not a thing: like the book you have in your hands or the chair you may be sitting in. It is, first of all, relational as its very essence, more like the relationality that underlies friendship or enmity than like a book or an armchair. Going further, derivatives are relations about relations. Specifically, their relative volatility in relations to the volatility of their underliers; for example, the volatility of the relationship between the dollar and the euro. The heartbeat of derivative trading and thus a derivative's replication is the magnitude and velocity of its volatility.

Like writing seriously about humor, capturing the derivative bet can be a tricky proposition. A liquid and legible style does not easily cotton to its inherent complexities. Nonetheless, the basic idea behind the derivative is compelling simple. There are only two moving parts: a bet on a relationship and a tango with time. The players define the bet in a contract in which the score depends on what happens—that is, the volatility or the price movement—to some other underlying asset(s), such as interest rates or the exchange rate between the dollar and euro. This bet is played out over some specified period of time determined in the contract. Time counts because the wager is on what the values of the underliers will be sometime in the future. Observe that the wager is on what happens to the relationship between the underliers—its relative variance or volatility—rather than what happens to the underlying assets themselves. And that it concerns what happens to the relationship of the underliers only over the specified time.

Given the contract's design features it is possible to offer a non-financial example: suppose I wager that it will on average be warmer in Chicago than in Boston in the month of January 2018. Now even if Chicago happens to have the warmest January on record (say 37 degrees) I would lose the wager if it were still warmer in Boston (say 39 degrees) and even if beginning midnight February 1 temperatures in Boston fell instantaneously to record-setting lows. For the outcome of the wager turns entirely on the relative change or volatility in the relationship between underliers over the specified time period. The financial term of art is *underlier*, though it is architecturally more accurate to view the underlier's interrelation as unfolding in its own relationship with the derivative. As constituted, the derivative creates a something akin to a capital meta-market in a parallel universe which, given the enormous monetary force driving the derivative markets, can exert a gravitational-like pull on the underlier's market.

As an aspect of capitalism's social evolution and the evolution of economies more generally, the derivative cannot help but stand in a historically specific relationship to the commodity. It is clear that the production of goods and services has existed always and everywhere before the derivative. And that capitalism has produced commodities since its inception. From this perspective, the derivative resembles a luxury good in the sense that hedging commodities with derivatives can be a helpful accessory to other technologies for managing risk, such as a downdraft in a good's price in the interval between a producer's investment of capital and the sale of the finished good. But production does not need the derivative to be successful. Nonetheless, the globalization of production and with that the amplification of the transnational flow of capital has resulted in the ascension and the empowerment of derivatives. A world in which there is heightened connectivity linked to increasing state fragmentation is part and product of the reformulation of the relationship between labor and capital. And thus between production and circulation, security and risk, subjective freedom and objective domination, the politics of the nation state and forms of deterritorialized governance. If we synthesize and theorize the inflow of evidence from the perspective of a social and historical reading of the derivative the following conclusion takes shape: *the derivative markets are the historically determined yet arbitrary means by which capitalism assigns value to capital at risk when it evolves a transformed platform for self-expansion whose mainspring is the circularization of nation-state–based production.*

What this means historically is that the derivative and its markets are separating circulation from production even as they are simultaneously generating new modes of connectivity and mutual dependence. It also means that derivatives whose success turns on assembling and circulating aspects of capital are neither dependent on, nor limited by, the structure of production. A kind of unlimited inc., derivatives have evolved to specialize on speculative wagers on assemblages of nomadic and opportunistic capital that circulate on markets of their making. The design of a derivative contract thus has no necessity; for it arbitrarily pairs and temporally brackets two arbitrarily selected aspects of capital to create a relationship. The derivative thus has no intrinsic value other than as an instrument that interconnects with parallax derivatives to generate a globally fluid market for capital, as a (re)source for collateralizing parallel wagers and thus for amplifying leverage, and as an instrument whose forecast of the future helps create the future it forecasts. This latter convergence can and does occur because a market's participants believe they can obtain a preemptory reading on the future price of an underlier (e.g., petroleum, exchange rates) by monitoring the relationship or volatility spread between a derivative's price and that of its underlier. This dynamic imbues circulatory capital with a self-referential and reflexive dimension: for the volatility of a derivative can induce volatility in its underlier which can motivate an amplification in a derivative's spread by, for example, reducing the number of participants in its market. Duly reflecting the extrinsic character of its value, the derivative contract is a determinate form vulnerable to all the uncertainties the world may throw its way. Thus formulated, a derivative wager epitomizes a speculative ethos because it stages a head-on collision between the deliberate and accidental, between a culture of calculation and the illegibility of chance. The present form of the derivative is how we—that is, metropolitan capitalist societies—have chosen at this point in their evolution to chance the capital in capitalism.

The basic idea of the derivative is the promissory gift. If one agent meets certain conditions he/she will receive some wealth from the counterparty. The idea stretches back mytho-historically to the Code of Hammurabi and the testament to the genesis of Jewish peoplehood. And so it has been noted that in Genesis (chapter 29) Jacob purchased an option costing him seven years' labor that granted him the right to marry Laban's daughter Rachel, though as circumstances turned unexpectedly, his prospective father-in-law reneged, thus producing an outcome whose surface appearance not only resembles a derivative but the first default on a derivative. The underlying difference is that where in gift based societies the concept of wealth and the agreement's annulment are founded on direct social relations (i.e., marriage), under capitalism both the derivative's pricing and the outcome of the wager are mediated by abstract risk. It is precisely this difference that is capitalism's signature: the duality of concrete and abstract. That the surface form of the derivative parallels the reality of the promissory gift imbues the former with a certain legibility. The overt form of the derivative contract fits a traditional slot in our understanding even if its underlying design represents a dramatic departure. Indeed, defining, as is often done, the derivative as nothing more than a financial contract is like describing the *Venus de Milo* as a double amputee.

That said, the derivative relationship opens the door to nearly endless possibilities because there is an extraordinary assortment of potential underliers.

Especially a capitalist economy whose global flows of capital are transcending, eliding, and discounting national frontiers, generates a continuous and expanding supply of underliers. The only limits are the imagination and creativity of the financiers, their collective willingness to risk capital for speculative purposes, and the capacity of the new derivative to generate a constant supply of tradable volatility. What we now know is that new derivatives create new volatility and new volatility creates new profit opportunities. It goes without saying that trader's trade, their sensibilities so hyper-directed to a market's unfolding that they neither need nor imagine a definition of the derivative. There is, in fact, a famous scene in Michael Moore's movie, *Capitalism: A Love Story*, in which traders are flummoxed when he asks them to define the derivative for him. It has, accordingly, been left to analysts to come up with a definition. However, attempts to craft anything resembling a definition of what a derivative is seem to invariably fail, mainly because they assume that its design is somehow invariant and rule governed.[1] This nature of the error is not accidental: it follows from capitalism's social epistemology which tends to treat *a contract* about *a practice* as the pairing of two object categories. But to the contrary, the derivative is a *generative design scheme*, evolved for responding to, anticipating, and sometimes engineering shifts in the character of the global financial markets. Where derivatives are concerned, the cast of characters is expansive, transient, and unruly, but choreographing their entrances and exits is less important than apprehending what all derivatives have in common: a generative scheme based on *(1) a time dependent wager on volatility, (2) the division and reassembling of capital, and (3) an amalgamation of variable and incommensurable forms of risk into an abstract cipher that functions as a social mediation.* Let me underline, the relationship of a derivative to its generative principles is more like that of power and money than that of vessel and water. The orchestration of these features—their structural assertion if you will—and the sociality that underpins it necessarily imbues the derivative with a logos whose form and effects are greatly removed from those of production. This generative scheme is the deep structure for the construction of an enormous number of derivative forms whose surface features differ, frequently dramatically so. Thus, for example, this scheme underlies collateralized debt obligations, interest rate swaps, and cross-currency contracts, three derivative types whose surface features are very different. This generative scheme constitutes the deep performative subject of derivative driven capital (Lee and LiPuma 2002). As Konings (2015) notes, apprehending derivative capitalism is difficult "unless we pay attention to the plasticity of its financial assemblages" (p. 271). That derivatives are products of the animation of a generative scheme means they are *relational* objects; they cannot, accordingly, be adequately captured or conceptualized through the fabrication and use of a thingly definition. I will try to make this become increasingly evident in the succeeding chapters.

As a political economy, the derivative is transformative because its economy is circulatory, contingent, and expansive, catapulting the economy it is generating beyond the conventional ways and means by which the nationalized production economy has sought to enclose itself. For a derivative driven economy, the most commonplace economic measures, such as gross domestic product—the *total sum* of *nationally-produced/exchanged goods and services*—is meaningless on every count. For derivatives, there is no cumulative sum of nationally produced/exchanged anything. Derivatives as an economic totality represent an indeterminate disparate aggregate, of globally-dispersed and replicating, abstract-risk-based contracts. What this indicates theoretically is that *it is only relationally that analysis can apprehend what is a derivative; that is, in respect to the co-features of their production.*

The Crisis of Economy

Martin has argued that the economic crisis manifests "a crisis of economy" in that it underlines the extent to which its exclusion of the political and its linkage of commodity production to national identity are being disrupted by the advance of the derivative (Martin 2013:102). More, a rupturing of the economic membrane consistent with nation-state-based production is necessary to its realization. This appears in several ways, first of all in the character of the crises it precipitates. In contrast to production, its systemic problems have absolutely nothing to do with an unwanted and unnecessary internal imbalance between production and demand. Rather, systemic risk is always present and systemic demise always possible because the derivative's replication and reproduction turns on the permeability and destabilization of its markets by (often unforeseeable) exogenous forces. In contrast to labor based commodity production, which has always sought ways to shelter itself from foreign competition (e.g., through laws that regulate the inter*national* transit of commodities), the economy of the derivative is necessarily an economy that must be constantly breached and compromised in order to sustain its very existence. Absent the production of volatility, the derivative and its markets could not exist. The reason is that it is volatility that motivates replication and thus circulation and as Bryan and Rafferty (2015) have noted "if they [derivatives] stop circulating, they become valueless" (p. 5). Because profits in derivative markets only derive from pricing volatility, they require a constant if measured supply of variance. More precisely and more socially, they require the social world to continually destabilize the market by introducing an array of exogenous disruptive forces that create inflections in the underlier's value. The financial community relies on models and forms of technical analysis which recognize the role of exogenous forces, but typically in ways that materially disguise their origination in the social. Financial economic reports typically conceptualize these exogenous forces on the image of natural phenomena. They see them accordingly as contextless forms of risk rather than as contingent consequences of the sociopolitical conditions of their production. They nominalize the forms of risk as discrete, independent, free-floating essences (such as counterparty, legal, or liquidity risk) that are inherently exterior to the social. The market replication of the derivative also assumes the presence and potency of relational concepts, such as a community of willing partners (i.e., counterparties), that the contract's technical pricing model excludes. Behind the backs of financial analysts and their technical models, the derivative composes itself and its market as dimensions of a space that is social, relational, and encompassing.

The evaporation of the always partial and provisional embankments of the nationally-oriented production-based commodity economy also appears in the phenomenon that the financial field refers to as contagion. In the field's own accounts, the infectious disease metaphor functions as a quasi-technical term. What it means is that economies that are productively independent may become financially intertwined and codependent due to their association by the derivative markets, such that a financially imperiled republic can create volatility and leveraged downward pressure on the currencies, interest rates, equities, and ultimately living standards of otherwise unrelated national economies. For example, through December of 2014, a precipitous dive in the price of petroleum motivated an even more precipitous dive in the Russian ruble due to Russia's great dependence on oil for its foreign exchange reserves (from 29 rubles to the dollar on December 1 to 79 rubles to the dollar on December 16). Given the regional linkage between major banks (and as importantly the presumption of such a linkage), the knock on effect from this financial shock included the destabilization of Turkish interest and exchange rates (for the lira), even though as a net petroleum importer Turkey's manufacturers and consumers are actually beneficiaries of a sustained decline in oil prices. And there is more: since petroleum is priced in dollars, the depreciation of the lira meant that Turkish producers and consumers could not capture the full benefits of lower oil prices. In other words, derivative finance has created a new interconnectivity in which its global markets can impart a trajectory to an economy that has virtually nothing to do with citizen's productive labor and products or their culture of consumption.[2]

The deterritorialization of the economy also appears in the fact, due to its arbitrary construction, there is no substantive difference between an original derivative contract and its synthetic avatars. To sustain the market's liquidity, derivatives abolish the limits to growth inherent in any regime of production. There is neither a limit to their multiplication nor a necessity to territorialize their creation or circulation. There is thus no inherent limit to the number, or number of differently designed, contracts that can be written against the same underlier, such as a national currency. Or the unfinite number of different underliers that the derivative, through innovation and marketing, can encompass. Any aspect of capital can be dissembled, multiplied to the extent of the demand whose outside band is the market's participants' fear of systemic default, and driven by the agents' capacity to financially harvest volatility. Even aspects of US Treasury bonds, such as their rate coupon, can and do have synthetic avatars. Indeed, a not uncommon arbitrage for hedge funds in 2014 was to be long corporate bonds and short synthetic treasuries (on the assumption that the Fed would raise interest rates, allowing the funds to profit from what they anticipated would be an ensuing collapse in Treasury prices). All of this said, the economy's de-nationalization is hardly transparent because the appearance of finance—especially for a media and mindset that is disposed by the recent history of capitalism to foreground institutions—is one in which a regulated banking system renders different "national" monies exchangeable (euro and yen) or different kinds of interest rates transactable (fixed and variable) when, in fact, both their commensurability and relative pricing are to a function of the way in which abstract risk mediates the circulation of derivatives.

An Economy of Financial Assets

The monetary size and limitlessness of derivatives has critical implications for the organization of the once national workforces and thus the conditions of our collective reproduction. For it turns out that if what finance conceptualizes as EuroAmerica redirects a substantial allotment of its most educated, smartest, and most entrepreneurial talent to the fabrication of derivatives, and if this mechanism of production evolves to reward speculation over prudence, and if governance agrees that regulation is unnecessary, the result will be burgeoning sums of increasingly complex risk-driven derivatives. *Speculation becomes the privileged ethos when the return on assets outruns the returns on productive labor.* On mainstreets across America, the basis of speculation (but also desperation) was that many homeowners converted their house into a fungible financial asset, their own private ATM machine. In the process, the cost of building a house (i.e., its replacement cost) became increasingly decoupled from the price of a house as a financial asset, this decoupling of a commodity from its cost through the securitization process the ground floor of the raging speculative housing bubble. In an economy in which asset manipulation appears to have displaced commodity producing labor as the touchstone and for some the tombstone of wealth creation, speculating on real estate—perhaps the most familiar, enduring, and tangible commodity—becomes the primary option open to those unschooled in the means and methodology of advanced finance. What has been little understood is that most people's only practical knowledge of an asset that is amenable to speculation, their only encounter with a commodity that can seemingly valorize its own value, is their house. And hence buying and selling houses became how ordinary people with ordinary production-based jobs sought to participate in an economy whose leitmotif is the ascension of finance at the expense of production. It is bad that so many failed and so horribly, and worse that they ended up participating in their own exploitation.

On Wall Street, the basis of speculation is and remains the constant compulsion to innovate and fabricate new derivatives, no matter how exotic or synthetic, to identify and capitalize on global capital flows. Then to attach these derivatives to the logic of leverage. Institutionally, the conversion of what were once private partnerships (e.g., Goldman Sachs, Morgan Stanley) into publicly traded firms spurred this speculative impulse as the firms transitioned from what were once risk averse and prudential partnership cultures into risk insensitive individualistic bonus cultures. This transition in firms' worldview and ethos was ordained by the logos of derivative driven markets which value bonus driven public firms over private partnerships (as measured and exemplified by the market's allocation of capital). Not coincidentally, use of the capital markets to capitalize once private investment firms was accompanied by the institutional creation of special derivative trading teams (See Tett 2009). Simultaneously, there was the transition from private "white shoe" relationship oriented investment firms to aggressive modern-day hedge funds. Whereas the former attempted to safeguard their clients' already accumulated wealth by assembling low-risk low-volatility portfolios of high grade bonds, the latter's success comes from speculatively capturing and cultivating volatility. This surfaces in the creation of bank production lines that sought to speculatively lend in order to securitize, the loans then assembled into asset backed securities (especially mortgages) and subsequently repackaged as tranches of collateralized debt obligations. An unanticipated result of the logic of this institutional transition is that the derivative that many thought would provide a market solution to discerning and disarming financial risk became the privileged tool of speculation, in the process magnifying risk systemically. It is hard not to conclude from this that the institutional design of the present financial system is partly responsible for generating the illegible and always potentially uncontainable risks that, given its penchant for math and statistics, it gives the illusion of managing scientifically. Read any money center bank report on the risk management of derivatives to realize that the statistics, charts, and equations serve more to legitimate the conclusions than to inform them.

Derivatives beneath the Surface

Where derivatives are concerned, the closer and more observant one gets the stranger they appear. The common idea that derivatives are a bet on a relation and a tango with time represents their surface appearance. The time bracketed bet is their necessary mode of expression just as the market is their necessary venue of execution. If analysis removes the laminate of their expression and execution, a deeper set of properties comes into focus. Properties that tie derivatives to a vision and division of the functions of capital under a supplementary regime of value. This new regime pivots on the way in which abstract risk mediates the global expansion of capital and the creation of socialized wealth outside of commodity production. The derivative thus ushers in the advent of the non-commodity commodity. By non-commodity commodity, I indicate that though the derivative is not a commodity, it adheres to the shape of the commodity form in that each derivative is both particular, as a wager on specific concrete risks (e.g., liquidity stop), and general as a social mediation of circulation. This is precisely how derivatives can "in aggregate, continually reproduce their own social existence" (Bryan and Rafferty 2015:5) and why they do not, in principle, accord a social character to that reproduction. Derivatives further adhere to the commodity's form in that the character of the mediation is also socially general. This is so because each abstract risk-driven derivative functions in the same socially mediating way, independent of their specific purposes. Derivatives thus rest their case on commodity based capitalism and the results of production focused labor even as they elaborate its reach and transcend the commodity's grounding in "ordinary" use values. Why this is the case has everything to do with the derivative's internal design and logos.

One necessary dimension of the derivative is that it is *a time dependent wager on volatility*. Derivatives price and monetize risk over a certain temporal distance from the instantiation of the now. The now is the virtual and spaceless moment of the contract's initiation. That every initiated contract expires at a certain set date is central to finance's understanding and pricing of the derivative because it allows for the conflation of risk and volatility. Near term expiration—whether it is set at a specific date or is triggered by the provisions of some contracts—means that volatility is risk because it must be dealt with forthcomingly. In this approaching moment, from their perspective inside the trade, the participants neither care nor contemplate whether the value at risk is ontologically real or fictitious. Derivatives contracts are intrinsically performative in that they fabricate the conditions of their own existence—much in the way that saying the word promise and its acceptance brings that promise, here, now, with certain conditions, into existence until its expiration. A derivative's utility as a value (directly or transitively for exotics) turns on its dynamic replication. Derivatives thus live in the interval between inception and expiration, continually creating a new now and a new what is, creating wealth by opening and closing continuously a gap (whose dimensions can only be delineated retrospectively) between some realized price and some possible impending futures. This movement captures the fact that derivatives do not inhabit the directional space of commodities—commodities yield wealth because the power of labor adds value in the time between the investment of capital and the revenues that the owners of production obtain when the commodities are sold. Rather, derivatives inhabit a space in which *wealth is created as a consequence of their volatility* conceived as a dispersion or "spread" around a mean that is represented and taken as the imaginary center of that spread.[3]

Volatility is important in and of itself, but also because the design of derivatives functionally leverages that volatility. This leverage lies in what is called the *convexity* of the derivative. Convexity means that change in the underlier's value and change in that of its derivative need not be symmetrical. Convexity allows that a change in the value/price of the underlier can produce a disproportionately larger change in the value/price of a derivative predicated on that underlier. The leverage thus stems from the fact that a small change in the state of the underlier can generate a large change in the derivative. During the crisis, the collateralized mortgage obligations were so toxic because a small number of defaults could generate enormous losses in the CMOs value.

The value of a derivative thus has a non-linear relationship with its under-lier. The result is that a derivative's price movement, such as the securitized instruments that precipitated the crisis, can be disproportionately larger than the movement of its underlier. This is expressed mathematically by what is called Jensen's inequality. Jensen's inequality is an attempt to give a probabilistic account of this non-linear relationship between underlier and derivative. Its ethnographic value lies in the fact that by offering a probabilistic treatment of inequality it recognizes the leverage embodied in the derivative.[4] The relative convexity of a derivative is therefore a measure of its power and influence upon the world. In the social world, student loans often have a high degree of convexity: if the graduates obtain high paying employment the return on the investment (essentially call options on their future) is disproportionately high whereas if they are unemployed or underemployed the return is disproportionately low and can easily lead to a judgment of default (from which there is little relief under the law). So under their present design student loans in the United States are rather risky because they compel students to leverage their future income stream in a transformative period of retarded job growth and stagnant wages.

For derivatives, the concept and pricing of volatility only occurs within temporal brackets. And derivative offer a new animated temporality. They offer in the first place an anxiousness of time in that their termination or finality is a horizon that is continually approaching. For time is always compressing and squeezing the interval between the trade's inception and expiration. Although it is easy to think abstractly of circulation as having a constant speed, in reality, the difference between the speed of derivatives and that of the commodity—their respective upper end speeds of volatility and circulation—is akin to the difference between a cheetah and a house cat. For globalization, when the world moves, derivatives move capital first and faster. The time of derivatives is the relocation and reanimation of the future into the present. This future is an imagined future or forthcoming, projected from the present and then read backwards so that an implied future (e.g., increasing interest rates) defines a forthcoming that transforms the present (e.g., a firm's cost of capital) across the interval stretching between now and a derivative's expiration date. Through anticipation and deduction, the derivative encodes temporality and trajectory as if agents calculate their realizations in advance, as though the logos of the derivative allows the participants to somehow get ahead of the social itself. From the continuous film of time, the derivative cuts out and enframes a particular interval—an interval that presents itself as a *forthcoming*. This is meant technically as an unfolding situation whose limits are set contractually, and which brings into existence for the participants expectations, memories, strategic moves in case . . . , and fears and anxieties about what might, could, should transpire. The derivative embodies an interpolation of the forthcoming that attaches the future to the present. Attaching the future to the present leads to an expansion of the now, but also its destabilization. For agents are condemned to anticipate a future they cannot know with any certainty, and so following the lead of economics they seek to scientize that future as a deterministic probability distribution. This is the essence of derivative pricing models, exemplified by Black-Scholes (Merton). The method is to define the temporal string from the present to the future as homogeneous, and to then read and reason backwards across the hypostasized interval to set a price that represents the point of contestation between the counterparties over the volatility of the forthcoming. Which is nothing less than a bet on the heterogeneity (or uncertainty) of the interval from the moment of a contract's initiation to its expiration. There are few things less present than a contract that has expired, the click of expiration wiping the slate clean for the next up trade. This use and redetermination of temporality is one of the critical things that serves to differentiate the derivative from the commodity.

In the space of commodity exchange and use values, it is transparent why agents consummate transactions. That agents occupy difference positions in social space all but guarantees a heterogeneity of interests and passions. This heterogeneity motivates the gap between value and price which, in turn, motivates the transaction. Simply said, buyers and sellers can agree on a price because they ascribe different use-values to the commodities they exchange. Sellers want to profit by trading commodities they have made or acquired whereas buyers value commodities in respect to the satisfaction of wants and desires. As Ole Bjerg (2014) explains: "the trade will come about at a given price as the parties invoke different measures of value that render the trade attractive to both of them" (p. 24). By contrast, the derivative is not a commodity and has no transparent value in the here and now (save as collateral for the leveraged purchase of other derivatives). The only measure to motivate the transaction is, accordingly, a calculation of the derivative's value in the forthcoming future, anywhere. Where use-values anchor the commodity in the space-time of the present, we frequently buy commodities that we consume immediately (e.g., a magnum of Barolo with parpandelle con tartufo), the derivative's value, because determined entirely in the realm of exchange, aims at a time in the future. A derivative can be priced because the participants consummate the closure of the bid-asked spread, this closure occurring if and only if the participants agree as to the derivative's net present value, but differ as to their speculative calculation of its forthcoming value.

The derivative differs not only from the commodity's form, but from other forms of capital instruments. The market can continuously value a derivative through its cycles of replication. In this respect, the derivative resembles debt instruments which are also embodiments of capital and can be continuously valued. Nonetheless, a derivative on, for example, a debt instrument such as corporate or treasury bonds differs from those bonds in significant ways. First, the derivative's price is pegged to and correlated with that of the underlying security. The derivative's utility can stem from the fact that it can price and disaggregate aspects of a given security that the security itself cannot price, such as the interrelationship between a security's specific risks and the volatility or risks confronting the market or the economy as a whole. For example, bond holders can use derivatives to disaggregate and price the risk created by clearing-house failure, accelerating inflation, or a flattening of the yield curve. Second, the derivative's results do not increase bond-like exponentially over time as its interest payments compound. For those who have a retirement account (e.g., 401K), a bond fund's interest reinvestment option exemplifies the effect of compounding. In sharp contrast, a derivative contract's value and utility (e.g., as collateral) decays over time as that contract approaches its expiration. Third, for derivatives, dynamic replication is necessary to their existence. For replication lies at the intersection of, and is determinative in creating, the relational dynamic between volatility and liquidity. The very possibility of capturing volatility depends on a contract's liquidity or tradeability. By contrast, bonds and other credit instruments have value in the absence of their dynamic replication because they furnish an income stream and because at expiration the issuer will redeem them at their face value. So the heartbeat of derivative trading is not an income stream, a return on capital, or even the directionality of the underlier: it is the magnitude and velocity of a derivative's volatility.

Although the derivative seeks to commodify risk, and the labor implicated in its production is abstracted from the concrete circumstances of that production, it is not a commodity, not even a derivative thereof. The reification of the relations of risk into a transactable thing (while critical to the derivative's social epistemology) does not make the derivative a commodity. As noted, the derivative is thus neither imbued with nor does it ever possess a concrete use value. A derivative's solitary value is as a wager, meaning that it is impossible to arbitrage surplus value by making a commodity at one price based on the foreknowledge that it can be sold at a higher price. Accordingly, the problem facing a use-valueless derivative is on what basis or criteria should the agents who co-produce a given transaction assign a price to it. The answer is that pricing is done on the basis of a given derivative's expected forthcoming volatility, measured as its degree of variance between the moment of transaction and its instant of expiration (e.g., 4:00 pm Eastern Standard Time on December 10, 2015). In the practice of trading (exemplified once literally and now mostly metaphorically by the "trading floor"), the derivative is priced in terms of its forthcoming volatility, including the possibility that that volatility will be so violent that it results in the default of the counterparty (hence the origin of credit default swaps). Where markets price commodities competitively, the pricing of (especially OTC) derivatives centers on the relationship between expected volatility and time to expiration. In 1973, the Black-Scholes (Merton) formula revolutionized the then budding derivative markets because it provided a mathematics for pricing any contract. The formula's math allowed market makers to price volatility independent of the underlier's directional movement. And this, in turn, made it theoretically possible, through a process called *dynamic hedging*, to expunge a derivative's directional risk (the risk that the underlier's value increases or decreases) and concentrate entirely on the profit opportunities afforded by its volatility. The qualifier here is the term *theoretically*, since in real-world markets traders can never completely effectuate either the *dynamic* or *hedging* part of the process. Nonetheless, traders often attempt to hedge their derivative portfolio in aggregate based on their intuitions and foreknowledge about a given market.

The ideology of finance says that hedging and speculation are distinct substantive categories. The ideology isolates the beliefs and desires of the agents at the moment of a contract's inception. This binary reading of the real—which is critical to the narrative that finance articulates to legislators inasmuch as it is fitted to a moral economy which values hedging over speculation—erases the interval and thus the temporality of the derivative and trading practices. The unfolding of actual trades foreground the fact that almost all trades imbricate the reality effects of hedging and speculation, and that practitioners only know retrospectively what aspects of the trading created these effects. Accordingly, hedging and speculation are best understood as a spread phenomenon, this trade here now occurring in a relational space whose horizon, from the forthcoming to the present, allows movement in all directions. Note that even the most unrequited hedge is also a speculation in that hedging involves not only the underlier's volatility (conceptualized atemporally as up or down) but mutable, fragile, which is so say, volatile beliefs about the forth-coming trajectory of that underlier. Hedging is also speculative because the agents tend to view it through the social epistemology of capitalism, with its substantialist bias. So though hedging is based on an hypostatized correlation (if y goes down/up then x should go up/down a corresponding and reciprocal amount), the participants grasp the correlation not as a parameter in their implicit model but as a real phenomenon. The correlation effect that grounds the hedge is taken as invariant and preordained. This view of hedging conceals the speculation that unknown or unknowable factors (including being ganged up on by other money managers) may derail the presumed correlation. Every OTC derivative trader knows from experience that an intended hedge can morph into an outright naked speculation, and that conversely two expressly speculative bets may end up offsetting one another. In sum, most derivative transactions articulate a changing mosaic of hedging and speculation. The des-ignations live in the always evolving spread between a trader's intent at the outset—from outright speculation or a fully articulated arbitrage—and a series of retrospective attributions as the contract arcs toward expiration.

This temporality imbues the derivative with a special susceptibility to the future's uncertainty. The rule of uncertainty necessarily socially implicates the derivative and its markets. For the challenge of time is to insure agents' col-lective belief in a market's future liquidity in the face of the unknowable edge of volatility created by the realization of the uncertain. What appears certain today may be thrown into chaos by a black swan (an un-anticipatable event) or by an overleveraged market's own internal dynamic. The optimal derivatives market walks a high-wire: for it seeks to embrace as much volatility as possi-ble without allowing volatility to become so excessive and uncontrollable that there is a loss of liquidity so disabling that the participants quit the market. Participants' collective faith in its forthcoming liquidity is the religion of the market, for derivatives especially. For this reason, behind its back so to speak, derivatives must invoke the performative power of rituality to instantiate col-lectively what each agent presupposes individually. It resolves the certainty of uncertainty shaped by the temporal interval and experienced by the sub-ject (each and every trader) as a projection into the forthcoming. The collec-tive belief that a contract will always have a value from now—its moment of initiation—all the way across the interval to its expiration holds on one con-dition: a market uses the power of rituality to objectify social relations. The participants must believe that this market, here, now, that I am trading into a forthcoming, is a continuous well-formed form. Where derivatives are concerned there is no alternative. For the participants, awaiting the moment of a contract's settlement (somewhere along the interval) must mutually, collectively presuppose the existence of that market as a durable space of operations, as an entity that will be there tomorrow. Otherwise there'll be no liquidity, no way to measure the effects of volatility, and therefore no way to determine the settlement price. The contingency of the payoff disowns all and any relationship to the contingency of the market. This rituality is reinforced to the point of facticity by traders' experience of successful trades, by bracketing and excluding the memory of failure as an impossible possible, and by mutually harvesting the power of equations and pricing models whose common use confirms that the market is a totality. The implicit agreement not to recognize practically what everyone recognizes—that markets can and do fail because their liquidity evaporates—surfaces ethnographically in the contradiction that every trader is individually aware that markets taken as wholes have amnesia about their past failures. Sociostructurally, a market is a formless form in that it is a space of relations whose surface appearance as a space of operations— that is, as a market—is *necessarily* as a durable, continuous, self-reproducing, well-formed form. The scandal of the market is that its very existence depends on the collectively held illusion that it cannot not exist. For every trader trading, the market is a technology that mediates between me and my similars; it must necessarily recognize us and be recognizable—so identifiable that we are able to collectively recognize its features without ever having seen them, like the face of god.

Derivative markets refer to uncertainty and risk as though their relationship is self-evident. Typically, uncertainty denotes those events that market makers cannot know about in advance (e.g., a terrorist attack) but will amplify volatility and result in an adverse outcome; whereas risk refers to events that are presumably knowable in advance (e.g., an uptick in inflation) and whose outcomes can be calculated as a probability. Beyond this commonsense standard, derivatives engage in a kind of deep play with the distinction between risk and uncertainty. Uncertainty motivates traders to trade going forward whereas risk represents the history of uncertainty read backwards. Net present value, the value of a derivative in the immediate moment, names the portal that mathematized models step through to translate uncertainty into typified forms of measurable risk. Both the types and measures of risk are precisely what uncertainty looks like when pricing models and practices render the future present. The derivative both compels and lures the agents involved to convene to price uncertainty as though it is indistinguishable from risk. From the ideology of a naturalized economics, risk and uncertainty are not just indistinguishable in traders' practices but ontologically and epistemologically. Whereas impending uncertainties are defined by the unknowable, inasmuch as the participants do not even know what they don't know, risk is defined by agents' sure-footed ability to harness what they know to maximize profits (e.g., by leveraging a derivative position). This view imputes a clarity—not to say participants' clairvoyance—to forthcoming events which erases the epistemic opacity. In reality, the derivative mediates the relationship between risk and uncertainty: for it must translate as a condition of its own possibility a probabilistic assessment of what will happen (e.g., if GDP accelerates then interest rates will rise; if the ECB cuts interest rates the dollar will strengthen against the euro; if Brazil elects a socialist president, then other hedge funds and proprietary trading desks will short the real) into a concatenation of types of risk that speculators can knowledgeably measure (e.g., counterparty, political, liquidity risk, etc.). This translation is necessary because to reach an agreement about a derivative's future value and thus its price requires a determination of its net present value which is not simply the result of the parties calculating that value based on the application of their expert knowledge, but their hyper-vigilance toward potentially impending changes (e.g., to interest rates) and their constant anticipation of other's decisions about that forthcoming to which they are all subsumed individually, indirectly, and in aggregate. And thus it turns out that one of the most powerful forces binding a market's traders together socially is that they must necessarily and simultaneously, over and again, confront the same progression of open ended horizons of externalities—social constituted externalities that range from the highly probable to the ungovernable volatility of the blackest of swans (e.g., no derivative pricing ever takes into consideration a terrorist attack on the White House or 10 Downing Street that results in the assassination of the president or the prime minister). These market makers are also bound together by the fact that they mutually apprehend these externalities by oscillating between a reflective vision (which scientizes these externalities as risks) and a practical vision which interprets changes in these externalities as adjustments to be made in the forthcoming recalibration of a derivative's price. In the end the most realistic view is that the derivative prices what it defines as risk through an indeterminate approximation of the pricing of uncertainty.

There is a technical dimension to finance's deep play of risk and uncertainty. The simultaneity of their conflation and difference appears in the way in which derivatives are evaluated. By, most famously, credit agencies such as Moody's and Standard and Poor's. Unable to untangle the uncertainty, newness, and epistemic opacity of derivatives such as collateralized mortgage obligations (CMOS), they simply equated these derivatives with less complex instruments, such as corporate bonds, that were inherently less volatile and for which there was long and detailed credit histories. Donald Mackenzie (2011) explains how credit agencies black boxed the complexities.

> The [credit agencies] permitted the economic value of different [derivatives] to be compared, both with each other and with more familiar, less complex instruments . . . by comparing the 'spread' (increment over Libor or other benchmark interest rate) offered by a given instrument to that offered by others with the same rating. This spread nexus was thus a way of turning what otherwise might be *radical uncertainty* into a form of order that—while never unchanging—is stable and predictable. (my emphasis)

This move turned "radical uncertainty" into measurable risk, even as the agencies acknowledged that the unknowns of the forthcoming were instrumental in driving a market's replication. Those who innovated derivatives knew this as well. So producer's of exotic derivatives, by openly comparing them with other credit instruments, could determine the combination of ratings and interest rates that would make the newly fabricated derivative competitive and liquid. The producers were essentially balancing what the buyers would demand above the "risk free" rate to offset the future's uncertainty with the security and legitimacy generated by a credit rating based on predictable risk. The key point is that both radical uncertainty and predictable risk would doom the derivative. Thus to capitalize on volatility, speculative capital must manipulate and play with their relationship in ways that simultaneously acknowledge and paper over the fact that uncertainty and risk will appear practically as a *spread*. And that importantly, the risk-uncertainty *spread* is always itself necessarily volatile. The only thing that can narrow or abridge the spread between risk and uncertainty is the one thing derivatives do not have: a time horizon so extended that it smoothes out the volatility.

The objective of dissembling and reassembling capital shapes the process of the production and circulation of capital itself, thus reversing the polarity of means and ends that defined the creation and allocation of capital under a regime of production. The logical implications of this reversal bear on the sociality of the derivative. To begin with, the main objective of the contract is no longer to reduce or reallocate risk (as is the case with insurance contracts for example). The derivative hedges or offsets risk only insofar as it advances the interests of speculative capital. This alters the character of risk. Societies in all times and everywhere have found ways to discern and disarm the specific concrete risks posed and sometimes imposed by circulation. Against the background of generality, the ascension of derivative markets has transformed the significance of risk. For now risk only matters quantitatively, in respect to how it enters into the calculation of a numerable price. The specificity of the risks do matter, of course, in the pricing of derivative contracts yet are immaterial to the creation of the circulatory structure and the liquidity of its markets. The derivatives market is, as it were, indifferent toward the creation of and market making in specific instruments. Critically, in contrast to the risk mitigation common to the sphere of production where specific risks are dealt with by specific actions (e.g., the risk of currency fluctuations is dealt with by making sure that most of a company's profits derive from same currency sources), the world's derivative markets reassign risk independently of the specific character of that risk. To the point where the derivative and its risks can be synthetic and therefore parasitic to some parallel product. So we can now see why *circulation's ultimate objective has become the objectification of risk itself.* More, this objective takes shape and substance independently of the will or volition of the market's makers. Conceptually, the calculation of risk turns out to be a means for the creation of a social (circulatory) form constituted by risk. This is a critical determination about why capitalism with derivatives constitutes a transformed form of the social.

That the derivative as a social form separates risk from the circumstances of its realization has certain implications. It allows derivative finance to define risk in terms of volatility. Risk becomes an inward looking category of the market, which then goes on to measure risk as the probability of the relative variance of a derivative's price. The use of a probability measure and its incorporation into a pricing model only makes sense if risk is conceptualized as a market internal category. The isolation of risk and its equilibration with volatility then allows the market to logically transform volatility itself into an object of production. And this is precisely the reality that has come to pass: an economy in which derivatives capitalize on the volatility that they actively create. While its mathematization certainly helps to impart an objective character to volatility, it also appears as eminently objective because it is now divorced and distanced from the specific nature of the risks that engender the fluctuations and because volatility, once it is defined as a measure of market internal risk, appears as an object that has a life of its own. The social epistemology of derivative capital imbues risk with an objective character that allows it to appear as a self-animating subject which can impose itself on the situationally specific actions of financial agents.

The derivative converts agents' reflective and practical visions of the future into a contingency that the market can trade. But this will only happen if there is a difference of opinion. In the space of the market, *the spread* names even as it grounds this difference of opinion by marking out the distance that the traders must dissolve for the transaction to take place. This means that the spread necessarily transcends the opposition that it stages as a condition of its own completion. The spread is, because it appears as and represents, the difference between "the bid" and "the asked" for a derivative, a difference that must be continually annulled to complete this transactions and every other transaction to maintain a market's liquidity. Though I am jumping ahead to a forthcoming discussion, it is worth observing that the negative performativity of the transaction, the way in which it annuls difference (between the bid and asked prices), presupposes the positive constitutive performativity of rituality in generating the fixed enclosure of the market, both of which disappear in what appears to be a law-like objective settlement of the settlement price. Every derivative transaction's singularity of price conceals both the spread and the ritual that underwrote its realization. The unfolding of the spread across the interval—that is, recalibrations of token prices which are typified—are subject to three critical types of transgression that radiate out from the market's center to the world at large. The first is amplification in the volatility of volatility within a market (due to fluctuations in the status of outstanding contingent claims); the second are recalibrations of prices due to the market's reactions to economic events and the actions of regulatory institutions, and the third are exogenous events, such as terrorist attacks. These exogenous events can, of course and historically, trigger increases in the volatility of volatility.

Despite the hyperbole that sometimes accompanies accounts of the ascension of derivatives, they can't displace commodities or subsume their use values. The ascension of circulation has come in the midst of a global rise in production levels. But there are two significant howevers. The first is that the wealth created in derivative markets is increasingly related to production through layers of mediating factors, as is the case for cross currency derivatives. These mediating factors can become so powerful that the "price" of a nation's money (e.g., Brazilian real or Thai baht) appears as a spread phenomena, the volatility and amplitude of exchange rates only partially and variably tethered to the state of that nation's production of commodities. The price of a currency floats in the spread between a nation's economic performance and the internal mechanics of derivative markets. Consider that the currency markets apprehend aspects of a nation's economic state—such as its inflation rate, productivity of industrial output, prevailing interest rates, wages, and the state of its debt obligations (especially in dollars and euros)—as exogenous forces that intersect with the derivative markets to inflect the price of that nation's money, which, in turn, inflects the availability and cost of capital. What this means is that not only are finance and industrial production increasingly internal to one another, but that they exist in a state of disruptive interdependence. This interdependence shapes an ontological discontinuity in that while the success of the real economy depends on minimizing and ideally even eliminating such disruptiveness and volatility, they are the lifeblood of the derivative markets such that the participants (e.g., global banks and hedge funds) in these markets seek to capitalize on and amplify precisely the forms of disruption and volatility that often harm production (e.g., by fostering accelerated sudden changes in interest or cross currency rates). Said another way, industrial production does best when finance volatility spreads are gradual, measured, and predictably return to the mean, whereas derivative markets thrive when spreads are as sudden, exaggerated, and large as possible without compromising liquidity.

The second however is that when commodities come under the optic of derivative markets—in order for use value commodities such as and especially houses to be turned via securitization into speculative wagering assets—the derivative must reconfigure the valuation process. For in addition to the directional risk that attends all commodity production, the derivative markets imbue the commodity with all of the risks engendered by the constant calibration of volatility across the interval. The derivative markets continually reprice commodities not on the basis of their immanent value but in respect to an impending and inherently uncertain future value. In this process, the derivative's forecast of what the commodity will be worth in the immediate future inflects the labor employed and the capital allocated to its production. By selling the commodity (think here of a new house) before it is realized as a worldly thing, which is as a use value, derivatives insinuate circulation in production by assigning floating and contingent values to the commodity. To speculate on a derivative driven commodity (exemplified by wagers on home prices) is to speculate on the spread between the directionality of prices and the spread engendered by replication in the derivative markets. A reality never more apparent than when the wagers are levered to and collateralized by the commodity wagered on.

The derivative arises in a constitutive relationship with capital, as the character of speculative capital is to use derivatives to dismember then reassemble capital itself. The speculation that produces wealth lies precisely in the way an investment bank or hedge fund, mathematical scalpel in hand, can dissect capital into its elementary forms of risk and then reassemble a new creature that takes on a life of its own. Redesigned on the plan of the derivative logic, capital no longer has allegiance to any national currency. Capital can be dissembled into its liquidity, money value in foreign currencies, reliability of repayment (counterparty default), organization of its ownership, money value in its own currency (inflation), relative price stability (volatility), politics of its governance (state oversight), perceived image of its issuer (be this a national state or a corporation). These aspects are extracted from capital, variously according to the design of a derivative's maker, and then reassembled into an abstract risk-driven instrument whose future value is bestowed a present price, first through the application of a mathematized pricing formula (the Black-Scholes model) and then through readjustments traders make in light of all those realities the mathematized model excludes.

The exchange value of a derivative is the resolution of a difference though the settlement of and on a price. However, the exchange value of a derivative is not a necessary expression or mode of appearance of value if value is conceived as a function of the social abstraction of labor; rather, the exchange value of a derivative is an expression of the social abstraction of risk implied across a finite temporal interval, read from back to front and then progressively forwards until the contract expires. And while there is a use value to some derivatives, as a means of hedging (currencies or interest rates, most notably), they do not implicate labor and are, anyways, of fractional importance in that they are dwarfed by pure speculative wagering. If a derivative has value it is only because the derivative objectifies abstract risk such that the conjuncture of different dimensions of capital can mediate their differences. This value is a function of the knowledge about the future that the derivative conveys to the present, that is, the accuracy with which it captures the risk embodied in a particular re-articulation of capital over some immediate future (e.g., Japanese interest rates in respect to a credit default swaps index on yen denominated corporate bonds reading from December 31, 2013, to the present). The forward value of this derivative contract is based on the information and terms codified in the contact. The derivative suggests that there is another source of value that does not lie in the commodity based concept of labor, but in the labor expended to produce the interconnectivity of capital, circulating globally.

Derivatives and Crisis

The relationship between derivatives and crisis will only become evident once the analysis reveals the internal dynamic driving their markets. That said, any discussion of derivatives must indicate from the outset that if capitalism flourishes through crisis then derivatives would seem to be its most advanced expression. This relationship is due to the centrality of volatility as the source of wealth, and thus the raison d'être of the markets themselves. The implicit aim is to always walk a tightrope in which a market has as much wealth-producing volatility as possible without having so much volatility that it causes an impairment of liquidity. For traders, a perfect derivative market is one in which they can continually arbitrage volatility, and thereby generate wealth, because the market retains its liquidity despite the volatility of volatility itself created by the market's life-producing subsumption of uncertainty. Understanding this relationship will eventually lead to the theorization that the immanent dynamic of a derivative market (and thus a foundation of the present crisis) lies in the give and take between the necessity to arbitrage volatility and the amount of risk (e.g., through leveraging) necessary to keep that market's volatility worth arbitraging.

For now, note that the standard narrative is that crisis is something that happens to derivative markets. The narrative spins an account about how a market that is sailing along smoothly can encounter bouts of turbulence much in the same manner that a ship at sea can encounter a violent tempest. What was once a journey on untroubled waters becomes so problematic that the ship can founder and sometimes capsize, requiring rescue from the authorities in the form of extramural infusions of capital. This storyline has a certain persuasiveness due to its familiarity: for it implicitly equates the failures that may befall the derivative market with those encountered by the equity markets. Exemplified by the steep prolonged decline in stock prices precipitated, as the economic history of the twentieth century underlies, by an economic recession or the onset of war.

But this narrative does not do justice to the relationship between crisis and the derivative markets. Indeed, once the analysis illuminates the temporality of the derivative markets, it will turn out that they are prone to crises of their own making, crises that ensue because their internal design magnifies to a great power small changes in the value of the underliers. Left to its own device, the DNA of a derivative market and the structure of the competition between participants will result in a dynamic relationship between volatility and leverage such that a derivative market is prone to germinate the seed of its own systemic impairment. Two examples will provide an idea as to the direction of the analysis in the forthcoming chapters. The market's crisis tendencies appear in the fact that a decline in volatility, which in production based markets leads to increasing stability, often ends up amplifying the instability of a derivative market. The reason is that a sustained decline in volatility will lead to a compression of margins and thus a decline in the profitability of the volatility arbitrage, which, in turn, will motivate traders to compensate for the decline in profitability through the increase use of increasing leverage. And as leverage amplifies two things happen: it becomes increasingly difficult to hedge outstanding positions, and small changes in the value of the underlier can (due to convexity) generate huge changes in the derivative. A second example comes from mutual fund managers in the equity markets—the kind of funds that average citizens and institutions (e.g., university endowments) are likely to invest in. To beat the benchmark index (e.g., technology) against which the financial sector measures the managers quarterly performance, it pays the manager to speculate on equity derivatives, from simple options to more exotic instruments.[5] This move is institutionally "rational" despite the fact that it leverages the fund because the derivatives are not part of the benchmark index, which means that any gains are pure alpha. The downside is that massive derivative losses can cause the fund manager to liquidate much of his underlying stock/bond portfolio, which, in turn, will only serve to further destabilize the derivative markets. On this reading, the crisis tendencies of derivative markets are not rooted in the relation between the markets and the precarity of the outside world. Rather, these tendencies lie within the basic design of the derivative markets themselves.

Derivatives and Money

Ole Bjerg (2014), in a work that examines the philosophical underpinnings of crisis capitalism, explores how the dynamic of the derivative's temporality inflects the ontology or foundation of money itself. Picking up on the argument by Bryan and Rafferty (2007) that derivatives constitute a form of money, Bjerg shows that their culture of circulation also motivates money-center banks to create as much credit money[6] as is necessary to satisfy the seemingly ever escalating demand of the derivative markets. The derivative is therefore systemically transformative because it represents the emergence of a self-expanding, self-valorizing money form. The dynamic of expansion-valorization is that the emergence and crystallization of the derivative as a store of value, means of exchange, and deferred payment motivates the creation of additional money, which, in turn, allows for the expansion of the derivative markets. This expansion of credit money is the primary source of the speculative capital that fuels the growth of derivative markets and helps create the bridge to the real production economy. Reflecting on this reality, Bjerg observes:

> Trading in financial markets is not just about the redistribution and circulation of existing money. As trading volumes grow, financial markets themselves generate their own demand for more money to come into being in order to service transactions in the market. This means that not only is debt and credit money the oxygen of financialization but the growth in financial trading also leads to the financialization of money itself. (p. 195–96)

The basis of this dynamic is a new temporal horizon for credit money in that it must anticipate the creation of derivatives which are their own "quasi"-money form in that they function, when within their sphere of circulation, parallel to the stores of credit money they embody. In this sphere, derivatives can serve as collateral for a loan, payment for a debt, a means of exchange for another derivative (as in the case of a swap), and a unit of account for calculating an institution's liquidity.[7] And so with Ole Bjerg we can conclude that the self-valorizing, symbiotic expansions of the derivative form/trading and credit money creates a temporal dynamic that is reconfiguring "the ontology of money itself" (p. 197) in that the production of money no longer corresponds to the production and circulation of goods and services. There are two real-world indices of this transformation (the analysis of which lies beyond my objectives): (1) especially since 1973, the increase in the quantity of US dollars continues to dramatically outstrip the growth in production, and (2) the velocity of money coursing through the production based economy continues to fall. What this says is that circulatory capitalism has created a home for the creation and animation of money that is essentially extrinsic to production.

One reason this is critical, especially for the governance of the economy, is that the training of economists and central bankers has indoctrinated them with theories that cannot accommodate this new reality. Despite the recession and the ensuing deleveraging of the economy, they are fearful that increasing the money supply will semi-automatically lead to inflation. The fear follows on the premise that injecting money into the banking system is equivalent to stimulating the demand for goods and services. Based on the production centric economy that held sway for more than a century—and which gave rise to economic theorems such as Say's Law—the assumption is that the financial system will naturally and invariably transfer the injected money, via loans such as revolving credit facilities and mortgages, into acquisitions of capital goods and the other means of production and into funding consumer purchases. But it turns out, of course, that having injected—through several rounds of quantitative easing—almost a trillion dollars into the financial system, the Federal Reserve cannot materially stimulate consumer demand or push inflation above even 1 percent. Despite dire warnings by neoliberal economists about the great perils of monetary stimulus, warnings that emanate from models based a nation-state production-centric economy, there has been no inflation, alternative currencies such as gold have remained moribund, interest rates on government bonds have declined, and the dollar has risen rather than fallen against other currencies. Eight years after the crisis (2016), everything that was supposed to happen on account of great monetary expansion has fallen into nothing. Nonetheless, it remains hard for those who economic habitus is rooted in the production based "system" of national-based capitalisms to accept that their economic theories and models require more than minor readjustment. The new reality of circulatory capitalism is that global transnational trading networks and derivative markets are absorbing almost all of the newly "printed" dollars.

Derivatives and Wealth

In respect to the creation of wealth there are two foundational questions: why should derivatives trade and why should people trade derivatives? Put differently, why should derivatives have value and why are their values tradable to the point and with the result that derivative create wealth? Wealth that is, in the most literal sense imaginable, the wealth of society (Meister 2013 and Martin 2014).[8]

Now it is obvious that derivatives can enrich the anointed few: as illustrated in bold colors by news stories about decadent houses in the Hamptons (Long Island, NY), new Lamborghinis, and parties extravagant to the point of obscenity. It is thus also obvious that derivatives can distribute wealth as this is, after all, the essence of the zero-sum game that underwrites wagering of all types. And if by wealth is meant only the commodities that capitalism generates in and through the production process through the mediation of labor (concretely and abstractly), then derivatives are little more than a hole in the economy that permits finance to siphon off wealth created elsewhere to advance its singular, predatory interests. The problem is that this productionist view does not account for what is a real amplification of wealth or explain why finance has become a larger and larger share of the economy. To say, as is said in some Marxist circles, that financial capital is creating a burgeoning separation between value and wealth is anachronistic. For the existence and expansion of the separation does not begin to explain the sources of this wealth, the sociostructures that produce and reproduce it, or the use of this wealth to lobby, cajole, and intimidate the politics of the present.

The more current account it would seem, meaning one adequate to the facts, is that financial derivatives have value and create wealth but on a different order of economy than production. An order of economy that is the character of the present. Where the creation of value/wealth in the sphere of production turns on and is mediated by labor—as the work of Postone (1993) has illustrated beyond any reasonable doubt—its creation in the sphere of circulation turns on and is mediated by the risks capital encounters in its movement across boundaries. What is called globalization, the term fostering the illusion that the process is emanating worldwide like a radio signal when in reality it names a metropolitan neoliberal ordering in which social and economic life has become simultaneously globalized and interdependent, yet increasingly fragmented and statelessly decentered. In this context, the circulation of capital cannot but generate volatility in that circulation is and amplifies the transgression of difference. Private sector, cross-border flows of capital between often anonymous counterparties encounter and thus transgress differences in culture, currency, organization of the financial field, political forms, and juridical regimes to cite the most transparent differences. Such transgressions of difference generate risk, or more precisely a plethora of risks of different orders of magnitude. These risks motivate the innovation of instruments to quantify and price risk, necessarily abstractly. The derivatives that embody risk embody value in the same way that an immunization has value: they offset the risks of transgression. The difference—and this is all the difference in the world—is that for the derivatives markets to come into existence and continue to exist to offset risk they must continually attract speculative capital, which because they are organized by the logic of the capitalist market whose only motive force is differential monetary opportunity, can only be achieved if they continually generate their own disease (volatility) to immunize themselves against. The derivative markets thus depend on their being sufficient volatility to attract speculative capital, but not to the point where it proves fatal, meaning the cessation of liquidity/life. There is accordingly a meta-use value to the derivative in that it preserves the system for the mitigation of risk created by circulation across difference. The contracts thus generated possess real value because they represent income flows (in, for example, the case of swaps), can be used as collateral for the purchase of other securities, and can serve as a contingent claim on the wealth of society. To put it differently, this generation of value (and societal wealth) is intrinsically connected to a mode of circulation founded on risk in its derivative form: which is, as I will clarify, an abstract aspect of the dissembling and assembling of capital. Implied in this is a certain historical specificity: for it is only with the advent of circulatory capitalism in the 1970s does risking capital become a derivative that can mediate circulation socially. In the same vein, the derivative is the form of value and wealth consistent with a global order that depends on capital flows among interdependent yet fragmented and stateless decentered entities. In a delimited way and with a very different intention, the derivative markets are a replacement for the World Bank and International Monetary Fund who specialize in managing global flows of capital under a regime of production-centered, nation-state–based capitalism.

To say that derivatives organize the flows of capital—between types of securities, currencies, and geographies for example—is tantamount to identifying their regulatory capacities. As Martin (2013:93) notes, their culture of circulation takes on the regulatory functions that where once the sole province of governance. In this sense, the circuits of derivatives do away with even the semblance of the notion that there's a political that stands outside the economic. The derivative market can engender constraints and imperatives that delimit and sometimes determine what, for a government up against these constraints and imperatives, a rational optimizing decision is. A reality that the crisis underlined for EuroAmerica when its governments felt compelled to rescue the banks but was already well understood by emerging market economies through their experience with the global markets' exercise of control over their currencies and interest rates, and thus over their internal fiscal policy. In the globalization of capitalism whose spearhead is the globalization of capital, the derivative is "a figure of regulatory capacity in its own right" (Martin 2013:93).

There is more to the story. Derivative creation produces a new form of, and new collateralizable assets, which, in turn, have a multiplier effect on the money supply. This expansion allows for new wealth production which derivative markets access by trading volatility—volatility which has been socialized through pricing mechanisms such as the Black-Scholes formula. The derivative can create wealth by socializing volatility because the social is already a form of abundance of value. This is true because the social reverses the second law of thermodynamics: expenditures of energy/the labor of derivative creation and circulation leads to more complex forms of organization. In this case, the reproduction of the form (e.g., globalized corporation) through the mitigation of the abstract risk and looming volatility generated by circulatory processes that transgress difference (between as noted currencies, cultures, legal systems, monetary regimes, logistical structures, and so on). What derivative markets define as desire is their own permanent state of near emergency—high volatility with endless liquidity.

Living in this fragmented and decentered space of globalization, yet functionally designed for connectivity, the derivative is dependent on the social for all of the forms of transgression that render it necessary. Without its embeddedness in social life, the global circulation of derivatives could not exist. This reality notwithstanding, all that is social is precisely what derivative markets' pricing mechanisms disavow in the interests of the mathematization of finance. But this also means, quite paradoxically, that the social is necessarily self-expanding because it is the source of the contingency (forms of risk) that motivates the recalibrations of the derivative, which, in relay, keeps the markets in motion or liquid. The differences across space and time created by the social are the author of the derivative's necessity and also the sources of the protean mosaic of uncertainty that allow derivatives to generate a self-sustaining market.[9] What finance calls political, country, counterparty, currency, regulatory, and interest rate risk are nothing less than some of the socially created differences that motivate replication. The social is thus the author of the necessary ontological gap between a derivative's price and its value, for trades can only take place when the participants agree on a derivative's price, temporarily closing the spread, but differ as to its value over the duration of the interval.

The second part of the original query is why trade derivatives. The easy answer is money, status, and excitement amplified by compulsion. This is undoubtedly true but it doesn't explain why a derivative market should attract big money in the first place or why the participants willingly participate. The deeper answer goes to the intersection and interplay across the temporal interval of a culture of calculation with the illegibility of chance. And the ways in which this interacts with the leverage inherent in the derivative form. Each derivative transaction embodies an attempt to arbitrage the relationship between calculation and chance through agents' reading of the forthcoming. The attempt to arbitrage this relation is coded as probability, although as Eli Ayache

(2010), himself a derivatives trader, explains in an article entitled *The End of Probability*, this view misunderstands and misrecognizes the market's reality. Ayache reports that everything in his experience says the realities of existential uncertainty so encompass and overwhelm the act of trading that probability represents a retrospective interpretation; it is nothing more than an intellocentric fiction that supports the illusion there is a genuine prospective calculus of derivative pricing.

At any point in time, market participants can calculate the volatility of an outstanding derivative in two methods. They can measure its historical volatility by calculating how that derivative fluctuated over some period in the identifiable past or they can calculate its implied volatility by looking at its anticipated price at expiration and then reading backwards to the present moment. Both of these are formal measures defined by a culture of calculation. Typically using the mathematics of the Black-Scholes derivative pricing model or some variation on its provisions. What the model calculates is the leverage inherent in a given derivative. As noted earlier, this necessarily implicates convexity. Traders capitalize on convexity because it means that fluctuations in the value of the underlier can produce a disproportionately larger change in the derivative predicated on that underlier. Take for example a security (the underlier) that is trading at 100. On this security there are three call options that expire in 60 days. The market prices the schedule of options as follows: the 100 strike price is $3, the 105 strike price is $2 while the strike price of the 110 call is $1. If at expiration the price of the underlying security is $112 then the following outcomes result: holders of the 110 call earn $1 on their wager, holders of the 105 call earn $5 ($7 minus the $2 premium), while the holders of the 100 call earn $9 ($12 minus the $3 premium).

Consider the leverage and the generation of returns that stem from the fact that a relatively small percentage change in the price of the underlier (in the example 12 percent) can generate a much larger change in the prices of the derivatives (100 percent on up), and that the percentage earned turns on the convexity of the graduated options. Consider also that a participant can amplify the derivative's intrinsic leverage by borrowing the capital used to underwrite the purchase. So, to continue the example, if a trader borrowed $30,000 at 6 percent interest and used the funds to purchase 10,000 calls at the 100 strike price, the return on the investment of $300 (the interest on the loan) would be $90,000 (or 30 times the original speculation). For the record, the derivative featured in the example is called *a vanilla*—the metaphor of the most common flavor meant to indicate that it is the simplest and most transparent derivative type on a gradient that ascends toward increasing rare and complex colorations, called exotics. And so there has evolved a complex culture of calculation that specializes in calibrating and capitalizing on the volatility, the convexity, and the leverage available.

But this culture of calculation is only worth the effort if it intersects with chance and therefore uncertainty concerning the shape of the forthcoming. For if the Black-Scholes formulation provided not only a precise but an accurate account of the derivative's volatility across the interval, then there would be no reason to trade it. Replication would be inert and inconsequential because there would be nothing to motivate agents to trade and thus make the market liquid. This is where the illegibility of chance much matters. For the presence of numerous, often unforeseeable, forms of transgression subject derivatives to unpredictable volatilities. These forms of transgression that inflect pricing range from forces that are endogenous to the market (such as the forced liquidation of a security due to a margin call) to exogenous events, from natural disasters and terrorist attacks to political events, economic conflicts, and changes in law/governance. What motivates wagering is agents' variable and differential knowledge and expectations about how these transgressions will influence the volatility and thus the price of the derivative being traded. These transgressions, which are outcomes of chance that result from the many uncertainties inherent in the transit across an interval inundated with all sorts of volatility inducing social realities, intersect with and are amplified by the convexity of the derivative.

Originating Abstract Risk

The evolution of derivatives is important because they are the functional form that speculative capital assumes in the marketplace and because they are the structural form that circulates risk. Speculative capital takes this form because derivatives unify in a single instrument the objectification of multiple kinds of risk even as they mask the forms of uncertainty that loom on the horizon. This evolution has two dimensions: in their first dimension, market makers have continually shaped and reshaped derivatives to help mute the risks created by specific concrete situations (e.g., depreciation of the dollar against other currencies such as the euro or yen); in the second dimension, derivatives have evolved as objectifications of abstract risk. It is this second dimension that has come to define and determine the globalized flow of capital via these new derivative instruments and what distinguishes this form of monetary circulation from the long history of global lending and borrowing. The objectification and abstraction of risk has evolved as a process that has cumulative and compounding moments. In the initial moment, the financial community has adopted a methodology that detaches any risk from the social context that created it and, consonantly, from the relations in which it is immersed. The practice is to classify a given situation as risky (i.e., non-arbitrage) and then abstract the element of risk from the social, economic, and political circumstances that defines the situation. Practice then removes the identifiable risks to an analytical space where they can be considered independent of these circumstances. Over the past forty years, this process has been institutionalized through generative schemes for inserting these instances of risk into a classification system, thus transforming sociohistorically specific instances of risk (e.g., mortgage defaults under the extraordinarily leveraged conditions that prevailed from 2007 to 2012) into instances of a universal type. In what has been an expanding classificatory scheme, derivative market participants recognize the following as classes of risk: interest rate risk, redemption risk, regulatory risk, counterparty risk, credit risk, liquidity risk, transaction risk, directional risk, and so on, this generative scheme classifying any identifiable possible variable as a form of risk. This nominalization fits a historical trajectory in which finance treats each type of risk as an ontologically real, concrete object. This view of risk has, in turn, permitted finance to amalgamate the various typed tokens into an abstract form in the derivative. The financial innovation was to reduce the plurality of variegated incommensurable forms of risk to a singularity: risk in the abstract. The modus operandi is to abstract the various concrete situationally specific forms of risk into a homogeneous unity so that market makers can determine the price spread of the risks borne by a given derivative. It is the process of detachment and reassembly that fabricates the objectification of abstract risk. Note that this constitutes the blueprint for the innovation of collateralized mortgage obligations in which individual mortgages are detached from the concrete local conditions that generate risk (e.g., falling home prices due to the dismantling of a town's industrial plant because it does not contribute to increasing a firm's shareholder value) and then reassembled into tranches of abstract risk bearing derivatives.

It should be made clear that what has crystallized is *not* two separate types of risk, concrete and abstract, but two inseparable dimensions of risk involved in the creation and circulation of derivatives. The dimensions of risk differ depending on whether they appear as concrete and specific instances of risk or as an objectification of the totality of relations that generate risk-taking.

What defines the modern derivative markets is that it is this totality of relations that is priced, circulated, and speculated upon. This abstract quality amplifies the sociality of the object, the derivative, in ways that, paradoxically, mask its sociality by subsuming, equilibrating, and quantifying all of the variegated forms of social relationships material to the reality of specific concrete risks. CMOS combined in a single derivative and therefore priced as a totality all of the variegated typed risks—counterparty, interest rate, liquidity, income, etc.—associated with the financialization of the US housing market. Accordingly, the risk that the housing market would collapse in numerous regions simultaneously, the risk that a substantial number of (typically heavily leveraged) mortgage borrowers would become unable to service their loans, the risk that imperiled collateralized mortgage obligations would threaten systemic collapse, the risk that interest rates would precipitously rise or fall, the risk that government sponsored entities would withdraw their support, and much more are combined in a single derivative, quantified, and then priced accordingly. Though unaware of the theoretical weight of their statement, this is what commentators indicate when they say that what characterizes today's financial system is the commoditization of risk: namely, that the vast ensemble of socioeconomic relations that engender specific risks (re)appear as a singular homogeneous object.

A culture of finance in which the derivative is the general form of the product being circulated is generating a new form of mediation specific and instrumental to the growing independence of the circulatory system. Increasingly, the real economy is not driving the financial system; instead, the financial markets are driving the real economy. The risk based derivative is thus a historically new means of suturing the circulatory system. This means of suturing circulation is compatible with the forms of interdependence characteristic of the production centered economy, even as it is more than beginning to direct and dominate its trajectory. And because the derivative markets have become the world's largest and most influential, the creation of new means for objectifying risk, exemplified by the process of securitization, becomes the critical basis for dealing with the connectivity that the capitalist structure of globalized production currently demands. Risk has become a very peculiar and particular sociological object: to mitigate specific and concrete risks through the use of derivatives, risk must be abstracted and monetized; and, to deal with connectivity, it must be instrumental in the creation of a circulatory sphere organized around speculative capital's fabrication and trading of derivatives in volatile markets.

This is extremely different from the concept and character of risk under a regime of production based capitalism in which the function of banks was to allocate capital to the most progressive firms. Under this previous regime, risk is not organized, it is not abstracted or commodified. Companies and their bankers deal with specific risks through specific means, issuing, for example, corporate bonds of different durations to help offset the risk of rising interest rates. By contrast, in an economy where derivatives are the constitutive edge of the financial markets, households, communities, and firms cannot mitigate the risks created by financialization through direct economic action. The end result is that as capital markets animated by speculative capital lead to the autonomy of these markets, risk emerges as a social mediation, as the principal means by which persons and companies organize their interdependence. Risk does this by serving as the objective means of organizing the sociostructures of the market. Entirely anonymous agents and organizations are brought into a relationship by virtue of their participation in a market of risk-based transactions. In ways analogous yet distinct from the role of abstract labor in the realm of production, risk itself constitutes a social mediation in that it encompasses and subsumes the forms of connectivity possible via direct economic action. This is essentially no more than a socially informed description of what securitization is (in contrast, for example, to the traditional financial practices of Fannie Mae which functioned more in the time honored manner of ordinary insurance). So derivative markets are socially mediated by a form of risk that they both presuppose and produce. Further, in addition to the usual and concrete functions of risk mitigation, like hedging a portfolio subject to interest rate volatility (what JP Morgan was attempting in 2011 when its London division executed what it presumed were offsetting derivative bets on different bond indexes which are themselves derivatives of the underlying instruments), risk in its abstract form serves as a self-mediating agent within the system of circulation that creates a specific market.

Abstract risk is neither everywhere nor has it always been: rather, it specifies a historically emergent function of risk in restructuring the capital markets. And within that process, the organization of capitalism's design and dynamic. In this capacity, a derivative's function in mediating connectivity globally and reproducing the market as a totality is independent of the specific risks it attempts to commoditize. So each derivative is both qualitatively particular in its attempt to capture a determinate ensemble of identified risks, and socially systemic because it enables the abstract risk which mediates the production of the market. More, the forms of concrete risk matter because they are the sources of socially-generated volatility. For example, interest rate risk refers to the forthcoming volatility in an interest rate; political risk refers to the volatility in a nation's regime of governance and regulation; counterparty risk refers to volatility in the capacity and the willingness of the participants to pay off a contract. And so on. What this means is that abstract risk must synthesize in order to price volatility in the abstract.

If we review the history of derivative markets it becomes clear that what makes risk systemic is not the truism that risk (and uncertainty) is common to all sorts of economic transactions; rather, once risk exists in abstract form it can take on the greater function of mediating the production of connectivity itself. And because each derivative calculation of abstract risk, each replication of the derivative, functions constructively in the same way, it constitutes a general mediation specific to the entire market system. The mediation is thus systemic because it interconnects the variegated forms of specific concrete risk, thus defining them as quantifiable through the same mathematical procedures (exemplified by the Black-Scholes model) and because its character is system wide and abstracted from any and all sociohistorical contexts. When viewed from within a given market, a concrete risk (e.g., the depreciation of the dollar, or the appreciation of the euro, or an uptick in mortgage rates) is particular and created by a fluid and heterogeneous circuitry, such as the deliberations and decisions by a central bank. But as abstract risk, it is an individuated dimension of a homogeneous and systemic mediation which aims toward the reproduction of a market as a totality. It is precisely what agents must posit, collectively and unconsciously, to imagine the market as a totality such that the market remains liquid through numerous iterations of itself under circumstances that are constantly changing, requiring those involved to continually recalibrate prices. Though this totality is always out of reach because it is impossible to disembed risk from its contexts of production, it is the directional dynamic of circulation, a dynamic that supports the illusion that stochastic models can adequately capture the risk in situations of uncertainty.

Because risk has come to mediate the sociality of derivative markets, agents who participate in these markets do not recognize or accord a social character to risk: rather, risk appears to be the objective and formal output of exogenous factors, such as changes in macroeconomic forces. Abstract risk subsumes concrete specific forms of risk and, simultaneously, mediates the creation of the liquidity that creates a derivatives market. Accordingly, abstract risk appears to be undeniably objective in that it appears to a market's participants as a uniform and general sphere of unavoidable abstract necessity that functions naturally in a law-like manner. Simply stated, no abstract risk, no liquidity, and thus no derivative market. Based on this logic, weaknesses in a firm's value at risk model, the acceleration in subprime loans, and hedge funds progressively leveraging their portfolios, increases risk in precisely the same way that a prolonged drought increases the risk of crop failure. What is evolving is a historically specific apprehension of the world in which the internal structuring of the derivative products and their function as socially mediating forms conceal the relationship between the action of the derivative markets and the realities of real human beings. Only retrospectively did market participants notice the connection between derivatives that game the mortgage markets and the capacity of homeowners to finance their homes and maintain their communities. Even though, as in the case of CMOs and CDS, the derivative markets are responsible for creating risk, the determination of risk is such that a corporation's, pension fund's, or investment bank's own needs appear to be the source of the necessity. The culture of financial circulation conflates the reality that economic activity everywhere contains risk with the fact that it is crafting a historically specific and socially constituted form of risk: abstract, discrete, and quantifiable risk. The two forms of risk are conflated under the cover of an apparently indisputable necessity: investment firms must distribute risk to stay in business over the long term. That was exactly what JP Morgan was attempting in setting up the derivative position that eventually went south to the tune of six billion dollars (Dominus 2012:34). Evident here is a mode of misrecognition that rests on an inversion of social reality in which the most powerful form of contextualization possible manifests itself as a decontextualized necessity. The evolution of finance is such that the foundational acts of objectification that reproduce abstract risk and the reproduction of objectification through the circulation of specific derivatives mutually conceal each other. Accordingly, there appears to be no connection between the engineering of a wager against mortgage obligations, in the form of credit default swaps, and the ability of homeowners to finance their mortgages. From the standpoint of principals in corporations, hedge funds, and proprietary trading desks, because the risks associated with the circulation of tranches of mortgage loans appear to be entirely impersonal, objective, and formal, they see the desire and decision to offset risk as an entirely natural response to an objective reality that they did not create. Nonetheless, this risk is inescapably social because its genesis is sociostructural and because it is founded on processes those in the finance have engineered in the course of their collective history and acquired through their mutual participation in the field.

The Genesis of the Derivative Markets

The derivative can never escape the question of risk and decision making under uncertainty. The speculation that imbues a/the market with liquidity and thus life itself is possible only if agents' decision making involves the imbrication of calculable risks and unknowable uncertainty. Derivatives turn up the volume on risk-taking, partly through the derivative's convexity and inherent affection for leverage and partly through its creation of connectivity. This is a connectivity that turns on reformulating and repackaging the risks associated with the increasing global connectivity of capital in the context of increasing fragmentation and the declining relevance of state-based regulation. What has evolved are circulatory regimes in which abstract risk serves to mediate the relationship between the institutions and individuals that participate in these markets. The question is how did this evolution come about? Why did the supercession of the historical relationship between production-based capitalism and national identity—illustrated by the "made in" labels on commodities—lead to the ascension of a capitalism whose globalizing cutting edge is the derivative and its markets? On the issue of risk and its abstraction, the discourse of finance economics is as faint and intermittent as a radio signal in the mountains. For the most part, finance fetishizes the socially constructive abstraction of risk as the natural and neutral amalgamation of singular, objective, concrete risks. But for all of this the question of its origination remains.

For capitalism, the globalization of EuroAmerican finance has become a substantive category. What this means is that new institutional forms are deploying through the use of derivatives and global derivative markets enormous and still expanding sums of speculative capital. The qualitatively different ascension of circulation centered capital invites us to entertain the question of to what extent its rise has redirected the foundational logic of production centered capital that, since its inception, has progressively sought to bind work to wealth, virtue to value, and production to place. By contrast, the directional dynamic of the modern finance seeks to detach the price, profitability, and allocation of capital from the fundamentals of the economy, particularly the state of production, the social welfare of the producers, and the economic needs of the citizens. Even, as theorists such as Randy Martin (2014) have observed, the logos of the derivative based markets seeps into and inflects the economy of sports and the arts. On many levels this logic is entirely different from that of production. Recall that investment banks (such as Bear Stearns) created synthetic mortgage obligations for premium hungry longs so that other speculators could short the very same instruments. Temporally boosting liquidity and permanently systemic risk. Even ordinary familiar economic categories like supply and demand take on a particular and peculiar complexion when market-makers can artificially whip up new supply to satisfy heightened demand for a product, as in the construction of the aforementioned synthetic mortgage obligations. The supplies of risk-driven rewards are limited only by the leverage allowed; accordingly, the supply of risk can potentially be dialed up to any power, exponentially increasing the affect of finance on the "real" economy. Not surprisingly, a rising refrain in academic and popular accounts is that these detached financial markets have become instrumental in shaping every aspect of the contemporary economic context. The epicenter of concern is the character of the implications of these capital markets on everything from the provision of commercial loans and mortgages to the topography of global and national redistributions of labor (Panitch and Gindin 2012). Another way to conceive this is that *capitalism globalized is a product of, even as it produces, an interconnectivity between the episodic crises of finance and a continuous crisis of work.*[10]

There is not only an historical perspective on this transformation but the reality that analysis cannot justifiably decouple the character of that transformation from its formative history. So from a sociohistorical perspective, the capitalist circulation of money and commodities that began in earnest in the nineteenth century appears to be taking on a new direction which foregrounds a logos and a conception of social value that was there in an embryonic and covered up state since capitalism's sixteenth-century inception. Although this expansion was long in the making, dating at least as far back as the sixteenth century Dutch (Schama 1988), its dominant world dominating form only fully emerges at the start of the nineteenth century. Its developmental logic animated a process of perpetual expansion, punctuated by several rounds of amplified globalization, with the end result that capitalism engineered an increasingly interdependent worldwide political economy based in commodity production and founded on a single, self-universaling division of labor (See especially Arrighi 1994; Harvey 1989; Postone 1993: Sewell 2005; Wallerstein 1974). While financial and mercantilist capital were present from the outset, and importantly so, this form of national capitalism valued production over circulation, labor over risk as a source of value creation, productive capital as against its more speculative cousin, and the territorialized state (as exemplified by the proliferation of nation-states from 1800 to 1973) over more localized (especially world cities) and supranational forms of political organization (e.g., League of Nations).

In marked contrast, the new circulatory regime is less state territorial based, more culturally diffusive, violent in ways more abstract then tactile, economistic in its self-understanding, marked by the ascension of a speculative ethos, the abstraction of risk, a monetized subjectivity, and above all, founded on a reorganization of the relationship between production and circulation. In this respect, the ascension and ascending powers of the EuroAmerican financial markets is very significant because it is a mainspring for the restructuring of a global political economy that had been dominant for two centuries. It is important to be clear on this point. The rise of a culture of financial circulation does not and cannot replace production; rather, what it does and what requires attention, is its ability to economically displace and materially inflect the shape and trajectory of production and the financial circuitry and with that the shape and trajectory of capitalism. And all of this in the process and interests of its own creation, expansion, and valorization.

Taken globally, it could be argued that capitalism appears to heading toward a contradiction that is being played out partly in its constitution of space. The contradiction consists of a structural tension between forms of economy mediated by labor in which the allocation of capital is directed toward and governed by the ambitions of production, the economies of China and the other BRIC nations stand out, and a historically emergent form of economy socially mediated by risk in which the allocation of capital is directed towards speculative and derivative interests. The structural contradiction stems from a EuroAmerican derivatively driven economy whose markets must continually destabilize production—by, for example, using monetary force to amplify fluctuations in cross currency rates—in order to generate the volatility upon which they depend. Read all the way to its logical conclusion the implication is that derivative capitalism is not only foregrounding a form of value that superimposes itself on the value created by producing labor, it is doing so in a way that is engendering a fundamental contradiction.

The fulcrum year is 1973. Not 1973 the calendar year, but the longer version that stretches from the fall of 1972 through the winter of 1974. To the point where the term contemporary financial markets refer to the structure and evolution of the markets from that fulcrum point onward. Prior to 1973, cross currency rates and interest rates (across a wide assortment of bonds) were extremely stable. The principle role of capital was to fund the production centric economies of the United States and Europe, determining that the primary mission of money center banks and the financial markets was to assemble and direct capital toward more successful franchises. The ascendant economy that followed on the end of the Second World War was founded on an organization of production in which a "domestic" corporation accumulated raw materials and then, using unionized labor, transformed those materials into use value commodities. Most of these commodities were distributed and consumed domestically, a lesser sum shipped overseas to foreign markets. This was not, of course, the whole of the economy: but critically, the domestic production of use-value commodities by unionized labor was its dynamic and symbolic core. This organization of production tended to create an antagonistic alliance between management and labor, to align producers and consumers, and to define the primary mission of the state (e.g., to maintain the national infrastructure, regiment exchange rates at which raw materials could be bought and finished products sold, hold interest rates within a fixed slow moving band, guarantee an adequate level of competition among domestic firms).

The history of this transformation, global in scale though increasingly definitive of fragmentary localities, has yet to be written. Nonetheless, at least in outline, the narrative of transformation begins with the diminution of the economic boom that the end of the war animated for some twenty years. During this period, American followed on by recovering European corporations absorbed raw materials from South Asia, the Middle East, and Africa, from which they produced capital and consumer goods most sold domestically with some exported transatlantic and some back to the sources of the raw materials. The demise of the economic expansion coupled with the ascent of the export based economies of first Japan, followed on by what were called the Asian Tigers, led to a new form of globalization in two directions. Emerging market nations began to export finished goods to EuroAmerica and EuroAmerican corporations began to import system components (e.g., automotive breaking systems) used in their production processes. In *The Making of Global Capitalism* (2012), Panitch and Gindin note that, beginning in the late 1960s, the globalization of American corporations was associated with the shift "from trade linkages across national spaces of accumulation to the development of transnational productive spaces characterized by the crisscrossing and straddling of borders via networks of production" internal to these fast globalizing companies (p. 112). This ascendant globalization process created problems of interconnectivity that went beyond the purview of the nation-state and its inward focus on domestic production. The then existing institutions of EuroAmerican states had no way to accommodate the reality that these "transnational productive spaces" inevitably, mutually dependently, interconnected national currencies, interest rate regimes, political economic policies, and legal and financial systems.

A very differently fabricated mosaic of risks would be brought to the doorstep of these firms. Risks which were beyond the ken of familiar cross-national agreements. This transformation would ultimately involve the concurrent and imbricated reorganization of metropolitan production and production in these emerging economies (exemplified by the BRIC nations), the acceleration in the creation and global dissemination of information, the emergence of the dollar as the undisputed de facto world currency (e.g., by 2013, the BRIC nations conducted more than 75 percent of all their inter-nation transactions in dollars), the ascent of a politics that valorized financial asset-based wealth creation and the unyielding discipline of the market to replace the work of governance. Neoliberalism names, the ideology of the "free market" encodes, and the liberalization of metropole and emerging market economies serves to forcefully instantiate this historical development. And there is without doubt more moving parts to the history, singly and in conjunction with one another.

That said about the history yet unwritten, two catalytic events of 1973 were the devolution of the Bretton Woods System that had regulated exchange rates since 1949 and instigation of an oil embargo (Mitchell 2010) that set off an inflationary fuse which led to the removal of interest rate ceilings (Van Dormael 1978). The rescission of government control precipitated a marked increase in volatility across both currency and credit markets (Das 2011:73). Effectively, there was a privatization of risk. The risks that governance had once absorbed as part of its national mandate would now be absorbed by the market. And as if choreographed, 1973 is the year of the genesis of the derivative market, whose internal elaboration would lead to different instruments of price insurance or hedging on foreign currencies, interest rates, and equities markets. While this was only the very beginning, a dynamic had been set in motion that would swiftly shift the centers of financial power and control from government institutions to increasingly deregulated and speculative markets dominated by risk-driven derivatives. It is no accident that in January 1974, when Gerald Ford assumed the presidency, it seemed only natural to appoint William Simon, a legendary bond trader at Salomon Brothers to be Treasury Secretary, and Ayn Rand's noted acolyte, Alan Greenspan, to become chair of the Council of Economic Advisors. Where finance was once conceived as a means of funding production, events had conspired to so reverse the economic polarity that business and government increasingly viewed production as a means of funding finance. Literally and progressively, increasingly the role of our national wealth was to help collateralize the financial markets just as the function of our national debt was to keep them liquid.

If the place of derivatives in the EuroAmerican economy was limited to providing insurance, allowing production based firms (in manufacturing for example) to hedge against fluctuations in currency and interest rates, then the girth of derivatives markets would have remained circumscribed. The necessity to hedge is intrinsically limited by the amount and location (outsourcing) of the goods produced.[11] Though it went mostly unnoticed at the time, beginning in the early 1970s growing competition from Japan and South Asia compelled EuroAmerican capital to reorganize itself. As more and more industrial production was outsourced to the Far East (first to Japan and the Asian Tigers and then amplified by the emergence of China) the demand for capital by industrial firms stagnated, leading to an overabundance of capital. It is important to highlight what in retrospective was a world transformative contrast. In the post war period, American firms were in a cycle of self-expanding production. As the historian, Steve Fraser (2004) notes: "between 1950 and 1973" industrial companies reinvested "70 percent of corporate profits" back into the company and funded some "93 percent of these capital expenditures out of internal resources" (p. 488). The recession of 1973 and the rise of Japan and Southeast Asia permanently changed this dynamic. EuroAmerican industries were placed on a different track in which many of them continually generating substantial amounts of capital that they could no longer profitably reinvest in the expansion of their productive capacity. Some of this excess liquidity found its way into technology and the dot.com start-ups, eventually so indiscriminately that it fomented a destructive asset bubble. Corporation also directed this excess liquidity to the creation of financial arms (non-bank banks) only tangentially related to production. Perhaps an even more telling indicator is that firms began allocating this constant abundance of excess capital to propping up their own stock prices by repurchasing shares, our analysis indicating that for industrial concerns in the s&p 500 (minus their non-bank banks), more than 50 percent of their increase in real earning per share (i.e., adjusted for inflation and extraordinary items such as writedowns and asset sales) since 1973 have derived not from increasing production and profitability but from reducing the numbers of outstanding shares. Significantly for the ascension of circulatory capitalism, this overabundance of capital has found a home in the derivatives markets. Free capital walked into the waiting arms of hedge funds even as the enormous availability of capital would motivate the creation and recreation of hedge funds, proprietary trading desks, non-bank banks, and sovereign wealth funds that would come to specialize in deploying this surplus capital.

The institutional sign of modern finance is the appearance of many versions of speculative investment vehicles.

Global commodity production, especially oil, made its contribution. Petroleum is denominated in dollars and the most robust producers—exemplified by Saudi Arabia—have limited opportunities to reinvest their huge earnings domestically. The result is that since 1973 there has been a constant jet stream of petrodollars into the hard currency economies of the United States and European Union. The current estimate is five trillion dollars (OECD 2012) and growing due to what appears to be an extended period of what are comparatively high petroleum prices (at least by historical standards) brought about by the exponential growth of Chinese and Indian demand. All of these sources, both collectively and singularly, have and continue to generate what, given the needs of production, is an over accumulation of capital in EuroAmerica. This gargantuan supply of surplus capital—now measured in the dozens of trillions of dollars (BIS 2012:6)—has entered the structure of financial circulation as *speculative capital*. This is a huge non-production directed, continually expanding pool of mobile, nomadic, and opportunistic capital that institutions and agents allocate to gaming volatility through the tool of derivatives. In short order, hedging receded far into the background, making up today no more than 1 percent of the OTC markets, the primary purpose of derivatives to create opportunities for speculative capital to place bets on credit, equities, currencies, and other assets. In this manner, a new type of functionally earmarked capital, speculative capital, had emerged as a force in its own right.

Speculative Capital in Corporate America

The emergence of this nomadic opportunistic form of capital deeply and permanently influenced the corporate world. For the logic of speculative capital says that the singular measure of a corporation's value is the price of its stock. And perforce the value of its management and employees which, in relay, defines the value of their compensation. This singular measure is shareholder value, an idea decades in circulation but unused prior to the ascension of speculative capital.[12] And, in short order shareholder value would emerge as the organizing concept of speculative capital as inflected into the domain of equities. As such it bears the birthmark of the derivative. Shareholder value is simultaneously a practical (evaluative) construct used by market agents (e.g., fund managers), a concept that is a point of reference by companies seeking to attract new capital, and a particular kind of object and objective constructed by economic theory. Capitalist firms have always sought to make fast money, turning over capital as rapidly as possible, but they were invariably driven by other rationalities such as the firm's long term trajectory and communal and national interests (as biographies of even the most cut-throat capitalist, J.D. Rockefeller and J.P. Morgan come immediately to mind, attest). But speculative capital has relatively little tolerance for the subordination of short term profit for long term corporate development, let alone for social concerns that cannot be justified as a veiled form of advertising.[13] So it should occasion no surprise that the ideology and empowerment of shareholder value also begins its assent to prominence in long year of 1973, as the deterioration of US firms in the face of Asian competition conjoined with the increasingly availability of speculative capital (See Khurana 2002 for an analysis of the 1970s initiated evolution of this ideology).

The influence of shareholder value decrees that management out of a sense of self-preservation is motivated to focus foremost on maximizing quarterly earnings in any way possible, less speculative capital flee the stock driving its price down precipitously, leaving it vulnerable to a hostile takeover (e.g., through a stock swap or leveraged buyout) by a corporation that has "hit its numbers" and can attract capital, or leveraged buyout firms specializing in the extraction of immediate profits [usually by financially dismantling the company "in whole or part for a quick cash profit" (Brooks 1987:29). In the hands of speculative capital, shareholder value is a historically specific means of the regulation of corporations, whose mode of legitimation stems from the coronation of the concepts of speculation and the market as agents of the greater good, and from the behavior of so many corporate executives who came to see their employment in much the same way that colonial administrators viewed theirs: as the fabrication of a fiefdom that could vanish at any time instantaneously (e.g., from a hostile takeover) from which they are entitled to extract as much compensation as the company's board of directors would approve. The two key aspects of shareholder value's social epistemology, which represents a culmination of the shift from commodity to derivative, are (1) the equation of a firm's value with its market price (and therefore the price discovery process); and (2) the corresponding assumption that the market constitutes an objective and impersonal arbiter of a firm's value.[14] The ongoing result is that through its large influence on the credit, currency, and equity markets, speculative capital is inflecting the financing of the real economy, and further burrowing into the logos of the reproduction of production.

Speculative capital has elevated the notion of *shareholder value* to the point where participants have come to see it as the privileged and unquestioned measure of any firm's success. From this view, the slope of a company's stock price is the singular measure of its success in generating shareholder value. One image can thus be the complete story: when a equity's price line begins on the lower left and rapidly ascends upward to the right then speculative capital deems the firm, its executives, and its employees to have fulfilled their principal objective, and to have won the freedom to management the business free from intervention and from a leveraged buyout by what in the euphemisms of finance are called activist investors. Driven by the logos of speculative capital, almost every mutual fund prospectus claims that its manager(s) overriding objective to invest in those companies dedicating to maximizing shareholder value. Even funds that seek to invest in socially responsible companies (e.g., those promoting alternative energy) invoke the mantra of shareholder value, usually by claiming that it is possible to find responsible firms without sacrificing investors' returns. But a reality effect of speculative capital is its temporal compression of an investments' horizon. This short-term perspective powerfully influences production by, paradoxically, divorcing the process of the allocation of capital from the temporalities of the production process. And indeed what we now find is that on average financial firms will hold stocks for periods much shorter than either product cycles or secular business cycles. For most actively managed mutual funds, the time horizon of their equity investments has shrunk until it is now mostly quarter to quarter. This is critical because financialization has compelled most households to become passive investors who must entrust their savings (e.g., retirement) to fund managers. What's more, the returns from passive investments (in stocks) have been growing faster than the economies in which they are ensconced. The result is that the total quantity of funds entrusted to professional mangers continues to increase, and with that their power and compulsion to influence firms to focus foremost on satisfying the demands of speculative capital as opposed to the markets for their products, the needs of the community in which the firm is located, or even the long term prospects for the corporation. The ascension of fast money hedge funds and the power of speculative capital to compel financial agents (e.g., mutual funds) to accept the primacy of shareholder value has elevated the shareholder over the stakeholder (such as supplies and employees) and distilled a firm's (social) value down to the market's estimation of its share price. And those who have come to inhabit an equity market oriented by the principle of shareholder value are compelled as it were to measure a company's value derivatively, based on whether or not speculative capital approved of the way management allocated capital.[15]

The logic of shareholder value is thus allowing speculative capital to abstract the corporation from its own body, dispossessing the firm of whatever divisions, employees (e.g., outsourcing), and attributes (e.g., an over-funded pension fund that a hedge fund can tap to leverage the firm's buyout) that the holders of speculative capital see as potential sources of unlocked profit. Like the derivative's vision of capital, the corporation is something to be dissembled and reassembled based on its immediate progress in increasing shareholder value. Each day, hedge funds charge teams of analysts to scour the balance sheets of the world's corporations to uncover hidden sources of "value"—meaning aspects of a firm that can be monetized but are not reflected in its share price. Though rarely connected, the notion of shareholder value is what the logos of the derivative looks like when adapted to the equity environment. The valorization of the concept and of the financial practices that surround shareholder value are also marking a change in our understanding of the corporation and its reproduction socially. Indeed, a critical way in which the equity markets have come to incorporate the logos of the derivative is the diminishing difference between capital and corporation. The capitalist corporation is increasingly becoming identical to itself in that the difference between its underlying form and its surface form is disappearing: so that the corporation's only purpose is the valorization of value. Especially the rise of hedge fund "investors" animated this transformation. A corporation became considered less a social organization than an engine for generating capital. Where the corporation once had certain purposes that lay outside of itself—that is, the interests of the stakeholders in the firm—the motivating force of the shareholder driven firm is value itself. Essentially, profit becomes a means to a goal (satisfying speculative capital) that is itself a means of defining a form of derivative capitalism. The social telos here has become profit for profit's sake, driven by a process (perpetually increasing shareholder value) that exists for its own sake. The logic of shareholder exposes the logos of the derivative: the directional and quantitative expansion of capital within a circuit of its own design. That is, as noted, abstracted from the body of the corporation.

It is important to observe that capital has always been protean. It has never had a determinate form or finality. Under the regime of production, capital appears as money or commodity depending on the perspective on its cyclical movement. The ascension of the derivative imbues capital with an additional and complementary dynamic as it transits from credit money to risk-driven contract to

credit money (when the contract does expire). The possibility of this complementary dynamic has been inherent and latent in the structure of capitalism.
Capital has always borne the birthmark of debt, risk, and the interest that is
its compensation, although in the formative years of capitalism (when Marx
was preparing and writing *Capital*) the power of production and the contribution of labor were the epicenter of economic reproduction. Whereas in
production, value always appears as the objectified materialized form of money
or commodity, neither mode of appearance is necessary nor determinative.
What defines the rise and empowerment of circulatory capitalism is that self-
valorizing value now also appears in the objectified yet highly dematerialized
form of the abstract-risk risk-driven contract. Currency and commodity have
thus become historically overlain with a socially imaginary cipher and a contract. In this respect, shareholder value encapsulates and articulates the alien-
ated form of corporate relations that possesses, and is possessed by, an inner
temporal dynamic that is giving rise to a particular way in which we convene to
risk together. Each contract and each transaction is a progression in a complex
circulatory sociostructure in which social relations themselves—here the sociality of the corporation—increasingly appear in their derivative form.

This shift in the way people viewed corporations led them to imbue the
notion of shareholder value with a presumption of functionality which, in
turn, helped motivate the evolution of a new regime and technologies of analysis. The idea was that equity markets functioned most efficiently when investors take the price assigned by the market as the only legitimate indicator of
a firm's success. Though the stock price is itself a derivative of the underlying
company, and options on that firm's stock price are essentially a derivative on
a derivative, "the Street" (shorthand for the institutional participants in the
markets) came to apprehend a stock's price and the pricing of its derivative off-
shoots as the most reliable, transparent, and tradable indicators of a company's
future. This spurred the rise of what the market refers to as technical analysis.
In contrast to fundamental analysis which seeks to understand and then evaluate a firm's business (analyses of this sort begin with the Dutch invention of
capitalism), technical analysis evaluates a firm exclusively on the basis of the
trajectory and volatility of its stock price. It is indicative that financial sector
spending on technical analysis has grown from an estimated ten million dollars in 1973–1974 to north of ten billion today. Technical analysis came into its
own during what came to be known as the technology bubble. For it was the
perfect tool for valuing tech companies that, having no earnings and never
having had any earnings, had no fundamentals to evaluate. Such stocks paral-

leled derivatives in that their embodiment of risk was what was being traded. They were venues for speculating that traders could exit or unload their position before the uncertain expiration date of the stock's collapse.

Their has evolved since the mid-1970s increasingly large, indiscriminate, dark pools of speculative capital that provide the ammunition for these buyouts. For hedge funds and other purveyors of speculative capital, the central struggle of twenty-first-century capitalism is between speculative capital and the managers of production based capital (such as the CEOs of major corporations) rather than between capital and labor, the principle site of struggle from the industrial revolution up through the Fordist period (from the early nineteenth century until the late twentieth century). Indeed, the production centered approaches of theorists such as David Harvey (1989), Fredric Jameson (1984), and J. Lyotard (1984), for all their virtues, could apprehend the ascension of a postmodern world only in terms of the disassembly of Fordist production, ignoring the still ascending influence of circulatory capital on the cultures of capitalism. This has been, of course, nowhere more true than in the dissemination of the speculative ethos that animates the flow of derivatives to especially the American public, motivating the metamorphosis of the American house from an inviolate homestead to an increasingly leveraged financial asset. In a different venue and with different effects, the financial markets applied much the same logic to public corporations. As such, corporations become their present exchange value (i.e., their market capitalization), the singular mission of stakeholders such as managers, employees, and communities to help inflate this value. The frequently repeated, quasi-historical narrative constructed by finance tells how the rise of institutions armed with speculative capital and adept in the creation and use of new financial instruments rescued corporate America from its dismemberment at the hands of foreign competitors by forcing companies to align their values with those of circulatory capital. The narrative shapes an ideological, well-funded, and self-promotional reading of the evolution of capital which sees enormous virtue and profit in a financing system founded on speculative capital.

The Institutionalization of Speculative Capital

Along with the ascension of speculative capital and the development of risk driven derivatives, the final piece of the restructuring of the financial field has been a great transformation in the institutions that organize, engineer, and animate the markets. These organizations are the active institutional centers for the creation of the financial order. They constitute the social space of the social agents that, animating concepts and dispositions engineered in the course of their collective history and acquired in the progress of their individual lives, drive the socio-restructuring of capitalism in respect to the financial labor of capital. At its essential core, this reformation simply represents different ways of housing, financing, and naming the primary vehicle of circulatory capital: the hedge fund. Or more properly and less euphemistically, what are speculative investment vehicles (SIV)? More properly because the hedge fund names a diverse vehicle that is often highly leveraged and seldom fully hedged and because the majority are not funds at all but divisions of larger institutions such as investment banks and corporations. In economic history, the rise and flourishing of the SMV is the institutional crystallization of the concept dear to culture of circulatory capital that the value of an institution is its near rate of return. And since the transformative events of 1973, the dominant institutional change have been creation and empowerment of speculative capital investment vehicles.

The first major participant arises from the escalating involvement of commercial and investment banks in the derivatives markets. The increasing involvement of the banks in derivatives markets was crowned by the formation of proprietary trading desks. For practical purposes, the *prop desk* as it is called by *the street* (meaning Wall Street which is itself a euphemism for the active core of the financial markets) is a SMV or internal hedge fund that makes wagers (e.g., directional bets on subprime mortgages or interest rate spreads) with the institution's own capital. More precisely, it makes bets with the capital of the corporation's shareholders, typically using leveraged derivatives strategies to amplify shareholder value. Commercial and investment banks also manage, advise, and partner with an assortment of external hedge funds. As the annual reports for Goldman Sachs, Morgan Stanley, JP Morgan, and others underline traditional lines of banking (such as commercial loans) are simply less profitable than generating and wagering on derivatives.[16] The drive for profitability is a compulsion to create and circulate new financial products, including critically the impulse to design, market, and lobby for the forms of securitization that would detonate the 2008 crisis. Indeed, in the aftermath of the crisis the banks attributed their failure to regain their former profitability not only to the crisis induced impairment of their balance sheets but to the constricted profit margins on traditional banking activities and to what they saw as suffocating government intervention (epitomized by the Dodd-Frank legislation with its Volcker rule).

The second institutional player is the independent hedge fund. The steady decline of opportunities in long stock positions in EuroAmerican industrial sectors coupled with the appearance of volatility are the primary reasons for the advent and success of these more diversified, omnivorous, and global funds. In respect to investment vehicles nothing characterizes the financial period from 1973 to 2008 more than the unabated growth in the number, size, and leverage of EuroAmerican hedge funds, this growth propelled by their concentration on, and success with, financial derivatives. In contrast to the more conventional and more regulated mutual fund that has a narrower, more determined, and usually more conservative regime of investment objectives and available tools, the hedge fund is a barely regulated investing vehicle that manufactures and thrives on speculation. To give some indication of their ascendant power, diversity, and political leverage, consider that hedge fund holdings have risen from nearly nothing in 1973 to somewhere in the neighborhood of three trillion dollars by 2007. The petroleum producing nations have even created their own EuroAmerican based institutions to manage their speculative capital, that go by the name of sovereign wealth funds (which probably have somewhere in the vicinity of several billion invested in derivatives).[17] The hedge fund industry as we now know it, whose holdings and monetary firepower exceed the GDP of all but the most prosperous nations, is a very contemporary invention.

A third major participant are the financial arms of the major corporations. Originally designed to help their customers finance the purchase of the products manufactured by the industrial division and to implement hedging strategies, these financial arms are now growing faster than their manufacturing cousins and also becoming increasingly disconnected from production in that their financial activities, products, and global presence bear a much stronger resemblance to commercial banks and hedge funds than to conventional manufacturing firms. Some examples of this internal metamorphosis are GE Capital, the financial arm of General Electric, and GMAC, or the General Motors Acceptance Corporation. And as global derivatives markets mushroomed, the growth rates and profitability of the financial divisions dramatically outpaced their once predominant manufacturing parents. These now enormous financial machines are the "non-bank banks" of the money markets; they represent the corporate realization that the capital markets are far more profitable than plowing capital back into industries threatened by China and the other BRIC nations.

There is also another participant that is specific to a crisis whose roots lie in the mortgage markets. These are the government sponsored entities (or

GSES), especially Fannie Mae and Freddie Mac. Not however as designed or intended by the originators, but as they concurrently evolved in response to the reality that the greatest profitability lies in managing derivatives. They are important because their government affiliation gives them access to an almost endless pool of financial resources, they are directly involved in and are the most important financiers for the US housing market (the world's largest), and they were able to generate an enormous amount of surplus capital (free cash flow) which, in turn, gave them the ammunition to accelerate their profitability by setting up what amounted to their own, speculatively oriented, internal hedge funds. In this history, the aggressive entrance of commercial and investment banks into the global derivatives markets, the rapid rise and proliferation of hedge funds, the internal turn of corporations towards finance, and the redirection of government sponsored agencies are all mutually reciprocal outcomes of the transformations away from investing capital in commodity production toward wagering speculative capital. All of these new institutional forms, the proprietary trading desk of investment firms, the stand alone hedge fund, the non-bank banks of corporation, and the government entities, have all morphed into wagering machines that stand far outside the historical parameters of traditional banking.

The rise of these institutions has been instrumental in transforming the relationship between capital and the state. Toward this end, the financial sector has politically aimed its increasing share of global wealth, intellectual resources, and influence to undo the capital regulations of the past (e.g., on the amount of leverage that may be employed) and to help guarantee that new financial instruments remain unregulated.[18] Surely, a key element in the evolution of the financial field has been the dialectic between the ascent of a neoclassical economics whose commentary valorizes the unregulated market, marking it as an obvious recipient of the field's largesse, and a financial industry that pushes politically for greater deregulation based on its brute economic power burnished by the legitimacy conferred by economistic analyses. So the political objective of the hedge fund in all its institutional incarnations is to marshal its political leverage to permit speculative capital to create and circulate derivatives free of government oversight or regulation. That institutions centered around speculative capital have acquired such influence and legitimacy signals a significant historical turn in the organization of the political economy of late capitalism. In the competition among various economic fields for power over state power the financial field has come out victorious, nowhere more obvious than in the contention by numerous "free market" capitalist politicians (e.g.,

Mitt Romney and Ron Paul) that the government rescue of the automotive industry was a big mistake in contrast to the far larger, substantially less profitable, capital infusions extended the financial sector. The temporal process now in motion is one in which capital circulation detaches itself from both the production centered economy and from state regulation even as its ability to inflect the *real* economy and the governance of the nation continues to increase. And this on an increasingly global scale.

Conclusion

In broad outline, the history of the founding and funding of derivative driven capital underlines several mutually implicating features. The first feature is the co-evolution of the abstract risk based derivative driven by speculative capital. This history is defined by the societal reallocation of capital to a speculation and by the innovation of new techniques, instruments, and technical methods. These techniques, instruments, and methods serve to disassemble and reassemble capital in ways that allow the participants to wager on and price volatility. The result is a historically specific method to assign value to capital at risk via a dynamic of self-expansion whose mainspring is the financialization of nation state based production. The second critical feature is the evolution of a generative scheme for concocting derivatives. This generative scheme is based on a time dependent wager on volatility, a disassembling and reassembling of capital, and an amalgamation of incommensurable forms of risk into a singular abstract cipher. The third feature is that this co-evolution produces a social epistemology of concealment and misrecognition on the part of the agents. Hidden from view, not least the market's view of itself, is the character of financial markets as historical agents in which uncertainty will always commingle with risk, the deep presence of a financial habitus that animates the market-makers, and the relationship between the derivative markets and the real economy. This concealment and misrecognition is not some oversight or a mistake that clarification can correct; rather, it is a constitutive dimension of the real relations of the production of the derivative markets. The fourth crucial feature is that abstract risk is the foundation for the derivatives that circulate capital globally. Its abstract function is as the socially mediating form that allows the market to exist and replicate itself. As a result, the (re)production of abstract risk, which appears concretely as measurable volatility, has now become an end in itself. The fifth feature is the rise of a culture of finance that creates and valorizes a worldview and ethos founded on speculation. This mix of worldview and ethos encourages agents to equate investment with finance, or at least to see finance as the most profitable and desirable sphere of wealth creation. A gauge of this transformation is that the proportion of US wealth held in financial assets has quadrupled since 1973 (Calhoun 2010). Increasingly, the most productive investments, those having the highest return on capital, outstripping greatly the return on productive labor, are those concerned with speculative investments in, and wagers on, the global flows of capital.

The conclusion is here also a beginning. One view of derivatives, indeed the conventional view, is as financial instruments that were once attached to the economy, but somehow escaped through some yet to be uncovered portal. What is thus needed is for governance to rescue us by restoring the economy we've lost, closing down this portal so our collective thirst for money will not get the better of us and the cyclicity of crisis can be reconfined to the capitalist business cycle. The view is that once regulation has returned the demon beast to its cage, once our rational selves have quieted our animal spirits, things will return to normal. Translation: the nation-state production based economy will resume its dominance. But this view will not do if we seek a theory that is adequate to its object. The conventional view can only look from the outside at the great transformative effects of derivatives on the reorganization of time, value, money, risk, domination, and the other social ontological categories of a capitalism that has taken on new dimensions.

Viewed as a transformative force that is reshaping the economy and the social upon which it is founded, the derivative and its markets need to be treated as social principles, as structuring structures whose trajectory is to remake the world in their own image. If we conclude that the economy did not spring a leak and let out our animal spirits to toy with fictitious capital, then an altogether different project of understanding ensues. The most essential element of that project is to reinstate the social such that the transformative social generated by the arrival of the derivative comes into focus. Toward this end, the remaining chapters explore the sociostructures of the derivative and its markets.

·

Chapter 2

Social Theory and the Market for the Production of Financial Knowledge

The further you look inside yourself
The greater the distance you can see ahead
—SICILIAN PROVERB

The unconscious is history—the collective history that has produced our categories of thought, and the individual history that has been inculcated within us. —PIERRE BOURDIEU 2000:9

Derivatives fill the economy with risk the way floods fill the land with water, seeping into areas that, at first glance, seem to have escaped its effects. —EDWARD LIPUMA 2015

The story of the derivative is about its markets and its logos and the deep-seated compulsion for financial victory. The story is about the reformation of capital and the transformation in the pulse of capitalism's internal dynamic. But there is more in that the production and circulation of analyses about the derivative, its markets, and its political penetration is also a critical part of the story. If, as has been said, finance is a center of the knowledge economy, then analysis cannot separate the derivative from the production of knowledge and the economy of its circulation (Martin 2014). Indeed, however much the derivative conceals the social, it cannot help but showcase the value of knowledge and the enviable virtue of being in the know. More, the derivative serves to amplify the value of knowledge and of know-how because *intelligence* (about a derivative's future volatility and liquidity) is the milk of profitability. What this underscores is that our understanding of the derivative in real-time action is inseparable from our contestation over the production of knowledge. Nothing defines the field of finance more than the value of knowledge, which correlatively, also imbues deception with value. An assortment of forces combine to motivate financial agents to skew all moments of the progression toward knowledge that runs from legible data to useful information to actionable knowledge. The ever-present aim is to delimit and redirect its *strategic intelligibility*. Because the financial markets produce only abstract objects (such as derivatives), control over the production of knowledge is a principal stake in the game insofar as its opportunistic control underpins the markets for monetary and symbolic gains. Not surprisingly, then, assorted accounts of the markets and the causes of the crisis more than coexist; they compete for whose production and circulation of knowledge will sway a nested overlapping ensemble of audiences which range from the few (in the Federal Reserve for example) to the citizenry, domestic and globally.

There is thus a politics of knowledge that unfolds at the intersection of science, the financial markets, and state governance. Hence generating knowledge about the crisis and derivative markets confronts an armada of competing accounts. This includes critically empowered neoliberal discourses which are so muscular and thus so difficult to contravene precisely because they are canonized by all the powers of a world of power relations (exemplified by the Treasury and CNBC) that these discourses are instrumental in producing. Characteristically by shaping decisions and policies of those who dominate finance (at the Federal Reserve or JP Morgan for example), in the process affirming and amplifying the legitimacy of these (economistic) discourses as *our* principal sources of knowledge. Some heterodox discourses exist of course, think of Marxists such as David Harvey or of neo-Keynesians such as Paul Krugman; but at the end of the day their works point less to an alternative path to knowledge than to the vast difference between being and power. This production process should remind us that understanding can never divorce the force of knowledge from an analysis of that force inasmuch as what others believe are truths about financial markets are for its players sources of wealth, legitimacy, power, and status.[1] Consequently though not surprisingly, the market's capacity to reduce epistemic power to economic power has greatly determined the outcome of the struggle over the production of knowledge. One reading of the crisis is that the economic power of the financial field determined the outcome of this struggle. And thus the strategic intelligibility of what was known. What notions prevail, of the economy and the market, the character of crisis and its resolution, involves a struggle for power, control, and wealth played out through unequal competing productions of knowledge. The question of questions is how can we produce knowledge about the crisis and how do we apprehend the crisis through and against the knowledge produced about it?

The derivative was hatched in the cauldron of science, and more specifically an economistic version of economics which sees the path to prosperity as the emancipation of finance from politics and its warped regulatory hand. This efficient market theorizing then interconnected with, and was sutured to, analytical techniques already in train across the financial markets (Day 2009). What we can refer to as speculative monetary vehicles (SMV), meaning the proprietary trading desks of investment banks, hedge funds, and what are euphemistically called non-bank banks (e.g., GMAC), all publish technical analyses of the financial markets (e.g., charts of the price of gold in euro versus yen). More broadly, they publish analyses of the fundamentals of those economies that interest the markets (e.g., EuroAmerican). To this analytical mix there adhered a rapidly growing field of financial commentary, animated and advanced by the ascension of television channels and web sites devoted entirely to finance (CNBC celebrated its twenty-fifth birthday in 2014). Venues that are designed to analyze the news they discover and, in the own entrepreneurial service, may intentionally create. Joined to this ensemble were an increasing array of state and interstate institutions, such as the Bank for International Settlements (BIS), whose mission is to statistically track, analytically dissect, and suggest ground rules for the exploding space of derivative transactions globally. That for every point of view about the derivative there are multiple competing points of view about that view conceals the fact that, although these viewpoints compete, often antagonistically, at a deeper level they emanate from the same epistemology of the social. This sameness in the first degree underlines that the derivative markets shape a special frontier analytically in that *the game within the game turns on the production of knowledge itself.* A contestation of validity and of authenticity by theories, frequently dressed as descriptions, which appeal to science to confirm their evidence and canonize their conclusions. More, in this process these theoretics implicitly join to tacitly underwrite a historically specific theory of science predicates scienceness and the legitimacy it confers on the unquestioned implicit acceptance of an objectivist theory of objectification. That is, a theory which conceptualizes social relational objects as naturally occurring ones. A standpoint from which the derivative is an asocial unit of capital, solely circulating and held in orbit by the gravity of markets and our animal spirits. There is no understating the fact that analyses of the derivative and its markets are struggles over the production of knowledge, the production of the science that produces knowledge about derivatives, and this production as a common social good whose greatest good is to benefit society as a whole. As critical is the culture of circulation that mediates the translation of knowledge production into a lived politics. For this is the corresponding site of power, misrecognition, and shape shifting the truth. Democracy's capacity to "regain control over capital and ensure that the general interest takes precedence over private interests" (Piketty 2014:1) begins with, stands on, and ultimately rests with the production and circulation of knowledge about the economy. A little known truth of the derivative is that it can exist in its current form only so long as financial capital alone knows the truth of it.

Recounting the Collapse of Finance

In 2008, the collapse of the derivative markets created crisis and violence for the production-centered world of labor. A world that was once thought to stand on its own foundation apart from finance. This was not a punishing but passing storm; the harm and violence were not temporary. They did not subside when the financial crisis was officially pronounced dead or even when the imperiled banks had repaired their once broken balance sheets (Stieglitz 2010). The crisis metastasized, wounding the housing market and the sectors dependent upon new home construction, which, in relay, delayed the purchase of capital equipment, durable goods, and all manner of discretionary spending, thus fomenting a reinforcing cycle of anemic consumer spending, sluggish retail sales, and pervasive unemployment. Despite attempts at revision, the certain cause of our problems was the implosion of the derivative markets.

The present defines itself in its statistical prowess. And there exists an elephantine assemblage of facts, coded as percentages and statistical trends, to measure the impact and longevity of the crisis. And the documents will show that the crisis both inflects the entire economy and the entire duration of the economic cycle, changing as it were its tempo and responsiveness to stimulus. But it is also worth underlining that hard data, precision, and objectivity have their place so long as we disown the disassociative behavior that often accompanies the citation of numbers. And begin by recognizing that the hardship, pain, and despair caused by the crisis only amplified and compounded a deeper and more intransigent suffering in train since the early 1970s. As Piketty (2014) shows, for many workers and households the only growth industries over this period have been the expansion of debt and income inequality. To be sure, the financial community was quick to dust off the violins of contrition and making amends. And certainly a few financial firms went headlong into bankruptcy or were dismembered as the stories of Lehman Brothers and Bear Stearns and Countrywide remind. But that was not the half of it or even a smaller fraction. The real repercussions were as clear and as daunting as foreclosure signs on neighboring homes, an intransigent unemployment rate led by the layoffs in the housing and financial sectors, the government having to stage manage the costly rescue of finance institutions (e.g., AIG), government sponsored agencies (i.e., the Federal Home Loan Corporation), and automotive corporations (i.e., GM and Chrysler), the transference of risk and precarity from speculative capital markets to ordinary households, and a nation increasingly divided along the axis of privilege. Especially for those who had very little to begin with, the crisis so rapidly compounded their problems that it incinerated their lives before it registered in our understanding. To a point where moralizing seems oddly irrelevant given how deep and intransigent the human suffering. Seven years into "the recovery" the term itself is, for the underclass (the bottom 20 percent), little more than a cruel euphemism in that their incomes have actually declined substantially during the recovery period (Irwin 2014:5). What could have possessed us to view such suffering as a category outside the economic?

Seven years have passed since the financial crisis began to pull its markets and "the economy" down. And the crisis clock is still ticking, the economy gaining momentum only hesitantly and unevenly, underemployment remaining painfully high, new business start-ups painfully slow, wage growth for the working class stagnant, and disinflation still a concern notwithstanding the Fed's draconian measures. The production-based economy and its main source of funding, the global capital markets, are nowhere near what they once were in the decades leading up to the financial implosion. And neither have the forums of production broken on the wheel of finance. Despite a big stimulus program, followed on by several rounds of "quantitative easing," accompanied by interest rates that hovered around absolute zero and incentive programs to encourage firms to make capital investments, there persists a crisis of work. The grudging recovery in employment continues to coexist with underemployment (i.e., low wage jobs with no benefits), stagnant wages, and a workforce participation rate bordering at near record lows (under 80 percent). The demography of employment tells a still more troubling story. Workforce participation by those between 60 and 70 was reaching new heights, as they could no longer afford to retire, while participation by those between 20 and 30 tumbled to record lows, as those coming of age could not find work and certainly not work commensurate with their talent, education, or ambitions. Job creation is so lethargic that the number of jobs in 2014 was still more than a million less than when the crisis began despite an uninterrupted increase in the population and as disturbing the average hours worked and hourly wages (discounted for inflation) were both less in 2014 than they had been seven years earlier (US Bureau of Labor Statistics 2014). Mian and Sufi (2014) have used the big data sets now available to amass a mountain of statistical evidence which shows that the increasing debt loads and diminishing work prospects created by the crisis are continuing to decimate working class households. Interview after interview confirms that, like water filling the breached hull of a foundering vessel, the future of working class households seems to them determined by capricious, arbitrary, and unfathomable forces. Perhaps the most profound violence of the financialization of the economy is that for working class households the causes of their lives reside beyond their purview.

And there is a politic call as well. At a loss to understand, especially white working class households, and especially in the South, habitually personify their predicament by misrecognizing their reality. Often, taking their cue from Fox "news" and the endless entertainment of hate, they end up venting across the internet that their lives have become desperate and dark because Barack Obama has conspired against them and the America they personify. For these white descending working class families, Obama's blackness only compounded the despair at their lives' more general deterioration. The changing of color of the presidency and the cascade of minority voices on their ascension to becoming a majority (especially Mexicans) represent an end signal to life as they once knew it. They imagine themselves standing, stranded, on their front porches waving goodbye to good jobs for God-fearing people, living a family life in a stable cohesive community where everyone helps their neighbor, and where everyone is bred to do an honest day's work for a living wage. Unfortunately for them, a politics of misrecognition only answers the prayers of those in positions of power and wealth.

What is so striking is that the near death experience of arcane capital markets so thoroughly derailed the real economy. What is also striking is that the increasing systemic instability of financial markets has occurred in the context of increasing stability in the underlying economy (Bookstaber 2007:3).[2] Thus raising high the question of what exactly happened. Critically as well as morally due to the machinations of a speculatively driven derivative market manned by financial firms working unregulated frontiers in which capital became itself apart from everyday work-ways. And not just for the EuroAmerican hub, but globally as regions with "strong economic and financial fundamentals" also encountered turbulence that shook the very foundations of their economies, producing "a sharp V-shaped business cycle" (Filardo 2012:139, writing for the Bank for International Settlements). The world beyond finance could be forgiven for thinking that the "V" stands for violence and victimization by economic forces and circumstances not of one's own making. The fear—articulated in the minutes of the Federal Reserve's Open Market Committee meeting for July/August 2012—is that there is rapidly mounting evidence that the systemic damage precipitated by the crisis may subject the global economy to a life sentence of retarded and uneven growth (that no amount of central bank intervention can commute). The incipient fear too deeply feared to be acknowledged is that financial crises will reoccur perpetually if episodically because finance does not have any real incentive to adequately recapitalize the future. And none of the crisis' perpetrators have felt the pain of the penitentiary: the understanding is that, for big financiers, the theater of contrition is good so long as it is not accompanied by hard time.

If analysis rolls back the crisis clock to the beginning, the initial question is what precisely went so terribly wrong? What happened in 2008 that led George Bush's Treasury Secretary Henry Paulson, the former head of Goldman Sachs, the world's most prestigious investment bank, as extraordinarily wealthy as he was knowledgeable about the US banking system, to get down on one knee and beg Nancy Pelosi, the Democratic House Speaker, to support the administration in passing a bailout package before the credit markets seized up catastrophically (*The Guardian*, September 26, 2008)? What moved John Mack, the CEO of Morgan Stanley, to call his friend at Mitsubishi Bank in the dead of night, and invoking the Japanese tradition of respecting past relationships, ask for an immediate loan of ten billion dollars to prevent one of Wall Street's oldest and most storied investment banks from disappearing (Sorkin 2009:chap. 18–19)? What led successive CEOs of Citigroup (William Rhoades and John Reed) to conclude that the financial models used to price risk bore no relationship whatsoever to the real-world risks the bank did incur, and that the markets themselves were farther from equilibrium then from sanity? In short, what happened economically to motivate elevated men to stoop to desperate measures?

Especially as Alan Greenspan, Bernanke's predecessor at the Fed, had confidently assured the nation that contemporary capital markets were self-correcting, and that we were beholding the dawn of a new financial era in which risk was well understood and therefore expertly manageable. Indeed, in his congressional testimony (2006) Greenspan openly congratulated himself and the economics profession for devising a new more powerful set of mathematical skills and models that would allow us to understand (aggregate) risk and thus eliminate any possibility of a systemic failure. His argument was that installation of these mathematical tools, amplified by advancements in information gathering technology, all but guaranteed that the present, as expressed in the markets' prices (e.g., for houses and equities), would serve as a foolproof guide to the future. In espousing this creed, Greenspan was translating into public testimony and government policy the neoclassical supposition that systemic market failure is impossible. The economic position is that all risks are knowable, rational agents calculate these risks accurately, and without exception this causes (motivates) them to adjust and regulate their behavior accordingly. The systemic effect of these serial adjustments is presumably to allow the market's invisible hand to preserve its integrity and forestall the harm of crisis.[3] Thus the conundrum: while systemic risk and crisis are not apparently theoretically possible in the standard account of the derivative markets, they are certainly a reality of practice. And central to this reality is that although derivatives were responsible for the economic turmoil, it did not begin to portend their demise. Neither theoretically nor practically. Rather, the crisis announced that the structures of financial circulation, embodied in derivatives (monetarily and totemically), command a priority and privilege so immense that their salvation is inseparable from our own. A point that Treasury Secretary Geithner (2014:7) underlines lest we forget it. And so the Central Banks of EuroAmerica were moved to inject trillions of dollars of public monies in prioritizing the reanimation of a moribund derivative market. On exhibition here is the first law of power: *nothing more proclaims the structural domination of the financial field as when the entire structure is compelled (some would say condemned) to act on behalf of its reproduction.* The impression of this violent reality which has become our own begs speculation as to how speculative capital teamed up with risk-driven derivatives to create a predicament defined by speculative excesses and diminishing security. A predicament that we are apparently still unprepared for in more ways than we can imagine.

Framing Capitalism with Derivatives

Looking at the derivative with open eyes is revealing about the recent evolution of capitalism. What each passing day seems to underline in ways great and small is that the derivative and its globalization are the fulcrum of a transformed form of capitalism insofar as derivatives change the character of capital. The capital in capitalism now encompasses something different. And insofar as capitalism names a form of social life that informs the design of culture and subjectivity, then derivatives, their markets, and their market makers represent a significant transformation in the inner filament of social reproduction. They announce a sharp turn in the shape and substance of twenty-first-century social life. From this perspective, the crisis is a collect call from the economy telling us that the derivative is transforming the foundations and conditions of the social. The modern epoch features a historical pattern: the ascension and then decline of state-centric organizations of social and economic life. And with this decline the apparent primacy of the political over economic realities. Whenever the moment of the ascent of the state and the political, its demise and devolution originates in the crises of the early 1970s (LiPuma and Lee 2004), and the corresponding transformation in the character of capital. The self-unveiling result is the effervescence of a muscular neoliberal global order. Its general character is that social and economic life has become simultaneously globalized and interdependent, yet increasingly fragmented and statelessly decentered. In more than metaphoric fashion, the global order increasingly resembles a derivatives market. It is hard not to concede that finance is now spearheading the globalization of capital.

Two conclusions press themselves upon us. First, that the reformed global order is omnivorous in that it is encompassing all forms of economic life: capitalist, socialist, and admixtures of capitalist and non-capitalist economy. Such that differences in design and development are unfolding as different inflexions of a planetary ensemble of directives and constraints, imperatives and involuntary choices (Postone 2010:8). The analytical lesson underlined is that we cannot apprehend these global processes in local and contingent terms, however much these processes inflect localities contingently. The second conclusion is the necessity to pay attention to the now emergent economic order or pay the steep price of inhabiting a theoretical approach that is not contemporaneous with itself. The most critical because most hegemonic dimension of this economic order is the rise of cultures and sociostructures of financial circulation. That is, derivatives, their markets, and the logos that impels their global self-expansion and their colonialization and control of the capital in capitalism. This means analysis cannot apprehend this process in political and statist terms, however much this process inflects the politics of states and the state of politics.

Creative complexity in the leveraging of risk is a critical axis in the making of the financial crisis. For this is the home of the derivative as an instrument of speculation for speculative capital. The temporality of this circuitry is the present progressive. It began its ascension in the early 1970s–1973, the fulcrum year when the conditions for the rise of derivatives solidified—and has continued to matriculate to higher and higher plateaus of speculation, value at risk, market size, detachment from production, autonomy from state oversight, and the severity and duration of the global economic downturns precipitated by financial-induced crises. As theorists such as Harvey (1989:180–81) have observed, the conundrum that has beset capitalism from its very inception is what to do about over-accumulations of capital. The rise of derivative markets represent an answer that goes well beyond the inauguration of a new mode of regulation (as many Marxist theories rooted in production assert). The present situation is one in which circulation is siphoning off over-accumulation of productive capital in the de-industrializing nations of EuroAmerica even as it appropriates the new credit money created to stimulate a renewal of lost production. It then deploys this capital and the capital recycled from the escalation in commodity demand (for petroleum especially) for its own speculative ends. But what is evolving is not a simple reiteration of past rounds of financialization (as theorists like Arrighi suggest) because the derivative restructures the character of capital itself. What is evolving is a kind of duplex structure. At the surface level, the circuitry of finance is progressively detaching from production, creating markets that are far from the kinds of work that most citizens do and understand. But at a more structural level, circulation is burrowing deeper and deeper into production in ways generative of great reality effects—what I have referred to as the crises created by the crisis. The colliding of circulation with production at this deeper level is explosive to the point where each is riddled with the other's particular shrapnel. This is the narrative behind the interrelationship of the derivative mortgage markets to new home construction and the housing market. One critical result is that the imbrication of derivative markets with production, the derivative form of capital with the new forms of labor that are materializing in its wake, are re-forming the economy in ways exceedingly complex. This has sparked a chapter of economic heresy—

set forth by England's Lord Turner in his pointed commentary on the causes of the banking collapse (2009). It says that if EuroAmerican capitalism was once driven by creative destruction, it is now being derailed by destructive creativity. Drawn to idealization of creativity as a beatific good, we end up suffering crises summoned by our own demons. We have created a derivative based capitalism that has no capacity to discover the value of those capacities. Nonetheless, even in the face of such destructive creativity, neoliberal economics clings to the orthodoxy that finance's recovery indicates that the derivative induced crisis was nothing more than a small slip and fall, that unfettered markets are an inherent good, that the capital markets mastered a useful lesson concerning risk management, and that conventional economic models need only minor adjustments (Mirowski 2013). To the contrary, as the crisis and its aftermath underline, the derivative, its markets, and its logos lie at the epicenter of a great transformation that is testing our powers of comprehension.

The Problems Derivatives Present

For more than a few reasons knowing this transformation—which entails producing useable knowledge about how capitalism with derivatives changes us—is as difficult as it is necessary. The first is that contrary to the naturalized way that our culture presents them, derivatives and their markets are resolutely social. No matter its appearance or staging, the derivative is social at its essential core; sociality is constitutive of its markets, its logic of expression and expansion, its abstraction of risk, its speculative ethos, the design of the motivation driving the markets' makers, and its relentless penetration into the economy of the everyday of households everywhere. What is visibly economic about the derivative only and significantly names its appearance. It is important to be clear. Finance is a central and longstanding component of production-directed capital, and this hasn't changed in its basic elements. But what is new is that in addition to its role in the service of the commodity, derivative finance has become its own means of accumulation, self-expansion, and social instability. The political thesis unfolding across the analysis has the following shape: *the derivative constitutes a transformed way of producing and circulating wealth through a securitization machine that redesigns the design and distribution of risk implicated in the circulation of capital.*

The initial reason fades into a second about why it is inherently difficult to grasp the transformation at hand. This summons the essence of capitalism since the inception of the commodity form and capitalism's ascension as *the* mode of political economy and social reproduction. Namely, the sociality that founds a capitalist economy is concealed by its appearances.[4] Indeed, the peculiarity of the derivative is that the design and forms of its appearance conceals its social essence. And even more often persuade us and the market's participants to misrecognize that essence as an expression of our human nature in a formal efficient market. More, the economic phenomena, such as the crisis, which contradict the derivative's conceptual architecture (e.g., discerning and disarming risk) are forms of the appearance of those categories. The mutual creation of the structure of sociality and agents' practices are mediated by these forms of appearance (e.g., derivative pricing models) which fabricate a template for the notions, dispositions, and actions of financial agents. The participants' template—which I will explicate through Bourdieu's notion of the habitus—presupposes the transhistorical/transcultural fact of the market, risk, wealth, capital, and the derivative itself. So, for example, the fact that derivatives appear as ordinary contractual financial relations (e.g., an agreement to loan so many dollars at a specific interest rate for x number of years) hides the fact that they represent a new and historically specific way to dissemble and reassemble capital itself. And this is further concealed by the ideology of the contract which understands it exclusively in terms of a monetized relation between the individuals involved. *The argument is that the empirical categories—capital, risk, market, liquidity, counterparty, the derivative—that the financial field uses to analyze, price, and politicize derivatives are forms of the appearance of their underlying sociality and their interdependence with commodity producing labor.*

Grasping this transformation is also made difficult because it entails a change of direction in how to apprehend the economy. A change of direction that most people were unprepared for. Since capitalism's inception we have directed our gaze upon an economy founded centrally on production. Little analysis was aimed at how its agents and institutions harvested the revenue streams of the assets that finance might fabricate through slicing and dicing capital itself. No one conceptualized nor could they be expected to the immanent potential of finance and the ascension of a culture of financial circulation.[5] Operating locally, globally, in ways which transform the character of a people's, and all peoples,' social reproduction. For the economy, the concepts gleaned from two centuries of dealing with production-centric capitalism are simply inadequate to a capitalism that has become a transformed form. In a human way, those who study finance have been slow and loath to renounce the relevance of the standpoints they have learned and internalized and thus feel provide them with a tool that is ready at hand and historically vetted, however much these standpoints have become dated. This datedness has produced a bull market in end-runs, dismissals, and equivocations for those notions being left in the derivative's dust but still endowed with the epistemic capital and cache acquired earlier. The datedness is coded euphemistically in phrases like fictitious capital, one-off seven sigma event, the opposition between finance and "the real" economy, and the anachronistic idea that capitalism with derivatives is anomalous and/or temporary. What this says is that if we desire to begin to apprehend the transformed form that is modern-day finance, we must draw on the existing archeology of knowledge—already present but spread across many disciplines—to create an alternative theoretical optic. One with a social ontology and epistemology consistent with circulatory capitalism.

And then there is the mathematization of modern finance and the economics of its understanding. Partial differential equations and Gaussian copulas team up with lemmas and martingales to intimidate many who would otherwise investigate the culture of financial derivatives. The truth of the mathematization of finance is that the calculus used is well understood (the basic equation for pricing derivatives dates from the nineteenth century) and the numerics are also good. But there is a fundamental design flaw at the point where the mathematics claims to speak to what is ontologically real. The ensemble of assumptions that financial analysts use to underwrite the creation of the abstract space of events required to motivate the statistical models (i.e., the assumptions that fix that space's parameters and its internal characteristics) are so remote from the reality (i.e., economic transactions) that they purport to represent that the models do not and cannot produce consistently good results. The financial models simply skip over the deep epistemological problem of how to make the transition from mathematical spaces, which exist solely as ideal constructs, to the space of sociality which serves as the foundation of what, for humans, is the ontologically real.[6] The reality is that the mathematical results are accurate only probabilistically insofar as these assumptions happen (by happenstance) to align with the conditions that obtain in a specific financial context. Though coded in a technical object language, these assumptions conceal deeper assumptions about the nature of human agency and social structure. In practice, the equations are correct only serendipitously: when the assumptions happen to align with a socioeconomic reality that the assumptions remove. Especially in crises, when the risk of systemic failure is imminent, the gap between the assumptions and the underlying reality becomes unbearable. Notwithstanding its ultimate validity (or the critical judgment that mathematical statisticians are now beginning to render), the mathematics is important, very important and especially socially, because those who inhabit finance and economics unconditionally believe in the math. The financial community believes as an article of faith, economists as part of a covenant to be a pure science, traders as a jumping off point for recalibrating markets always in flux. Misused, arcane math, cloaking the crisis in a mist of scientism: what could be worse for the ordinary person seeking to understand the crisis to construct a political judgment?

So a certain kind of science is part of the greater problem in that the discipline of financial economics fixates on and then scientizes the surface categories. The thrust of the discipline is to present the appearance of the derivative and the overt acts of those who participate in its markets as the only reality. But even more, finance scientizes the surface categories by treating them as natural kinds. Its implicit ontology is that the categories are transhistorical, transcultural, objective forms which exist independently of any social and historical conditions. What I have referred to as an objectivist theory of objectification. Accordingly, the science of finance can apprehend risk, liquidity, time, volatility, and all other financial categories through the use of mathematical formulations originally devised for modeling natural phenomena. This founds the Black-Scholes model, far and away the most significant widely used model in finance. An analysis of derivatives must thus continually switch registers to order to connect the creation and valorization of the surface categories that are produced by their underlying sociality and their interdependence with the real economy of production-based commodity producing labor. For the social theoretical objective is to deconstruct the category *derivative* in order to reveal that it means so much more than a contractual wager between buyers and sellers; it specifies an emergent form of sociality, a structured and structuring structure that is re-determining the trajectory of social life.

Finance's Self-Analysis of the Crisis

The crisis announced and then confirmed the priority of the derivative markets as holding the economy captive. But the unraveling wrought by crisis also revealed in some remarkable, unexpected, and to orthodox economic thinking puzzling ways the sociality of derivatives. For each crisis bears the signature of the sociality repressed. And then the scare tissue. The crisis focused an immense amount of new scrutiny on the markets as those in the financial field—from the working press to the central banks—sought to discover what had happened. A critical and reflexive feature of the financial sector is that it valorizes and routinizes its self-analysis of the market. And by extension the crises precipitated by market behavior and the behavior of the market. A more than incidental feature of the derivative markets is that neoliberal economics assisted at their birth along the way installing a more general and inculcated sense that a science-like approach is the doorway to knowledge.

It is then not surprising that the first analyses of the crisis came from those in the financial community. As soon as the threat of systemic meltdown subsided there began a temporary but torrential stream of books, documentaries, newspaper articles, and conferences seeking to determine what had happened.[7] The accounts arising from the financial sector constituted something of a counternarrative to academic economic discourses in that their touchstone is the market's inefficiency. The narrative line is that inefficiency leads to destruction when a permissive environment (defined as low interest rates and a lax regulatory regime) lets out the dogs of our most primal economic instincts. This narrative line is telling insofar as it inscribes our existing ideology of the primacy of greed as the impulse engine of capitalism and then again its undoing and the corollary unsolved contradiction between the virtues of a free market and the need for regulation.

These first responders probed the genesis of the trouble instruments, especially collateralized debt obligations (CDO) (Tett 2008; Morgenson and Rosner 2011) and credit default swaps (CDS). Analysts (Gasparino 2009) examined the government's role in first assuming a lassise faire regulatory posture, then having to step in with a gargantuan bailout. Several accounts dissected the accommodative monetary policies of the Fed during the Greenspan regime (Fleckstein 2007; Wessel 2009) and the economistic model of the self-regulating economy on which they were based. These were complemented by big picture accounts of how the events leading up to the TARP unfolded (Sorkin 2008) and smaller reflections that chronicled the extinction of the once legendary institutions of Bear Stearns, Lehman Brothers, and Merrill Lynch, not to mention a pond full of smaller fish such as Washington Mutual (See Kelly 2009; Bamber and Spencer 2008; McDonald 2009). On the technical front, there were attempts to figure out how the credit markets surrendered their liquidity, and why the mathematically delineated econometric models designed to depict and predict these markets failed so miserably (Cassidy 2009; Leinweber 2009; Triana 2009; Morgenson 2011; Fox 2009; Talib 2004). Although many ways different, a thematic and theoretic connectivity punctuates these commentaries. Thematically, the common riff is that rapacious greed set loose in an anything goes unregulated shadow banking system motivated increasingly reckless speculation which inevitably led to the crisis and the bailout. These "native" accounts of how the derivative markets work highlight the competitiveness and compulsive commitment of those immersed in the game such that economistic belief in the existence of rational actors is itself irrational. These accounts underline that the notion of a rational market has no grip on how peoples' emotions and desires could not only induce irrational destructive behavior but, to those caught up in the game, make such behavior seem plausibly rational. These accounts approach but do not quite embrace what is social and systemic. Given their narrative arc, they are prone to fixate on the character of individuals besotted by greed or graced with wisdom rather than a financial system inhabited by agents with collectively instilled and complex motives. Virtually all the commentaries are framed as a teleology of the *visible present*, the story anchored to the now by vignettes which recount the outsized personalities and the breathless unfolding of events that led us to the precipice. This native viewpoint provides a valuable, though partial reconstruction of how markets work. These works point to an emancipatory politics of enlightened governance, though the force of the argument is adulterated by their fixation on agency (the latter a defect they share with postmodernist forays into understanding the crisis).

A second and official line of investigation was opened up by government agencies interested in legislating what had happened. The crisis signaled that the deregulation of regulation had come to an end, at least temporally until things died down and the financial industry got its second wind. *The Financial Crisis Inquiry Report* (2011) encapsulated the government's investigation. The report culled and collated data from various sources to demonstrate that the financial sector, led by markets for what are called Over The Counter derivatives, had become an empire of circulation. Where financial sector profits in 1973 constituted 7 percent of all corporate profits in the United States, on "the eve of the crisis in 2006" they "constituted 27%" of corporate profitability (2011:xvii). Financial institutions of all sorts assemble and deploy speculative capital to extract hundreds of billions in revenue, and it is estimated that the liquidation value of derivatives is somewhere north of 30 trillion dollars. Consider this in light of the fact that in 1973 both revenues and liquidation value were inconsequential economically (i.e., measured in the millions). Also as impressive, the face or notional value of all derivative contracts has soared from twenty million to roughly two quadrillion dollars.

The report portrays the derivative as a technical tool of finance, which due to a lax regulatory regime and too many rented regulators, broke out of its cage to ravage *the real* economy. The report offers an inventory of the contributing factors: excess speculation, inadequate risk management, a congenital lack of transparency, a systematic breakdown in accountability and ethics, the unrestrained securitization of assets, and the misalignment of financial incentives with the public good. This is how the financial crisis appears from an institutional public policy point of view. The report's conclusion is that change in the way financial systems operate simply got ahead of public policy and the institutional capacities of government, thereby allowing the greedy to use their technical know-how to pillage the collective coffer. The report is neither wrong nor explanatory: because no matter how comprehensive the compilation of localized and contingent factors it cannot illuminate the structural imperatives and constraints which lead to derivative markets and makers transformative of the very clockwork of capital's reproduction. This statist point of view proceeds as if the market is an always already well-formed form and as if the logos emerges from a retrospective and synthetic reading of the crisis was from the outset its only locomotive.

There is a third vector of insider analysis. The memoirs of those who oversaw the banking system and its unparalleled plunge into crisis. Almost all of the commanders of the regulatory agencies have felt compelled to write memoirs to recount their version of what happened, hoping as it were to get ahead of the oncoming train of history's production of knowledge about the crisis. The accounts are remarkable socially. For whether by Henry Paulson (2008), Alan Greenspan (2010), or Timothy Geithner (2014), the analyses are significantly similar efficiently so, as though orchestrated by the invisible hand of self-exoneration.[8] The accounts reveal much about the epistemology of the crisis through two inadvertent reversals. As though the contradiction slipped in unnoticed to the authors. The books acknowledge that the banks' rescues were one-sided and morally unjust inasmuch as they rewarded the very people who were responsible for the crisis. But they then rather quickly mitigate its implications and forego any culpability for their actions with the notion that a unilateral policy to rehabilitate the banks with public funds was justified by the resulting stabilization of the economy which, as they see it, benefited all Americans. The books are unanimous in claiming that given the economic models at their disposal there was no way to predict the crisis, but that once the financial system imploded these very same models were predictive in their methods on how to salvage it: namely, to direct our collective wealth to guarantee that the banks are solvent and the markets liquid. But this lapse is not the only contradiction. The authors all reference the fact that the financial market broke down systemically because the participants lost their shared faith in the market's liquidity due to collective uncertainty about their counterparties' ability and willingness to repay their obligations. They portray the crisis-time as devolving on the shared beliefs, desires, and judgments of those involved. But then, in what from their view appears to be a seamless transition to the ways and means of reanimating the stilled markets, they become hypertechnocratic in that they presuppose that the economic system is independent of the other dimensions of social life and that breakdowns in the financial markets are purely technical problems, such that restoring a given market for, say, commercial loans turns on fixing its hydraulic mechanism for pumping money through the economy. All the accounts have the tendency to dress ideology as expertise and to feign that what they knew was all that was possibly knowable. This leads, in relay, to the pretension that what they wanted to do, determined by their immersion in the habitus of finance, was what should have been done unequivocally. A key to this perspective is the implicit opposition which runs through the accounts between an economic logic—driven by the imagined natural laws of the market, competition, and money—as against a social logic driven by cultural norms of equity and fairness. And so the regulators shaped their thoughts and policies on the premise that the economic logic applied to the banks whereas a separate and social logic applied to the homeowners. The mind-set of the bank regulators is important because it allowed them to scientifically justify converting an economistic model of finance into this immense political operation. An operation whose political policy devolves from the belief system that the economics of the market dictates that rescuing the banks is more justified than helping homeowners. What is evident in every sentence is that their perspective precludes a self-reflexivity that would allow them to examine the social and economic conditions required to produce this perspective or inquire as to the sociostructures (of finance and governance especially) that are the condition of its exercise. Ultimately their accounts of the crisis are revealing in that they reveal that those charged with regulating the finance system could not recognize let alone analyze the conceptual contradictions and the reality effects—such as ignoring homeowners—resulting from the interdependence of their social positions and dispositions.[9]

Dissection of the crisis from inside finance, however much they may differ in their diagnoses and the wattage of their outrage have one thing in common. Their productions of knowledge all presuppose the social: its design the foundation and frame against which their narratives of the visible present unfold. In concert with, and reaction to, the work of their academic counterparts, these commentaries leave the social foundation and frame mostly invisible. The questions they ask, the solutions they propose, assume that what is economic dominates social life. In accepting this assumption, they join with Alan Greenspan and neoliberal economics. The inverted frame of the view is why we evolved to believe that the economic predominates over other venues of sociality to the point of eclipsing them. What transcendent understanding led to idea that what is economic is so godly powerful that it overrides other considerations to the point where we like models that theorize the economic independently of other dimensions of social life. Family, country, the construction of one's subjectivity, institutional position, and peer group standing—all co-contributors to what we circumscribe as the social—are, on the economistic view, exogenous and subordinate to an economistic logic.[10] But the thorn of bracketing the social runs even deeper. For the core operation of financial derivatives to game the volatility of fragments of capital made commensurate for some duration, and to treat these derivatives as a form of money that can collateralize debt, entails an immense social transformation in the character of capital. Fundamentally, foundationally, things deeply social are animating the transformation of the economic wrought by derivatives. Accordingly, accounts from inside finance, because they foreground the dominance of the economic and presuppose a social they're not equipped to account for, cannot describe or reveal the underlying sociality driving derivatives and their markets. Missing is any analysis about what imbues derivatives and their markets with an historically new internal dynamic, engenders a derivative form based on the abstraction of "concrete" risk, re*forms* the capital in capitalism, reframes and reverses the polarities of production vis-à-vis circulation, sets in motion a new logos, and in another more existential register motivates and valorizes new ways of being a person. However inadvertently, these accounts confirm that to apprehend the derivative it is necessary to shape an analysis that apprehends its sociality.

Visualizing Sociality

How then to visualize the derivative's sociality. How do we visualize just what a derivative is, how the derivative markets are produced and then reproduced in the face of potentially life ending crises, why their tentacles have come to reach down into the space of production and the household, and what motivates those involved to accumulate speculative capital to make intentionally enormously risky stomach churning zero sum wagers (and then wake up the very next morning and do it all over again). Essentially, how can social theory generate social knowledge about the work of derivatives. To do this, methodologically, it is necessary to carry out an ethnography of finance, but also attempt to excavate the sociality inscribed in so many of the received accounts. An ethnography, such as the one that I am conducting and which serves as one of the principal grounds of observation, consists of interviews with derivatives deal makers and traders, quantitative analysts (*quants*) and risk assessment managers. The interviews, which now number in the hundreds, provide critical insight into not only what the participants think about their practices but the affect and the sensibilities that move them. That make trading derivatives a life. Also in the tradition of participant observation, I have drawn on my own experience trading derivatives (such as currency and options) for my own account as nothing teaches a sense of the game like one's direct involvement. This evidentiary fold incorporates the technical accounts that those who participate in the financial markets create, circulate, and (when their predictions pan out) publicly celebrate about their own behavior and the inner workings of the market. Central to a socially informed methodology is an enquiry into methods, especially the sciencization of finance through the increasing use of numerologies and a near evangelical faith in mathematically-based models of the markets. (Essentially, a theoretical account of the theoretical accounts used to grasp the market which locates their economistic models as constitutive of the deep design of capital). The methodology I have deployed has sought to marry evidence from these disparate sources on the understanding that this is necessary to apprehend a reality as inherently complex as the financial markets.

To pursue this line of analysis which sees the present ascendant culture of financial circulation as socially and historically specific, I animate an approach that apprehends the derivatives markets concretely as the product of the relations between three realizations of the trajectory of the post-1973 financial field: the sociality embodied in the dispositions of agents that work within the derivative market, the sociality embodied in its institutions such as hedge funds and proprietary trading desks, and the sociality implicit, inherent, and buried in the derivative itself and in the structure of trading practices.[11] This implicates both objectifications of the social. First, the sociality that resides in the sociostructures shaped by the financial markets: the derivative, the market, the logic of speculative capital, the financialization of households, the emergence of risk as a social mediation, the instantiation of new forms of temporality, the exfoliation of an increasingly abstracted form of structural violence, the reformation of the economy toward forms of circulation as against production. Financial markets use these structures to monetize information, images, currencies, and through securitization assets of any kind (e.g., houses and cars).

Second, the sociality which, organized by the sociostructures it reproduces, is institutionally inscribed in agents' unrelenting competitions for status, conceptions of work, secular initiation rites, senses of belonging and self-identity, ideas of fairness and just compensation, images of emerging markets, an ethos endorsing speculation, quasi-choate schemes for balancing one's life plan based on a career in finance with one's familial attachments, notions of public/government service and philanthropy, a shared faith in mathematics, schemes for the construction of agents' subjectivity based on monetary acquisitiveness, and an immersion in a derivative logic that is nothing less than history naturalized. For journalists and other commentators who focus on what they take as "primal instincts" of greed and power, the financial markets are social in only a narrow sense. For finance economists who focus exclusively on the rational action of abstract categories, the markets are social in a rather different but even more narrow sense. Paradoxically, and this speaks to the internal character of capitalism, for the financial agents and the institutions involved, the more successful the inculcation of their habitus, that is the more those agents inhabit a common and unquestioned ensemble of standpoints, generative schemes, and dispositions, the more the social is obscured from their field of vision. The problem is an invitation: to clarity why financial markets appear asocial not only from commonsense and economistic standpoints but for those most invested in financial markets. Why the more embodied the sociality of finance is in the market's makers, the less social it appears to them. At issue is precisely what kind of social is it that does not appear so from insider's inside perspective?[12] At issue is, how do we grasp the derivative when its surface categories are designed to render their own reality invisible? We have come in a loop back to the starting question of what are the conditions for the production of knowledge about the derivative? Especially about its sociality.

The Market's Production of Knowledge

The appearance of appearances raises firstly the problem of the conditions for the production of the knowledge that agents use to reproduce the markets. What are the social conditions for apprehending the framing and reframing of a totality—the social practices that produce and reproduce the objectification of the market—when the same sentient subjects simultaneously inhabit, reproduce, and analyze that totality? The same knowing subjects surrender themselves to financial markets that they actively produce and reproduce through generative schemes embedded in their work regime. This is critical because these schemes, especially those animating the work of speculation, are ultimately comprised of economically rational calculations, other co-occurring modes of rationality (e.g., those that center on competition, position, and the creation of one's social persona), and a structure of desire bordering on—and sometimes crossing over into—an erstwhile drive for identity, self-accomplishment, and self-esteem. Knowing in all its states is important because financial markets are about the production of the agents who populate them, and hence about the production of subjectivities. What makes this important is that one of the most normalized practices is for agents to take the market and their own behavior as pure objective objects of investigation. Those who participate in the derivative markets generate a slew of technical accounts, originating in a plentitude of methods, from those that openly emulate science and statistics to others that secretly approximate magic, all intended, singly and collectively, to fathom what makes each particular market tick.

And there is more to the story. Unlike situations where the analyst is remote from the analytical object, either because the group in question does not take itself as an object of contemplation or because the object under investigation is an analytical category (e.g., revolutionary wars), derivatives are the object of multiple productions of knowledge whose spread ranges from deep insiders productions to state regulators to outsider productions. Analytically, they range from a physics of finance organized by economics to the analyses (fundamental and technical) done by the players in the financial markets to the creation of analytical screenplays by the financial media (such as CNBC). There is an intricate and triangulated dance featuring *parallax* productions of knowledge (e.g., by the US Federal Reserve), the market's *own* production of knowledge (e.g., by investment banks and rating agencies), academic accounts by economists, and the market *for* the production of this knowledge (e.g., investors/speculators). That said, the sociostructures of circulatory capital intervene: for their economic and epistemological dimensions often team up to skew the production of knowledge. Indeed, one might say that one of the important aspects of this production of knowledge is the reproduction of non-knowledge concerning the social. Non-knowledge of derivatives is the result and condition of misrecognizing the character and consequences of one's own experience. Such that knowledge of the social is not an explicit species of knowledge however much it may inflect the very existence of the market and the actions of the knowing trading subject—a subject whose understanding of and temporal prognostications about the social is actually a prerequisite for viable trading in a liquid market.

The making of non-knowledge is not to say that the social never enters the financial conversation. It appears all the time, except as an aside, a background human condition, a gesture toward a more real and complex world out there, an inscrutability of those who are different and distant in places like South Asia. And the social always appears albeit in a clandestine manner in discussions and discounting of risk. Though always in play, the social appears ultratransparently in foreign settings when analysts calculate what they refer to as political and country risk. Such risks turn social relations into abstract objects, as in the euphemized calculation that, in a real example, the favelas of Brazil may rebel against the capitalist free-market establishment by electing a socialist president which, given the global market's disparaging view of socialism (its dominant ideology), would lead to the real's devaluation, an escalation in interest rates, and thus a necessity for traders to incorporate an additional risk premium into derivative transactions (e.g., in an interest rate swap the party exchanging a floating rate for a fixed one would command a premium to offset the political country risks taken). Note that this methodology euphemizes the politics of the social as an abstract object reducible to a financial calculus. On exhibit here is the second law of contemporary power: *in a knowledge economy nothing more advances a field's social reproduction than command over knowledge's production.*

This means that any account of financial practice concerned with making the social visible must compete with other accounts that are aspects of the field's reproduction. And importantly, part of the field's officially canonized means for obscuring its sociality. This includes scientifically coded effort to uphold the idea that markets are independent and depersonalized objects that analyses can grasp entirely through mathematical and technical methods.[13] There is the belief is that these technologies are so robust they can absorb the financial reality to which they refer. Analysts simultaneously seek to chart, explain, and mathematize derivative markets from specific positions within the financial field even as they assume that their analyses emanate from an external view from nowhere, rendering them objective. These analyses construe the market as a spectacle: as an external reality best understood in terms of the market's behavior in pricing of assets, which, in relay, produces knowledge (and predictions about the future behavior of prices) that the players can then profitably insert back into the reality it has described. These forms of analysis, upon which billions of dollars are spent annually, presuppose a market of concrete objects determined entirely by asocial instrumental rationality. As will become apparent, the development and centrality of a logic of abstract risk, encapsulated in a single crystallizing number called a derivative's price, lies at the core of a historical reconfiguration of the way agents and institutions grasp financial markets. The circulation and acceptance of these analyses thus disseminates in a field legitimated form, a specifically asocial view of the market.[14] A characteristic dimension of these analyses is that under the guise of describing the financial market, they contribute to the constructing of a specific version of it. As the investigation unfolds it will become clear that the financial field's production of knowledge serves to complicate an understanding of its practices because the field's own self-revelatory products obscure its social character. Alternative voices must compete against the megaphone of the financial field's insiders.

The asocial view is also an interested view. It allows the politics that despite the bankruptcies, the shot-gun mergers, and the government bailouts, analysis can still vanquish uncertainty and contingency, and devise statistical technologies that can measure the risks derivatives' incur or the propensity of risk to escalate (and spin out of control in ways that compromise the life of an entire market). It also sanctions economistic and interactionist suppositions about what constitutes a financial crisis and what constitutes a legitimate theorization of it. These suppositions about rational actors, the uniformity of agent's information, and the closure and completeness of the market are central since they are the cornerstones of what I call the *illusio*. From this vantage, the efficient market thesis is the critical cornerstone of the illusio, for it functions as a premise of scholastic analysis and simultaneously as one of the stakes in the game. More than passing mistakes or theoretical inconsistencies, the illusio refers to the forms of misrecognition (of the social) that are components of *real relations of the production of financial circulation*. An illusio works culturally as social practice because its cultural envisioning of the social world, whose very existence the illusio must deny, becomes so deeply inscribed in its holders' foundational scriptures about the nature of the real, that they find it unthinkable not to apprehend their worldview (the model) and social reality (a market) as indistinguishable. Returning to the original question, the illusio is an important aspect of the management of knowledge and the conditions of the canonization of insight: for it says that new knowledge counts only if its content remains faithful to the worldview. Other forms of knowledge, most importantly the practically acquired and inherently more inclusive knowledge that traders employ to price derivatives in the real world but also knowledges generated by the other social sciences are dismissed as tangential and antidotal and thus unworthy of inclusion in a scientized model. Which thus raises the institutional question of where will our sources of understanding come from? What are the socio-intellectual conditions for producing the imagination to produce knowledge that cuts against the grain?

The question of the sources of economic understanding foregrounds the design of the academe, and with that the construction of scholastic theorizations as to the character of circulation. And here we begin with a conclusion put in service as an introduction to an alternative theorization of the structure of circulation: that we owe the bullet proof division between the anthropology of primitive societies and the formal economics of bourgeois capitalism more to the history of the self-positioning by the disciplines than to the actual economies found in the world. About this, there had long been an informal division of intellectual labor. Anthropologists worried about the typically non-western, marginally and partially capitalist, frequently still struggling postcolonial economies. Community based, primary production centered, economies or economic enclaves lying on the margins of capitalism. Places like the former Bantustans of South Africa, the remote, tribally ruled, mountain regions of Nepal and Ethiopia, or marginalized islands such as Haiti and New Caledonia. By contrast, economists focused on market-driven, capital intensive, globally integrated economic sectors where they appeared. So, for example, anthropologists and rural sociologists studied the Amazonian Indian populations working on the rubber and coffee plantations in the interior of Brazil while economists were charged with studying Brazil's burgeoning finance and petroleum sectors. There are, of course, no disciplinary rules about economic subjects, but as a rule the division held with only a handful of scholars camping consistently on the other's terrain. More importantly, this division of intellectual labor corresponds to a theoretical vision of the social. The idea is that sociality inundates the economies that anthropologists and wont to study; especially gift based economies are so intrinsically social that it is pointless to use concepts and tools developed for large scale capitalist market-driven societies. The countervailing idea is that where capitalism reigns supreme, the economic is an entirely independent domain, which renders it possible to craft methods and models which isolate and fixate on the economic. As though the economic is a separate and thus separable dimension of social life. Embedded in this formulation was an agreement that the epicenter of formal economic analysis would be production whereas anthropologists would foreground the sociology of exchange (Sahlins 1972). An accepted disciplinary distinction between formal and substantive economics[15] enshrined this vision and division of the social world, which not coincidentally corresponded to two distinct and non-conversant literatures.

However, it turns out that an analysis of the semiotics and structures of financial circulation is only possible if we reject this theoretical divide in favor of the view that all economies, even our own here, today, now, are necessarily substantive because they are inherently social. My position is that while capitalism, as exemplified by the markets for derivatives, is qualitatively different from any other economic regime, it is nonetheless fundamentally social. Critically, the economic aspects of the social are also fundamentally different, but no less social for being so. Nothing will illustrate this more than the social processes required to sanction agents to, provisionally, isolate the economic by placing themselves in contexts valorize those dispositions that sublimate or eclipse their investments in the social. Let it be said that if cultural anthropology has produced one incontrovertible conclusion, it is that for most of the history of humankind, societies did everything in their repertoire to produce persons who valued and valorized kinship and community above all else.

So let us being with an example of how the economic dimensions of finance are resolutely social. There are two dominant and simplifying narratives about the forces that motivate derivative traders to trade: innate rationality and innate greed. The first narrative underpins economic theories of finance, the second is the rebar of popular ideology. They represent the spread of possible interpretations that present themselves once the social is externalized. Both narratives and everything that falls in between (most notably behavioral economic accounts) create the illusion that humans come this way naturally even if the anthropological record culled from literally thousands of different cultures tells an entirely different story. Indeed, however natural it may seem to those who tune in to CNBC and Bloomberg, entertain the *Wall Street Journal*, or are schooled to an MBA, it requires a tremendous amount of social labor to produce persons (such as those interviewed), who, enframed within the market, voluntarily sacrifice their relationship with their wife and their children to earn money speculatively on bets which, on account of their enormous piles of sequestered wealth, has little marginal value to them as a medium of exchange for other commodities. For the first time in social history, we have—through an intense process of socialization that begins with children's mass media and ends with MBA training and the initiation rites of investment firms, produced persons defined by a deeply instilled monetized subjectivity: individuals whose core of self-esteem, identity, and self-worth is not centered foundationally around the creation of a family and a space of domesticity, the purchase of desirable commodities to support their family and index their worldly status, the admiration bestowed on those who ascend to a prestigious social position, the satisfaction of artistic or intellectual achievement, or the attainment of heavenly merit, but around the unending compulsive acquisition of money itself. It is not that these other ways of defining one's subjectivity are no longer present; rather that the financial field strives to foreground this monetized subjectivity because it is a better fit to the objective design of a field that extols financial victories above all else.

The terms crisis and greed have become fraternal twins in the media's usual characterization of the present. What the common notion of greed distils, albeit in a deeply ideological form, is that the goals of self-actualization that have stood at the center of most cultures for most of the history of humankind, the goals that shine forth in ethnography after ethnography about cultures from all corners of the planet, are reduced to occasionally and conditionally important notes, as complements to one's life rather than the very core of personhood and self-identity. The quest is for money in the abstract, which is money in its electronic form as a cipher and surrogate for the self. What defines those at the pinnacle of derivatives trading is that they are so preoccupied with and so deeply valorize their *acts of acquiring* money that money once acquired, diminishes in value inasmuch as it can only be exchanged for the things that money can buy (e.g., houses, cars, boats). As Michael Lewis's investor portraits in *The Big Short* (2010) indicate, their return for being on the right (i.e., profitable) side of a trade that cut against the wisdom of the prevailing market (i.e., shorting collateralized mortgage obligations), was that it illustrated to their peers and above all to themselves that they were the embodiment of an uncommon level of diligence, courage, intelligence, and competitive fire. The noticeable trait that high-stakes poker players and derivative traders have in common—which helps to explain why many of finance's most prominent deal makers are such avid poker players—is that money counts and there is accordingly never a limit or end to their desire to acquire it because money is the means of keeping score. Those in finance appear to be inordinately greedy, their desire for money seemingly insatiable, precisely because the sociospecific form of greed that defines the contemporary financial field is founded on the acquisition of money. It is founded on the performative creation of the subject through repeated acts of acquisition: a deep-seated non-conscious compulsion whose appearance in everyday practice takes the form of agents' competitive drive and their love for the financial game. Gobs of money are, of course, exquisitely useful because agents can use it to fabricate a lavish material world and index worldly success, but only acts of acquisition repeated again and again can make the kind of subject so deeply valorized by the financial field. Which begins to explain why derivative traders feel a compulsion to trade, remaking speculative bets and constructing new deals, working long days and then into the weekend, owning Ferraris and boats they only infrequently have the time to use, often refusing to take a vacation or vacationing with the computer screen and cell phone ablaze, long after they have accumulated tens of millions of dollars. Perhaps predictably, artists such as the poet-songwriter David Grey are the ones charged with telling us the truth, when he reveals "it is not the money we're after, but the howling ghost within."

What I am trying to get across in this sidebar about what motivates traders is that wherever analysis probes beneath the surface, it becomes evident that there is a deeper, more social, reality driving the financial field, markets, and agents. A place where the distinction between the social and economic makes little sense. While these markets are powerfully economic in the most robust sense of the term, they equally and unmistakably implicate questions concerning the social reproduction of the market, the restructuring of capital, the evolution of a speculative ethos, the creation of agents' subjectivities, collective senses of belonging and fairness and nationalism, an imaginary of the market, notions of anonymous sociality, agents' practical use of science, institutional means of trying to balance out collaboration and competition, participants' sense of immersion in a game, and more that is intrinsic to the financial field and its markets but goes far beyond any narrowly conceived definition of the economic. The primary aim, let it be said, is not to convince you that the economic is less than it appears, rather, that the creation and the practices of the financial markets presume the presence and depend on the power of a sociality that the financial field conceals as a condition of its own sociospecific production.

The Scholarship of Finance and Crisis

Questions thus abound if we acknowledge that derivative markets spearhead a transformation in the shape and substance of social life and in the reproduction of the social itself. Put otherwise: if making the derivative and its implications legible is important to everyone, from production centered firms to working class households and everything in between, why has scholarship been slow to address the ascension of a culture of financial circulation? Postone observes that "viewed retrospectively, there appears to be a relation between the nature and success of determinate paradigms in the human sciences and their historical contexts" and that the dominant approaches to capitalism "now seem to have reached their limits, unable to adequately grasp our current moment of transformation" (Postone 2012:227–28). Most significantly I would argue, the structure of financial circulation as embodied in the cultural concepts and practices motivate agents and institutions to engender a universe of speculatively driven capital markets. One reason, maybe the primary reason, financial derivative markets have (at least until the recent crisis) escaped sustained scholarly attention is because economics has built its models and methods, its theories and themes, around production. Whether in neoclassical or Marxist versions, the accounts were resolutely production-centered. A key effect of the magnitude of the crisis is that it has compelled even those economists who had turned a blind eye to the circulation of financial instruments to take notice. But this awakening awareness is not easily translated into action. Finance is not only arcane to begin with, its directional dynamic is toward greater levels of complexity—this is, after all, the characteristic arc of financial creativity and innovation. Moreover, high-money finance occupies a portion of social space that academics seldom encounter in their life or their profession. Much finance, and almost all of the circulation of exotic derivatives, happens behind closed doors as off-book transactions among cloistered counterparties—and deliberately so. Though the fallout from the crisis is real and visible, (foreclosures, persistent unemployment, broken communities), nothing, not even the social machinery of deal making that make it all possible, catches the ordinary eye of everyday experience. Commodity production is more visible and has a longer history than financial circulation.

A feature of social theory is a propensity to underestimate the power of theory in constructing the social. And thus also the economic as exemplified by the ascent of the derivative. What is said about financial markets emanates from two perspectives lying on opposing sides of an enormous chasm, yet linked by the fact that they are unwilling to take derivatives and their markets seriously as a source of social transformation. On one side is neoclassical economics, or at least an array of professional economists conditioned to allow economistic assumptions regarding finance. And though it was not true at the discipline's beginning, for at least the past half century finance economists have stood with their backs toward the social. Their doctrine is that analysis can grasp the economy and therefore its financial circuitry independent of the other spheres of social life. The main idea is that by fabricating models and methods that purify economic behavior of exogenous influence, it becomes possible to capture human action in natural science terms. If an economy and its markets are closed and complete, if a utility maximizing logic is the sole source provider of economic motivation, than it is possible to use the formal mathematical tools that natural scientists use. Indeed, the mathematical formula (i.e., binomial diffusion) used to price derivatives is a direct descendent of the method invented by the botanist Robert Brown two centuries ago to describe the randomness of the motion of pollen grains suspended in water. Exemplified in the work of economists such as Eugene Fama, Douglas Ross, Fischer Black, among others, the use of mathematical models based on Brownian motion imbues finance economics with the charisma of science. A pure object, analyzable through the use of a continuous, finite, and determinate stochastic process in which each successive event (i.e., increment) occurs independently of the previous (or future) event and the entire ensemble of events are normally distributed. The mathematizing of finance commandeers social space by reducing it an abstract formal space, the reduction an unavoidable byproduct of being able to transfer into the mathematical space only those properties of social life that conform to its requirements. This creates a most peculiar inversion of the real in which finance economists bracket, alter, and sometimes repudiate reality in order to make it conform with their mathematical tools. This methodological grail is invested with so much symbolic capital—adherents have won numerous Nobel Prizes in economics, have held lofty positions in government such as the Chairmanship of the US Federal Reserve and Council of Economic Advisors, and have been quoted and showcased by the media— and has become so deeply inculcated in the field's self-understanding of what doing economics is all about that it is unreasonable to think that many economists would admit, let alone introduce into their theorization, the idea that the economy is not a standalone analytical object ripe for the mathematical taking.

The reluctance of economists to adjust their theorization of the financial market in respect to the rise of circulation and the realities of the crisis flows into the stance of the financial field. For all its open public celebration of individuality, it is the cohesiveness and regimentation of the financial field that stands out, its ability to regiment the behavior and practices of its agents across statuses and below the waterline of their consciousness.[16] The circulation of similarly inculcated agents across a wide range of institutional positions is a critical dimension of the financial field's internal coherence and self-regulation. A dynamic underlying the crisis and the extraordinary rise of the culture of financial circulation is the triangulated relationship between the neoclassical paradigm of "the efficient market," the infiltration of this model into federal policy, legislation, and the habitus of the regulators (especially at the Federal Reserve), and the ways in which this model in its scholastic and regulatory realizations has burrowed into the practice of investment firms and their traders.[17] Intrinsic to the derivative markets is a rather problematic marriage between the virtual mathematized model of derivative pricing and formal regulation and the actual generative strategies that agents deploy to negotiate the hand to hand combat that is trading. These strategies are nowhere part of the derivative pricing model or efficient market theory. They reside in the parallel universe of agents' sense of, and feel for, the market. This is critical because it points out that one of the aspects of the production of the market is precisely the *relationship or spread between the virtual and the real*, between a scholastically conceived economistic model of derivatives and the lived practices of those who make markets in derivatives. One of the key findings of the ethnography of finance is that high degree of coordination and coalescence in the world view and the ethos of those who participate in the derivative markets. And thus the third law of power: *the financial field can never more prosecute a cohesive politics then when an ideology of individual choice conceals the regimentation of agents' economic positions and dispositions.*

So mainstream, neoclassically based, finance economics will be of only peripheral assistance in the mission of understanding the derivative markets. And the reason is that its accounts of financial markets presuppose and rest upon a sociality it cannot account for. Accordingly, there is no workable analysis of the production and the reproduction of the derivative markets or the character of a regime of work oxygenated by what is, historically speaking, a newly minted ethos of speculation. Similarly, its efficient market thesis cannot account for the deeply instilled sociality that underpins and inflects the expressions of instrumental rationality. Its advocates cannot adequately ground the concept of an efficient market (socially or mathematically) or account for its enduring success (in the face of catastrophic failure after failure). Finance economics cannot begin to account for the crisis because it cannot begin to explain why some of our most intelligent people, educated and experienced in finance and markets beyond all others humans, should have the frame, the opportunity, and the motives to do what they did. The truth is that finance economics is a sideshow to the present: for its lack of a theory of capitalism means that it has no way of accounting for capital's transformation at the hands of the derivative.

Accounting for this failure has lent authority to the quixotic explanation from (the emerging discipline of) behavioral economics that an outbreak of "*animal spirits*" caused the financial crisis. These spirits—which function practically in the behavioralist account as residual terms for cultural expression of sociality—are thought to be irrational impulses that, episodically, erupt from their cocoon in our brain stem and override our cerebral canons of economic rationality (Akerlof and Shiller 2009). While this recourse to animal spirits acknowledges the social, animal spirits being the negative imprint of unbridled utility maximization, the formulation provides little theoretical traction. At the level of the agent, behavioral economists construct experiments—about market trading—that pose only those questions that the economists ask themselves about trading. The problem is that the trader's viewpoint is often far more encompassing than the viewpoint from which the questions were produced. Critically because it encompasses and is oriented toward social relations, such as esteem from one's peers, that money can't buy. Behavior economics thus proceeds as if the concept of animal spirits that it has mobilized to render the financial crisis intelligible to observers who are trading outsiders who arrive after the event is the principal steering mechanism of the practices that produced the crisis.

At the level of sociostructures, things are also problematic. Inasmuch as behavioral economics presumes these animal spirits are part of our genetic makeup, it cannot begin to explain why at this historically specific point in time "the spirits" emerged in a sociospecific form. I will return to the behavioral economic account: for now observe that recourse to our "animal spirits" violates a cardinal rule of explanation which goes back to Aristotle. The rule recomends that it is impossible to account for the differences between two phenomena by reference to what the phenomena have in common. Accordingly, we cannot account for the difference between two states of the market, when it operates with normal liquidity and manageable volatility and when, alternatively, the market is so systemically impaired that it possesses little liquidity and enormous volatility, by reference to our animal spirits, precisely because their existence, as aspects of our nature, is presumed to be constant across time and space. If these animal spirits exist uniformly across all states of the market, they cannot explain why any one state emerges at a specific point in time. This error is a characteristic explanatory defect in all naturalistic explanations of things social. Ask any animal about the difference between nudity and nakedness.

On the other side of the divide lies those approaches which take capitalism as their principle object. Thus conceived, the financial field in general and the derivative markets specifically represent aspects of capitalism. Analyses undertaken from this perspective see capitalism as a system that is profoundly structurally distinct from other economic regimes especially in its inflection and redirection of the other dimensions of social life. The analyses center frequently on the mediations through which capitalist production works toward and succeeds in determining the social itself. Marxism is the theoretical viewpoint most closely associated with this formulation, though there is a substantial body of theorists who use this approach without enlisting in one or another of the Marxist schools. A reason for this quasi-association is that Marxists often, contradictorily, oscillate between treating capitalism as a historically dynamic system and thus one Marx could capture only at a certain period in its evolution (i.e., prior to the ascent of the circulation of derivatives and the corresponding financialization of everyday life) and as a finished historical totality whose properties are canonically laid out in the three volumes of *Capital* (1876). The latter standpoint has no theoretical space for an adequate account of financial derivatives, not least because this standpoint comprehends value as a concrete singularity that is immune to historical transformation. More, circulation remains simply the filament that links the labor based processes of production to consumption, even if its redesign allows for a more flexible accumulation process. The inflexibility of this approach also ends up treating culture and capitalism—here the sociality of the derivative—as having only the most contingent relationship. And, in that moment the political escapes. Accordingly, there is no way to elucidate how the transformation of the social brought about by derivatives might both exaggerate and disclose the great disparity between what the wealth of society is and what potentially it could be if we redirected the wealth that derivatives create for our collective benefit.

There are certain theoretical treatments that might allow for an analysis of financial markets (e.g., Postone 1993; Martin 2002; 2013): but at least for now they remain on the perimeter of mainstream Marxist thought. Thus Postone notes that the a weakness of much "traditional Marxism" is that it has backed into a future it could not apprehend because it conflates capitalism and its nineteenth-century configuration (2014:24). It is distressing to see how many Marxist accounts of the contemporary situations are still stubbornly centered around production, labor, and class relations. These readings of the present grasp derivatives as "fictitious" in the sense that capitalism with derivatives simply represents a new way of expropriating the pool of surplus value generated by production based labor. The esteemed Marxist economist Duncan Foley (2013) explains:

> Many types of income in capitalist economies, including interest, financial fees, speculative trading profits . . . arise as parts of the surplus value generated by the exploitation of productive labor appropriated through the assertion of various property rights. This dramatic phenomena of highly profitable "business models" . . . do not represent new modes of value production, but modes of participation in the pool of surplus value. (p. 257)

For different reasons than orthodox economics but with the same effect, this view marginalizes the ascent of circulation and the influence of the derivative and its market on capital. These analysts write as if Marx had not entitled his masterwork *Capital*. This perspective closes the door on how Marx might reformulate his theory if he returned to his historical project after derivatives had taken off historically. But suppose we take Marx's historicism and the immanence of his critique seriously and begin with the hypothesis that the category of value was not fixed once and for all the moment production centered capitalism assumed the stage. Suppose we assume that the category of value can itself undergo transformation, and that the derivative figures in this reconfiguration. Suppose we start by reopening the question of the relationship between labor and risk in the structuring of social reproduction. Suppose we assume that capitalism also has another dimension of value that resided in capital itself, and that this dimension of value once of minor importance in the structuring of the totality has now matriculated to the point where it increasingly appears as a structuring force in its own right.

Toward a Social Theory

Once we see finance as intrinsic to economy, and the production of knowledge and subjectivities intrinsic to both, an alternative perspective emerges. As does an alternative theorization of the social. This direction entails analyses that treat derivatives as global and intrinsic to the production of (abstract) value, and a perspective that treats culture and the production of knowledge (e.g., big data) as intrinsic to the social form of derivative driven capitalism. Moving in this direction initiates a call option on the future in the form of reconceptualized categories of the social and economic. And in the spirit of intellectual collaboration (to my mind, the polar opposite of interdisciplinary research), the analysis is omnivorous in consuming concepts from wherever they may arise. Indeed, to grasp the derivative it is necessary to fabricate, resurrect, and reposition concepts that may appear scandalously out of place. Concepts and arguments that rupture and dislocate the prevailing theoretical frameworks— orthodox neoliberal economics, various heterodox Marxisms, and postmodernism. But, I argue, offer out best hope if we chance to understand the present conjuncture. For the derivative, its markets, and its logos lie at the center of a great transformation.

It is hard to gauge the prospects for an improved theorization of finance. For much economic theory, the crisis seems to have only encouraged the disciplines to reinforce their perimeters. So creating a theoretical optic adequate to its object is troubled because it contravenes the present vision and division of disciplinary labor. That said, the choice is as straightforward as it is problematic: either we break down these intellectual enclosures and release ourselves theoretically or apprehending the transformation and the ascension of the derivative will remain beyond our reach. The essence of the real is that it defines our fate whether we recognize it or not.

Chapter 3

Outline of a Social Theory of Finance

A theory ought to be judged as much by the ignorance it demands as by the "knowledge" it affords. — MARSHALL SAHLINS 1976:76

Homo oeconomicus, as conceived (tacitly or explicitly) by economic orthodoxy, is a kind of anthropological monster: this theoretically minded man of practice is the extreme personification of an intellectualist or intellectualocentric error by which a scholar puts into the head of the agents he is studying—housewives or households, firms or entrepreneurs—the theoretical considerations and constructs he has had to develop in order to account for their practices. — PIERRE BOURDIEU 2005:209

The starting point and conclusion of this book is that understanding finance entails a social reading of the derivative. An approach seeking to grasp and clarify the social life of financial derivatives requires, at the least, an outline of the social theory of the practice of derivative creation and circulation. If the analysis foregrounds issues that would seem more properly to belong to finance economics, it is that economics not only bracketed these considerable issues, now pushed front and center by the crisis, economics bracketed any consideration as to why these issues should be bracketed.

A social approach begins with the principle that analysis cannot bracket any of the determinations that shape the financial field and its markets. Nothing can be set off in parentheses for the sake of theoretical elegance or ease. This compels the analysis to not only account for market phenomena socially, but to socially account for those dimensions of the financial field that remove the social from the field of play, in the process rendering it invisible. With this theorem in mind, the driving objective of this chapter is to lay out a topography of what we see as the deeply embedded problems that underlie any attempt to theorize and thematize modern financial markets. And to suggest a course of understanding nurtured by theoretical traditions that have been excluded from this discussion, let alone juxtaposed and commingled in ways that disregard disciplinary borders. This turn toward the social requires that we begin here and animate throughout the book a conversation between theorists such as Pierre Bourdieu, Frank Knight, Max Weber, Clifford Geertz, Andrei Kolmogorov, Fischer Black, Moishe Postone, and others who have long resided on isolated intellectual islands. This conversation is carried out directly and even more so in the very structure of the expositions. Collectively, they provide those willing to listen with a host of powerful oars—such as the concepts of habitus and of performativity—to help zephyr us upstream against the prevailing currents.

This redirection toward the social is significant because it founds a break with the approach that has come to dominant finance. This is an economistic approach derived principally from neoclassical economics. The main strategy of this approach has been to intellectually cloister itself by constructing a conceptual wall between the social and the economic, and to self-conceptualize itself as a natural science whose object lies outside of culture and history. On theoretical and evidentiary grounds I see this as an artificial and abstract division—a division that ends up producing a theory that fails to apprehend the principals whose unraveling was the bases of the crisis.[1] In great part because it devotes a considerable amount of its social capital to denying and concealing those principles. For financial analysis the worldview inscribed in this division tends to obscure the intimate relationship between the agents' culture and their economic behavior, and more generally, between the institutional culture common to the financial field and the market as the site of competitive, identity-making, profit-seeking strategies. This matters because the division precludes the very possibility of constructing a realist account of economic reason. Let us underline theoretically what every derivative trader knows practically: that there exists an extraordinary gap between the economistic models used to model the market and the realist economic reasoning that they use to trade the market. As the analysis unfolds it will become evident that a paradox of the expansion of finance capitalism is its investment in, and dependence on, a set of financial models (e.g., to discern and disarm risk) that systematically bracket the social forces of uncertainty, collectivity (i.e., social groups and identities), and performativity whose inclusion is the precondition for the success of those models and the perpetuation of the markets they attempt to model. The defining strategy of economics is to narrow the theoretical aperture to the point of excluding the social.

The countervailing strategy is to open up this space to the full range of social theorization. In the same vein, I seek to de-analytify the spaces of analysis by connecting dimensions of social life, exemplified by ritual, play, and work, whose analysis has been predicated on their separation. I reconnect the structure of finance to the agency of its participants. The trajectory is that analyses of practice must be tested on the pulse of these participants. Going further and reflexively, we take it as axiomatic that an analysis of the financial field must include the point of view from which it speaks, be this interpretation economic or socio-relational. At its core, the aim is to animate a theory that apprehends the character of *concrete financial relations* because it does appreciate the entire range of determinations that produce them socially. The lighthouse premise is that nothing is more practical than a theory of practice adequate to its object.

Against theory that reifies the economic, this approach is founded precisely on the concept of *the social*. While this concept is foreign to finance economics— at least in its contemporary incarnation—it has a history that traces back to the pioneering work of Emile Durkheim and Max Weber and several entwined lineages of successors that have materially refined the idea. A concept of the social is also an undercurrent in the economics of John Maynard Keynes and the entire generation of theorists who had suffered through the Great Depression.[2] The social has a specific reference. It constitutes the unmarked term that encompasses all of the ways in which concrete human actions enacted with sociospecific practices (such as executing a derivative trade) are the product of the organization (both institutionally and through the habitus)[3] of deeply imbricated social, economic, political, moral/ethic dimensions of contemporary life. The concept of the social seeks to capture the reality that, at the level of concrete human actions, these dimensions of our contemporary existence are intrinsically interwoven. Such that foregrounding one dimension or another is inherently a kind of action upon the social which, in turn, influences deeply the way we apprehend the world.[4] This notion of the social foregrounds the reality that human action is intrinsically collective. Concretely, this means that the buying and selling of a security, speculating on its forthcoming value based on the participant's willingness to assume an unknowable amount of abstract risk, is only possible for agents who have already acquired dispositions geared to the plural and entwined species of rationality (i.e., maximizing profits, producing subjects' self-esteem, competitive dynamic, speculative ethos, and even a sense of nationalism) that course through the financial field. Concretely, this also means that the dispositions that motivate each and every trade serve to combine a past (history) and a forthcoming; they speak to the relationship between the organization of agents' dispositions constitutive of the financial habitus and the structure of possibilities (e.g., wagering on credit default swaps) constitutive of the financial field at a given point in time. Concretely, the structures of the financial field and the specific markets are built into the cognitive and generative schemes that the agents implement in their attempt to apprehend the field and its markets. This real-world dynamic based on the relation between the structure of agents' dispositions and that of the financial field is the outcome of multiple and competing determinations. The hope is that curating a social approach will help ignite an analytical movement that honors the complex socialities inherent in the ascendancy of circulatory capitalism.

To do this entails foregrounding the issue of the creation of a sphere of financial circulation progressively detaching from production at a surface level even as it serves to restructure production at a deeper level. And leach into the political culture to the point of inflecting political outcomes (on issues such as employment and immigration). A social turn requires an appreciation of the whole and thus how entities such as markets devoted to derivatives come into being as recognizable and reproducible totalities. This leads us to foreground the issue of the production and reproduction of the financial markets as *socially imagined totalities* (a term carved out in the political writings of Charles Taylor [2004] to conceptualize how especially capitalist democratic nation-states create spaces of collective sociality). Expressly framed is the question bracketed by both neoclassical and Marxist approaches of how are markets realized as collective agents, and how do the markets sustain themselves as such. Answering this question of collectivity requires a theorization that is specifically social, and that illuminates the generative structure by which financial markets accomplish this. There are, of course, numerous accounts that reference the market as a totality, though so far there are none that adequately account for its totalization. Based on a theorization of the evidence, I argue that the objectifications of these markets turn on a performative dimension that harnesses and directs the inherent rituality embodied in social practices. While rituality may, at first blush, seem removed and remote from the world of finance, rituality is its modern secular form is, I will demonstrate, the hidden constitutive dimension of the innovation and reproduction of financial markets, including the derivatives markets. This analytic focus requires that analysis historize the concept of the market by illuminating the sociospecific and historically imperative character of modern derivatives markets, critically the forms of temporality and performativity these markets embody and motivate. The aim is to grasp a social whose arc is moving from away from the social that reigned during the salad days of pre-derivative capitalism; a transformative social that is emerging in the context of the restructuring of the relationship between production and circulation, in ways whose dynamic lies in how new forms of detachment involve new dimensions of connectivity.

The second principle of a social account is the true necessity of understanding the construction of the analytical object. These objects under investigation, the market(s), the derivative, and the work of trading, having been created by humans in the course of their collective history, do not come ready made. Such that a scientifically rigorous account—rigorous because its categories of knowledge (or epistemology) are true to its object of investigation—must come to terms with how these objects are constructed, socially and historically. When speaking of objects such as the market the first point is that they are not "objects" in the literal sense, the term a metaphor suggested by the design of the English language (Lee 1997). Derivatives are not concrete objects like the paper in this book or the heavenly bodies that orbit the sun; they are relational objects working within the socially imaginary one of the market. Relational (e.g., competitiveness, nationalism) and imaginary objects (e.g., the nation-state, capitalist markets, etc.) have no necessary existence: they can accordingly only exist because they are objectified in agents' practices and collectively interpreted as such. Through the office of collective belief these objects are brought into existence at socially specific historical moments as culturally real things. The point is that relational objects such as derivatives set within an imaginary object such as a market count because together we make them so. Agents' individual acts generate single transactions that crystallize as a collective action, engendering *a specific derivative market* that is then understood as an instantiation of *the market*. Think of the relations of buying and selling that take place within a market that the buyers and sellers have socially imagined as the site of derivative trades. (Such *capitalist capital markets* only coming into existence through their imagination and institutionalization in sixteenth-century Europe). In this sense, the notion of a financial field composed of markets is a kind of conceptual shorthand; it points to the construction of a methodology which appreciates that it is necessary to understand how a collectivity forges the foundational relational and imaginary objects that define the social, imbuing these objects with such an aura of factuality and inevitability that they seem self-evidently and singularly real.

The concern for concrete social relations and for a realist definition of reasons and motives flows inevitably into the issue of the habitus of work, specifically a newly minted *financial habitus* founded on a *speculative ethos*. At issue is how speculative wagers with speculative capital, until recently castigated as an enemy of the economy and contrary to a principled (e.g., patriotic, prudential, and godfearing) life, emerged as a deeply valorized dimension of financial work and asset management. A social approach cannot but begin in the understanding that there are always social and historical reasons for the realization and canonization of specific modes of reasoning.[5] The objective here is to apprehend and ethnographically describe how financial agents make speculative wagers on derivatives that exhibit definite but unstable regularities, yet are not the result of either a pure economic rationality or the mechanical effects of exogenous constraints. From this perspective, what analysis needs to understand is how, on the playing field of concrete social relations, the financial sector aligns the positions of trader, quant, and manager with their corresponding dispositions. This is critical because recalibrations of a market that lead to its real-life reproduction can only occur because agents willingly cross the frontier between model and practice, and because they apprehend this transgression as the work they do in the financial workplace. This requires a socialized account of reason that makes a place for a working knowledge of financial work. This is a knowledge of financial work that works because the knowledge locates itself within the practices of a workplace condemned to more than just monetary meanings.

One shorthand to conceptualize what we are doing here is to say that the embodied sociality of the habitus takes the place of the economist's abstract invisible hand. This reorientation foregrounds the participants' agency and the conditions of its production. Accordingly, the analysis seeks to apprehend finance as a socially specific mode of work, one whose epicenter lies in the creation and the valorization of a specific kind of subjectivity, critically what I will delineate and analyze as a *monetized subjectivity*. This version of subjectivity, based on a perpetual acquisitioning of money (money serving here both as an exchange value and as the store of value of repeated winning wagers), is specific to the relationship between the markets and those who are willing to play the game of betting speculatively, a derivative's game that presents itself to those caught up in the market and addicted to its rewards as imposing its own necessity and self-evidence. This mode of subjectivity appears to be outlandish, atavistic, preoccupied with avarice, consumed by narcissism, a delusion of sorts only to those who apprehend the derivative markets from a perspective outside the arena in which the participants play the game. This concern with subjectivity underlines that what motivates financial agents to invest in the game is more complex, more social (and more interesting) than either the scientific notion of utility maximization or the popular notion of greed can convey. At issue is the way in which investment firms use all the resources at their disposal to mold those they hire into very particular kinds of subjects. The notion of the flesh and blood subject points to the work of finance in a real-life workplace as the site where individuals attempt to create themselves as people. The point is critical because abstract agents, abstracted from the real concerns and conditions of their lives, fixated on money and nothing more, motivated solely by utility maximization gone haywire, bear little resemblance to the real persons or concrete social relations that imperiled the financial system.

One final point about illuminating the darkened space of the social. The concept of practice that defines our approach to the crisis attempts to comprehend both what agents apprehend about a practice from living within it and what about that practice goes beyond the limits, and lies outside the perimeters, of immediate apprehension. We will find that it is necessary to break with participants' ordinary experience of the financial world in order to account for their experience. This separation is necessary because everyday experiences invariably arise and take shape from specific positions within the field. Accordingly, the participants cannot but see and grasp the financial field, especially the market, from the particular positions they occupy within the field. This positionality results in a real but only partial and perspectival picture of the encompassing structure of relations that generate a person's actions. To give an example: traders on the proprietary trading desk who are speculating daily with enormous sums of an investment bank's money have a different experience and vision of finance from the mathematically trained quants who reside on a different floor of the building and specialize in abstract models, both groups more often than not distant and segregated from the views and capacities of upper management. A socially scientific rigorous account would take this organization into consideration. It would thus seek to create a theoretically driven method that would allow analysis to appreciate this social structure of relations.

Crisis and Liquidity in the Markets

Why should the crisis provide a platform to reassess the financial field? The short answer is that the crisis ripped apart the financial field, in the process revealing its hidden structuring principles and calling into question the prevailing analytics of finance. Few phenomena, short of the Great Depression of the 1930s, have so visibly and materially destabilized the US economy, thus bring to the fore the question of why and how did these markets fail systemically. As the US Federal Reserve, led by Alan Greenspan and then Ben Bernanke, would observe (Congressional Testimony 2009), the immediate cause was that the circulatory process that imbues life into credit markets had become paralyzed due to the evaporation of what the financial sector refers to as *liquidity*. Liquidity is more than a memorable metaphor for the fluidity of capital. It is financial shorthand for assessing the economy's capacity to circulate capital—this circulatory pump being both a distinguishing feature of capitalism and its lifeline.[6] Quite simply, no capital, no capitalism, financial or otherwise. That was Bernanke's message. The free-flowing circulation of capital is the necessary condition for the existence of a postmillennial economy whose cutting edge is circulation. Central to this new economy is the circulation of speculative capital, the use of technology to shape and animate flows and counterflows of capital, and the technologically amplified circulation of images that inform agents' decision-making processes to wager speculatively and globally.[7]

But there was also another message, a subtext to the discourse on crisis. For as the character of the problem unfolded across the markets, it became clear that for the financial community there is an unrefined consortium of terms that implicitly reference the social. Especially the concept of liquidity in concert with *counterparty, arbitrage, and volatility* constitutes the nucleus of a small ensemble of distilled and deeply veiled expressions for the sociality of circulation. The crisis peeled open an economic terminology whose hidden inner core is resolutely social. It underlined in an unexpectedly powerful exemplary fashion that a counterparty is not an abstract objectification, but real, deliberative social agents who can consciously chose not to participate in any financial transactions. Similarly, the idea that financial markets are uniform, homogeneous spaces (the concept derived by disallowing arbitrage) turns out to be only partially true and only under certain socially constructed conditions that are aborted when crises erupt. By the same token, volatility denotes agents' assessments—itself a confluence of their beliefs, desires, and judgments about the market—of the influence of events on the recalibration of a derivative's prices. These terms represent the manner in which an economics that has redacted the social deals with its determinations, their uses during the systemic meltdown to explain its causes providing a kind of encrypted confirmation of the necessity of dealing with concrete social relations. Thus the journey to unveil the social can capitalize on the crisis because the unraveling of the credit markets exposed the sociality embodied in what appeared to be purely economic. What's at stake is complex though the necessity is transparent because the wounds are still open: it is critically important that we understand how financial markets work concretely because these markets now possess the existential power to bring down the economy. On this score, finance economics offers little relief; for it can never explain the destruction of a market precisely because it brackets or discounts the forces responsible for a market's innovation and replication—forces that are eminently social.

To his lasting credit—although he hasn't been given credit for it—Robert Pasani, CNBC's eye on the floor of the New York Stock Exchange, got to the hidden heart of the conundrum when he ascertained that "liquidity is a religion" in which the market had "lost its faith" (September 27, 2008). The participants once possessed a confidence of belief in the markets, a confidence not based on empirical proof but on their trust in its agents and institutions, and this was gone. What Pasani grasped was that liquidity is something that the participants in a market provide one another, but that they only do this under certain circumstances that have much more to do with their collective state of mind than with the clockwork of the market. Behind his remark is the idea that liquidity is a pseudonym and reification for the *social relations* that allow *individual* agents to construct the *collective enterprise* that is a market. Just as in their own ways are the notions of counterparty, a homogenous (arbitrage free) market, and the volatility that underwrites the recalibrations that make a market possible practically. Perhaps ironically, this is nowhere more radiant than in respect to the derivative markets. However much they appear deliberately not so, derivative markets are an ultimate expression of a social imaginary brought into being by the play of concrete social relations. The exposition must ground itself in these relations because they interpolate and mediate—through, for example, the recalibration of prices—the dialectical relationship between the always contingent and often unpredictable flows of events and the construction of a market as a totality. Those who inhabit the financial field imagine a (derivative) market as a totality on the order of a concrete object such as a house, which has doorways through which agents can enter and depart, and windows through which sights and sounds can impress themselves on the inhabitants, but which nonetheless constitutes its own singular and identifiable territory in socio-financial space. Such totalities have a peculiar characteristic: they are self-identifying in that the financial field christens them with proper names, such as the CDS market or, more finely, the Greek CDS market. The successful circulation of these names as standing in a one to one correspondence with a given market is itself one cog in the generative scheme through which the participants' practices reproduce a market as a totality. A good example is the circulation and citations of reports whose subcutaneous premise is that the CMO market is a clearly bounded analytical object whose trajectory can be charted because it possesses a past and a future.

Once analysis foregrounds history and the social, the term market itself requires additional specification. Although the word *market* appears identically across the whole financial landscape, and financiers do construct derivatives that use ordinary securities (e.g., stocks and bonds) as their underliers, contemporary derivative markets are historically unique inventions because *their very existence is inseparable from their liquidity*. Unlike ordinary commodities (such as houses) or production based businesses (such as home builders) *derivatives have no intrinsic value*.[8] They have no ordinary use values because they are intrinsically nothing more or less than a wager, a zero-sum wager between competing counterparties about some extrinsic outcome. This design feature accounts both for their extraordinary expansionary powers and their fragility. It follows from their basic design as contractual relations about the volatility of other relations—what was exemplified by securitization.[9] What this means is that a derivative market, and by extension all of the complementary markets linked to it, can continue to exist only if its agents have faith in its liquidity (and an operational faith in a pricing mechanism based on the principal of non-arbitrage). As such, the issue is what generates and sustains faith in such a market; what undermines it? How do derivative markets produce and reproduce liquidity over numerous iterations of themselves? Or, from the other side, what drives those who participate in a derivatives market to stare down contingency and collectively recalibrate prices, thereby sustaining that market's liquidity?

What makes this so important is that the stilled heart of the crisis was the almost complete evaporation of liquidity in the credit markets. Financial institutions were frantically hoarding rather than circulating capital because they feared that their counterparties might be covertly insolvent and that derivative pricing had become inefficient. Market makers were gripped by a potion of fear and anxiety that the next event would be streaming news of their counterparties' demise. The agents and institutions that make markets had lost faith in one another and hence in the markets themselves. This collective loss of faith was by no means unwarranted. Due to a rapidly failing American housing market, an unknown and perhaps unknowable number of financial firms were caught up in two concurrent and mutually reinforcing deleveraging cycles:

one involving home mortgages, the other securitized instruments. Lenders were suffering an accelerating accumulation of non-performing assets (exemplified by subprime loans that had gone south). These non-performing assets were eviscerating their balance sheets which, in relay, meant that a broad range of other financial institutions, from hedge funds to insurance companies (e.g., AIG) to government sponsored agencies (e.g., Fannie Mae) to investment banks (e.g., Lehman Brothers) that had bought or guaranteed mortgage-based derivatives were rapidly being pushed further down a road called insolvency. The specter of insolvency the very definition of an unsuitable counterparty in markets founded entirely on liquidity.

The hoarding of capital by institutions large and small was a symptom of paralyzing levels of uncertainty about the future health of their counterparties and derivative markets generally. A deep and suffocating *uncertainty* took control because financial agents and institutions were emptied of *faith* in the solvency of their counterparties and the markets' efficiency. Across Wall Street and beyond, the electronic screens showed no bids for the mortgage securities and other derivatives offered. It was as if agents' collective faith in the markets had been put through an industrial shredder, moving financiers to shut down the circulatory pump that created the economy's life-sustaining credit lines. The evaporation of liquidity meant that the buying and selling of the broad assortment of securities (e.g., retail mortgages, commercial paper, corporate bonds, etc.) only extrinsically connected to the derivative markets, securities responsible for animating the flows of capital through the production economy had ground to a halt. The systemic peril was that the EuroAmerican financial system would collapse. Richard Sandor, a pioneer of financial futures (that is, exchange traded derivatives) who had coined the term *derivative* to describe these futures contracts, cringed because he understood that "financial institutions go bankrupt not from negative equity, but from having illiquid assets" (Sandor 2012:203–04) which, in a kind of relentless chain reaction, destroy the assets of other once healthy institutions, portending systemic failure. This chain reaction in which bad banks take down good ones is what the economic literature refers to as contagion (the term contagion a biomedical metaphor that conveys the image of a virus which spreads of its own accord, an objective, impersonal, conscienceless agent that operates independently of the social). Financial failure on this systemic scale would threaten a deflationary spiral, which once out of control, could all too easily ignite a global depression that would almost certainly foment political unrest.[10] The situation was so grave that the US Federal Reserve, the Treasury, in an uneasy alliance with European Central

Bank (ECB), began to implement what would turn out to be a drumline of rescue plans, quantitative easings, bailouts, and regulatory restructurings to avert economic cataclysm. Unrecognized as such, the great structural power that the financial sector had accumulated since its build out from the 1970s—its institutions not only too big but too interconnected to fail—was realized as an "elective" governmental decision to bail them out financially.

A tenet of social analysis is that the social invents and reinvents itself; it is not an evitable outcome that naturally comes to stage as a polished product, but it the product of ingenuity and the redirection of agents' generative schemes of creativity. So it should not surprise that when thinking about a social approach to finance innovation is a good point of departure. For this very human capacity lies at the intersection of the individual and the collectivity, especially as invention and its canonization is a main engine of history and transformation. Creativity and ingenuity are not absolute; they only have uptake at specific historical conjunctures when the innovation proposed meshes and aligns with the social institutions and habitus then defining the field. The credit crisis which shook the financial universe is not akin to an earthquake or other natural disaster, it is the product of forms of innovation deeply linked to social and historical conditions. Focusing on innovation and creativity is a means of understanding the progression of contemporary finance from the perspective of the agents and the institutions involved. The social take away is that for the financial field, crisis does not lie in its stars but in itself.

The Historical Innovation of Crisis

The financial markets have always been a dangerous place, the rise of risk-driven derivatives making them more so. But the storyline is also about innovation and markets' continual rebirth and resurrection. The narrative arc of this story begins with the genesis of instruments and markets, not at the end with revelations about the impending crisis that consumed the capital markets in a fire-sale of assets. A critical design feature of the capital markets is that expansive innovation is the fuel that propels them forward even as they reconstitute the underlying social forms that create the institutional space and intellectual possibilities for such creativity. Keep in mind that it is the invention of liquidity dependent derivatives which allowed houses—for us perhaps the most tangible and useable of all commodities—to become a financial asset. Securitization as an innovation is essentially a synthetic form of circulation based on detaching the exchange value of what was once an ordinary commodity from its use value. A singular feature of the modern era is that the competition among banks meant that if they were to increase their earnings and thus their shareholder value (the leitmotif of success and thus the mainspring of compensation), this entailed higher and higher volumes of increasingly leveraged and speculative deals, and the innovation of new derivative products. From the standpoint of circulation, innovation, speculation, and creation of hedge funds and proprietary trading desks were all pieces of the transformative process.

In the beginning there was Michael Milken and his junk bonds, and turning the page forward to the present the securitized instruments that the financial community christened collateralized mortgage obligations (CMO) and credit default swaps (CDS). What makes this significant is that these instruments are not like lower life forms, born fully formed and genetically predestined to live and die in a certain way; rather, humans breathe life into and nurture these innovations in their quest to engender recognizable types of instruments and markets for their circulation. The historical context is that unprecedented disruptions to EuroAmerica markets that began in 1973 helped to create and reinforce a perspective that financial markets had taken on a life of their own. The markets now defined by a level of amplified and persistent volatility that appeared increasingly estranged from the state of the underlying (production-centered) economy. This new financial context gave rise to a new sensibility in the rising generation of financiers that finance was about the invention of instruments aimed to calculate, control, and capitalize on the fact that interest rates, business solvencies, cross currency ratios, and securities' prices had entered an era in which high volatility was the new normal. If the contemporary history of the rise of circulation reveals anything, it is that the character of the derivatives and their markets as well as agents' motivations are social inventions. A tenet of social theory that an event's genesis can be as revealing as the event itself radiates across a universe in which the regeneration of profit, symbolic as well as economic, turns on the continuing innovation of new products, great and small, conventional and exotic. To accomplish this finance must mobilize the agency and interests of those who inhabit the field.

For those who like to mark beginnings with dramatic personae, the story starts with Lewis Ranieri, a legendary bond trader at now defunct Salomon Brothers. As the first turn of globalization evolved (what come to be known as the emergence of the "Asian Tigers"), production based manufacturing jobs began a steady decline across the central plains of the United States while circulation based jobs in technology, logistics, tourism, and finance were expanding along the eastern seaboard and sunbelt states especially California. A mismatch developed in that there was an enormous accumulation of capital across the hard industry regions, such as the Ohio Valley, even as the demand for capital in these regions fell as reinvestment became unprofitable. By contrast, along the eastern seaboard and the sunbelt regions the demand for capital was increasing, as employment and populations expanded and with it the demands for capital. Seeing the mismatch, Salomon's bond trading desk began to hypothesize a number of often fanciful ways to reallocate capital from the Midwest to the ascendant capital hungry regions. The chosen innovation was to create a new kind of bond by assembling a batch of mortgages from the growing economic regions to absorb the over-accumulation of capital in the fading industrial regions. Salomon would gobble up mortgage loans made by local banks, repackage them into a tradable bond, and then set the bond into worldwide circulation. To do this, Ranieri had to turn what, at the time, was a unique and innovative token into a recognizable type with a liquid secondary market. This leap from singular instrument to marketable type required Raneiri and his team to fan out across the country to persuade bankers and lawmakers that mortgage bonds were genuine financial instruments with real economic value, that buyers and sellers could value/price the bonds objectively by relying on a mathematized formula, and that Salomon Brothers would direct its substantial capital to maintain a market for the bonds to thus insure their liquidity. This is the inauguration of the financial alchemy of *securitization*. The term coined by Ranieri was so appealing because it connoted an improvement on an existing market rather than a newly innovated instrument with uncharted speculative potential.[11]

Ranieri and his team were bonds traders who had personal and highly interactive relationships with their clients, which meant that they were attuned to the needs of the now burgeoning hedge and mutual fund industry. So their next innovation was to reorient the compass from the reallocation of capital to their potential end buyers of mutual funds, hedge funds, and the like. The next move was to divide the single mortgage backed security into differentiated security types. They sliced the bonds into tranches based on credit quality and maturity, and then fabricated bondlike certificates based on what their model told them was a greater risk/greater reward profile.[12] Ranieri and his team was able to transform what were improvised securities into recognized types by creating the self-fulfilling imaginary that these securities were part of self-expanding market with growing participation among cutting edge investors. Salomon Brothers' vaunted history and high status, as well as Ranieri's personal reputation as a financial visionary, were critical elements in canonizing and legitimizing securities, which unlike ordinary stocks and bonds had no price history (and thus could not be objectively assessed on any terms, fundamental or quantitative/mathematical). Buying such derivative and unproven instruments was in itself a speculation, but one motivated by the comparatively enlarged yield and secured by Salomon's reputation. However much it make appear so retrospectively, there was nothing inevitable about the fabrication of collateralized mortgage obligations (CMOs) or their acceptance by the investment community. This financialization of the housing market entailed innovation, the arduous labor of convincing regulators and the investment community, and a growing sociohistorical willingness to see speculative capital positively.[13]

Once bankers figured out how to detach the financial instrument from the underlying assets, and then instituted a market for such derivatives, the door to innovation swung even further open. Any type of standardized loan could be packaged into a collateralized debt obligation, and soon student loans, car loans, and credit card debt had entered the world of securitization. Note that the design of the collateralized obligations embodied a number of unintentional inventions. The derivatives where no longer anchored to production (e.g., of housing), but to circulation as expressed in and through the flow-throughs of money, that is, liquidity. *In the sphere of production, money expresses the deep commensurability and facilitates the exchange of commodities; whereas in the world of derivatives, money simply expresses and facilitates itself.* The result is that the underlying asset can itself become as abstract relation. And insofar as a derivative is nothing but a wager on the volatility of this abstract relation, there are no natural limits to the size of the market because the wagers and leverage are limited only by the willingness of the participants to assume risk and discount uncertainty. A new financial world was opening up in which the constraints and limits of traditional banking—that is to say, banking rooted in the structure of production—were becoming remnants of an older less dynamic economy.

Enter Peter Hancock from JP Morgan Chase. True of his postwar generation, he assessed that in the emerging cyber-financial world profitability would depend on product innovation, which in turn, would arise from computing power tied to industrial strength mathematical models. Determined to drive innovation in ways unimaginable to traditional banking, his team, called the derivative marketing operations, would specialize in innovative products. And, indeed it did. In the new era, banks generated the most profit and thus shareholder value by fabricating deals (e.g., leveraged buyouts) rather than by holding an inventory of loans which earned nothing by comparison yet required the banks to maintain capital reserves in the event of default. JP Morgan thus invented a way to make the loans disappear: a synthetic CDO using swaps. The loans would be bundled into an imaginary derivative, and buyers would agree to insure the bundled loans in exchange for the loan's revenue stream. And then during one of Hancock's brain storming sessions that as usual oscillated between playfulness, moments of folly, and creative outbursts the derivatives marketing team realized they could slice the synthetic CDO into tranches based on the mathematical calculation of implied risk. They could segment the derivative into separable, graded tranches: a hierarchy that would be based on the relationship between an obligation's premium and priority of owners' claims to its cash flow. Again, what made this work is that Morgan had the size and its management the ethos to insure a liquid market in these new securities. What all this proved was that the historical financial context and the inventive dispositions of bankers had both changed so dramatically that what was once unthinkable (conceptually and ethically) had become all finance could think about.

But this is hardly the conclusion of the story; the derivatives team at JP Morgan had invented a generative scheme for transforming new and singular debt instruments into recognizable and therefore saleable types. They had created a template that allowed agents to attach the formula of the synthetic debt obligation to all sorts of new derivatives schemes (critically mortgages), in the process producing a transposable narrative that could locate any specific customized derivative—here, now, in this form—as an instance of a recognized derivative type. Because the market's participants are inculcated with a similar (though historically new) palate of concepts and motivations, they grasped the fabrication of new derivatives (such as those synthesized from subprime mortgages) as simple expansions of a recognizable type, which, for the financial community, meant that these derivatives were manageable sources of profit because there was an accepted model (that of David Li [2000] based on the Gaussian copula) that could accurately predict their future behavior or price volatility. In the context of the ascent of circulatory capitalism, finance became a quest to continually invent and improvise new forms of securitization that could game volatility.

A number of people scattered through the investment sector came to realize that as securitization evolved, many of the newly minted derivatives provided fertile ground for speculation, these speculative wagers having the effect of producing markets with increased volatility and risk. Such was the case with the risk attached to collateralized mortgage obligations. Driven by the speculative ethos that had come to permeate all the derivatives markets, the impulse was to game this risk by betting against (shorting) the health of these obligations. As detailed by Lewis in *The Big Short* (2010), Michael Berry, the hedge fund manager of Scion Capital, was one of the first to see that the mortgage market was deeply compromised. Betting against CMOs entailed invention as there was no way to short these obligations. The innovation was to transpose the generative scheme underlying credit default swaps to the mortgage market. The challenge was that pools of mortgages are different from credit swaps in that homeowners default one at a time. But Goldman Sachs and the Deutsche Bank devised a formula in which buyers of these swaps would be paid incrementally, as the individual mortgages gave up the ghost. Firms like American International Group's (AIG) rapidly came to specialize in the very lucrative market of selling CDS to insure the endless stream of CMOs. Indeed, in time, a strange and inverted reality came into being in which speculator's demand for CDS—that is, their desire to short the mortgage markets—moved financial firms to create synthetic mortgage obligations which was itself feasible (and also profitable) because the demand for CMOs far outpaced the number of people applying for mortgages. What the financial field did was to invent an entire speculative world of the circulation of CMOs and CDS that was attached by a single thread to the real economy of production. That thread was homeowners who had learned and then turned their house into a financial asset.

The Mechanics of the Financial Crisis

The thrust of these innovations is rooted in and capitalizes on a changing financial landscape, a new chapter in the capitalism's history in which the creation and circulation of strategic financial products is front and center. This foundational change in the character of capitalism centers on the rapid ascension of an increasingly autonomous system of financial circulation. The dynamic driving this evolving system is the innovation of instruments, the abstraction and bundling of uncertainties into quantitative risk, and the proliferation of speculative capital. A daunting feature of this system is that has a directional dynamic of accelerating complexity, coupled with increasing connectivity and secrecy so that financial institutions and agents are profoundly interdependent yet mutually opaque. This quantum interdependence in which each individual's fate is inextricably bound to the fate of the collectivity is a direct outcome of derivative traders' unending demand for greater liquidity.

There is more. Greater liquidity allows for greater leverage because the cost of borrowing depends on the lenders' perception of how easily and efficiently they can offload their borrowers' collateral in the event of default. If these lenders share a collective faith and investment in the liquidity of the market for the collateralized securities—that is, if they are tightly interconnected—then the cost of leveraging derivatives wagers decline. And the opportunities for speculative capital increase. And the connectivity born from the demand for amplified liquidity "feeds right back to the source of the complexity" (Book-staber 2007:145), meaning that the very existence of a derivatives market will depend on the participants' collective faith in it. Central to this faith is agents' shared belief that no matter the overall complexity generated by their myr-iad positions, what they refer to as "the market" will orchestrate the orderly liquidation of these positions. For if everyone was liquid or sought to liquefy (sell) their positions at once, then that market would cease to exist as such and the implicit covenant, instilled by virtue of their participation in the financial space, would be broken, as did occur during the credit crisis. One result of this directional dynamic toward complexity is that it is rather difficult for even interested outsiders to crack open finance's speculative logic and instruments.

One way to open up the financial field is to take a look at the derivatives and the speculative logic that defined the crisis. Technically, the liquidity crisis stemmed from the collapse of collateralized debt obligations (CDO), though others forms of structured debt and credit insurance (credit default swaps) also joined the band. None of these instruments were created for or traded on regulated exchanges, like the Chicago Mercantile Exchange or the Chicago Board of Trade where derivatives were originally invented and traded. Rather, like almost all (more than 90%) derivatives they are non-exchange traded over the counter (OTC) products. This means that they are neither standardized instruments nor are they subject to regulation by the Securities and Exchange Commission (SEC). In the "vanilla" version, a mortgage lender would originate a portfolio of mortgages of whatever quality and varying duration, an invest-ment bank (the now defunct Bear Stearns specialized in such loans) would bundle the loans into a package, the credit quality of the loan portfolio was evened out and upgraded by purchasing insurance (e.g., Ambac) thus securing a AAA rating, after which the investment bank peddled the product to buyers, warehoused the CMO until it could find a willing buyer, or retained the CMO for its own account. To the world at large, the entire processes of bundling, pack-aging, slicing up, and selling the debt obligations were opaque because banks did this through off-balance sheet vehicles that (1) were under no regulatory obligation to report what they were up to and (2) were precarious because their finances depended on a liquid cooperative short term debt market (e.g., commercial paper). In this manner, a loose affiliation of individuals and institutions circulated somewhere in the neighborhood of one trillion dollars of suspect loans through the financial system.[14]

The various sectors of the financial field—the investment institutions, the financial media, the regulatory bodies, and the finance economists of academe—did not begin to comprehend the systemic harm posed by the accelerating creation and circulation of these securitized debt instruments. Michael Lewis (2010) comments on the pervasiveness of this blindness:

> Inside of three years, credit default swaps on subprime mortgage bonds would become a trillion dollar market and precipitate hundreds of billions of dollars' worth of losses inside big Wall Street firms. Yet, when Michael Burry [cited above] pestered the firms in the beginning of 2005, only Deutsche Bank and Goldman Sachs had any real interest in continuing the conversation. (p. 31)

As far as Michael Burry could tell, no one in the financial community could see the looming systemic problem. Such comprehension was an outlier in their conceptual universe because their intellectual habitus, derived directly and indirectly from their exposure to neoclassical economics, predisposes them to adopt an objectivist perspective concerning the evaluation of empirical data (e.g., from the housing sector). This perspective grasps financial markets as created from direct and immediate influences. Any markets is, and can thus be grasped as, the sum of its rational surface-level interactions. Alan Greenspan was an example and exemplar of this perspective, when in his commentary on the housing market, said that housing prices were accurate and just reflections of the aggregate of the interaction between supply and demand, and that the use of securitized instruments to finance housing was a well-constructed mechanism for dispersing the risk of mortgage default across a larger pool of investors. CMOs were thought to enhance the security of the credit system by dispersing risk literally across the global universe of risk-on investors (e.g., from the state of Florida's main employee pension fund to an ensemble of Icelandic banks). The financial media, financial economists in positions of power (e.g., Treasury), and federal regulatory bodies concurred (at least tacitly) not only with Greenspan's assessment, but with the validity of the objectivist paradigm upon which it was based. Accordingly, the financial field en masse treated any suggestions about reining in the financial markets as an affront to established economic knowledge and therefore contrary to the interests of the union. Unregulated capital markets represented the point at which scientific knowledge intersected with the conservative crusade against big government in the service of the kind of efficient economy that would help us maintain our international standing, doubly imperiled by the rise of the BRIC nations and European financial centers. One element of the power of the financial markets to cause an economic crisis is that the production of financial instruments went hand in hand with the production of knowledge, the financial field as a whole lacking any notion of totality and therefore the systemic or system wide affects that can occur above and beyond the space of empirical interactions.

The key problem, as the forthcoming chapter on temporality will develop, is that circulatory capital is subject to a treadmill effect. One of the crucial properties of this treadmill effect is that what seems to be rational in the short term for individual actors is eventually systemically irrational and destructive. In the CDO market, the treadmill took the following form. On account of their outsized returns—on what appeared to be AAA-rated instruments according to the ratings agencies—the overall demand for CDOs increased exponentially. Demand increased rather dramatically because CDOs offered a large *risk premium* for a AAA-rated bond—the risk premium being the difference (or spread) between the CDO's interest rate and that of a riskless Treasury bond. Increasing demand tended to depress buyers' rates of return (as more participants bid for the same securities), which should have led to a decline in their profitability. Lower interest rates, lower return. Many participants refused, however, to acquiesce to the lower returns dictated by a system-wide decline in risk premiums (El-Erian 2008:20−21), objectively because their incomes and positions depended on earning outsized profits and subjectively because they are immersed in the speculative ethos permeating the financial sector. Given the enormous quantities of capital available at that time (due in substantial part to Greenspan's accommodative monetary policy), the most alluring strategy to sustain profitability was to progressively amplify the portfolio's leverage. This leverage consisted of borrowing less costly short-term money to finance the purchase of longer term CDOs. This strategy was possible because two cycles of leverage were feeding off of one another: homeowners were financially leveraging their houses and fund managers their portfolios. Essentially, the two entwined markets were being driven towards a mutually animated instability by a self-reinforcing directional dynamic.

To offer a straightforward example of the benefit, should a hedge fund or a bank's proprietary trading desk boosts its leverage to 30:1 (i.e., one dollar in capital for every thirty dollars wagered), a 2 percent return on one billion dollars would leap from $20 million to $600 million. A minor return on capital had thus magically matriculated to a stellar 60 percent. By borrowing capital, those who manage money could put more money to work in what they considered to be their best investment strategy. This strategy was successful so long as their income stream from their CDOs was greater than the cost for the borrowed capital. But the strategy had a crippling systemic flaw: because it was undertaken by many institutions at the same time, it only augmented the demand for CDOs at an even greater rate, which, in turn, motivated an acceleration in the supply of mortgages being fabricated and circulated, hence leading to an ever increasing demand to write new mortgages no matter the solvency of the borrowers (See Barth 2009:chapter 3), even as these additional supplies of increasingly speculative and unsecured mortgages served to further depress risk premiums. Worse, the decline in premiums and therefore profitability only encouraged the addition of even more leverage, which only served to perpetuate the treadmill until many investment firms were leveraged at ratios that, to this very day, they can scarcely acknowledge. As the bar of profitability was raised higher and higher, each new height becoming a common plateau, speculative capital offset the prospects of declining profits by taking actions that greatly magnified the possibility of tilting toward, then into *systemic* failure. What is more, the "insurance" that companies, most notably the American International Group (AIG) made available to shore up the CDO—credit default swaps—assumed that systemic failure was impossible. And as the author of these swaps, AIG special products division, was under no regulatory obligations to retain anywhere near the capital reserves that would be required in event of a systemic collapse, it operated as through the markets were as efficient and self-correcting as Greenspan had asserted. Everything depended on the CMO market remaining liquid, and for several years running the participants' faith was warranted and rewarded by a titanic tide of money, self-esteem, renown, status, and power, until of course the cascade of mortgage defaults erupted and ruptured the participants' faith in first this market and then immediately others due to their interconnectivity. No one knows what would have been the outcome of a complete financial meltdown, for the capital markets or the real economy in EuroAmerica and globally. That constitutes a technical asocial summary of the genesis of a systemic collapse that most, and the most important, government regulators and finance economists deemed to be impossible.

Nonetheless, three social points make their initial appearance. The first is that the securitization was inherently bounded up with a strategy of euphemization, from the actual mortgages themselves to their final assemblage as derivatives (i.e., CMOs). A critical and distinctive feature of a social approach that differentiates it from anything done in finance economics is an awareness that the management of knowledge is a decisive element of the political culture of financial circulation. This is why statements by the Federal Reserve and Treasury, as well as the financial sectors management of the knowledge (including its management of secrecy and silence) selected and circulated by the financial media is very significant. The second point that radiates here is that because human systems are always intrinsically social, analysis cannot grasp the properties of these systems or their potential for failure by focusing solely on individual actions, cumulatively or otherwise. Indeed, the conundrum that haunts *finance economics is that it seeks to model the regularities of human behavior (mathematically), yet has no account of how capitalist societies generate these regularities.* Unbeknownst to its own conception of itself, it does not address the issue that underpins its analyses of how markets work, the implication being that it can have no corresponding analysis of what happens when these regularities are broken on the wheel of history—that is, a systemic crisis that compromises the market as a totality. For the real question is not why a market is efficient or inefficient, but why a market is mostly only conditionally and partially efficient to the point where its overall functionality is relative, oscillating, sometimes disappearing altogether for varying durations. Finally, contemporary capitalist systems, including in its own way that of financial circulation, are vulnerable to a powerful treadmill effect as the pressures generated by market-determined competition push capital further and further out onto the precipice. The derivative markets especially have an inherent propensity to go through a leveraging cycle followed by a deleveraging cycle whose momentum can cause a market to spin out of control and lose its liquidity. What this means socially is that the speculative behavior that was the catalyst of the crises is not the sum or outcome of individual decisions. Quite the contrary, its field-wide adoption and systemic implications are the result of a socially created collectively instilled disposition that (like a rehearsed orchestra without an official conductor) steered individuals' decision-making processes in a specific direction. Moreover, the structure of institutional rewards that has become the industry standard, particularly the calculation of bonuses and the attribution of statuses based on immediate profits above all contributions, has served to encourage the expression of this speculative disposition. As one trader put it, "no one asks how, only how much."

Conceptualizing the Financial Markets Socially

Conceptualizing the sociality of the market is inherently complex, so much so that finance economics foregoes the question entirely, offering instead a formula that conceals its presupposition of asociality under the apparent neutrality of a straightforward empirical definition. The standard account accounts for the market by what it does: a market is an institution in which some aggregation of rational agents engages in transactions that define an asset's price (See Fama 1976 for the classic statement and Sullivan and Sheffrin 2003 for an updated but similar formula). The definition which says that the buying and selling of a commodity defines its price depicts an effect of people's actions when they participate in a market. On the view, what is called the market is the means, the aims and ambitions of its participants the ends. Socially speaking, the market does not exist, for it is no more than an irreducible entity that services the demands of its utility maximizers. What is crucial is that insofar as the economistic definition does not recognize the market ontologically it cannot possibly provide the social specification necessary to specify the market, any market, as a socially analytical object. Seeking to grasp what a market is by plotting and pricing its transactions is, ultimately, no more enlightening then learning how to knit by unraveling a sweater.

A review of the economistic view reveals its true character: namely, that it is not an account of the production or the reproduction of the market. It is no more or less than an empiricist description of a market's transactional character once that market's underlying generative principles come into existence. Both as an objective structure that can be institutionalized and as dispositions inculcated within the agents involved by virtue of their participation in the market. The problem is that the economistic view has some severe limitations. The most serious of which is that it incapable of revealing the foundations of a market that are produced and reproduced through the sociality and collective history of its participants. Thus, the approach tells us nothing about how or why the participants come to recognize a newly innovated product (such as Ranieri's collateralized debt obligation) as a commodity type. It tells us nothing about why these agents would believe a commodity, particularly a derivative, is sufficiently liquid that they are willing to buy it or accept it as collateral. It lacks any concrete market specific account about what motivates agents' transactions (to, for example, in a certain market at a certain time, go all in on a speculative wager). It has no place for the social conditions, such as attending business school or the indoctrination given initiates by investment banks, that imbue agents with the capacities, dispositions, and vision to apprehend a market and its products in such a remarkably similar manner. And finally, this approach ignores how the structure and history of *the* market and *a* market—including legalization through the twenty-first-century state (Fligstein 2001)—produce this effect. Consider by way of analogy that a description of the effect of our actions when we participate in a graduation ceremony—we bear witness and celebrate the confirmation of the degrees—tells us nothing about the structure of the modern university, or its creation and evolution as a social institution (beginning in fourteenth-century Italy), or why agents are existentially motivated to enroll and attend even when the return on their "investment" is uncertain. The graduation ceremony actually presupposes and is founded on the structure and history of the university as well as the inculcation of a disposition to become educated as a dimension of the sociospecific production of an individual's future, life trajectory, and subjectivity. In other words, an account of what is happening, no matter how empirically factually on point, cannot account for the structuring forces that frame the event or the construction of the beliefs, desires, and judgments (aka intentionality) that motivate agents to invest their lives in it.

What this tells us about the commonsense definition of the market is that behind the curtain of what can be expressed in the object language of ordinary experience lie deep theoretical problems. Problems that the empirically defined, descriptivist formulation cannot begin to address because it has no concepts for giving an account of the production of the structure of the market or the motivations of its participants. There is neither a theory nor a description of demand: that is to say and do, an account of what financial agents demand, sometimes at the level of compulsion, from their actions. As the analysis will show these include money, self-esteem/worth, a sense of accomplishment, competitive satisfaction, institutional status, public recognition, economic security for their family. Indeed, these problems are so difficult and dimensional that the leap of least resistance is to ignore them, leading to the observation by Douglas North (1977) that economic journals are replete with analyses of market behavior, but not of the market itself: the construct that these analyses presuppose. From a social theory vantage, the crisis was a collect call from the economy reminding us that the union of a commonsense notion of market with a mathematics abducted from natural science is a poor substitute for the rigorous construction of the market as an analytical object.

North (1977:33) offers that this omission of the market is "peculiar"; I think it's necessary and motivated—as is the literature's omission of any analysis of the work that (re)produces the market. An approach that has no account of the market is saddled with the problems generated by the reality that the inevitable, unavoidable tensions and friction characterizes the production of the financial markets in that they integrate different forms of sociality originating at different levels of abstraction, and orchestrate these forms of social relations over specific contexts for action. What this means is that a social analysis of the financial field would need take into consideration the structure of financial circulation, the structure of the markets as frames for practices and actions, and the structure of the agency (concepts and motivations) of market participates. It would examine how, within the sphere of financial circulation, do the formative principles of the derivatives markets and those of the financiers' agency mutually produce and reproduce one another. Indeed, an adequate social approach would seek to structurally locate the financial field within the compass of post-1973 capitalism, but without offering any ontological privilege or free conceptual ride to either the notion of the market or to work and workplace. On the contrary, a social approach would interrogate both the character of the market and the character of the work performed by the agents involved in innovating and iterating derivative markets. The term commonly used in finance, that of *market maker*, captures more than it intends. A social approach would also necessitate self-reflexivity: here by deconstructing the ideology of finance and how the illusio thus created informs the way in which the financial community, state regulators, and the (trans)national public visualizes financial practice. As the approach underlines, this set of problems is not only social and sociospecific, but so deeply imbricated that the most realistic understanding is to view them as a set of overlapping transparencies on the same problem: namely, the character of financial markets. The contention that the problems don't exist or cannot be dealt with methodologically because they are too social to be mathematically intractable will no longer suffice. One might say that this is the price of the financial crisis on the market for conceptualizing financial markets. There is also a complementary view from the history of science: that the ascension of circulatory capitalism reveals the extent to which existing economic paradigms are rooted in, and constrained by, the historical conditions of their conception.

The Principles of a Social Approach

This chapter makes the argument that is simple in its statement yet complex in its enunciation. That to apprehend the financial crisis, and the corollary crises it created, to apprehend the character of the derivative, its markets, its logos, and its globalization it is necessary to set out the theoretical and thematic principles that found a social approach to finance. For those willing to look, there is ample evidence that appreciation of the social is essential to the theorization of the derivative and its markets, especially markets prone to systemic risk. The objective is a theory adequate to its object: adequate in the sense that it comprehends the markets as constantly transforming forms that are created structurally and reproduced manually through the agency of their participants. That is our view which sharply contrasts with the dominant neoclassical approach, and also with Marxist approaches that continue to fixate on production and eschew the realm of circulation. We can enumerate and summarize these principles as follows.

> *Multiple Determinations.* To be adequate to its object, analysis must embrace all of the determinations instrumental in producing the financial field and its markets. Analysis cannot bracket or abstract from the real for the sake of a model's tractability.
>
> *Historical Specificity.* An analytic of finance must locate the present conjuncture within the evolution of capitalism: specifically the ascension, increasing independence, and influence of circulation. It must thus frame the analytic in respect to how the form of value motivated by financial circulation compounds and overlays the form of value created within production-based capitalism.
>
> *Theoretical Openness.* The analysis must consider all of the theoretical traditions critical to an understanding of the financial field, not least those implicated in the fabrication of its ideology. The sociostructures of derivative finance have evolved in such a way that no discipline can by itself grasp the transformation that it is bringing about.
>
> *Social Collectivity.* The analysis must ground itself in the reality that human action is intrinsically collective such that individual behaviors invariably presuppose, and are valorized by, their social foundations. The analysis must accordingly be grounded in an account of how financial markets objectify themselves as self-reproducing totalities.

Agency's Production. The analysis must be grounded in a sociospecific account of agents' ethos, motivations, and the production of the subjectivity of the participants. The sociostructures of finance, including the logos of the derivative, are only reproduced through the actions of its agents, operating practically. The analysis must apprehend the objective structure of the dispositions that the financial fields recruits for, and further inculcates subjectively within, its agents, that is, the construction of the financial habitus.

The Doctrine of Realism. The analysis must provide a realist account of economic reason: that is, the actual structure of rationality of the participants, including the intersection and competition among the different modes of rationality. Importantly, this realism must encompass not only the full complement of agents beliefs and desires, but agents' embodiments of dispositions and sensibilities oriented to the financial spaces they inhabit.

Social Practice. To grasp finance as a lived-in reality, the analysis must apprehend the character of concrete financial relations: which is, finance as a socially specific mode of work. This entails our immersion in the world of everyday finance, armed with a theory that is aware of itself theorizing, most importantly the limitations on theorizing practice without destroying its principles of construction.

Self-reflexivity. The analysis must be self-reflexive; it must ground the analysis in its sociohistorical context such that it includes the point of view from which it speaks. This means questioning the conditions of the privilege of knowing phenomena, such as a derivative market, in which the investigator does not necessarily participate in its reproduction. This also means treating the derivative markets not as a spectacle, an objective preformed form to be interpreted via analytical categories, but as a matrix of concrete problems whose resolution is practical.

These are the principles that, from my perspective, found a social approach to the financial field and its markets. Putting these principles into practice is by no means easy, although an approach that attempts to do so is, I would argue, our best chance for understanding how the derivative and its logos work.

At the chapter's outset, I noted and quoted several sources to the effect that the systemic crisis caused by the cascading impairment of the financial markets was unusual historically in that occurred in the context of a thriving production-centered economy. Both in EuroAmerica and globally in emerging economies. I noted that derivative contracts are inherently time encapsulated in that they have origination and expiration dates, and that the mortgage derivatives market had an internal temporal dynamic that propelled it toward instability. Examining this set of issues directs analysis to the relationship between the structuring forces of derivative markets and their temporal dimensions. All markets are statements about the future insofar as they register the way in which the present participants presently discount the future. With this in mind, the following chapter deconstructs the derivative markets in terms of their temporality which sets the stage for an analysis of the sociospecific generative principles and schemes that produce the concrete relations of the derivative markets at this historical conjuncture. Which is, the concrete *social relations* that allow *individual* agents to construct the *collective enterprise* that is a market. For systemic failure occurs in and through the actions of agents operating within and constrained by social practices. As does systemic success.

Chapter 4

Temporality and the Financial Markets

The crisis foregrounded the question of how and why can derivative markets evolve toward systemic failure. Precisely what kind of temporal dynamic can cause a once robust market to end up in chaos? A chaos so disruptive and so debilitating that only external intervention can resurrect the market. What is thus necessary is not only the recognition that markets can fail but an account—however preliminary—of the inner clockwork of market failure. The chapter addresses the question of the contradictions inherent in the growth of a derivatives market, leaving aside the more global question of whether, given the value dimension of finance capital, the *form of growth* animated by the derivative is intrinsically problematic. *My argument is that a free derivative market will self-engineer a temporal progression in which it experiences continually increasing levels of abstract risk, eventually reaching the point where even small market disturbances can trigger a systemic breakdown. Consonantly, the propensity for instability that may induce failure is built into the market's internal temporal dynamic.*

For the financial markets, time is a complex and collective noun. It is also a pivotal dimension of their sociality, though to this point their relationship to time has only been the subject of an ancillary commentary. Insofar as markets, derivative markets most of all, are enframed by time, and this in many forms, it is thus necessary to frame the investigation by setting out the linkages between time and the markets. The financial field can, in fact, be described as temporal estuaries in that its sociospecific modalities of time intermingle and continually play off of one another in what amounts to an endless loop. To re-include the determinations of time is to embrace what is social about the financial markets. For the recognition of time, other than as a pure externality, reopens the question of the history of capitalism in respect to financial circulation, and thus the issue of the production of the capacities and dispositions that drive circulation. It reopens the question of the internal directional dynamic that propels the derivative markets toward increasing complexity and instability (i.e., what I have referred to as *the treadmill effect*). And it problematizes the relation between formal abstract time and, what is so different, the temporality of agents' practices, which, in the lived world, is the focus of their investments in the market and their continual adjustments to what they anticipate is going to happen. Consider an example that combines all three of these questions: that being invested in a derivative market posits a forthcoming that precludes its failure, a market's systemic collapse a possibility that exists hypothetically so long as it does not come about, until that is the situation that has been precluded appears forebodingly as something already there irremediable, provoking a deep palpable fear that spreads involuntarily across the bodies of the participants, those involved testifying to sweating, swearing, becoming hyper-vigilant and unable to sleep due to currents of fear and anxiety coursing through them, these volatile emotions fighting with the rational expectations that lies at the core of their scholastic training in mathematized economics. For they must decide under conditions of enormous uncertainty, decide now, here, in the forthcoming moments whether to shut their eyes and offload their positions at any price, thereby saving at whatever cost what is left of their capital and their reputations, or do they stand pat, waiting out and praying for the market's swift return to normality—meaning a restoration of liquidity, price discovery, and something approaching equilibrium—all the while afraid that time may not be on their side, the objectified market objectively rendering its verdict no matter the technical accuracy of the analysis. This constitutes a depiction of the reactions and strategic dilemmas of many SMV managers (e.g., Clifford Arness of Applied Quantitative Research) during the meltdown in August 2007 (Patterson 2010:209–241), a delineation of concrete social action that turns on temporality because the strategies agents' deploy are invariably crafted in respect to their implicit comprehension of how time works practically within the structure of the cognitive and motivating forces that define today's markets (e.g., a strategy to buy or dispose of a given derivative based on our interpretation/calculation of our competitors' actions at what we understand to be a particular stage in the market's (d)evolution, the difference between a temporary correction that beckons a buying opportunity because the market will snap back momentarily and the onset of systemic failure that precipitates margin calls being all the difference in the world in respect to the survival of a hedge fund).[1] Market crises serve to foreground time, the social efficacy of time never more apparent than when there is an interminable interval between trades— that is, a dearth of liquidity—because the participants have lost faith in the price discovery process and in their potential counterparties. For concrete social action, a market's temporality is never more powerful or threatening or more likely to provoke fear, anxiety, and consternation than when nothing is going on. Letting time takes its time, a hallmark of primitive, non-capitalist economies, is not a viable option for derivatives markets.

The financial field has many dimensions of temporality, and complexly so as some dimensions are nested inside of others. There are a handful that are specially critical to the project of making the social visible. The first is the historical trajectory of the financial field, especially since the field has been transforming dramatically since the early '70s. At one level, this concerns the evolution of its principal institutions in respect to the sociostructures of capitalism, specifically institutions now geared to innovate new products, assemble and deploy speculative capital, and manned by agents inculcated with a speculative ethos. *The defining feature of the historical rise of circulatory capital is the dialectical coevolution of speculative capital, hedge funds and other speculative capital investment vehicles, and the abstract risk driven derivative.* At another more granular level, this transformation concerns the evolution of new species of temporality, forms that reach beyond the limits of finance and influence (some would say corrupt) other dimensions of our social economic life, not least housing, but also education (Martin 2012), governance, and role of the corporation as a stakeholder in the life of the community. So at the heart of the argument is the understanding that what shapes these institutions, agents, and practices is a transformed form of finance defined by sociospecific temporalities and their modus operandi. They encompass a new tradition of the new that proceeds under the sign of innovation, the mathematical calculation of the new form of abstracted risk, the creation and expansion of a new form of investment vehicle, and the decoupling of the temporality of production from that of the circulation of capital. This is significant because the ascension of circulatory capital brings with it a peculiar temporal dynamic which is constitutive of the particular immaterial form of production that is the derivative.

The second dimension of this temporality is the internal dynamics of the financial markets that is animated by the present-day structure of circulatory capitalism. As indicated earlier when dissecting the crisis of 2008, the derivative markets are subject to a powerful treadmill effect. At agents' ground zero, the contestation for compensation, this treadmill is animated by the now triumphant notion of how competitive markets drive shareholder value/return on equity. The treadmill for derivatives is defined by a powerful directional dynamic toward market entropy which reveals that crises and near crises are intrinsic to derivatives markets. There is accumulating evidence of this from orthodox microeconomics no less, though it lacks the theoretical tools and intellectual habitus to adequately frame these evidentiary insights. The microeconomic studies point a finger at the problematic relationship between the temporality of real world events and the abstract formal temporality that underwrites the finance markets' uses of calculation. On a larger, more theoretical scale, a rising tide of quantitative analysts, led by Emanuel Derman (2011), have underlined the degree to which simple linear models cannot capture complex temporalities.[2]

The third dimension is the temporality of the abstract risk that founds and drives the derivative. This centers on the temporal horizon specific to the finance market in which the objective is to neutralize, offset, or otherwise hedge the risks created by duration while simultaneously capturing the profits engendered by volatility. For profits in such a zero sum game turns on anticipating the direction of volatility created by abstract risk. Based on the participants' consensus as to the directional volatility of one or more components of a derivative's abstract risk, profits depend on the market recalibrating its price in a favorable direction. Given an ideology that reifies the market, the financial field explains recalibration through a formulaic repricing narrative which makes it appear as though the derivative has repriced itself. This sanctions and normalizes statements such as: credit default swaps on Greek/Spanish sovereign debt are now *pricing in* the *possibility* of growing political *and* counterparty risk, the dollar-euro contract is now *pricing in* the *prospects* of volatility *and* political risk *on top of* the considerable interest rate risk already priced in, or mortgage obligations are now *pricing out* the possibility of volatility *and* redemption risk due to Fed intervention. What is analytically critical about these rear view accounts of the causation of repricing is that they identify and in the process reify the derivative as the agent doing the repricing, a narrative tack that depends on eliding or removing the social circumstances of recalibration.

This observation about pricing directly segues to the fourth dimension which is the temporality created by the constant recalibration of the derivative in the face of the flow of uncertain events. This temporal contingency is only (ironically) nullified in the case of pure arbitrage, the condition outlawed by derivative pricing models. Time is one of the paired variables that design and define any derivative contract (the other being volatility or price fluctuations). By their very design, derivative contracts start at and expire within predefined temporal parentheses. This calculation of future probabilities brackets the markets internal temporal dynamic and posits the functional capacity to successfully discern and disarm the uncertainties of history. Finance economics limits the temporalities of the market to abstract formal time, seeing them as certain, reversible, and propelled by the transhistorical logic of utility maximization. This in sharp contrast to the actual practices of the markets and its participants who use their economic reason to override and discount the temporality of the mathematized model. Finally, there is the form of temporality that defines the workplace. Inasmuch as people's lives and careers are about the threads that link their present to their foreseeable future, how they internalize and live within the cultivated time of finance shapes their subjectivity and thus their behaviors. As this final dimension is inseparable from the habitus of work, I will defer analysis to the investigation of the financial habitus. Although rarely spoken as such, in the form of time is to be found the form of market-making, its concatenation and melding of temporalities, most visible when crisis is at the door, the foundation of the relationship between the derivative markets and the greater social that encompasses them.

The Temporal Dynamic of Derivative Markets

A wide array of commentators who live close to the market, from central bankers (Steinherr 2000) and economists (Friedman 2012:343) to finance journalists (Olsen 2011; Patterson 2010) and money managers (El-Erian 2008; Bookstaber 2007) have observed that derivatives markets are so inherently unstable that even their volatility is often extremely volatile. There is also evidence that as a market evolves it tilts toward or cycles through progressively increasing levels of leverage (increasing risk), complexity, and instability (Financial Crisis Inquiry Commission 2011; Kroszner and Schiller 2011), as shown by the evolution of collateralized mortgage and credit default markets from 2005 through 2008. Speaking from the standpoint of the agents, Ho (2009) notes that products and markets that "predominate one year, employing entire floors of people, can be decimated the next, the department previously devoted to them shrinking to one or two desks" (p. 235). What her interviews underline is how these markets reach a crescendo of activity (as increasing leverage amplifies the aggregate value at risk) and then frequently, often rapidly devolve as they become systemically impaired. Those in finance capture the degree of impairment in the distinction between *a desk and a market,* the commonplace understanding is that it is one thing for a desk to disappear (due to shriveled liquidity, which could potentially be revived) and quite another for a market to disappear (meaning total systemic impairment). These devolutions are no longer unexpected, those involved having learned to normalize a progression in which a new (or even a newly revived) market first begins to gain traction, picks up momentum as it draws in new entrants, then experiences ascending risk and volatility as competition increases relentlessly, followed by instability and a downward trajectory as the liquidity evaporates when player after player is compelled to deleverage their portfolios. History shows that the real world imbues this progression with all manner of twists and turns and above all specificity, such as (ironically, given how much the financial sector inveighs against them) government regulations (like the Volcker rule) which may help prevent a market from spinning out of control by delimiting leverage.

One way of reading the evidence of crisis is that especially derivative markets are recursive. They are internally driven by a treadmill effect which means that as these financial markets evolve temporally they are apt to become increasingly unstable. The argument is that a free and unfettered derivative market—meaning a market which is not inhibited by regulatory and/or liquidity constraints—will self-engineer a temporal progression in which it experiences continually increasing levels of abstract risk, eventually reaching the point where even small market disturbances can trigger a systemic breakdown (whose sole remedy is the intervention of an external agent such as the US Federal Reserve or European Monetary Authority). The more successful a market is at generating outsized profits, the more rapidly it attracts new speculative capital due to the intense competition between SMVs, which, in turn, and on account of the same competitive forces, motivates increasing leverage in order to juice returns in order to obtain compensation, competitive success, and also self-esteem. So the more profitable a market is, the faster and farther its temporal progression is likely to go and the more people who will be involved. There is what might be called a pathologically progressive impulse to modern derivative markets. It was for this reason that by the time the financial crisis occurred, investment firms had acquired or were financing some twenty one out of the top twenty five subprime mortgage lenders (Patterson 2010:197), actively participating as it was in their own eventual troubles. This treadmill effect and its regulation—whether internally or through government intervention—lies at the core of the economics of the culture of financial circulation.

The first taste of the dynamic powers of the treadmill effect came almost a quarter century before the 2008 financial crisis, when in October 1987 the stock market went into unconditional freefall. On the single day of October 19, the s&p 500 index, comprised of the largest and most stable firms on the exchanges lost twenty three percent of its value. The centripetal force driving the huge decline was, especially by contemporary standards, an astoundingly simple derivative strategy known as portfolio insurance. It employed stock index futures and options in a dynamic fashion to help institutional money managers hedge their positions in the event of a stock market decline. The strategy's purpose was to increase the temporal window so that the managers would unwind their equity positions with minimal damage. Known as dynamic hedging, the money managers would short an ever increasing numbers of contracts as the equity markets fell, their short position in futures offsetting their stock losses. Here, the treadmill kicked in, for as more and more futures contracts were executed, the buyers not only insisted on sharply reduced prices and thus amplifying risk premiums, they, quite rationally, hedged their own long futures positions by shorting the underlying stocks. This rational behavior drove security prices down further, which in turn, initiated a new round of dynamic hedging as institutions shorted more futures contracts, motivating buyers to initiate a new spate of sell orders. When the market had tumbled by thirteen percent, a smattering of buyers stepped in on the reasoning that the best firms had become inexpensive on a fundamental basis (e.g., a growth rate that exceeded their price to earnings), but they quickly regretted their decision to the point where most were forced to liquidate their positions before the sun set that day. The locomotive had been dialed up to derailment and the following day, October 20, ushered in the prospects of systemic collapse. The astounding fall had decimated the value of institutions' collateral positions which, in turn, precipitating a flood of overnight margin calls. By morning a tsunami of sell orders had accumulated, but there were no buyers. Even the specialists whose designated job it was to make a market in specific stocks had retreated, discretion being better than bankruptcy and unemployment. In a word, the market was no longer liquid, even if the underliers were quite different from present day derivatives in that they were companies embedded in the real production centered economy, companies with real cash flows and earnings. That Procter and Gamble stock was illiquid did not mean people had suddenly stopped buying Tide detergent or stopped feeding their pets (unlike derivatives the stock market is not a zero sum game). With stocks not trading there was consequently no way to calculate an accurate reading of the stock index futures, which meant that the futures contracts at the core of institutions' dynamic hedging scheme also had no discoverable value. At this point in the treadmill, the only way to resuscitate the market by restoring its liquidity is through external nonmarket intervention. Due to the reality that the stock market was composed of real economy companies and the participants were prevented (through federal regulations) from using the leverage ratios, which would later become commonplace (leverage was capped at no greater than four to one), this was possible and feasible. The Federal Reserve led by Alan Greenspan called the investment banking giants, centrally Goldman Sachs, Salomon Brothers, Morgan Stanley, and Lehman Brothers, and underlined that the Fed would backstop their stock purchases, supplying as much capital as necessary. The CEOs called their head floor traders: at this juncture, the floor traders then informed the specialists who made markets for the S&P 500 that the firms would work cooperatively (rather than competitively) to finance buy offers large enough to open any of the frozen stocks. The firms' remedial action was successful: the financial firepower and the institutional credibility was sufficient to reanimate liquidity and restore confidence, thus reversing the treadmill spiral. Note, however, that it required external capital backing and cooperative action, the very essence of nonmarket forces, to restore liquidity and reverse a downward reevaluation of prices that was independent of the underlying economy and companies. The invention of securitization and synthetic instruments, because they have completed the abstraction of finance from the real production centered economy, perfect the treadmill phenomena that first became visible with portfolio insurance.

The lure of derivatives is that they promise a return much greater than what is the presumably risk free return on sovereign debt or investments in production based capital. However, an outsized rate of return has the effect of attracting new participants into the market, thereby increasing the demand as well as the volatility due to the introduction of mobile speculative capital. What the street refers to euphemistically as fast or hot money. Because no one wants to get left behind, financial professionals pirate the profitable ideas of their peers, copycatting others' trades being a recognized and oft commented upon strategy. In finance, lucrative trades quickly become crowded trades—the adjective *crowded* a term of art in finance to indicate increasing SIV participation. For individual agents, fixated above all else on their own short term competitive position, this imitative behavior is eminently rational. The reason is that market participants have adopted the notion of shareholder value for publicly traded firms such as Citigroup or Goldman Sachs, or return rate on invested capital for hedge funds such as Greenlight Capital or Citadel Investment Group. For banks and corporations' non-bank banks, shareholder value is enunciated in their stock prices, the trajectory of these prices mostly determined by their quarterly earnings reports and conference calls. The key metric for increasing shareholder value is accelerating revenue growth (the Street acronym is ARG). For hedge fund manager, whether they attract capital or suffer outflows is a function of their competitive rate of return, this rate critical in that their over-all compensation is typically structured as a formula that weighs both the per-centage of assets under management and the portfolio's rate of return. What this means is that there are three key characteristics of the structure of incen-tives: they are short term, competitive, and entirely monetary. Everything is designed as a short term monetary competition among the fields' participants. Under these conditions, no one can afford to pass up a profitable derivative position no matter the danger lurking in the future. So the treadmill effect re-creates at each stage the unresolved chase for profitability at its core.

This social structure guarantees that lucrative trades will rapidly attract enormous capital inflows. Increasing demand will then depress buyer's rates of return as more participants bid for the same position. Indeed, a charac-teristic of the financial markets is a temporal compression in which a firm's margins are becoming wafer thin at an increasingly accelerated pace. The ini-tial response to lower rates (i.e., margin compression) is that some partici-pants amplify their leverage, which, in relay, compels the other participants to increase their leverage ratios to remain competitive. Otherwise their (profit) performance will pale in comparison with their peers, thus squeezing their compensation and their standing. A critical dimension of the logic of the tread-mill is that the progression of a market requires that the participants progres-sively boost their levels of value at risk. The hedge funds directly, their investor sources of fast money once removed. What this means is that the appearance of unforeseen problems and therefore risks—that is, essentially, problems a market's pricing mechanism has failed to discount (e.g., a sovereign default)—can precipitate giant swings in volatility that redetermine and reinforce one another. These swings in volatility are further exaggerated when highly lev-eraged hedge funds are exposed to long-term assets (such as mortgages) but have "fast money" funding that can be withdrawn on short notice. The inflows of speculative capital can rapidly reverse their polarity, exemplified by hedge funds shedding their derivatives positions even as their investors withdraw the money that funded the positions. Each hedge fund desires what their desires collectively preclude: the liquidity to liquefy their positions as the buyers vanish.

Such a market gravitates toward instability as agents, often reassured by quantitative models that predict a restoration of equilibrium, initially attempt to withstand the outflows of speculative capital, and then if the selling only gains momentum, capitulate and try to sell before it is too late and what little liquidity remains vanishes (into the dark well of disbelief). The recent biography of the derivatives markets underline that the accentuation of volatility engenders existential fear and anxieties in those exposed to amplified levels of risks, leaving them conditioned to pull the trigger—that is, do whatever is necessary to liquefy or even out their positions—on even unsubstantiated rumors of contrary news. Under these conditions, sudden and precipitous downdrafts in prices (sometimes for reasons which have absolutely nothing to do with the derivatives in question) can create margin calls and thus compel a substantial liquidation of positions. This selling further increases volatility which leads to further liquidations, the particular market now on a downward tilt that can all too easily become irreversible and precipitate systemic turmoil. Few outside the financial sector realize that in August 2007, prior to the fall of Lehman Brothers a year later, the portfolios of several major hedge funds collapsed, forcing other funds to sell into a falling market which, in turn, led to a catastrophic downward spiral that nearly shuttered a broad range of derivative markets (ironically, *Turbulent Times in Quant Land* posted on the Lehman servers chronicled the deleveraging). The important point is that evolution of circulatory capitalism has created derivative markets whose social structure determines that as they evolve over time what is rational in the short term for individual actors can become destabilizing even lethal for the market as a whole. The very design of derivative markets has led them to internalize a temporality that will continually foment crises, potentially to the point of imperiling their existence. Financial crises, according to the analysis outlined here, are not simply random consequences of "Black Swan" like events; rather, the crises induced by these events are the consequence of a structural tension or flaw intrinsic to the temporality of derivative markets.

Within the financial field, economists have begun to point out some of the forces identified here. There is a certain descriptive awareness that increasing leverage can cause debilitating problems. It is hardly an accident that the economist most responsible for highlighting the implications of leverage, John Geanakoplos, was chief of Fixed Income Research at Kidder Peabody before becoming an academic economist. In a recent paper, Geanakoplos (2011) concludes that "the current crisis is a clear example of a leverage cycle crash" (p. 393). His review of the evidence shows that the evolution of a leverage cycle conforms to a script in which "leverage become very high and the assets [e.g., CMOS] are concentrated in the hands of natural buyers [or optimists] who have borrowed large sums of money" to acquire them. The stage is now set where the advent of "bad news . . . causes asset prices to fall" forcing "the leveraged natural buyers or optimists to sell assets to meet their margin calls, thus realizing their losses." Their departure causes assets prices to fall more because the assets fall into "less optimistic hands." If the bad news is 'scary' [i.e., if in the author's own words, such scary news amplifies *"uncertainty"*] then lenders demand more collateral thereby compelling the borrowers to deleverage their portfolios (p. 392, italics in original). This description recounts the opening progression of the treadmill effect, even if neoclassical theory is at a loss to locate leverage cycles within the overall dynamic of derivative markets.

Once this deleveraging is out of control it can lead to what Guillermo Calvo and his associates call "sudden stops" in liquidity. Their research on the empirical foundations of sudden stops in liquidity (Calvo, Izquierdo, and Mjia 2004) comes to two key evidentiary conclusions. The first conclusion is that seemingly exogenous forces and events which lie outside a market appear, in some inexplicable way, to penetrate the market and cause an irrationally abrupt evaporation of liquidity. While economic theory suggests this should not happen, the evidence suggests otherwise, as "scary" news increases the uncertainty and undermines participants' faith in the market. And as observed, the market cannot remove or marginalize these exogenous forces/events because the very existence and replication of the market is based on the volatility they foment. Their second conclusion is that the severity and duration of the breakdown in liquidity corresponds to the market's internal structural vulnerability, such as highly leveraged security positions that are vulnerable to forced liquidations. What their empirical research is confirming, albeit through the prism of an economistic theory that does not know what to make of such observations, is the temporal unfolding of the treadmill effect in which a market's increasing vulnerability allows for seemingly minor and "foreign" events to trigger what can become escalating waves of uncertainty, fear, and disbelief for the market's participants, the result of their collective suspension of belief in a market believed to be compromised, an unpredictably sudden stop in liquidity. To press the issue further, Geanakoplos's (2011) conclusion that to prevent a reoccurrence of the liquidity crises the government needs "to manage the leverage cycle" underlines the inherent dynamic of the treadmill.

The social analytic goes well beyond analyses in technical, economic terms. For it argues that the imbricated co-evolution of speculative capital, hedge funds, and risk-driven derivatives have engendered markets that have a specific internal dynamic and directionality. Central to this dynamic is the category of risk because risk is the essence of the wagers that speculative capital articulates through the derivative. It is a primary relation that founds the relations of contemporary finance capitalism. It creates a field of social life in which the participants are dominated by their need to assume risk and feel compelled to maintain this domination, whose not so euphemistic name is market discipline. This imperative motivates market participants to progressively increase the amount of risk that they quasi-voluntarily assume; yet, in so doing, they cannot but contribute to the total amount of risk borne by the market as a totality. That is, systemic risk created by agents' mutual loss of faith in their counterparties and realized as their mutual retraction of liquidity. This risk is rooted in the character of the derivatives that define finance capitalism—that they constituted solely by exchange value—and by a deeply inscribed compulsion of temporal necessity to perpetually increase this risk. A dialectic is set in motion in which each new retention of profitability through the amplification of leverage and thus risk becomes the base level of the abstract temporal frame of reference. Agents can succeed competitively only if they give in to this dialectic, its collective iteration the way in which risk becomes an attribute of a market as a totality. Though constituted through practice as wagers on derivatives, such as the various concrete risks associated with a specific mortgage obligation, risk becomes a systemic determination that can bring down the market independently of what is happening on the concrete level. The is the modus operandi of finance derivative markets because risk is simultaneously a concrete speculative activity (a performative wager here, now, for this set amount) and a socially mediating activity that imbues a market with its systemic cohesion. Grasping the temporal dynamic allows us to explain structurally why a financial market in crisis (*pace* 2008) will price individual securities well below their fundamental value: meaning the price(s) they would fetch in a liquid market. This gap between price and value is not, as conventional wisdom would have it, a matter of the market "mispricing" these securities temporarily, but of the temporal unfolding of a market as it approaches the crisis point. Said another way, the price of concrete risk expresses the temporality of systemic risk. The "mispricing" gap is a signpost that indicates the internal structural state of the market wrought by the treadmill effect.[3]

This account of the ascension of circulatory capital founded on directionally dynamic markets points to two contrasting forces, the necessity to amplify risk and the necessity to preserve the market's integrity, that are fundamentally different. Nonetheless, they are bound together as two moments in, as argued in the previous section, the historically specific incarnation of the financial markets. The real outcome, hidden from view until it was foregrounded by the crisis, is a dynamic in which the two contradictory forces produce an intrinsic structural tension. This structural tension is social, and decisively so, in that it lies *within* the logic of speculative capital, the institution of its investment vehicles, and design of the derivative. This inner contradiction does not determine in any linear way that a particular derivative market will necessarily collapse systemically, but it does ground its immanent possibility. Especially in the absence of regulation, whether this be national government regulation (e.g., Dodd-Frank), the regulation imposed by exchange traded derivatives, or the financial market's own self-regulation of OTC markets (which would require a collective self-reflexivity that seems rather unlikely at this juncture). An approach that apprehends the immanent possibility of systemic market failure as intrinsic, structural, and social allows the realization that the secession of crises and near crises are not unpredictable results of extrinsic forces (e.g., government policy-created incentives that cause institutions to assume excessive risk or the field's uncritical acceptance of a wayward Gaussian formula that motivated the widespread mispricing of risk). Rather, the propensity for instability that may induce failure is built into the market's internal temporal dynamic.

The Temporality of Risk

In addition to the evolution of a culture of financial circulation and the market's directional temporal dynamic, there is also a temporality to the kind of risk that drives the derivatives markets. This temporality refers to the specific relations of time that shape the behavior of derivative markets by shaping the time horizons of those who participate in them. Structurally, the temporality of financial flows centers on the short term, indeed, the shortest term possible. This is realized and exemplified in speculative capital's quest for arbitrage opportunities, a situation in which counterbalancing positions effectively neutralize the risks generated by duration: the time lag between the initiation of a derivative position and its set expiration date. This creates a directional dynamic toward the compression of time, both in terms of any derivative position(s) and in terms of turning over speculative capital as expeditiously as possible. Supercomputerized, high speed, algorithmic trading which compresses the duration a trader holds a position to fractions of a second epitomizes the compression of time and rapid turn of capital. Though on the surface, this appears to be a question of the amount of time, a sliding scale of duration of more or less, a more social approach sees it as a further qualitative determination of the market.

The reason for this is that time itself constitutes a form of abstract risk. Time is a ubiquitous form of risk definitive of every derivative of every type. Within the sphere of production, primitive and capitalist, producers minimize the externally generated risks they encounter by lengthening their time horizons. They reduce their exposure to production's uncertainties by adopting a long term perspective on the understanding that environmentally motivated fluctuations in returns on everything from livestock to capital will eventually iron themselves out if given a long enough time. By contrast, an inverse set of risk conditions determines the sphere of circulation. Because every derivative has an expiration date and because the time period bracketed has no external referent—the relationship, for example, between the housing and mortgage industries is continuous—time is both a source of and a quantifiable dimension of risk. Duration is thus a summation of the length of exposure to abstract risk on account of the correlation between time and volatility (due mainly to the technically unaccounted for repercussions of contingent events which traders, in contrast to derivative pricing models, always take account of practically without ever pricing them technically). Accordingly, for speculative capital, the mitigation of risk depends on the compression or neutralization of the effects of time: volatility, market instability, and the apparition of contingent events that compromise the balance sheets of the SIVs and thus the market's liquidity. The directional impulse is thus aimed directly at the short term. This temporality of compression has a qualitative effect. For speculative capital, the means of connectivity, the derivative, becomes the end in itself, serving as its source of profit and reproduction. The emerging reality is a culture of finance that shapes social forms, such as abstract risk, creates new technologies, such as the mathematics of derivative pricing, and institutes new contractual arrangements that allow the derivative markets to turn in on themselves. This self-referential, temporally compressing, monetization of abstract risk generates derivative markets whose construction of time bears no necessary relation to the temporality of underlying markets or the temporality of its institutions, including financial institutions. This is clear in that the duration of collateralized mortgage obligations have no necessary relation, and indeed have had no relation, to the temporality of home building, government programs to spur homeownership, the creation of concrete mortgages of specific durations, or the economic cycles of the production centered economy. To return to the example of the 2008 crisis, the prices, volatility, and viability of home mortgages were determined by markets whose temporal design has little to do with what was once the real economy. Instead, it was the temporality of the mortgage derivative markets that drove the creation and financing of subprime mortgages, imposing its short term logic on housing by transforming a market once dominated by fifteen and thirty year mortgages into a casino of mortgages destined to have the time horizon of the rapidly flipped property or the economic windfall that would by needed to satisfy the large upcoming balloon payment. Subprime mortgages their underwriters knew were destined for a short life, although more than long enough to create and package new synthetic mortgage obligations to meet the demands of speculative capital. A peculiar world is emerging in which the unfolding of sociohistorical realities, exemplified by the long term relationship between homeownership and the fiscal solvency and solidarity of many US communities, reappears as securitization: the quasi-autonomous circulation of unregulated, temporally compressed, socially decontextualized derivatives. The point is that, through our mode of governance, we have granted the derivative markets the right and the capacity to impose their structure of time on other dimensions of social life.

The Temporality of Contingency

A defining feature of modern capital markets, and a context for the production and circulation of financial derivatives, is that they are oriented toward, and are wagers on, the future. Not some indefinite future, but a forthcoming insofar as financial instruments, particularly derivatives, are founded on points of initiation and expiration. They all involve expectations and forecasts about the future, rendering them susceptible to price swings or volatility of unknown duration. This temporality is internal to the markets inasmuch as the instruments which agents buy and sell are inherently time-bracketed. They are predicated on forecasts about, and their payoffs a result of, expected values (price) in a circumscribed and discernable future. It follows logically that time (t) is one of two independent variables in the (Black-Scholes) formula used to price derivatives. The transparency of the future—the relationship between time and certainty—is thus of great significance in framing financial practice.

The temporality of derivatives is toward a near term, probabilistic future in a self-correcting market, which is, a market that uses forthcoming time to rectify mispricings of securities. Because every derivative has an expiration date and because the time period bracketed by a derivative has no external referent, derivatives construct time as a source and quantifiable dimension of risk. The market's participants consider time as a source of risk because the longer a derivative is exposed to market forces, the greater the possibility of volatility. As observed, under these conditions, the mitigation of risk depends on the compression or neutralization of time and further on creating a calculus that measures and predicts the chances of damaging volatility. The idea that became ascendant as derivative markets evolved, an idea endorsed by neoclassical economics, government regulators, and equivocally by the derivative trading community is that analysis can determine the price trajectory of a derivative. I say equivocally because the derivative markets embrace two antithetical notions of the forthcoming; two very different notions about how the future eventuates. The first is a concept of future events based on the economistic model whose underlying scholastic claim is that in the financial markets uncertainty has no future because finance has taken possession of the tools, technology, and know how to turn a future once understood to be inherently uncertain into probabilistic distributions of quantified risk. The second is a practical notion of the future used practically by those who participate in the derivative markets. This concept, which is rooted in the habitus of the agents, takes into consideration the continual contingency of events, constructing a spectrum based on agents' immersion in the encompassing social world, ranging from contingent events that are not unanticipated to black swan events that seemingly come out of nowhere. This worldly immersion produces in agents a sense, at once cognitive and intuitive, of how the space that encompasses a derivative market inflects the recalibration of prices, agents taking into consideration not only their own interpretations but how they think other participants will interpret the same senses. This sense of the world is omnivorous, embracing such disparate information as perceptions of the speculative inclinations of different SIV managers (on a sliding scale from conservative to gunslingers), consensus on the behavioral tendencies of regulatory agencies, the intuition that the German central bank is predisposed to adopt a monetary policy that will err on the side of disinflation (because it remains mindful of the inflationary chaos that was instrumental in the ascension of Nazism), and so on embracing an almost endless inventory of agents' constantly evolving senses of the world that encases the market. The result is that the practice of trading unfolds as the determinate price set by the derivative pricing model, at which point the traders then override the model as they reset, renegotiate, and thus recalibrate a derivative's price by interpolating the changing flow of contingent events through the prism of their senses of the world.

The first conception of the forthcoming time, which is inscribed in the economistic mathematized model, has over the past forty years changed the infrastructure of theoretical knowledge. Its captivating concept is that the key to making the right bets and unlocking profits is to harness the notions of risk and probability in order to accurately price implied volatility. Looking back, the ascent of the notion of risk has marginalized the notion of uncertainty. Especially for managers who can grasp neither the intricacies of trading nor the mathematized models fabricated by the quants, the aura that surrounds the guarantee of calculation helps to elide some of the fears and cautions that attend uncertainty. The crystallization of a speculative ethos that moves institutions and agents to assume huge risks—exemplified by the multi-billion dollar hedging debacle at JP Morgan in 2012, some four years subsequent to the crisis—goes hand in hand with the assurance that there can exist a certain certainty about markets' futures. The view inscribed in the economistic models is that the temporality of derivative instruments is under scientific control because derivatives have expiration dates and because it is possible to forecast the intervening volatility. Not even the credit crisis and the economic turmoil that ensued has been able to dislodge this view of derivatives. So the narrative of the derivative in synch with the mathematics of its pricing removes uncertainty and minimizes temporality, which is nothing less than the claim that derivatives are immune from contingency. They somehow exist outside of the social and historical.

The persistence of this view notwithstanding, one of the lessons of the crisis is that derivative markets will always live in the republic of uncertainty. Uncertainty in its most distilled and multivariate form, rather than risk as a measurable variable. Both evidence and interviews confirm what an earlier generation of economists would have predicted: that cascading waves of uncertainty and the coils of fear that they induce when security's prices become dark and counterparty trust evaporates underpinned the crisis. This uncertainty is an enlargement and loss of control over the normal current of uncertainty that courses through financial markets. A corresponding lesson of the credit crisis is that derivative markets are founded on the fabrication of knowledge, or, more precisely, what the markets' participants understand as useful information that allows them to solve the concrete problems that they confront. Especially for leveraged positions in complex markets, their most pressing and persistent quest is to uncover and use practically insights that help them to hedge against uncertainty. Here, the crisis and its systemic ramification were highly instructive about the future of uncertainty. For it foregrounded and magnified the fact that there is a decisive difference between the *absence* of information (about security prices or the solvency of counterparties), *noise* or information flows irrelevant to decision making under uncertainty, *information* or steams of useful and usable data, and *knowledge* which entails the stitching together of this data so as to reach a practical conclusion. But also as Fischer Black (1986) realized in his now famous paper on noise: it is virtually impossible to tell them apart prospectively. Indeed, it is only reasoning backwards from the trade's outcome that one can ascertain with any certainty what important information was missing, what information was relevant and what irrelevant to the outcome, and whether or not the trader's conversion of information into practical knowledge was done with sufficient accuracy.[4] Reasoned to its logical conclusion, Black's thesis on "noise" says that uncertainty is where knowledge goes to die because it can inhibit agents from executing what from a rational calculated standpoint should be a profitable trade. What is more, collective market wide uncertainty can lead to a recession of faith in that market which appears in practice as the disappearance of liquidity. That is, a systemic crisis.

For all of its aspirations to be scientific, finance economists is founded on certain suppositions about social action and practice that have no empirical foundation in the way individuals actually behave. One of the more central and general suppositions is that agents collectively apprehend the future with near perfect certainty. The concept is that market participants must possess both an accurate and precise understanding about how markets will behave over some infinite future. They will divine clear and correct beliefs about what will happen to security price, currency, or interest rate volatility in the foreseeable future. Benjamin Freedman, an economic insider, summarizes "the assumption that has governed most [neoclassical] economic analyses for the past four decades": "the assumption is that all agents (act as if they know) the processes that govern the particular realizations [of random variables], including the structural relations among them as well as the distributions of the underlying random influences" (Friedman 2012: 341). The assumption is that the model of the market constructed by finance is indistinguishable from the model that agents use in practice, and that this model allows participants to know and foresee the future because it accurately mathematizes risk. They also know with certainty that their counterparties are financially sound and that price discovery always reveals the single true price. This would come as extraordinary news to anyone who professionally trades derivatives, so much so that when I introduced this supposition to practicing traders more than a few shook their heads in disbelief and observed that it was so terribly distant from their experience of the markets that they found it difficult to believe anyone could hold such a notion. There is, to sharpen the point, an extraordinary gap between the abstract notion of certainty posited by finance economics and financial traders real-life experience of deep uncertainty. What the ethnography reveals is a confusion between an economic model of reality and the reality of that economic model, the assumption of rational expectations placing into the mind and finance practices of the participants the model that the scientist has constructed to account for their reality. For the question is not what rational expectations participants *should* have, but the risks that they actually attach to their expectations. In real life, agents seldom know nor act as if they apprehended the processes that orchestrate the realizations of random variables; they act according to the ensemble of social, economic, and psychological motivations that has been inculcated within them based on their position in social space (which is why the depression generation and the post-war generation habitually attach different levels of risk to their expectations about the same security).

Elie Ayache (2010) points out what is more than implicit in Fischer Black and what derivatives traders know as a matter of practice: that derivative pricing begins where the derivative pricing model ends. The reason for this is that the pricing model excludes as a condition of its (mathematized) production precisely the entire space of contingent events, implicit knowledges, and relationships among the participants that constitutes the basis of derivative pricing. Once the traders know the calculated implicit volatility and thus the decontextualized price of the derivative, they then override the model based on these other considerations. What characterizes these other considerations is that they are rooted in the social. More, if the price set by the model was determinative or final there would be no economically rational motivation for trading derivatives, which means that the economic rationality of derivative trading stems from the variances or recalibrations generated by the introduction of an inherently uncertain social. The very possibility of a market founded on profitability depends on these contingent events, the implicit knowledges brought to bear in interpreting them (including what counts as a contingent event), and the relations among the participants (e.g., which siv managers will buy into what is an avowedly risky derivative instrument because they are desperately seeking additional yield to help catch up with the benchmark indexes and/or their peers). All of this in stark contrast to the primitive market, culturally founded on explicit kin and community relations that the market is customarily designed to reproduce above all else. Observe socially that the relationship between the derivative pricing model and traders' real-world pricing of a given derivative depends on an overriding process that is rarely explicitly recognized as such, and then only by traders when they retrospectively dissect a transaction (e.g., "my sense was that they would accept the price I quoted because they did not fully understand the risk incurred or that a better price was available"). The result is that the financial markets have a kind of bipolar personality: an economistic mathematized persona that figures in a firm's or regulators modeling of risk, and a real-world persona based on the way in which the social habitus of traders calibrates and recalibrates the flow of contingent events. One can observe here that one of the principal problems with a VAR, or value at risk, model is that it must always start from a risk neutral positions that is in principle unknowable.

Belief in rational expectations was not always the orthodox view. Economists like Keynes worked on the premise that there was an ineluctable uncertainty about the future, especially the future of the securities markets. In his *A Treatise on Probability* (1921), then again in his general theory some fifteen years later (1936), Keynes argued that due to the irreducible uncertainties that course through the markets, agents' decision making is not probabilistic in the statistical sense, but rather a matter of situational logic and deeply imbued dispositions (that is "animal spirits"). In the same vein and year, Frank Knight (1921) distinguished between risk and uncertainty. Uncertainty denotes those situations in which the participants have no secure command over the range of factors that might influence the outcome or their relative force in its determination. The universe of probabilities and their interrelationship is itself an unknown probability. Risk, on the other hand, refers to those specific situations in which the participants can generate a comprehensive inventory of all the probability distributions of upcoming events. Under these conditions, the participants in question could accordingly (1) identify all of the risks involved and (2) scientifically quantify those risks. In his article on *The Limitations of the Scientific Method in Economics* (1924) Knight argued that the basic limitation of risk based analyses is that uncertainty governs most situations, including the possibility of making a profit in the market.

Indeed, almost everything that finance economists think is a risk, actual derivative traders treat as an uncertainty, even if they follow the vocabulary of economics and call them risks. *The single most compelling feature of the practical act of derivatives trading is the existential tension engendered by having to make decision after decision under relentless uncertainty.* Often the only thing that is certain is the uncertainty. And the fact that the uncertainties are multi-dimensional. The demise of Lehman Brothers underlines what traders always knew: there is always the possibility that one's counterparties may be or become insolvent and thus unable to pay up. The credit crisis illustrated that contrary to and beyond what economistic accounts assume there is genuine counterparty uncertainty insofar as it is impossible to accurately quantify the future well-being of portfolios made up of changing assortments of volatile securities that are interconnected in unknown ways. A famous floor trader (Arthur Cashion of UBS Securities) depicted the crisis through the language of uncertainty, noting that the problem is that "we don't know what we don't know" about the solvency of the counterparties in the financial system. The derivatives trader, Nassar Saber, submits that his experience is that uncertainty about one's counterparty materially inflects derivative pricing (1999).

A different yet equally extraordinary uncertainty permeates the practice of trading, particularly the circulation of OTC derivatives. Across the trading desks of all types of investment firms, information about prices of specific derivatives and information that affects these prices (e.g., the relative solvency of a counterparty) are hard to come by, unevenly distributed, and circulated through communication channels that are typically insular and interested. Often there is a scarcity of concrete information and the floating of competing contradictory narratives (e.g., about the outstanding "book" or positions of specific investment firms), resulting in a lack of trust in the circulating information. Trading desks attempt to amplify their own intelligence, dissemble in ways intended to increase the ignorance and confusion of competitors, even as they may shield others from information (e.g., that the firm's clients could have obtained better pricing for a security elsewhere). Especially when market volatility soars, and securities' prices seem to veer far off course due to waves of selling pressure, uncertainty reigns and information is at a premium.

Peter Muller was the leader of Process Driven Trading (PDT), an elite derivatives division within Morgan Stanley so hidden and secretive that only the firm's most senior management was aware of its existence. Muller notes that when markets are on the verge of breaking down—as happened repeatedly during the crisis—there is not only an absence of liquidity but of knowledge. The initial impulse is to ring up hedge fund managers and proprietary trading desks and try to determine who is selling and who is not. Knowledge is essential because uncertainty begets volatility which triggers even more and more violent volatility. But seeking to distinguish knowledge from noise turns out to be rather difficult because few are willing to reveal their hand, and those that do may be bluffing. Muller compares this to poker in that no one knows who is holding firm through the volatility and contractions in liquidity and who is bluffing, putting on a stalwart front so that they can unloading their rapidly depreciating securities in an illiquid market. As Scott Patterson (2010:161–165; 218–220; 227–229) illustrates in his exposition of Muller and his derivatives team, uncertainty radiates so brightly when the (equilibrium based) models break down because uncertainty was always underlying the market.

The disposition to accumulate and protect information is powerful, so powerful in fact that members of the same firm often and deliberately fail to share vital trading data with one another. In practice, because OTC derivatives trade on a complex market riddled with uncertainty many securities will have multiple prices simultaneously. Contrary to what economic models of the market say, the restoration of a unitary price through arbitrage rarely occurs in such cases because price discovery is virtually impossible. This absence of transparency and the creation of multiple prices simultaneously for the same security is not an accident or one off event but an objective. One of the ambitions of trading houses (e.g., Morgan Stanley), inscribed in both institutional practices and the dispositions of its traders, is to do everything possible to eliminate or tilt price discovery. The collectively held secret is that sometimes this entails gaming the financial disclosure laws. What is at issue here is not probabilistic risk, but the extremely concrete and very social production and management of uncertainty.[5] Traders deliberate try to circulate misinformation about prices—the term misinformation in the financial markets a euphemism for a lie that appears credible and is therefore effective based on the symbolic capital accumulated by its individual and/or institutional producer. So derivative traders not only confront uncertainty, they also actively amplify it to advance their own interests. In the world of finance, knowing how to play "the game" requires agents to master the generative schemes for amplifying uncertainty which, correspondingly, is the knowledge that they animate to detect others' attempts to muddy the waters. That is, agents advance their self-interests by packaging and circulating "noise" (foregrounded in the constant swirl of rumors that course through the market) as though it was genuine information. In the world of concrete social practices, agents often do everything in their power to prevent and preclude the possibility of accurately calculating a derivative's volatility.

The uncertainties also include what is, more than a little euphemistically, called "headline risk"—meaning economically influential events from the space of politics, governance, and environment (e.g., the BP oil spill in the Gulf of Mexico). This class of uncertainties encompasses all those events (exemplified by a terrorist attack) for which no feasible and/or possible hedging strategy exists. What this means for traders is that cross currency rates and interest rates are intrinsically uncertain because there is no way to forecast accurately what these events will be, how other agents and institutions—such as the Federal Reserve—will interpret any succession of events, or what action they might embark on collectively or singly. In great contrast to the abstract model which assumes that agents can hedge all and any (probabilistic) risks, real-world traders engage a world in which they are uncertain of even what all the possible uncertainties are. More importantly, the state of uncertainty—that is, agents changing estimations of the future—is market defining because it motivates investors to oscillate between holding more of their assets in cash and less of their assets in cash than would be warranted in a world defined by probabilistic risk alone. The premium that cash more often than not commands is not irrational or a product of our animal spirits; it is the price that specific historical agents willingly assume to take an action that precludes the untoward consequences that may befall those who do not take into account an uncertain and therefore precarious future. This current may at times flow in the opposite direction when agents become in the now famous phrase irrationally exuberant. So it is not surprising that across the United States in the years leading up to the crisis, the rise of the speculative ethos corresponded with higher indebtedness and an overall decline in the cash premium (US Treasury 2008) as investors assumed that the exuberant state of collective economic opinion as expressed in the upward slope of equity, credit, and housing prices, and circulated through the public sphere by the financial media, was the distillation of a correct summation for the future prospects and trajectory of the American (and global) economy. However, once the crisis shattered this faith, there was a violent return to cash (and cash equivalents) to the point where a trillion dollars idled in money market and short term US Treasuries yields were so depressed that they sometimes temporally turned negative (on an absolute return basis).[6] Seven years into the crisis, the Federal Reserve had kept short term interest rates at near zero and created and injected hundreds of billions of dollars into the economy through rounds of quantitative easing, yet a great amount of assets still sat in idle stationary cash (the "sidelines" as it is called by the Street in another of its many sports metaphors) because so many potential investors remained immobilized by their fear of the uncertainties that might lie ahead. The most rational expectation is to realize that our expectations are rarely purely rational. Or, more precisely, can encompass many, sometimes conflicting modes of realist economic reasoning [what the economic literature begins to only partially capture with the diffuse, and still rather heterodox, notion that an ensemble of individuals, such as the participants in a market, many have "heterogeneous beliefs" and therefore nonconforming dispositions about that market and its future (See, for example, Vogel 2010)].

In the final analysis, without an appreciation for the uncertainty that courses through social life, there is no way to develop an analysis of liquidity and thus of the performative relationship between liquidity and the market as a totality or whole. There is no way to appreciate that *liquidity in the face of uncertainty is a foundation for the production and reproduction of the market.* It is the need to produce the religion of liquidity in the face of extended uncertainty that compels the totalities that are the markets to find ways to reproduce themselves socially—that is to say, through the practical actions of motivated agents. For economics, uncertainty translated into manageable risk, which is then further reduced to a determination (a market defined by ideal liquidity, no counterparty risk, and perfect price discovery) permit the use of mathematical models at the expense of an understanding of the actual real-world operation of the markets. In the end and without knowing it, finance economic's account of the market is so abstract and removed from the real that it actually precludes the very possibility of the market as an actual entity. No wonder then that the 2008 systemic crisis has become an impossible to explain occurrence that seems to motivate not concern and curiosity but avoidance. Either absolute avoidance in that financial economic analysis proceeds as though nothing worth analyzing had happened or it has recourse to formulations that are too abstract and removed from the realities of the market to say anything meaningful about concrete social and economic relations. Coming to terms with the state of finance is of more than scholarly concern: for it is hard to ignore that the ascent of circulatory capitalism, with its proclivity for allocating available capital speculatively in risk driven derivatives, goes arm in arm with declining productivity growth (and thus employment) in EuroAmerica. The argument for having derivative markets is that they allow us to hedge and distribute risk. The reality is that the inherent uncertainty of the future coupled with their own temporal dynamic or treadmill means that these markets cannot hedge and actually serve to concentrate what is the most crippling and contagious of all risks: that of systemic failure that both goes global and bleeds into the real economy.

A poster child for economic accounts that too abstract and too removed from market realities to say anything meaningful about concrete social and economic relations is *Liquidity and Crisis* (edited by Allen, Carletti, Krahman, and Tyrell 2011). Its stated purpose is to address the fact that an "important reason for the global impact of the 2007 financial crisis is massive illiquidity in combination with an extreme exposure of economically and politically relevant parties to liquidity needs and market conditions" (Intro. p. 3). This gesture toward the real notwithstanding, the articles cannot escape their intellectual heritage. They pivot around formulations such as a "decline in the supply of liquidity" (Allen and Gale 2011:112), "aggregate liquidity risk" (Bhattacharya and Gale 2011), the misbehavior of the value of money [(as in "the value of money is not well behaved" (Allen, Carletti et al. 2011:11)], and a plethora of other terms and noun phrases that treat concrete social relations as though they were abstract objects. From a social standpoint, four methodological tropes lie at the heart of finance economics. (1) Concrete social relations are transformed into abstract objects (e.g., liquidity) which are imputed to have a life of their own. (2) These abstract objects then interact with abstract general agents constructed by bracketing off the specific social and economic characteristics of the concrete agents. In *Liquidity and Crisis*, the abstract agent, "financial intermediaries," encompasses institutions that are fundamentally dissimilar and had extraordinary different relations to the market's construction of liquidity. The abstract agent, "financial intermediary," encompasses institutions as fundamentally dissimilar as investment banks like Goldman Sachs, non-bank banks like GE Capital, hedge funds such as Soros Investment, Vanguard Mutual Funds, the Baton Rouge Community Savings Bank, and the California State Pension Fund. (3) The concrete agents that comprise the abstract agent are posited as behaving uniformly in respect to the abstract objects, because they all behave as economically rational, utility maximizing entities in a hypostatized economy. (4) This allows for the production of imaginary ethnography in which an author will declare, for example, that a financial intermediary faced with a certain circumstance (e.g., increased risk) will invariably behave in a certain manner (e.g., implement hedging strategies). Historically speaking, sometimes so, sometimes not, which begs the question of what actually determines their behavior. Twenty-six articles and some seven hundred pages later, the reader of *Liquidity and Crisis* is not one bit closer to understanding what about liquidity was instrumental in creating a real-world crisis. Not once in all those pages is Goldman Sachs, Bear Stearns, AIG, Morgan Stanley, Lehman Brothers, or Fannie Mae even given so much as a mention. There is also no mention of agents speculatively-driven trading in CMOs and CDSs. And as conspicuously absent is any mention of the political power of the financial sector to influence regulatory regimes and government responses to the crisis. In other words, the predicate of analysis on these terms is the banishing of the real.

Once analysis recognizes that the problem that lies at the very foundation of derivative markets is the iteration of liquidity in face of deep uncertainty over the solvencies of counterparties and the discovery of prices, and that the only viable way to accomplish this iteration of liquidity is to generate and institutionalize a frame (or totality) that motivates the production of regularities in behavior. The objective is to grasp the dialectic by which the actions of the participants (re)produce a market as a frame even as the instantiation of that market (on the model of the market) canalizes agents' behaviors so that they are regular and recognizable. Though by no means predetermined. In sum, understanding the character of the recent financial crisis and, more generally, how financial circulation has evolved to work requires an account of the space of the market.

Chapter 5

Theorizing the Financial Markets Socially

The most interesting aspects of any living market are the volatility, magnitude, and breath of its inefficiency.

From the standpoint of capitalism and even more so from the standpoint of finance capital, nothing is more luminous or foundational than the market. The market names the institution and transactional space where capitalism realizes itself. This purview is so transcendent that theorists of many persuasions—from neoliberal economists to traditional Marxists—habitually conflate capitalism with the market. As though the market was the definitive defining feature of capitalism. This is nowhere more true than in respect to the derivative market. The view so powerful we may call it the official view is that the market stands at the epicenter of finance and even more so the circulation of derivatives. It is a conception of the space of operations wherein the economy of derivatives take place and capitalism organizes the allocation of capital.

Yet, for all of its centrality and significance, the analysis of the derivative never entertains the question of what exactly is a market and how through the practices of its participants does a market or any market produce itself? The question can be stated more precisely: how through the act of replicating the derivative does a market reproduce itself? Analyses of the derivative seem to forget that the market is not simply a setting in which the agents execute transactions, but the means whereby the positing of trades becomes possible. Bizarre as it may seem, a defining feature of theories of crisis and market failure (or, correspondingly, the impossibility of failure) is that they have no theory of the market that derivatives presuppose. About this idea, the view taken here is that without a theory of the structure and reproduction of the market, we can grasp neither the crisis nor the normal functioning of the derivatives market.

There is a notion of the market that courses through the normative narrative of the financial community and most finance economics. Call this the market with a capital M. The market with a capital M is the prevailing idea that markets by their very nature possess an ontological integrity that transcends space and time. The idea indigenous to neoclassical economics, now embedded in the narrative of the financial media and in business school curriculums, is that the reality of the market does not depend on the workings of culture or history. The market is the bedrock of commerce, it exists wherever and whenever there is a circulation of goods. This idea of the market is taken by the participants, and by the public discourse that surrounds the markets, as the unquestionable foundation of the many specific markets. These specific markets exist as institutions; they are the sites for the circulation of securities, the provision of liquidity and recruitment of counterparties, the deployment of speculative capital and hedging strategies, and the changes in securities prices that trading discovers. But for all its centrality to theory and methods, the market as a concept, as an institution, as an ensemble of practices, a site for governance, and not least as an object of legitimizing ideology, financial economists have done little to construct the market as an analytical object. Or apprehend the market in terms of the lived world of concrete social financial relations. Or as a modern species of totality that moderns invent and reinvent to enframe their financial practices—that is, as a historically contingent social imaginary, an imaginary that agents construct by virtue of their participation in the culture and practice of financial circulation.

The chaos that the markets have experienced in recent decades, topped off by the systemic meltdown in 2008, have given writers cause and opportunity to call the market in question. Writing from both sides of the investing platform, as a derivatives trader who capitalizes on his practical knowledge of financial practice and as a quant who constructs stochastic models to forecast derivative prices, Elie Ayache (2011) invokes the notion of contingency to problematizes the orthodox view of markets. Ayache argues that derivative markets continually encounter contingent events that by their very contingency cannot be accounted for by the kind of probabilistic model that founds the mathematics of financial derivatives. Each event is a singularly whose regularity is accordingly only known retrospectively. An event can only be typified or integrated into a set post festum which, concordantly, means that it is impossible to identify in advance the variance the event will precipitate. For Ayache, there is here a deep contradiction manifest in the fact that the "derivative *market* is not part of derivative pricing theory" (2011:26, italics in original) for finance economics. Its abstract suppositions of state prices, absolute liquidity, perfectly probabilistic risk, riskless counterparties, and so on create necessary values for any given derivative. But, as Fischer Black observed in a similar context, if derivatives' values are necessary and known then there is no logical reason for agents to make a market in these derivatives. Imagine a poker game in which all the cards are dealt face up before the betting begins: there would be no game. Ayache's point is that using these abstract suppositions constitutes such a selective and skewed apprehension of the real that the "market precisely happens after the book is closed and done with" (p. 26). From a social perspective, two significant points appear that center on totality and habitus. The first is that the theory of derivative pricing has no theory of the market that it must necessarily presuppose for the economic activity that it seeks to models. The second is that the economic vision enshrined in derivative pricing theory collapses the practical economic reasoning of market makers into theoretical, deeply logo-centric rationality, even as it dispenses with a methodological consideration of the lived difference between theoretical and practical forms of economic reasoning. So taken to its social conclusion, Ayache is pointing out that the economistic treatment of derivatives presupposes but cannot explain either the market or the generative schemes instilled in agents for dealing with contingency.

Following Nassim Taleb account of the black swan and the enigma of randomness, Ayache argues that because events, due to their singularity, have no interpretation within standard mathematical treatments, analysis can only apprehend the causes of an event retrospectively. This creates a backward looking narrative in which the event serves as the ground for the discernment of its causes. Ayache following Talib's lead suggests that it is through this narrative that the economist imbues in the derivative trader prospectively the presumably perfect knowledge of the causes divined retrospectively (e.g., in the creation of martingales). This view in hand, Ayache retreats only slightly when he contends that "the derivative trader needs the probabilistic models. . . . precisely because he needs to go beyond them" (p. 27). In contrast to hypostasized markets, actual derivative markets constantly recalibrate prices. In fact, there is never *a* price as the *spread* between the bid and the ask demonstrate. That this spread must always be continually reconciled if a market is to exist, remain liquid, is precisely why the market price is the input instead of the output in any derivative pricing model. The result is even as traders use these models the fact of the recalibration of prices means that traders rewrite the market continually in ways that the theoretical models cannot capture. What Ayache could go on to say here is that agents' generative scheme for "rewriting the market" is embedded in their habitus, which is the inscription of the constituted that structures the constituting. Relying on the Bergsonian philosophical tradition, Ayache unites these two moments in the idea that *"the reality of the contingent event is the same as the reality of the market"* (p. 28, italics in original). Though articulated in a different language, the contention is that a derivative market as a socially constructed totality and its participants' responses to contingent events are intrinsically inseparable. Ayache's account, in other words, brings us to the doorstep of totality and the habitus.[1]

The Problematic of the Market

It constitutes a problematic—meaning a problem that founds and foments ancillary problems. The problematic is the character of financial markets as social creations. Where constructively does a financial market come from and how is that market produced and reproduced through the collective action of anonymous agents? One answer is to say that a market is simply the natural inevitable outcome of people's need to trade, these trades driven existentially by their pecuniary instincts, that is, greed. But this commonsense apprehension, incorporated into finance economics, avoids rather than explains the creation, structure, or transformation of the financial markets (as part of larger change in the global structure of capitalism). This empiricist view of the market is a prisoner of appearances, housed in the penitentiary of abstraction. Markets as we now know them have not always been: most of humankind's history, stretching many thousands of years into the past, took place prior to invention of the market, and even in the near past the market has not existed everywhere, especially not the form of the market that has come to define capitalism (Postone 1993), particularly in its circulatory incarnation. Analysis must thus address the problematic of the market because markets are social inventions and because financial actions, such as trading derivatives, take place within a frame of their own design. More, the new financial frame constituted by the ascension of derivative markets calls for and rewards new expressions of agency, which in turn, foregrounds the question of what are the cognitive and motivating structures that collectively disposed those who inhabit finance to become attached to new schemes of financial behavior.

Nothing exemplifies the imbrication of markets and motivations like the work of speculation; the drive to initiate the speculative wagers that roiled the EuroAmerican financial markets could never have been created, consecrated, and circulated without a specialized derivatives frame. That is, a real social entity whose realness is known and felt because it enframes, orients, and canalizes the motivated actions of those who participate. The founding question is how do "we" come to collectively believe in a type of totality, *the market*, which serves as the template for the creation and institutionalization of specific markets, which all appear to be instantiations of the "market" type? How does the financial field produce and reproduce collective agents?—such as an equity, mortgage, commercial paper, or merger acquisition market. How is what agents do within the market—their attempts to produce themselves individually through the deals, strategies, and trades they enact—lead to the production of a market as a totality? This focus on the totality is not to say that different markets do not become institutionalized or that the history of certain markets has not been characterized by their progressive institutionalization (particularly as the standardization of practice can minimize some uncertainties); rather, that what economic agents may seek to institutionalize is precisely the social totality, and that the standardization and formalization of their practices is itself one of the notable strategies used by different markets to totalize themselves. This is significant to public comprehension in that the more institutionalized a market is, the more publicly visible that market becomes. With the result that the most institutionalized market, the stock market, has become the commonplace paradigm for how markets work, when, in fact, the design of the OTC credit derivative market bares little resemblance to the stock market, and it is much more economically significant in that it is exponentially larger (by a factor of a hundred), more global, and directly implicated in the functioning of the real economy. Let us reiterate, because it points to the heart of the relationship of public knowledge to political oversight, citizens' normal engagement with commodity markets and even their encounters with financial markets in the form of stock purchases provides precious little insight into how the derivatives markets work or their implications for our collective well being.

Analysis can also probe the character of the/a market from the standpoint of the phenomenology of practice. When a trader examines the sequence of trades on a specific market, the succession of bid-asked spreads and prices which present themselves could not possible appear as replications of the same market if that trader did not know that each transaction represents the market, wagered from different points of view about its future direction. The fact that market-makers are able to draw together all of these prices and perspectives is dependent on their knowing cognitively that the market's agents can trade successively in this way. While no trader can ever observe the market in its entirety, its conception as a totality is nonetheless the intelligible structure which imbues the wagers that replicate the market with strategic meaning. It is on these grounds that we can justify the presupposition of a *market's* marketness because, as Ayache notes (2012), traders locate themselves inside the market in the middle of its events (p. 22–23). Ayache's point, born of his experience trading, is that the trader is a body of knowledge in that his body and senses are precisely that familiarity with the market born from immersion in it. Traders cannot thus but apprehend the market's particular form as enclosing a specific space of operations for derivatives. In this space of operations, traders are able to assimilate, thread together, and respond to the volatility of bid-asked spreads and gyrations in prices only because they have already acquired the market as a totality. And that this fact of the world requires no further examination. In the throes of market making, a trader does not imagine *the market* or think himself imagining it: for he knows from experience that his sensibilities are already better informed than he is about what move to make next. This is why derivative traders see an unmistakable analogue and affinity between what they do and the professional athlete who, in playing the game, must assume the totality of the game and rely on their deeply instilled sensibilities to play it well.[2] the reality of their dependence whose business is playing the game There is here a true phenomenology of market making in which traders conceive a market's practical unity as the correlative of its conceptual unity.

We are now in a position to formulate the problematic of the market, not least the derivative markets which are the driving, compulsively innovative edge of the circulation of capital. How to explain agentive-driven contingent transactions whose consummation is predicated on the collectively held presupposition of the existence of a market that the transactions produce by virtue of their consummation. At issue is how the work of dynamic recalibration calls forth the socialized subjectivity of the participants' belief in the market's totality, even as that totality serves as the imaginary abstract space for the calculations (exemplified by derivative pricing models but also encompassing all the other forms of knowledge intake streams gained from immersion in finance), which passing through, and pinging off, the bodies of the variously positioned participants, motivate the market's recalibration. By design, a derivative markets has no necessity in law or in tradition, this freedom being the essence of a compulsively creative, unregulated, over the counter market. Although the word *market* appears identically across the whole financial landscape, and financiers do construct derivatives that use ordinary securities (stocks and bonds) as their underliers, derivative markets are singular historically unique inventions because *their very existence is inseparable from their liquidity.* Unlike ordinary commodities (e.g., houses) or production based businesses (e.g., home builders) *derivatives have no intrinsic value.* Intrinsically, they are nothing more or less than a zero-sum wager between competing counterparties about some extrinsic outcome. A derivative market must thus shape and instantiate its own principles of formation. What needs to be explained socially is how the rituality inscribed in the concrete social relations of the work of buying and selling performatively objectifies a derivative market. This performativity is necessarily sequentially prospective then retrospective, as constituted prospectively in the *posting* of a bid and asked price (which instantiates liquidity) and retrospectively in the *execution* of a trade (which instantiates the counterparties and new price discovery or recalibration). In a truly social account, the ongoing dialectical relationship between the existential moment of dynamic recalibration and the social collective instantiation of the market is mediated by posting and execution, both of which arise from the generative schemes, dispositions, and inclinations inculcated within the participants by virtue of their immersion in the habitus of finance. This habitus is taken for granted by traders; it is the water in which the sharks swim, aware of its currents, the changes of temperature, and the appearance of prey and predators, but not the weight of the water.

Forward and Backward

And so a social approach that gave all of the determinations their due would problematize the market both as a system/totality and as a mode of work/practice done by reflexive agents/subjects. A derivatives market is thus a sociospecific space designed for a particular mode of agents' practice: that is, behaviors (e.g., the use of speculative capital to circulate risk driven derivatives) linked by the connectivity of the cognitive and motivating structures (e.g., profit, ambition and competition, risk-taking, self-esteem) that drive these behaviors. The burning question is why is it that the determinations that reproduce specific markets lead to markets that, temporally, are regular and "rational" but only partially so, episodically followed by periods of amplified volatility, sometimes so great that liquidity vanishes and the markets court systemic failure. The question that every analysis seeks to sidestep, as a condition of maintaining its theoretical cohesion which is no doubt the best indicator of the question's significance, is why are the derivative market's regularities so irregular? It would be easy to demonstrate, as measured for example by the constant yet oscillating persistence of arbitrage opportunities, that a derivative market (in response to exogenous and internal forces) will oscillate between varying degrees of regularity and efficiency, interspersed with episodic brushes with disorderly trading,[3] any one of which can matriculate into a full-blown crisis, especially so when the market has progressed toward amplified levels of systemic risk (and the only way to, as it were, reverse course is for deleveraging to go supernova which is what happened in 2008). In real markets, whose conditions of existence can never escape trade decision-making under varying degrees of uncertainty, agents are always confronted with a play of options (whose importance crises exaggerate) which are both multiple yet delimited by the market's conditions, the decisions reached (e.g., to sell, hold, or increase one's position) owing their direction and efficacy to the shape of the relations between those engaging in them and those who are the object of those actions. The critical point that is affirmed and reaffirmed by the ethnography of real markets composed of concrete relations is that markets are inconsistently regular at best and self-destructive at worst. This being the case because their participants must invariably make decisions under uncertainty, including uncertainty as to what forces (e.g., a collapse of the Chinese banking system) will materially influence the markets' future, this uncertainty combining with the structural constraints imposed by the markets and the common collective dispositions instilled in the participants. These dispositions (e.g., to speculate) tend to produce behaviors characterized by oscillating and sometimes nonlinear degrees of freedom (mathematically self-evident when a market varies by four or five or six or more standard deviations as did indeed occur during the crisis). What defines a social approach is that it understands this question of regularity as intrinsically related to the question economistic approaches elide: namely, what are markets as social inventions. Specifically, what is the sociospecific character of recently invented derivative markets as dimensions of, and transformative of, contemporary capitalism.

Numerous societies, all to a greater or lesser degree, use markets to distribute an extraordinary range of goods and services from condiments like salt and pepper to magical ceremonial spells, from climate exchange contracts on carbon emissions to collateralized mortgage obligations. These societies set up relations among agents which mediate the circulation of socially valuable things, the term *market* the label designated to describe these general mediating relations. That a market is inherently a set of relations—exemplified by the performative acts of buying and selling that animate it—means that any attempt to accurately delineate what a or the market is must begin with the understanding that it is not an object category. Recognizing this reality is important because the intrinsically social process of objectification never more subtly governs scholastic and commonsense analyses then, when unrecognized as social, it leads to the unreflexive naturalization of that process. These naturalizations treat relational categories as though object categories, creating a kind of ontological mistake, which once committed, can seemingly never be commuted. On these grounds, the market, and with that any specific market, is intrinsically different from concrete object categories such as houses, books, tools, football fields, automobiles and any of the innumerable other objects that make up our daily lives.[4] Quite the contrary, the market is a relational category on the par with nationality, ethnicity, kinship or even more quotidian categories such as friendship. A distinctive feature of relational categories that distinguishes them from object categories is their extreme social and historical determination. Which is another way of saying that there could have been alternative histories in which the nation or derivative markets were either never invented or socially canonized. One indication of the difference between object and relational categories is that it is comparatively easy to translate object categories from one culture to the next, from one historical era to the next— what language does not have terms for water, rain, or agricultural products like corn or wheat—whereas relational categories are much more difficult to translate in that there may be no straightforward term for nationality, ethnicity, market, or culture. Relational categories are defined by their connectivity, the reality of the categories sustained through the beliefs of the collectivity as manifest in their use by the speech community and through the processes of institutionalization (e.g., a legal definition of what a market is, a physical site where agents conduct the market as on the New York Stock Exchange, as embodied in the traditions of investment firms).

But there is more in that the relations of *a market* are enframed socially within the imaginary totality of *the market*; that is, relational categories such as the market can be objectified and institutionalized in ways which lead to the construction of a totality, or in a slightly different language, a system. Cultures can transform certain relational categories, exemplified by the nation and its vision of peoplehood as embodied in our concept of an American nation and identity (enframed in the opening salvo of the Declaration of Independence as "We the People"), into socially imagined totalities. This creation of a collectively imagined, thus social, totality requires a conjunction of quasi-ritual forms of objectification with a deep process of institutionalization, including and importantly the construction of a financial habitus. If a market—a derivatives market for example—is a historically specific means of circulating relations about relations (i.e., wagers based on the volatility of underlying relation) through social entities like contracts, then the market that enframes it must also be sociohistorically determinate. So the social logic of the culture of financial circulation creates both an abstract general form, the market, that serves as the totalizing frame for the specific sets of relationships and forms of connectivity that create particular markets, even as actions of agents in the production of these particular markets reproduces the concept of the market. The linguistic standpoint is also revealing: when we examine how those in the financial community use a term as pervasive as the market, the evidence clearly reveals that the market in the singular, as in the mortgage market, the commercial loan market, or the equity market denotes the enframing imaginary, whereas a market refers to the relationality produced and reproduced via the interactions among the participants. Numerous statements produced in the midst of the crisis such as "the mortgage market is dead; simply put, no one wants to make a market [in mortgages] due to the [extraordinary] level of uncertainty" (Bill Gross, CNBC, 12 November 2008) exemplify this duality. Or, a slightly different version in the words of Matt Ridley (2007), chairman of England's imperiled Northern Rock Bank: "we were repeatedly advised that liquidity in wholesale markets depended on loan quality" when in reality "liquidity dried up across all wholesale markets, making no distinction between loans of different quality" (p. 19). The statement implicitly contrasts the wholesale market as an entity with the actions of its participants, who put rationality aside "for much longer than even the most extreme forecast" (ibid.:19). The entire distinction between an asset's fundamental market value and the price market participants assign to that asset [a mainstay of the literature on crisis-inducing asset bubbles since Keynes (1936: chapter 12)] presupposes that there is a distinction between the imaginary of the market and a market enacted existentially by agents making decisions under uncertainty. Suffice it to say that we can multiple these examples ad infinitum because the distinction, yet mutual implication, of totality and relationality is our cultural concept of the market: the one put in play by EuroAmerican capitalism and then circulated globally to the historical point that it exists wherever capitalist markets exist, which, increasingly, means everywhere. What is so significant socially, as we will see, is that *a market enacted as a continuous set of transactions functions (remains liquid) because its agents presupposes the market as a(n imagined) totality, even as the very existence of that totality depends on the continuity of those transactions.* The derivatives markets are not only founded on this relationship, they take it to an exponentially higher power because their very existence is detached from any use values.

The most vexing problem for modern science has been coming to terms with the underlying sociostructures of modernity itself. As evidence one could cite that for modern economics the most vexing issue is grasping the character of the contemporary capitalist economy and markets. Capped by the transformation and ascension to power of circulatory speculative capital. Certainly a sign of this conundrum is the propensity to conceive the derivative and its markets as object categories, when, in fact, they push the relationality and socially imaginary elements of the market almost to their breaking point. For after all, the dissolution of the relationality constitutive of the derivative markets, which is to say, their liquidity, is what can precipitate the imminent collapse of the imagined totality, aka systemic failure.

The Appearance of Totality

A social approach to the financial markets seeks to theorize the character of these markets as structures endowed with a directional dynamic. This requires a concept of social totality. For this is the only way to capture the reality that a financial market is a system of relations and properties sustained through the collective genesis and implications of their participant's actions. Derivative markets do not reproduce themselves by virtue of some clockwork of perpetual motion. Quite the contrary, they require human effort, concrete, considerable, and above all collective. From the standpoint of concrete social relations, the foundation of (derivative) markets is the embedded processes by and through which agents objectify the totalities that they participate in, by virtue of their participation in them. The significant question that can all too easily be ignored is what "invisible" aspect of work (re)produces the whole? This dimension of financial production is invisible in that the reproduction of the market is an unintended consequence of actions whose very efficacy presupposes its existence. No one sets out to deliberately reproduce the market; nonetheless, agents' concrete goal directed acts of making money, inventing and selling new products, position-climbing within an institution, increasing their senses of self-worth and status, competing against their peers, and so on reproduce a market. The argument is that derivative markets possess not only a surface performativity, observable in the wagers placed, the derivatives created, and the way each iteration of a market calls forth a response from its participants (such as consciously maintaining or revising their strategies), but a deep performative structure in which these very same actions are founded on a determinate social imaginary of this or that market which reproduces and stabilizes the market in question by presupposing its totalization, or, in a different language, its systemic character. What this indicates is that an understanding of the derivatives markets must begin with their surface properties.

The first of these is that a derivatives market appears as a space of operations which allows agents to place certain kinds of speculative wagers. This space of operations is the socioeconomic enclosure in terms of which the agents activate their beliefs, desires, and judgments, such as their disposition to calculate the value at risk or the potential gains in a certain way. It is also the point of view from which the agents in this space of operations determine what appears to be extrinsic to the market, how and why they might deliberately introduce information or noise to gain a competitive advantage (noise being exogenous data made to look endogenous and thus important enough to influence other's decision-making processes), and their degree of certainty about what is uncertain and unknowable about the forthcoming. Other analysts have also observed that markets attempt to carve out a space of operations. The Callon group (operating from a science and technology studies view) has described this production of quasi-bounded economic space, such as the credit derivatives market, through the concept of "framing" (Callon 1998, 2007; Latour 2005; MacKenzie, Muniesa, and Siu 2007). Michael Callon writes that "framing is an operation used to define agents who are clearly distinct and dissociated from one another." It thus "allows for the definition of objects, goods, and merchandise which are perfectly identifiable and can be separated not only from other [extrinsic] goods but also from the actors involved" (Callon 1998:17). This frame or space of operations allows the participants to create and typify a specific interaction, to devise and describe a given transaction as, for example, a bet on the volatility of the euro-dollar relationship. Intrinsic to framing is the inculcation within the markets' participants, by virtue of that participation, of a sense of the limits of the market, a sense of approximately how far they can plausibly push their generative schemes for creating, marketing, and typifying this or that derivative. Traders realize this sense of limits in their everyday practice when they weigh a particular move that they would like to make— e.g., inventing a derivative that allows for a wager on the relationship between the volatility of the Brazilian real and the London interbank rate (LIBOR)—with their assessment of this derivative's objective chances of success. And so also its profitability with everything that that entails. The limits of the framing, and thus also its expansion, can come about because an institution spots a perceived need (e.g., for a CMO squared) or a request from a client for a tailored derivative. The financial field reserves the term, *exotic*, for these tailored, often situationally specific derivatives that stretch, even transgress, the participants' sense of the market's limits. Financial firms find it relatively easy to create a need in that speculative capital's predominant need is new sources of profitability. Speaking to this point, a former analyst (at Citigroup and Merrill Lynch) wryly observes that if one bank offered a derivative "with a somersault, than a second offered the same with a somersault and pike, while a third marketed one with a triple somersault and a pike ending in a double tuck" (Das 2011:73–74). What appears a surreal treadmill is set in motion in which a derivative market's directional dynamic is not only toward increasing leverage but toward increasing complexity as the marketing of products to speculative capital requires the constant expansion of the market's limits. The why, as one hedge fund manager put it, is that everyone wants to be a "profit monster." What is perhaps less obvious is that the expansion of a market serves a socioeconomic function in that, as in the original example of Salomon Brothers and Ranieri's invention of mortgage obligations, it favors large institutions with the financial capital, the workforce, and the interconnectivity to make a market in a "new" derivative. Although it ultimately falls short theoretically,[5] the Callon group's foregrounding of the way a market frames interactions underlines the necessity of appreciating the social (re)production of the totality that makes this possible.

From an evolutionary standpoint, from a history of exchange that stretches back into prehistory, what is secretly remarkable about this frame or space of operations is that it is organized around and defined by a form of agency that appears to be the very antithesis of the social. At its most existential level, a derivative market turns on a form of performativity in which each participant imagines a world/market of imaginary others, similar in mind and interests. Made obvious by its absence, a key property of these markets is that there is no necessity for the participants to know, or even know of, one another in any other than a technologically mediated way. Face to face interactions, personal exchanges, direct communications: all happen often and often superficially. But they are sidebars to the central dynamic founded on technologically mediated agency and work. The relations that make the market are technologically mediated in manifold senses, from algorithm[6] driven high speed trading to the use of purely technical models to found economic reasoning to the deepening disposition that anonymity is preferable to interpersonal communication. Technological mediation has the reality effect of masking the underlying sociality of the market's (re)production and of amplifying agents' sensibility that the market will exercise a sharp, objective, and quantifiable determination over their behavior. The objective and autonomous character of the technology becomes a simulacrum for the market's objective and autonomous character, at least as apprehended from the standpoint of the participants, meaning that the machinery and its programming have become a part of the market's sociality. It not only interconnects agents; it mediates their sociality in a historically specific way because the participants grasp this form of mediation as the epicenter of their lives and of the financial lifestyle. The view is rather transparent in the myriad comments from traders about having no choice other than to spend their entire day glued to a arsenal of computer screens, flickering quotes and trades. Fischer Black, afflicted with (a then undiagnosed) syndrome in which the individual shuns social interaction but frequently has an affinity for subjects like math, once suggested in a characteristically oblique phrase, while he was working at Goldman Sachs shuttered away for days in his office, that his personality was especially adapted for the new financial markets. Noting that the markets don't require personality.

In more theoretical language, a critical social dimension of derivative markets is the realization of what I refer to as *anonymous sociality*. This involves an existential performativity: the attribution of a culturally specific sociality—that is, a mutually expected repertoire of beliefs, desires, and strategic judgments concerning *the* market and *a* market's behavior (e.g., its price action)—to an anonymous other/counterparty whose only self-presentation need be nothing more than the electronic trace of an other's trade on a screen. Agents both impute this intentional repertoire to others and interpret the actions of others predicated on it. They assume that the structure is reciprocal and recursive in that others interpolate their behavior in the same way, however anonymous these others may be and irrespective of the reality that the transaction(s) appear on the screen may be a computer generated trade: for everyone is predisposed to take for granted that the trading programs themselves embody this intentional repertoire. The trading programs like the minds of their creators and the minds of traders generally have, in this way, a standardized use value that participants use to create exchange values (trading profits). The labor involved in creating a derivative product, executing a trading strategy, or building a computer trading program objectifies itself performatively not only as buying and selling, but as the performative objectification of "the mind" of anonymous sociality. That is, a sociospecific and social repertoire whose power to frame a market of anonymous operations and delineate its limits derives from a surface animation of creating, buying, and selling that conceals a deeper performative process of objectification. For a derivatives market founded on anonymous sociality to work—to work meaning that the market sustains its life-giving liquidity—this repertoire of beliefs, desires, and judgment must be more than the means by which agents individually formulate their moves and countermoves, it must acquire the force of a social determination whose systemic effects occur, as it were, behind the backs of the market's participants.

Designing this repertoire of beliefs, desires, and judgments, and installing them in a community of financial agents, requires considerable psychosocial labor, such as directed processes of recruitment and indoctrination. The audition, selection, and training of new university recruits by the leading investment houses, such as Goldman Sachs and Morgan Stanley, centers on an initiation rite in which the recruits (to survive the cut) must acquire a mastery of financial practice, this mastery including the acquisition of a worldview whose mainspring is how markets work and how to work the markets. As is clear from those I interviewed, knowing how markets work is inseparable from knowing what are the beliefs, desires, and judgments to expect from others in the market. Only those who "know" their anonymous counterparty can conjure and make the right moves. The appearance of totality appears here in what it means for a plurality of agents to know—both in terms of agents' knowing and their knowing how. This is the point at which what agents' know about the intentionality of some anonymous others intersects with their knowing how to use this knowledge to set up and execute a competitive wager. The necessity to acquire the field's intentionality appears to be entirely objective and impersonal, so much so that the severe demands placed by financial institutions' on their new recruits (mostly from prestigious universities) to acquire this structure of intentionality appearing to be nothing more than orienting them towards the true north of operating within this frame. Karen Ho's (2009) ethnography of Wall Street describes in great detail not only how the firms hammer this ensemble of beliefs, desires, and strategic judgments into their agents, but that the agents apprehend its inculcation as in their interests. The frame is such that one's own need to be successful, to win the game against one's anonymous others, appears to be the source of the necessity. That agents everywhere and in all times need to have some appreciation of the intentionality of their interlocutors, conceals the great sociospecific labor required by the financial field and its institutions to produce a concept as seemingly at odds with itself as anonymous sociality.

The analysis will necessarily return to this point when we analyze the design of the financial habitus. But it is worth considering here just how well the various pieces of the financial field's spaces of operations are mutually reinforcing, each serving as a kind of redetermination of the other. So the anonymous and faceless other is an aspect of, and reinforces, participants' sense that the market commands an impersonal and objective determination over what they can and they cannot do. It appears to the agents that they are immersed in frame whose intentionality they must adapt as their own as a matter of survival, institutionally and competitively. This is how this repertoire of beliefs, desires, and strategic judgments presents itself to the participants; its seeming inevitability and its immanence an expression of the operational reality that they experience, both objectively in respect to how a specific market works concretely and subjectively in terms of their self-creation in this framework or space of operations. Importantly, both the production of the market and this sociospecific intentionality, as products of the peculiar form that labor takes in financial circulatory capitalism, imbue themselves with an objective sensibility so forceful, so overdetermined, that it borders on an aura (Compare with what serves, for us, as the key foundational account of the design features of labor in capitalism by Moishe Postone 1993:chapter 4). There is here an existential performativity in that the actions that the participants engage in again and again, month after month, reproduce and reinforce their sensibility, raising its realness to a near unimpeachable certainty (in the sense that counterfactuals are summarily dismissed), that the operational frame and the forms of intentionality that it sets constitute an independent autonomous reality that stands over and sometimes against the participants because it can, at any moment out of the blue, exert a capricious and ruinous determination over their lives. That can redetermine their futures and fortunes in the event of serious failure, as interviews with those displaced and sometimes discarded by the crisis underline in stark terms. There is more than a little irony in that the participants sum up and objectify the results of this performative impulse in the viewpoint, typically couched in a humor that is at once real and feigned, that they live and work in the world's most luxurious ghetto. As one hedge fund trader put it in a one line review that presupposes the space of operations: "who else saves their ass [financially] by working the [computer] screens for twenty fucking hours, then goes to a [hotel] bar and celebrates with Crystal."

The subtext here is that a market, as represented in and through the trades that electronically appeared on his screen, was going to saddle his hedge fund with deep losing positions that would precipitate a margin call, so he manipulated the beliefs, desires, and judgments of others through the hyper-vigilant implementation of a trading strategy which permitted him to (the term of art is) "flatten out" his positions without letting on to his anonymous others that his portfolio was extremely vulnerable and therefore could be taken advantage of (that is, if other market participants read his vulnerability, they would enrich themselves as his expense, coincidentally, exactly what he would do if the situations were reversed).

Totality and its Recognition

A certain recognition of totality is immanent in the reality that though the market is intrinsically social, the participants experience the market as a crystallized form that encompasses them. This social dimension is externalized through agents attributing to the markets a kind of imputed agency. This externalization (which is also necessarily a kind of mystification) which sees a market as both objective relations and an agent appears in the conception that a market is simultaneously the sum of its economic transactions and also possesses has an independent intentionality of its own. This agency surfaces as an objectification of totality in sharp contrast to the existential flow of trades, deals, and new derivative products. This duality appears in the forms of thought associated with the market, exemplified on a daily basis linguistically with market analyses that begin: "The market thinks . . . has decided . . . wants . . . believes . . . feels relieved that . . . is concerned by . . . is afraid of uncertainty," and so forth. It has been noted, often and correctly, that the participants' representations reify and personify the market and that they describe the market's behavior through an assortment of metaphors (as in "the market believes that it can digest middling unemployment data"), but what I would like to indicate here is that the very creation of a antimony between an abstract asocial agency and a space of everyday utility maximizing transactions presupposes a social totality. The understanding of which is precluded by the antimony itself, an understanding that would begin by theorizing how precisely concrete financial relations, in all their social specificity, produce and reproduce a social imaginary totality.

Analytically, attempts to grasp the market have focused their aim on the second dimension of the antimony: the utility maximizing agent insofar as this is by far the most mathematically tractable of the two (though one should not overlook the forms of technical analysis which assume that the market is an abstract agent whose patterns of behavior, if interpreted correctly, can predict its future).[7] On this view, what is called the market is essentially a means; the aims of its agents the ends. Thus the market no longer exists ontologically: for it is simply an irreducible entity that serves the interests of utility maximization. But such a market can't exist and has never existed for the reason that the participant must embody mutually intelligible and institutionally coordinated concepts and dispositions for a market to coalesce in the first place and then convene in the future.

Indeed, the deeply systemic character of the 2008 crisis underlined that economic analyses that proceed from the standpoint of the individual utility maximizing agent are problematic. The very design of the rescue illustrated that because financial markets are organized at a systemic level, they are necessarily more and different than the sum of their individual parts. What this means analytically is that it is impossible to apprehend these systemic properties by tallying up the actions of those who trade a market. It is not that individuals' actions are unimportant: rather, because they constitute a different dimension of social reality, individuals' actions make a different contribution to the production of that particular reality. Consider, by way of analogy, that it is impossible to grasp the general structure of wars in Vietnam or Iraq simply by compiling a list, however accurate and comprehensive, of what the participants did (e.g., exchanged gunfire with the enemy, reconnaissance, threat assessment, formed bonds of solidarity and comradeship, created an informal economy with the civilian population, and more). Accounts of the wars (e.g., Caputo 2006; De Fronzo 2009) indicate that these are accurate descriptions of soldiers' behaviors. Nonetheless, these accounts are also unequivocal in indicating that aggregating individuals' behaviors does not begin to explain the structure or the impetus for these nation-state based conflicts. Rather, the soldiers' combat actions presuppose the sociospecific structuration of warfare at this point in history as well as the existence and state institutionalization of the imaginary of the nation. The point to be made is that analysis must apprehend the systemic properties of any totality on its own terms—it is never reducible to, or a straightforward aggregation, of anything smaller. The social conclusion is that the financial markets must be grasped on their own terms. This is critical to the present because a market's systemic properties set the conditions for its systemic failure—which is nothing less than failure at the level of the social totality. Which begins to explain why the seizing up of the credit markets provoked a sudden turn toward the social by a financial community that under "normal conditions"—meaning free flowing liquidity—shunned any reference to the social.

Consider here the majority report as to the causes and conditions of the extraordinary contraction in liquidity (US Government 2011; Morgenson 2010; Barth 2009; Bamber and Spencer 2008). According to the financial community's own assessment, the breakdown in liquidity turned on systemic properties, principally the relative interconnectivity of the counterparties, the overall (non)transparency of their balance sheets, and high multiples of leverage imprinted across the market. It was not any solitary instance of interconnectivity, (non)transparency, or excessive leverage which motivated a near universal withdrawal of participant's faith in the credit markets, rather, as our interviews will attest, their "native" intuition about their overall cumulative effect when nearly everyone embraces the same speculative financial strategies. Critically amplified by these forces complexity and technologically mediated character, which the agents also took into consideration. Within institutions, this complexity matters because it corresponds to an increasing division of competencies between a firm's management and its traders (exemplified by the proprietary trading desk). It is now common knowledge that CEOs and CFOs of the living (Bank of America, Citibank, and Morgan Stanley), as well as those of the departed (Bear Stearns and Lehman Brothers) only obliquely comprehended the systemic nature of the risk their firms had assumed or the systemic repercussions of an entire industry assuming massive amounts of pseudo-quantified risk (as indicted in the Financial Crisis inquiry report 2011). This lack of comprehension was nothing less than a lack of appreciation of the inherent connectivity that constitutes a totality. Due to this comprehension gap, the upper echelon could not discern the difference between precision and accuracy: they could not grasp that the seemingly precise calculation that what were called super senior tranches of debt had zero risk of default was worthless because the accuracy of the calculation could never rise above zero. The agents involved were conditioned to misrecognize the reality that the viability of their practices depended wholly on the totality remaining intact. To put this another way, the senior management of the financial institutions were focused on the appearance of a totality as a concrete space of operations, grasped as a frame in which their derivative traders sought to maximize profits, rather than the structure of a totality founded on a socially constructed imaginary.

The view of senior management provides insight into how difficult it is for the participants, even those benefiting from an elevated vantage point, to discern the market's systemic properties. Derivative markets especially are prone to naturalize and normalize their systemic properties, so that caught up in the whirl of a machine with so many moving parts, markets appear to participants to simply be how markets are. This would not make a huge difference if the state had in place a regime of regulation designed to preserve the systemic integrity of capital markets. This would entail rules and regulations that curtailed the progression of the treadmill effect by, for example, limiting leverage or the velocity of speculative capital. In addition to government offices and officials whose very deepest allegiances are to the public rather than the financial sector, a well-functioning regime of regulation would require a belief in, leading to an account of, financial markets as social totalities. An understanding that derivative markets are self-degrading would legitimate regulation. It is here that the commanding position of the efficient market thesis becomes significant: for its advocates see it as nothing less than a scientific description of economic reality. From the end of the Second World War until the present the growing hegemony of the efficient market paradigm has banished the creation of an adequate account of the financial markets. However, it turns out that an approach that brackets the production of the financial markets as totalities cannot thus take account of their social systemic properties, including critically the conditions for the amplification of systemic risk that induces failure. More, the efficient market thesis is an argument for financial deregulation insofar as it celebrates speculation as an indispensable source of liquidity and price discovery while it dismisses the possibility of systemic risk. At best, this perspective can recognize systemic implosions as unfortunate and unexpected outcomes, as the "noise" (See Black 1986) in the system that somehow became a deafening roar. No less an authority then Fed Chair Alan Greenspan confirmed this, when in his testimony before Congress (on October 24, 2008), he expressed "shocked disbelief" that there was "a flaw" in the invisible hand thesis that markets are constitutionally "efficient" and "self-correcting," and hence immune to the kind of systemic meltdown that had propelled the real economy into a deep multi-year tailspin. Some say the visible boot of what most of us know as economic reality had left its imprint on the maestro [Greenspan approved of, and reportedly circulated copies of Bob Woodward hagiographic account of him, entitled, perhaps a touch prematurely, *Maestro: Greenspan's Fed and the American Boom* (2000)]. The significant point is that the financial field's own theory of the market, theoretically precludes and dismisses an appreciation of the market's systemic foundations. So one of the market's most distinctive properties is its misconstrual of the properties of its own production.

Another critical feature of a market is that it turns on the dynamic between types of financial instruments and agent's real life acts of classification. There is a performative relationship between the innovation or fabrication of a derivative and its circulation or marketing. This relationship turns on the evolution of the generative schemes that agents intuitively access to typify what are, in OTC markets, typically singular one of a kind situationally tailored derivatives. The issue is how agents collectively come to accept the typification of such a product (i.e., token derivative). This issue is of more than scholastic interest: recall that one of the genesis of the credit implosion was that the financial field securitized mortgage obligations and credit obligations as though their differences were immaterial (Tett 2009:170–71) to determining their relative safety and price. On advice from academic council, the financial sector treated credit and mortgage derivatives as different incarnations of the same instrument type, when, as the subsequent systemic crisis would underscore, they were fundamentally different beasts.[8] It is therefore a touch ironic that mainstream finance skips over the assignment of singular derivatives to specific general categories as a transparent unproblematic exercise. To take a relevant example, the social, sometimes contentious and negotiated act of classifying a tranche of collateralized debt obligations (CDO) appears, specially retrospectively, to be nothing but a simple technical assignment. For those who are conversant with semiotics, the financial community treats individual tokens or instances as clearly labeled indexical icons of a definitive type, when in practice, the innovative impulse of the financial field, driven by the compulsive sense of competition that permeates its agents and institutions, all but guarantees that the types of derivatives in play are fluid and evolving, and the individually tailored derivatives, very frequently sold as off balance sheet over the counter transactions, are anything but clearly labeled.

Any blindness to the difference between type and token erases the practical act of classification, thereby rendering it all but impossible to explain the dialectical, back and forth process by which agents create new derivative (deals and instruments) on the model of past productions even as they fit singular derivatives to established types in order to price and sell them to an audience which is both yearning for profit yet skeptical and fearful of being embarrassed. Economistic thinking cannot help but construe (and fetishize) the creation and pricing of a derivative as an abstraction to be mathematized rather than what it is from the standpoint of the participants: a concrete problem to be solved practically using all of the resources at their disposal, including agents' sense of the "mood" of the market (e.g., the collectivity's present appetite for risk-on trades), their appreciation of how their potential counterparties/buyers will see the product as fitting into their strategies (of competition and compensation), their assessment of how this transaction will satisfy their needs not only for money but competitive success and institutional standing, and the larger reality that, as a now retrenched dealmaker blithely phrased it, "practically no one that I dealt to [pension and hedge fund managers] when I was at Bear [Stearns] got the process or the math of how the thing [derivative] was priced: all they wanted was yield and my assurance they weren't going to get screwed" [suffer an embarrassing loss]. As will become evident when we examine traders' habitus, their behaviors are driven by a practical logic that only partially overlaps with the abstract theoretical logic of economistic accounts, and more constructively, is founded on agents' investments in social values.

The typification of a token, transforming a singularity into a type, involves a performative act. Some tokens are unproblematic in that they appear to be exact replicas of existing tokens already in circulation. A new derivative appears to perfectly copy existing derivatives, with the end result that the successful uptake of the act of classification is so thoroughly expected that the classificatory act appears inconsequential, so long that it is successful of course. But there are other instances, whose propinquity is a direct function of derivative sellers (i.e., banks) incessant need to continually create new products to help counteract the effects of the treadmill in a mature market: decreasing margins, expanding leverage, and amplifying risk that serve to limit new demand even as it pushes the market towards a breaking point. In these instances, the act of classifying the derivative almost invariably courts struggle, and this in two ways: the typification of the derivative by the innovating institution and the typification of the level of risk (e.g., A, AA, AAA) by a credit rating agency, such as Moody's or Standard and Poor's, either directly or by reference to a previous *typified* rating of this *type* of derivative. This struggle is played out within the innovating institution as analyses and debates concerning the right method for pricing the derivative in question, and in the marketplace through rating buyers' willingness to accept a certain risk-return based pricing schedule. This was particularly important in respect to the cmos in that all the rating agencies graded the new products entirely in respect to their classificatory type, showing little or no concern for the specific mortgages including in a particular tranche. Recall hedge fund manager Michael Berry's amazement that most of the investment banks would allow him to hand pick the tranches of mortgages to short via credit default swaps (Lewis 201).

What Happened to the Social: Its Removal and Return

A distinctive feature of the financial field is that the social as such is exogenous and ephemeral, its affects episodic and transient; yet, at the same time, the very same social is constantly reconstituted as indispensable to the field's very existence. This foregrounds the question of just what happened to the social. How did the financial field come to canonize models and methods that regard what is social as irrelevant to the field's production and reproduction. Not everyone, of course, believes this. But it is, nonetheless, the hegemonic perspective. It appears as an unquestioned presupposition in derivative pricing models (e.g., Black-Scholes), in analytical treatments of market behavior (e.g., Studies in Nonlinear Dynamics and Econometrics), in the technical analyses conducted by financial firms (e.g., Standard and Poor's), in federal and state regulatory regimes, in the texts used in the leading business schools (e.g., Wharton and Harvard), in the commentary on the markets circulated through the print and electronic media (from the *Wall Street Journal* and CNBC to the blogosphere), and, increasingly, in the political rhetoric of those seeking government office. What makes this particularly interesting historically is that the elimination of the social was syncopated with the rise and empowerment of a circulatory capitalist sphere configured around speculative capital and the globalization of unregulated financial instruments.

The social is radiant in primitive economies, this being one of the chief findings of anthropology in its investigation of how people in other times and other geographies made a living. The economic anthropology of its leading theorists, Marshall Sahlins (1972; 1976), Clifford Geertz (1973; 1995), and Pierre Bourdieu (1973) all underlined the deeply social character of the economies that they studied. More, the founding theorists of finance were cognizant of the social right up into its twentieth century maturation. So Leon Walras (1909), Frank Knight (1921, 1956), John Maynard Keynes (1956) and a generation later even Fischer Black (1973, 1975, 1986) theorized about financial markets in ways that incorporated social insights and respected the reality that human agency transcends a purely instrumental logic.

Now, it is one thing for financial participants, engulfed in the whirl and urgent immediacy of practice, having little reason to go beyond an intuitive and practical grasp of everyday deeds and results, to misconstrue and/or misrecognize that the market and their motivations are foundationally social. It is quite another for the *social* science of finance economics to misconstrue and misrecognize the dimensions of sociality constitutive of their analytical object.

So what happened to the social if it was radiant for most of the history of humankind, including capitalism right up through the professional economics of the great depression? Why did the social become invisible?

In the aftermath of the Second World War, the reputation of the natural sciences, especially physics and mathematics, soared. They were widely heralded as having saved EuroAmerica scientifically through the perfection of the atomic bond, and of ushering in a nuclear age that beckoned a better world. Commercials that touted "better living through chemistry" filled the airwaves. The US and British military has pioneered the creation of operations research, a new discipline (led by physicists and mathematicians) which sought to solve real-world (thus social) problems of decision making under uncertainty through the redirection of mathematical and statistical methods (Gass and Assad 2005:chapter 4). Also ascendant were efforts to create computer programs whose thought processes (i.e., artificial intelligence) could make decisions under uncertainty (Poole and Mackworth 2010:6–9). This historical context (which is only hinted at here) seeded a number of disciplinary attempts to naturalize the social. In step with this historical impetus, what would become mainstream neoclassical economics developed models and methods that set aside the social in a quest to fabricate a "natural science" of the economy. Or, at least, a natural science-like account of economic markets and behavior.[9] As Philip Mirowski (1989) shows economics sought to matriculate to sciencehood by treating the economy as a natural phenomenon to which the instruments of physics (mathematics) could be applied. The key premise was that markets resemble natural entities and are thus for all theoretical purposes, efficient, closed, and complete.[10] They operated systemically according to purely economic principles and rational decision making under uncertainty. So conceived, it becomes legitimate to analyze financial practice using mathematical notions that were formulated in respect to the natural world (dispersion of gases). In setting this path, 1973 proved the tipping point. Fischer Black and Myron Scholes imported the mathematics of Brownian motion into finance. This (Nobel Prize–winning) strategy seemingly "solved" the vexed problem of how to price the derivatives that would come to dominate the financial markets in the upcoming decades. Although the evidentiary basis for the formula was sketchy and there were some unresolved problems (it doesn't take supply and demand into account), the financial sector rapidly routinized and institutionalized the use of binomial diffusion equations in what was assumed to be a perfectly efficient market. So for fifty years the direction of finance has been to redact and reduce all dimensions of the social in the interest of constructing a mathematically tractable economics. The notion—that morphed into a clear directional dynamic—is that there could be a natural science of the economy which had liberated itself from the goal driven, creative, culturally-saturated, persistently transformative, and therefore inherently messy, character of human action.[11] To do this, what is social had to be removed by detaching the economy from other dimensions of social life. As we will see when we deconstruct the "illusio" of the efficient market, the analysis of the financial markets has taken place under the sign of the excommunication of the social in the interests of forging a mathematics of efficient market behavior.

This mathematization of finance suggested the advancement to a new level of (its culture of) control over the market's uncertainties and risks. Those in the financial workplace were, of course, aware of many instances when security prices, like circus animals who had forgotten their tricks, veered (sometimes wildly) off course, but they assumed and finance economics affirmed that these gyrations (departures from the normal curve) were of short duration, episodic, and too small to ever spawn a systemic crisis. From the standpoint of Alan Greenspan (Woodward 2000:20–7) and other adherents of the efficient market paradigm, that market forces muted these gyrations proved that the market was efficient, rational, and thus internally asocial. The credit crisis notwithstanding, most academic economists, especially finance economists, remain wedded to the understanding that markets must be inherently efficient. There are three social reasons for their continuing allegiance. The first is that the cultural valorization gained from being recognized as a natural "hard" "real" science is very alluring. They understand that more symbolic capital attaches to those disciplines that use mathematics as opposed to words to present their findings. The second is that most human practices, most of the time, possess discernable regularities. Like an orchestra without a conductor, financial markets and participants tend to reproduce themselves in only slightly transformed patterns (this regularity lasting only so long as the critical conditions for the reproduction of the totality remain intact). That most (but not all) agents adhere to these regularities means that (absent a systemic crisis) the financial markets tend to appear as only slightly distorted distributions, which in turn allows efficient market advocates to ignore the distortions (i.e., market imperfections) and (re)interpret the results as evidence of a market behaving efficiently.[12] Third, everyone in finance economics is professionally aware that the efficient market view has become institutionally attached to an entire gamut of awards and rewards, ranging from monetary compensation and university tenure to research grants, government positions, and academic prizes. There is thus a wide array of powerful, socially embedded incentives to accept the paradigm and set aside the problem of its underlying presuppositions.

As observed, everything went well enough until the financial market's embarrassed the model and its advocates. The graphic problem was that the model and its champions had dismissed as impossible precisely the kind of systemic failure that occurred. Some finance economists who had bronzed the triumph of the efficient market paradigm felt compelled to marginalize the financial crisis by declaring that it was a one off event, like a meteorite striking Wall Street. However, the main response in the academe was to have no response at all. Or to produce accounts which treated the decimation of liquidity as a natural phenomenon that had nothing to do with the character of the system or the agency of its participants (Allen, Carletti et al. 2011). But especially for the players on the frontlines, the meltdown gave rise to the realization that the financial field and its markets rested on an unacknowledged sociality. They had, after all, to confront the immediate existential crisis of plunging prices due to the evaporation of liquidity and the palpable fear of insolvency that gripped the markets. They could not dismiss the question of why the market had become paralyzed, or retreat into scholastic accounts that are removed from practice. So these commentators, drawing on their own experience and involvement in the financial markets, offered the observations that: "liquidity is a religion;" "it depends on faith and trust," on a "collective belief in the markets." We were informed that "the currency of the markets is confidence." And so to "right things" we (used in its collective sense) "need to restore people's faith in the markets," we need to "redeem their broken trust," and "purify the markets by exorcising greed." Day after day, commentator after commentator, from every corner of the financial community from public officials to mutual fund managers, appeared on CNBC and Bloomberg and repeated some variation on these themes to explain why credit markets had tumbled into a hell of their own design. A Dantean like hell in which what was frozen was liquidity. These unalloyed references to religion, faith, redemption, and a collectivity that transcends the individual, everything the finance field conceptualizes as the inverse of the economic, constituted an acknowledgement that the social has an unrecognized constitutive power. For finance economics, the character of crisis was the mark or symptom of the appearance of the social.

It is worth remarking that those in the financial field find it next to impossible to think or frame problems socially. Their disposition is to frame problems technically, in an object language organized around common oppositions. For example, in arguing against a proposed ban on OTC derivatives, they submit that it is important to distinguish between the tool and its user. In this case, between derivative instruments and the ruthless speculators who pushed the system to the brink. However reasonable sounding, this is a false opposition socially. For what we know about agents is that they adjust their strategies to the potential of a given instrument just as they seek out and create instruments that allow them to execute their speculative strategies. The strategies of the users and the use of the instruments are symbiotic, each adjusted and readjusted to the conditions present in the financial field at any point in time. Derivative instruments cannot but inscribe the history of the use that speculators have made of them, which is, leveraging speculative capital. This incapacity to think socially also underlies the celebrated "moral hazard" argument. Commentators have argued that the reason traders speculated so recklessly is because they knew the government bailout would spare them the consequences of their actions. Note the argument's asocial design: it quasi-automatically transmutes an effect of the crisis—the bailout of some impaired firms—into the cause of all firms' actions. The switch eliminates having to explain the social production of knowledge: How "did" "could" "would" agents, reasoning under uncertainty, come to the certain conclusion that the government would bail them out? How did this knowledge become so widely institutionalized that, when the music stopped, many investment houses ended up with worthless and illiquid tranches of CDOs? Under what mental formula would agents reach this conclusion given that, historically, not everyone was bailed out—exemplified by Lehman Brothers but also by firms such as Bear Stearns which essentially disappeared. Could we, for example, imagine Bears' senior management issuing a memo which said "speculate to the hilt, the worst that can happen is that our personal stock becomes worthless and we're devoured by our hated rival JP Morgan Chase"? So the social question of the production and circulation of knowledge remains, especially as many investment firms "acted" as though they would be bailed out. One might refer here to Einstein who theorized that "belief in the action of demons is found at the roots of our concept of causality." Here the shape of the argument excludes the social by identifying a demon—the US government's bailout policy—that caused agents to make insanely speculative trades. One might also refer here to the poet who cautioned that "you have been in full command of every plan you've wrecked; but don't take a cowards explanation and hid behind the cause and the effect" (from Leonard Cohen's song *Alexandra Leaving*).

Believing in the Market

Now it also turns out that religion is an unexpectedly apt metaphor: for the modern American circulation of faith is an unregulated market where all commitments are over the counter bets on salvation. Critically, it declares what anthropologists steeped in gift-based exchange have known since the pioneering work of their ancestors (esp. Marcel Mauss and Claude Levi-Strauss): that totalities, including the market, are social fictions made real by collective belief and sustained through the name that we have canonized for the power and persistence of belief—namely, faith. A financial market is a social imaginary; a deeply institutionalized imaginary to be sure endowed with a name, ratified participants, bodies of received knowledge, registered firms, a codified history, and so on; but it is an imaginary nonetheless. A market objectifies itself institutionally much in the manner that a nation institutionalizes itself through the creation of a state (such as the institutionalization of US nationness in the Treasury Department or Federal Reserve Bank). From our standpoint, it is neither an accident nor some opportune metaphor that a crisis-torn market began to speak in prayers, its commentators drawn to formulations that suture the health of the market to inscriptions of faith and belief normally attributed to religion. Even more, in calling for the restoration of faith and belief, these commentators are, without intending to, invoking a performativity which attends religion's frequent accompanist: ritual. We should take the financial community's self-assessment seriously. Indeed, I see its references to religion not as a mistake but as a crisis induced moment of self-reflexivity. And thus a sign of where to look analytically. I will not suggest the argument that religions in a capitalist society tend to fetishize ritual in order to hid its economic dimension (though this is so, there being a real economy to ritual),[13] rather, I will suggest that the structuring of the financial field and its markets turns on their rituality. Our reading and theorization of the evidence leads to the argument that rituality underwrites the collective vision that founds the creation of socially imagined totalities.

It is clear that the answer to the question "what is a/the market" is neither simple nor obvious. The market as a social totality or frame is simultaneously a practical relational construct, a marketplace that is a site of work, and a particular kind of "analytical object" constructed by economic theory. This multidimensional presence of the market serves as a framework and constraint that frames the actions of financial firms and the participants, the regulatory policies crafted by agencies such as the Federal Reserve and Treasury, the picture drawn by the media, and the sciencization of the market by finance economics. What all the players have in common is that they share this image of the market, unconditionally; they circulate this image without thinking they are circulating an image, switching fluidly among the various facets, their collective belief influencing their market behavior even as it underwrites their confidence in their interpretations of the behavior of anonymous co-participants. Syncopation of belief is essential: indeed, the argument that will unfold across the length of the book is that the market as a totality is nothing less than an *ontologically real social fiction* that agents quasi-automatically produce through the grace of collective belief.[14] And that it is the continually iterated rituality inscribed in the everyday practices of the markets' agents that breathes reality into this fiction. Read from a social perspective, the centrality of belief is the underlying, unacknowledged theme that appears throughout former Treasury Secretary Paulson's account of the struggle to restore faith in the deeply imperiled credit markets of 2008 (Paulson 2009). Though he recounts his deeds in colorless description, the supposition guiding his actions is that agents' decisions to restart making a market under uncertainty turns on the revival of their collective faith in a market's integrity. Indeed, we now know (through the Freedom of Information Act) that the Federal Reserve in collaboration with the Treasury paid north of one trillion dollars for this outcome (Morgenson 2011:1).

Chapter 6

Rituality and the Production of Financial Markets

The ascension of financial derivatives and their markets has forcibly foregrounded circulation. Not just in its logistical mission as the filament that connects production to consumption, that represents how one pregiven form carries on a material and symbolic conversation with another, but as the means by which these forms, such as the ascendant financial markets, constitute themselves as such. And do so in a sociohistorically specific manner. Following the contours of this transformation, this chapter originates in a shift of perspective: a 180-degree revolution from crystallized forms to circulatory structures. What appears to be a slight shift in the optic of understanding, an adjustment suggested by the globalizing processes now in train, reverberates theoretically, frequently in unexpected ways. Once we accord circulation equal ontological weight, categories such as rituality and performativity come suddenly into new perspective, and the canonized opposition between presumably well-formed forms—primitive society and capitalist society—begins to dissolve. But also to reestablish itself on altogether different ground. From this different ground, the critical difference that separates capitalism from, even as it superimposes itself upon and encompasses, the diversity of non-capitalist forms of social life stems from the historically revised way in which capitalism uses production and circulation to create sociality. There is disciplinary resistance—that has always been the story—but the ascent of cultures of circulation, exemplified by the ascension of the derivative and the fast growing power of financial markets globally, compels a reinterpretation of the concepts that I have used to apprehend the social.

There's no point in wasting time: in the land of power, time is seldom on the side of science. In contrast to politics which is a voting booth literally and figuratively, science is a weighing machine in which the theorization or the finding with the most gravity eventually prevails. With an emphasis on eventually, precisely because the politics of our day seeks to produce voices that mimic those of science, in the process confounding and muddying the production of knowledge, the implicit objective to efface the voices of science much in the manner that a silencer quiets a gunshot, making its report appear distant and diffuse and complicated by other sounds.

In a spirit of reinterpretation, what follows begins with an effort to undo a principle dualism upon which the social sciences' sociohistorically specific account of the social has resided. Thus the quasi-foundational dualism between "primitive" and "modern" where the former rests upon a socially robust but economically rationally compromised practices of ritualized exchange, while the modern market awaited only advances in science to be mathematized into an apparently objective and sovereign space, termed *the* economy, that brackets off and misrecognizes the very sociality that is the condition of its existence.[1] In a synthesize of what once served as figure and ground, the present work will transit from an analysis of rituality in the context of primitive exchange to the rituality constitutive of the financial markets now roaming the earth. The critical link is the presumably non-economic categories of performativity and rituality. The aim is to show how performativity operates throughout to socially instantiate a form(s)—such as a market—in such a way that its objectification can serve as the ground of practice (the trading of inter-temporal derivative contracts). Developing the notion of performativity in respect to circulation will lead to a reconceptualization of totalities and the means by which they can serve as platforms for the production of wealth.

Anthropology and Economic Disciplines

I begin with a conclusion put in service as an introduction to an alternative theorization of the structure of financial circulation: that we owe the bullet proof division between the anthropology of primitive societies and the formal economics of bourgeois capitalism more to the history of the self-positioning by the disciplines than to the actual economies found in the world. About this, there had long been an informal division of intellectual labor. Anthropologists worried about the typically nonwestern, marginally and partially capitalist, frequently still struggling postcolonial economies. Community based, primary production centered, economies or economic enclaves lying on the margins of capitalism. Places like the former Bantustans of South Africa, the remote, tribally ruled, mountain regions of Nepal and Ethiopia, or marginalized islands such as Haiti and New Caledonia. By contrast, economists focused on market-driven, capital intensive, globally integrated economic sectors where they appeared. So, for example, anthropologists and rural sociologists studied the Amazonian Indian populations working on the rubber and coffee plantations in the interior of Brazil while economists were charged with studying Brazil's burgeoning finance and petroleum sectors. There are, of course, no disciplinary rules about economic subjects, but as a rule the division held with only a handful of scholars camping consistently on the other's terrain. More importantly, this division of intellectual labor corresponds to a theoretical vision of the social. The idea is that sociality inundates the economies that anthropologists and wont to study; especially gift based economies are so intrinsically social it is pointless to use concepts and tools developed for scalable, large scale capitalist market-driven societies. The countervailing idea is that where capitalism reigns supreme, the economic is an entirely independent domain, which renders it possible to craft methods and models which isolate and fixate on the economic. As though the economic is a separate and thus separable dimension of social life. Embedded in this formulation was an agreement that the epicenter of formal economic analysis would be production whereas anthropologists would foreground the sociology of exchange (Sahlins 1972). An accepted disciplinary distinction between formal and substantive economics[2] enshrined this vision and division of the social world, which not coincidentally corresponded to two distinct and non-conversant literatures.

However, it turns out that an analysis of the semiotics and structures of financial circulation is only possible if we reject this theoretical division in favor of the view that all economies are necessarily substantive because they are inherently social. What is especially significant is that the original disciplinary division, occurring in the context of the rise of structuralism in anthropology and neoliberal economics, assisted in the entrenchment of two critical theoretical flaws. The first was the supposition of an irredeemable historical break between primitive non-capitalist societies and modern capitalist societies. Levi-Strauss's distinction between hot and cold societies and the neoliberal supposition that a feature of modernity was the inevitable expression of the economically rational agent (that had been suppressed by tradition). Mainstream Marxists also implicitly endorsed this distinction by assuming that capitalism—founded on a commodity driven, class organized, market based distribution of wealth—was so powerful and totalizing that it subsumed and vanquished primitive forms of social life. This distinction so conceived, the ritualized exchange of reproductive goods/gifts had nothing to do with the market exchange of labor extracting commodities. This irredeemable break meant that there was no way to conceptualize the passages—that is, an historical interval that unfolds as a spread of possibilities—from non-capitalist primitive societies to capitalist social forms in respect to a genuine theory of the progressions from the former to the latter. What is missing is an archeology of transformed forms—that is historically, primitive forms of practice (such as and especially ritual) which capitalism transforms in ways which recontextualize and reconfigure that phenomena while retaining its instrumentality, in, for example, the reproduction of social totalities. What is apparent once we reconnect the forms of economic life analysis no longer has to treat Durkheim's constructivist account of ritual and Marx's immanent critique of capital as though they represent incommensurable analytical tracks. Weber is also brought back into the conversation both through his writings on ritual and his conceptions of social status and institutional position. The Weberian contribution reminds us that reproduction is mediated by persons whose economic positions and position-taking strategies (e.g., the allocation of capital) occur within, and are oriented in respect to, a collectively constituted space.

The second flaw is that the division between formal and substantive economics was conducive to slipping into a shadow account of the reproduction of a totality. What both substantivist and neoclassical economics had in common is that they bought into a capitalist ideology that the integrity of social totalities—markets, clans, a culture, an economy—is ontological and thus preanalytical. While Levi-Strauss (1949) and a whole generation of anthropologists focused on the exchanges of women and gifts, the analyses invariably presupposed the prior integrity and identity of the social groups conducting the exchange. As Bourdieu would latter suggest (1971), once this ontology is rolled into place both the transgressions of the social groups and the interval between gift and counter gift become irrelevant. By the same token, finance economics fixates on what market do, in the process presupposing the market's integrity as the ungrounded ground of practice.

Through these moves, circulation is made to disappear. Specifically, all forms of circulation unfold in time, imbuing them with a temporality that is nothing less than a collectively anticipated forthcoming in which events of paying-off punctuate, even as they generate, agents' sense of periodization (from an extended exchange cycle to a derivative's expiration date). This ontology brackets the reality that circulatory processes continually undermine and dissemble groups and other formations of totality, even as these circulatory processes are the source of the group's (the totality's) reproduction. We can see that reproduction depends on the volatility or change immanent in circulation but only on the condition there are processes in place that mitigate volatility to the point where it does not threaten the functioning of liquidity and hence the totality's continuity. Inserted into this language, the bottom of Ayache's claims about the recalibration of derivatives is that the temporal interval permits, and is the reflection of, all manner of transgressions. Ayache's exchange traded derivatives represent the point where the rituality of the market is so institutionalized and routinized that the social reproduction of the market appears to be each event's non-event. All well and good, and so perfectly invisible, until normal "expected" volatility breaks down due to transgression and a market's liquidity disappears, thereby endangering its existence (exemplified by the crashes of 1987 and 2000). In counterpoint to Ayache, Derman's observes (2014) that the pricing models which drive the circulation of derivatives are prone to "behave badly" because they lack a real theory of the interval as a spacetime of uncertainty in which the transgressive power of the exogenous factors the participants believe matter (e.g., change in the Fed's monetary policy) as well as the internal mechanics of the market can and do make themselves felt. Derman's exotic "over the counter" derivatives name the point where the rituality of the market is so exteriorized that the market's social reproduction appears to be systemically natural.[3]

So our position is that while capitalism, exemplified by the market for financial derivatives, is qualitatively different from any other economic regime, it is nonetheless fundamentally social. Critically, the economic aspects of the social are also fundamentally different, but no less social for being so. Put another way, capitalism founds itself on a distinctive specific form of sociality, but this form of sociality is no less social for its distinctiveness (exemplified by its asocial appearance) nor is it less inclined to use the performative power of ritual to reproduce itself. The path from primitives to derivatives goes through the rituality constitutive of the social. Nothing illustrates this more than the social processes required to sanction agents to, provisionally, isolate the economic by placing themselves in contexts which valorize those dispositions that sublimate or eclipse their investments in the social. Let it be said that if cultural anthropology has produced one incontrovertible conclusion, it is that for most of the history of humankind, societies did everything in their repertoire to produce persons who valued and valorized kinship and community above all else. The goal was to produce persons who radiate dividuality (above individuality) in that their "self"-interests are indistinguishable from the interests of the collectivity inasmuch as the crystallization of those interests arise in and through a person's relationality with others.[4]

However natural it may now seem to those who tune in to CNBC and Bloomberg, entertain Barron's and the *Wall Street Journal*, or are schooled to an MBA, it requires a tremendous amount of social labor to produce persons (like those encountered), who, enframed within the market, voluntarily sacrifice their relationship with their wife and their children to earn money speculatively on bets which, on account of their enormous piles of sequestered wealth, has little marginal value to them as a medium of exchange for other commodities. For the first time in social history, we have—through an intense process of socialization that begins with children's mass media and ends with MBA training and the initiation rites of investment firms, created persons defined by a deeply instilled monetized subjectivity: individuals whose core of self-esteem, identity, and self-worth is not centered around the creation of a family and a space of domesticity, the perpetuation of the family and lineage, the purchase of desirable commodities, the status rewards of social position, the attainment of public recognition, the satisfaction of intellectual achievement, discovering spiritual peace and fulfillment, or the reward of heavenly merit, but around the unending acquisition of money itself. What the common notion of greed distils, albeit in a deeply ideological form, is that the goals of self-actualization that have stood at the center of most cultures for most of the history of humankind, the goals that shine forth in ethnography after ethnography about cultures from all corners of the planet, are reduced to occasionally and conditionally important footnotes, as complements to one's life rather than the very core of personhood and self-identity. The quest is for money in the abstract, which is money in its electronic form as a cipher and surrogate for the self. What defines those at the pinnacle of derivatives trading is that they are so preoccupied with and so deeply valorize their *acts of acquiring* money that money, once acquired, diminishes in value inasmuch as it can only be exchanged for the things that money can buy (e.g., houses, cars, boats). As Michael Lewis's investor portraits in *The Big Short* (2010) indicate, their return for being on the right (i.e., profitable) side of a trade that cut against the wisdom of the prevailing market (i.e., shorting collateralized mortgage obligations), was that it illustrated to their peers and above all to themselves that they were the embodiment of an uncommon level of diligence, courage, intelligence, and competitive fire. The noticeable trait that high-stakes poker players and derivative traders have in common—which helps to explain why many of finance's most prominent deal makers are such avid poker players—is that money counts and there is accordingly never a limit or end to their desire to acquire it because money is the means of keeping score. Those in finance appear to be inordinately greedy, their desire for money seemingly insatiable, precisely because the sociospecific form of greed that defines the contemporary financial field is founded on the acquisition of money. It is founded on the performative creation of the subject through repeated acts of acquisition: a deep-seated non conscious compulsion whose appearance in everyday practice takes the form of agents' competitive drive and their love for the financial game. Gobs of money are, of course, exquisitely useful because agents can deploy it to fabricate a new material world and index success, but only acts of acquisition repeated again and again can make the subject so deeply valorized by the financial field. Which begins to explain why derivative traders feel a compulsion to trade, making speculative bets and constructing new deals, working long hour days and then into the weekend, often refusing to take a vacation or vacationing with the computer screen and cell phone ablaze, long after they have accumulated tens of millions of dollars.[5]

In essence, as analysis probes beneath the surface, it becomes evident that there is a deeper, more social, story of the financial field, markets, and agents. A place where the distinction between the social and economic makes little sense. While these markets are powerfully economic in the most robust sense of the term, they equally and unmistakably implicate questions concerning the (re)production of the market, the creation of agents' subjectivities, senses of belonging and fairness, an ethos of speculation, nationalism, an imaginary of the market, notions of anonymous sociality, the agents' sense of immersion in a competitive game, and more that is intrinsic to financial markets but goes far beyond the economic realm. My objective is not to convince anyone that the economic is less than it appears, rather, that creation and practices of the finance markets presume the presence, and depend on the power, of a sociality that the financial field conceals as a condition of is own sociospecific production.

To his lasting credit—although he hasn't been given credit for it—Robert Pasani, CNBC's eye on the floor of the New York Stock Exchange got to the hidden heart of the conundrum when he ascertained that "liquidity is a religion" in which the market had "lost its faith" (September 27, 2008). The participants once possessed a confidence of belief in the markets, a confidence not based on empirical proof but on their trust in its agents and institutions, and this was gone. What Pasani grasped was that liquidity is something that the participants in a market provide one another, but that they only do this under certain circumstances that have much more to do with their collective state of mind than with the clockwork of the market. Behind his remark is the idea that liquidity is a pseudonym and reification for the *social relations* that allow *individuated* agents to construct the *collective enterprise* that is a market. Just as in their own ways are notions of counterparty and a homogenous (arbitrage free) market. Perhaps ironically, this is nowhere more true than in respect to the derivative markets. However much they appear deliberately not so, derivative markets are an ultimate expression of a social imaginary brought into being by the play of concrete social relations. The exposition must ground itself in these relations because they interpolate and mediate—through, for example, the recalibration of prices—the dialectical relationship between the always contingent and often unpredictable flows of events and the construction of a market as a totality.

Now it also turns out that religion is an unexpectedly apt metaphor: for the modern American circulation of faith is an unregulated market where all commitments are over the counter bets on salvation. Critically, it declares what anthropologists steeped in gift-based exchange have known since the pioneering work of their ancestors (esp. Marcel Mauss and Claude Levi-Strauss): that totalities, including the market, are social fictions made real by collective belief and sustained through the name that we have canonized for the power and persistence of belief—namely, faith. A financial market is a social imaginary; a deeply institutionalized imaginary to be sure endowed with a name, ratified participants, bodies of received knowledge, registered firms, a codified history, and so on; but it is an imaginary nonetheless. A market objectifies itself institutionally much in the manner that a nation institutionalizes itself through the creation of a state (such as the institutionalization of US nationness in the Treasury Department or Federal Reserve Bank). From our standpoint, it is neither an accident nor some opportune metaphor that a crisis-torn market began to speak in prayers, its commentators drawn to formulations that suture the health of the market to inscriptions of faith and belief normally attributed to religion. Even more, in calling for the restoration of faith and belief, these commentators are, without intending to, invoking a performativity which attends religion's celebrated accompanist: ritual. Indeed, I take the financial community's self-assessment seriously. I see its references to religion not as a mistake but as a crisis induced moment of self-reflexivity. And thus a sign of where to look analytically. I will not suggest the argument that religions in a capitalist society fetishize ritual to conceal its economic dimension (though this is so, there being a real economy to ritual performance),[6] rather, that the structuring and reproduction of derivative markets turns on their rituality. Our reading and theorization of the evidence leads to the argument that rituality underwrites the collective vision that founds the creation of socially imagined totalities. This is anything but straightforward; for a market when viewed (and conceptualized) from the standpoint of the agents appears as an aggregation of individuals (maximizing self-interested competitors); whereas these same agents, when viewed from the standpoint of the totality which allows that market to exist as such, appear as a network of dividuals. Moreover, it is the connectivity between the partible dimensions of the agents involved, that is, their dividuality or elements of their personhood used to create the totality, that, pre-supposed in the act of trading, grounds the possibility of their self-interested maximizing, competition as individuals. The appearance of the person/trader as a singular individual—that is culturally, as a "thinking object" endowed with the capacity to self-commoditize its own labor—is the necessary appearance of a market that is necessarily constituted on other terms.

The notion of the transformed form calls forth two big questions. Questions whose answers repair or at least clarify the flaws originating in the received view of the arc from primitives to derivatives, from non-capitalist into capi-talist society. The first is what is the essential character of the rituality in its pre-capitalist incarnations; and second, how is this rituality transformed and instrumentalized to the sociospecific context of modern financial capitalism. Let us begin with the anthropological maxim that a careful consideration of particular instances can reveal more general considerations. Due to its almost universal importance in pre-capitalist societies, the analysis will take *ritual-ized marriage exchange* as our ritual object, and a highland society of Papua New Guinea as our ethnographic subject (in large measure because there is exten-sive data on these societies prior to their encompassment by nation-state capital-ism). Our objective is to illustrate how rituality is the engine of the performative objectification of totality.

Performativity and Ritual

So where to begin with performativity. Especially as performativity has been much discussed across a range of disciplines, although certainly not with the sociostructural implications that we attribute to it. Let us start with the sup-position that performativity is intrinsically social and social life performative. Making performativity a critical part of the foundational character of the social. The single reason for its centrality is that the objective structures of the social (including markets) can reproduce themselves only in and through the *performance* of agents who, acting on their own behalf (interestedness), do things whose collective result is to reinstantiate these structures in the face of the corrosive effects of circulatory forces. This point needs to be italicized because virtually all analyses' point of departure is the stabilized moment *after* the structure's reinstantiation. This objectivism substitutes what agents have objectified, a system of products (e.g., markets, financial instruments, etc.), for the principles and performative practices of their innovation and reproduction. Which takes place at the crossroads where production and circulation not only intersect, but are mutually constitutive (e.g., the innovation of a derivative always carries the intent of its circulation just as insuring its future liquidity informs the production of that derivative). Accordingly, analysis cannot apprehend the structuring effect of agents' performances if its standpoint removes the implications of circulation. Either by considering reproduction as a pregiven preordained processes which exists somehow prior to and thus external from the participants' practices (e.g., ritual) or, alternatively, as a vacant a priori framework that individuals fill in individually in whatever manner their preferences and circumstances dictate (e.g., the economistic account of the market as the crystallization of individuals' transactions).

So agents' performances are performative precisely because these performances reconstitute the sociostructure and functionality that circulatory forces are constantly compromising (to a greater or lesser degree). Performativity re-objectifies the form or sociostructure and conserves its functionality (the ability of a market to organize the flow of derivatives) in the face of the volatility and disassembling effects that the unknowns and uncertainties inherent in circulation invariably variably throw up. As to the structure, the objectification of the form is the recertification of the platform (e.g., a market) that the participants must mutually presuppose in order to create and execute the strategies (e.g., one agent selling a put the other buying that same put) that constitutes the event. The magic of performativity is that *the social* structures the event without being there as such, not least because traders trade so deeply in the moment that the social disappears: for the social is existentially consequential only if it fails and liquidity stops. On the side of agency, the participants' existential interest in the event/performance is what imbues their lives with significance and purpose; it is what motivates them to willingly take on the uncertain risks animated by the event itself, which, due to the uncertainties (e.g., transgressions) that attend wagers on the future or the forthcoming, can never rule out the possibilities of failures or misfirings (everyone knows cautionary tales of the best laid plans, the locked in can't miss wagers, that ended in loss, disgrace, conflict); ultimately, it is this existential interest that motivates the agents to invest in the event's outcome and in so doing to take actions which reproduce the objective structure.

Although many accounts of things social have invoked what amounts to an implicit theory of performativity, it is with the work of the twentieth-century philosopher John Austin that the subject gains the foreground. In *How to Do Things with Words* (1962), Austin observes that English has utterances (such as I promise, bet, and baptize) that create the situation they instantiate. These performatives are distinct from ordinary descriptions in that they are not statements about the world which may be judged as to their existential truth or falsity. Performatives work when agents correctly attach a specific utterance to a socially specific context (as when at the signature of a marriage ceremony a justice of the peace says "I now pronounce you man and wife"). Analysts also observed that language performatives often noticeably appear in social situations that are fully constructed rituals (such as baptism and marriage) or are imbued with elements of rituality (such as court proceedings and oaths of office). Austin identified an often ritually infused means by which the social performatively engenders itself; so not surprisingly, specialists in ritual soon began an extended if uneven flirtation with the concept.

Stanley Tambiah used the concept of performativity to link content and context. He showed ethnographically that Thai coronation ceremonies posit and presuppose the cosmology that the ritual exemplifies (Tambiah 1985). The coronation locates this king, here, now, as genealogically linked to a heavenly cosmology that the ritual's performance presents and represents as simply another chapter in the temporal continuity of a hierarchical religious political order. Another celebrated pioneer in ritual studies, Victor Turner, invokes performativity as the answer to the problem of how rituals create "a time out of time," and a space of liminality, in which they suspend, annul, or overturn the quotidian structures of the social order (such as the status difference between king and commoners or between the clergy and the laity) in order to construct a metacommentary about that social order (Turner 1969; Turner and Turner 1978). But perhaps the most explicit appropriation of the notion of performativity lies in the work of Roy Rappaport (1979; 1999). He argues that ritual's performativeness is essential in creating social clarity (by turning symbolic statements into indexical events), in canonizing the liturgical order (by performing a liturgical order the participants demonstrate to themselves and to others that they accept unconditionally that liturgical order), and in establishing the social conventions that define what is right and righteous. Thus, "rituals do more than achieve conventional effects through conventional procedures; they establish the conventions in terms of which those effects are achieved" (1999:126). The "logos" of performativity thus stands at the epicenter of the social, leading Rappaport to view "ritual as the basic social act" (p. 137), which, brought to its logical conclusion, necessitates that although there is as many "ritual contents" as there are social systems, "the ritual form is universal" and necessarily so (1999:31). What all these theorists appreciate is that the objectification of the social and the structure of practice is tied to the performativity inherent in ritual. Nonetheless, the notion of performative has presented something of a conundrum: on the one hand, it excites because it appears to hold an extraordinary amount of theoretical potential; on the other, attempts to use the notion of performativity never seem to live up to their promise. What is missing is a theory of performativity of the social.

It turns out that it is rather unfortunate that the study of performativity began with analyses of the explicit linguistic performativity common to Indo-European languages. Unfortunate because most of the world's languages do not subscribe to this form of performativity and even those that do rarely do so in the transparent and explicit manner of English. The Bantu languages of the southern cone of Africa have, to give one example, an extensive array of conditionals that can, under the right conditions, function as quasi-performatives. Indeed, there is a good argument to make that the importance socially of linguistic performativity is directly related and proportional to the emergence of the social contract as a highly critical surface form of juridical, state based, capitalism (the promise codified in the contract; the baptism of a name/trademark; the awarding of a patent with its declaration of originality, or the pronouncement of a contract). In it all, the analysis of performativity has centered on language and the presumably enclosed space-time of ritual, only occasionally venturing out in ways that are ultimately socially mute—mute in the sense that they're not generative of further analytical advances.

The alternative history of performativity—which grants equal ontological status to production and circulation and thus refuses to privilege one over the other—begins with the understanding that performativity is ubiquitous and social. It being a precondition for the reproduction of sameness and a form's totality. Totality and the act of totalization have an extensive biography, though too often its conceptualization succumbs to the contours of capitalism's social epistemology and the notion is essentialized (on the template of the commodity). The alternative reading is a theoretical starting point that does not ontologically privilege either totality or circulation, and with this a starting point that refuses to elevate objectification over performativity. On this approach, a totality is the product of agents' collective and therefore social imagination of an abstract space of events that the agents hypostatize to be closed, complete, and self-referential in order to ground and frame the eventfulness of practice. The totality is nothing less than an *ontologically real social fiction, fictive* in that they are historically contingent and socially created (e.g., it's conceivable that nation states and derivative markets were never invented) and *ontologically real* in that they ground and enframe real world events (e.g., an official from the US Treasury endorses the domestic derivative markets). There is nothing about a social totality that guarantees its reproduction absent the collective labor of its participants (thus the European Union is a first imagination of an alternative platform in which the nation-state form is a less consequential totality as the ground and frame of practice). On the approach developed here, totality and circulation are paired, inseparable, and frequently syncopated temporal refractions on the production of actionable social spaces.

Performativity is a thus necessary dimension of the social due to the necessity of reproducing a form's integrity. To objectify the form as a totality graced with an identity (embodied in the transparency, segmentablility, and giveness of a form's name such as the collateralized mortgage market, the Eagle clan, the city of Miami, or for that matter the Hell's Angels) in the face of recurring volatility and potentially disassembling effects created by the circulatory processes necessary to carry out that reproduction. What this means is that performativity is not confined to ritual or certain linguistic events, but is implicated and instrumental in the reproduction of all those social forms and sociostructures involved in circulation. Which encompasses all the socially meaningful ones, from nations and financial markets to universities and street gangs. But so long as analytics understand the concepts underlying objectification, sameness and totality, non-performatively they (meaning all the analytical traditions founded on an objectivist account of objectification) are condemned to presupposing the objectification of the forms that they analyze. Presupposing a form's objectification is tantamount to naturalizing and neutralizing all the social labor—agents' strategies, risk taking, and maneuvering—required to sufficiently counteract (not always successfully) the volatility created by circulatory forces so as to preserve or restore a form's liquidity. This liquidity is nothing less than the capacity to re-engage those processes of circulation necessary to its reproduction. The rise of a "derivative logic" (Martin 2012) as a principle of the production of the derivative (based on the disassembling and reassembling of capital) references the generative scheme (creation of an exotic derivative based on this principle) that agents (such as quants) employ that serve to performatively reproduce that derivative market. The nonperformative perspective is the dominant one defining the many theoretical traditions that privilege production over circulation, the form over its social reproduction in sociohistorical time, the logic of theory over the logic of practice, and the pointillist position over the actions that agents take across an interval of position-taking in respect to a spread of possibilities. The only way to put this is that an adequate account of financial practice demands a theory of performativity and that apprehending performativity requires an immanent account of objectification.

To foreground circulation, the temporality of reproduction, the logic of practice, and agents' strategizing across the interval is to rediscover the force of risk, uncertainty, and volatility. Indeed, what makes performativity so socially indispensable is that it works to counteract and ameliorate the threat to a form's integrity wrought by volatility and risk/uncertainty. So the rituality of an event is performatively successful precisely when it reproduces a form's integrity and thus the maintenance of its liquidity in the face of whatever volatility is instigated by the unfolding of circulation. This may range from the threat to a patriclan's identity brought on by the influx of non-agnates to the threat of a security having multiple simultaneous prices to the threat of a derivatives market terminating due to the withdrawal of buyers and sellers. All of which result in a loss of liquidity. So the critical concern is the reproduction of the form's form in the face of the extant volatility and the risk/uncertainty of future volatility due to the strategies that are being implemented today. Performativity re-objectifies the form's form, albeit as a transformed form that appears ideologically as a conservation of identity, so as to conserve a form's liquidity. Inasmuch as circulatory forces disassemble all social forms, these forms must continually reobjectify themselves, from major practices such as full-tilt rituals to the iteration of a proper name designator (e.g., the x market, the y clan).

Reunification of performativity and objectification leads to a reconceptualization of totality that turns it from a permanently installed crystalline form to one that needs to be continually re-objectified. This continual process of re-objectification has its own social consequences: it means that the forms thus formed will be provisional, positional, and perspectival. Some examples are helpful. A clan's integrity and identity as a social form is provisional insofar as its internal composition changes over time as a condition of its reproduction (people come and go); its identity is positional in that the clan's formness is in respect to other clans' recognition of its form as a genuine example of clanness (it has a legitimate genealogical structure); and it is perspectival in that a clan's formness depends on one's standpoint in social space (a clan's boundaries appear as a spread ranging from unconditionally permeable to impermeable under all conditions). Capitalist markets follow a comparative logic. A derivative market is provisional in that its financing, liquidity, and participants are changing constantly (sometimes to the point of disappearing altogether); it is positional in that its definition and position as a market is in respect to other markets (so that derivative markets were once recognized as little more than venues for gambling); and it is perspectival in that its integrity depends on one's position in financial space. The forms objectified serve as ontologically real fictional spaces for launching both the flows that destabilize them and the performatives that reobjectify them. All, and this is a big all, that's required is that the agents implicated maintain their collective belief in the form's integrity amidst the destabilizing effects of circulatory forces. This maintenance dependent on the small rituality of everyday acts—such as advertisements for a market, anthropomorphic reports of a market's behavior, the serial execution and posting of derivative trades—and on special occasions the grand rituality of full-tilt ceremonies and (only apparently paradoxically) the rituality inscribed in counter-ceremonial, i.e., crisis, events (such as the Federal Reserve celebrated infusion of liquidity to help stave off systemic failure of the *commercial paper market*).

Performativity is simultaneously positive and negative performativity. One might say that the simultaneity of the plus and the minus is what makes performativity perform. Thus ritualized marriage exchange presupposes the non-integrity of the clan through its explicit recognition of the presence of non-agnates (difference) even as their act of appearance in the ritual (canonized by their contribution) presupposes a sameness in the first instance. The positive reproduction of the clan's integrity/sameness always presupposes negative performativity as well. For a totality's recreation of sameness through the *effacement of difference* erases for the collectivity, that is to say at the level of the social dividual, what everyone knows to be true for the individuals involved, that is, that they were once bona fide outsiders prior to the ritual construction of a sameness. By a similar act of magic, the positive reproduction of a market's integrity/totality necessarily presupposes the non-existence of illiquidity and price opacity and the impossibility of systemic counterparty failure. The performativity that silently objectifies the market as a socially imagined totality erases collectively, that is at the level of the market, what everyone knows to be true for individual funds (that they may "blow up" and become failed counterparties that drain the market of liquidity) and for singular one-off events, crises. What has evolved is a peculiar social epistemology whose defining moment is that the agents involved, in order to create the conditions of profit, impose a form of misrecognition on themselves, bracketing and thus devaluing as singular and episodic (counterparty and market failure) what they know from experience can be collective and systemic.

Exemplifying Performativity

As noted earlier, there are a number of accounts of performativity, especially in the literature on ritual and more recently in respect to the derivative markets (Callon 1998; MacKenzie 2009). Their virtues notwithstanding, there is a missing dimension which is an exploration of the forms of performativity and their constitutive relationships with social practice.[7] It will turn out that there are variegated forms of performativity, that they are frequently inclusive and at times imbricated, and that where they differ is in the relative transparency and participants' (mis)recognition of their objectifications of the social. To give the analysis ground, the analysis theorizes this relationship of performativity to practice through an ethnographic example.

Our ethnographic example comes from the Maring people who live in a remote and rugged terrain in the western highlands of Papua New Guinea. The Maring are divided into twenty clan clusters, each cluster comprised of four or five exogamous, patrilineal clans (anthropological speak for clans that marry out and trace descent through the male line). The most socially central ceremony in Maring society is undoubtedly ritualized marriage exchange, without which clans could not reproduce themselves materially or symbolically. Viewed retrospectively, these exchanges deliberately appear as preordained, riskless, and non-controversial objectifications of normal social relations. Viewed prospectively, however, the situation looks much different. And much more performative. When viewed prospectively, exchange rituals appear as a spread of possibles across a temporal interval in which the actual ceremony is the punctuation of a rituality which begins before that ceremony and which continues after its execution.

The ignition is the agreement by two clans to arrange an intermarriage. The Maring recognize four distinct types of marriage: sister exchange, patrilateral second cross cousin, iterative exchange (characteristically with matrilateral kin in a "sister" clan), and outside transactions (with geographically distant clans). These types are significant in that they determine the character of the compensation, the obligations that are publicly animated as promises, the kind and amount of goods and services that clan members exchange, and the obligations that fall to offspring of the union. There are perfectly aligned unions in which the intermarrying couple fill the precise genealogical slots, but more often than not there is genealogical dissonance such that the respective clans—both internally and with one another—must come to an agreement on the type of marriage that is being consummated. For example, there are numerous negotiated "sister exchanges" that clans arrange between one man's true sister and another man's patrilateral parallel first cousin (a daughter of his father's brother). Such marriage proposals involve risk as they may be contested and ultimately misfire, when typically some fraction within the clan rejects the union by refusing to ratify the classification. What this says is that these negotiations foreground *type token performativity*: a process of typification in that singular instances are recruited to a recognized type, such that, from a classificatory standpoint, that marriage now appears as an indexical icon—that is, a perfect instantiation—of that type. The key point is a classification is only as socially real as the valorized acts of typification that instantiate it. Just as singular token events/unions become socially real via their typification. The upshot is that analyses and models that reduce the classificatory process to a mechanistic operation that requires no discussion distort and misunderstand the reality in progress.

The marriage typified, among other considerations the participant's agreeing on a marriage compensation payment (from the groom's clan to that of his wife) that is always an amount large enough that it can only be collectively assembled, the stage is set for the organization of the ceremony to begin. It is in the process of the ritual's preparation that its totalizing effects start before it commences. Which is why the performativity of a ritual has already accomplished much before the ceremony's performance.

A patriclan is a (re)production group which is theoretically composed of all those persons who share a common male ancestor. But it is also a territorial group that practically includes members whose presence is mediated by and the result of the continual circulation of people from other clans. Each ritual marriage exchange is a singularity in that the clan's membership is constantly in flux. So when clan leaders indicate that a ritualized marriage ceremony is to take place, that the clan's women should harvest taro and yams and gather firewood, that the leaders are contributing sacrificial animals and request other's support, the request is constructed so that it embraces (or does not embrace) a husband living on his wife's clan lands, a man residing with his mother's brother, a woman living alongside her in-married sister, a woman who has been adopted by her matrikin, and so on through all the possibilities presented by the culturally sanctioned circulatory routes. All of these non-agnatic agents can negotiated whether they can or will contribute labor, food, and sacrificial animals to the bridewealth payment. The act of acting, and having the action accepted, of signaling one's approval by gathering foods or firewood, or by donating an animal to the compensation, advances the ritual and begins to redefine the totality. When, to give a common and illustrative example, a woman adopted at an early age gathers firewood and taro for the feast, and participates in the ritual, and then recognizes that the men of that clan have become forbidden marriage partners (although, had she remained in her natal patriclan, they might be preferential partners) her "induction" presumes a performative (re)creation of totality. Indeed, when the clans assemble for the ritualized exchange they stand across from one another as totalized entities—the participants who are participating are all equally clan members by virtue of their authentic participation. There is a *constitutive performativity* in that the ritualized exchange presupposes the totality of the clans that are reconstituted through the ritual. There is a reobjectification of the clan as a transformed form of itself. Moreover, the exchange of wealth presupposes and certifies the efficiency of the ritual by transforming its consequences— the reconstitution of these clans, here, now, publicly—into the premise and predicate for further practices. This constitutive performativity produces two embodiments of history. The collectivity appears as an objectification of the ritual as objectified in its clan name, the specifically named territory on which its member have gardened and buried the bones of ancestors, in its record of the clan's exchange relations which also determine the necessity of ritual, and in its narrative accounts of military ventures, consummated treaties, labors, migrations, new settlements, and other foundational fictions of the clan group. The totalizing effects of ritual are also embodied in agent's dispositions, attitudes, generative schemes, motivational structures, and notions of the sense and acceptableness of actions. When, for example, a man who is residing with his wife's clan contributes to a bridewealth payment on behalf of one of its members and then shares in the reciprocal gift, or when conversely, he remains materially silent when his father's clan seeks to assemble a bridewealth payment, there is a kind of complicity between his social position and his disposition to instantiate or deactivate a specific clan affiliation, a complicity organized offstage by ritual's capacity to foreground totality at the expense of circulation.

The ritual involves a kind of transubstantiation. Within the context of the ritual, every member of the wife-givers' clan shares in the gifts, including women from the wife-takers subclan and clan who have previously married in. And conversely, when wife-givers reciprocate a small counter gift to their affines, always from pigs nurtured on their clan lands, every member of the wife-taking (sub)clan shares in that pork irrespective of where they originally came from. The subordination of social memory, of what people know, to the construction of a totality can take place because the ritual creates a hierarchy of value that brackets what they remember, the single objective intention of reproducing the group outweighing those aspects of persons that interrelate them to other groups. In so doing, clan members have not forgotten where their wives and in-laws came from. Even less are they enacting a role in which they are pretending to forget. They are entering into the spirit and enframement of value created by the ritual, which, in elevating the values of nurturing, belonging, and groupness, expects of people objectively what they subjectively expect of themselves. By creating a performance that is, in Rappaport's words "not encoded by the performers" (1999:24), ritual insures that there will be a close correspondence between the recognized positions and the dispositions of agents to act in a certain way (exemplified by sharing) so as to produce a totality. In another register, because the ritual is concerned to foreground disinterest, to produce connectivity between groups, it creates a temporality-bracketed perspective from which substantially imbricated (sub)clans, (sub)clans that have internalized one another on a continuous basis, appear as autonomous third person collective agents. That is, the groups appear as performatively objectified totalities that can engage in exchange. Constitutive performativity is thus the foundation of the production of the socially imagined totality and thus the logos of ritual as the basic social act.

But it is also the case that due to the power of circulations, the matter of clan membership cannot be settled simply by enumerating who is present. There are members who are not present because they are working a faraway job, receiving a foreign education, recuperating in an urban hospital, or living with another group on what is presumably a temporary basis. When the exchanging clans have assembled on the collectively maintained ceremonial theatre, each clan's leader makes a speech in which he first introduces the clan collectively, and then makes a specific point of "calling out" by name all of those persons (plantation workers, politicians, students, etc.) who are absent but nonetheless clan members. There is here a *citational performativity* in which all those named are to be counted as official participants in the ritual marriage exchange, meaning that they are equally responsible for and responsive to the obligations, debts, affiliations, rights, and promises created by the marriage exchange. This citational performativity contains a negative space in that for a person to be absent, yet excluded from the citation, is to be publicly disenfranchised from the clan.

The most visible dimension of performativity, and the one that has to date dominated analytic discussions, is *pragmatic performativity*. This form of performativity is the most transparent and thus most likely to be officially recognized. It can have both repetitive and indexical moments. Repetitively, the continued use of same territorial sites for ritualized exchanges molds the physical landscape so that it bears the trace of past exchanges and is preadapted for forthcoming ones. (Much in the same way that when on a university campus people repeat the same shortcut across the grass, their actions eventually result in a new and recognizable pathway between sidewalks). The obvious aspect of repetitiveness is that by continually realigning a platform—be it spatial, technological, mathematical—with a social practice the more they become adapted to one another (i.e., the path across the grass is more recognizable and easier to manage which motivates more people to take it).[8] This form of performativity points to syncopation that can evolve between a technological design and the expectations of the agents that use it. The predications of economic models invested with symbolic authority can thus serve as self-actualizing forecasts when the users of a model collectively believe in and use its calculations to organize their actions. MacKenzie (2006) shows this syncopation was the case for the Black-Scholes options pricing model until the unexpected 1987 crisis after which traders collectively tempered their belief in its accuracy (LiPuma 2014).

The indexical moment stems from the fact that ritual performances are not simply a symbolic representation or expression of some social reality, they are components of the messages they seek to convey. The performative act sets out the conditions and criteria for judging the felicity of the promises or the futures inscribed in the ritual. That is to say, the probability of deliverance. It is one thing for a clan to declare that it can fulfill all of the obligations created by the marriage; it is quite another to demonstrate this indexically by proffering a magisterial compensation payment, assembling a large clan turnout, and then executing the ritual with literally military like precision. The clan's size, wealth, and self-regimentation is itself a critical example of it being able to fulfill its obligations. The ritual sacredly promises that the clan will mobilize those resources in the future to fulfill its stated obligations. To put this systemically, ritual's indexical iconic power annuls the risks of circulation by making the intentionality of the agents transparent in that it must be publicly declared as the forthcoming of the relationship. In this way, the ritual seeks to dampen and socialize volatility in order to mitigate the directional risks created by a clan's outstanding vulnerabilities. In another language, ritual is the primary means by which clans create the sociality that allows them to hedge against a host of downside risks (e.g., an increase in population size that allows a clan suffering a shortage of garden land to exploit an affine's borderlands).

Finally, the uptake of any ritualized marriage exchange depends in good part on the discourse or narrative about the ritual that the participants constructed and circulate. Or, occasionally dispute. Which induces volatility (to the point of violence) because and to the degree the dispute not only calls this specific ritual into question but implicitly reveals the arbitrariness of the objectifications. Such disputes can spill into violence for good reason culturally: they undermine the groups' permanent and transcendent vision of themselves and diminish the wealth the exchange created. Mostly however, the depiction of the type-token performativity as cosmologically valorized and thus legitimate as well as an account of its pragmatic performativity in fostering an amplification in the quality and flow of goods and services figure in this narrative. The exchange was a sum-sum game in which the values circulated presently and as futures increases everyone's wealth. The narrative takes it as axiomatic that the typification of the exchange was transparent and indisputable, that the compositions of the clans were the only conceivable compositions, that everyone who was included citationally accepts the full burden of the social responsibilities incurred, and that the community of the excluded excepts and recognizes the results. There is here a *retrospective narrative performativity* founded on the widespread circulation via especially the public speeches of its high-status participants, leading to the collective and collectively ratified acceptance of the account. This narrative, which presumably simply explains the success of the ritualized exchange, is actually an instrumental part of its uptake or success because it crystallizes the conditions for future transactions. One feature of this narrative is that it embodies an economical generative scheme which quasi-magically transforms and canonizes correlations (between a marriage and its outcomes) into positive causations. This mode of performativity expunges the ambiguity—that there is never only a single interpretation or a guaranteed outcome—that was the condition of the staging of the event.

It is critical to underline—because this begins to signal the real difference between a capitalist economy and non-capitalist econom*ies*—that the ritual creates wealth through the amplification of sociality. A form of wealth that is socially and historically specific to that society because the agents exchanged ritually and the objects set in motion will embody the sociality of their makers. A "wealthy" clan is thus a clan whose calculated strategies have resulted in an abundance of sociality, whose existential manifestation is as a stockpile of contingent claims. That is, an accumulation of claims on others' requital of the socially inscripted gifts they have consumed.

Virtually all social practices have some elements of rituality. What makes ritualized marriage exchange instructive is that it exemplifies a codified, cosmologically valorized, full-throttle ritual, meaning that its rituality is explicitly foregrounded such that there is great visibility to the forms of performativity that generate the objectifications of the social. In contrast, capitalist markets exchange conceals and misrecognizes these ritualized forms of performativity; but they are no less performative for doing so.

What Is a Market Performatively?

I have argued that the annulment of the social is a necessary social feature of the culture of financial circulation. And with that the annulment of the rituality that allows the performative constitution of a market. Ironically, the derivative markets above all others are performative, owing to the fact that the instruments have no use or intrinsic value and must therefore ultimately refer to an underlying reality that is not a derivative and does not obey a derivative logic. All derivatives, particularly OTC (over the counter) derivatives which constitute the vast majority, are non-exchange traded and thus need not conform to any standardized design. Exchange traded derivatives, by contrast, trade the inflexibility of standardization for the certain alignment of token and type and the liquidity of each trade's counterparty. The fabrication, pricing, and circulation of OTC instruments must entail the enactment of *type-token performativity.* The market's makers must typify specific singular derivatives (even if that type is formulated from an admixture of different derivative types). Meaning further that each act of buying/selling that financial instrument is instrumental in performatively objectifying it as a specific type of derivative (such as a super senior CDO tranche). Typification is necessary because a market cannot price a singularity or use it for collateral. No matter how it may look retrospectively, derivatives are not born with clearly stenciled names or with transparent pricing instructions. What is required is an act of classification which defines *this* token as an instance of *that* type—an act which always presupposes the power and legitimacy to impose that classification. This is precisely why and where the reputation, symbolic capital, and financial firepower of the market's market making institutions comes into play. These classifications also shape the mental space of trading, predisposing those with a sense of that market to adjust their expectations to the probabilistic assessments of that instrument (e.g., that super senior tranches are bulletproof or that lower tranches have a specific risk/reward profile).

The functionality of the derivative is central. For the derivative to function as a speculative bet, as capital, or as collateral for a loan that leverages a wager depends on the existence of an energetic market. The ontological reason is that bereft of any use value the derivative has value if and only if there exists a market for its circulation. A point that the succession of crises have underlined. The raises the question what is a market to a critical problematic in that a market's functionality depends on the willingness of its participants to reproduce a stream of liquidity in the face of uncertain volatility. The standard supposition is that *the market* is an ontologically given well-formed form. But this view does not and cannot explain how the derivative emerged as a form of wealth, how the market for its expansion reproduces itself, or the conditions of failure and the appropriation of the public treasury.

If we critically pose the question "what is a market," or more concretely what is the derivative market on which these instruments trade, the answer is neither simple nor obvious. For the market as a social totality or a frame is simultaneously a practical construct, a marketplace that is also the site of work, and a particular kind of "object" constructed by economic theory. This complex multifaceted conception of the market frames the actions of financial firms and participants, the regulatory policies crafted by the Federal Reserve and Treasury, the picture drawn by the media, and the sciencization of the market by finance economics. What all the players have in common is that they share this image of the market, unconditionally; they circulate this image without thinking they are circulating an image, switching fluidly among the various facets, their collective belief influencing their market behavior even as it underwrites their confidence in their interpretations of the behavior of anonymous co-participants. Syncopation of belief is essential: indeed, the argument that will unfold across the text of our analysis is that the market as a totality is nothing less than an *ontologically real social fiction* that agents quasi-automatically produce through the grace of collective belief.[9] And that it is the continually iterated rituality inscribed in the everyday practices of the markets' agents that breathes reality into this fiction. Read from a social perspective, the centrality of belief is the underlying, unacknowledged theme that appears throughout former Treasury Secretary Paulson's account of the struggle to restore faith in the deeply imperiled credit markets of 2008 (Paulson 2009). Though he recounts his deeds in colorless description, the supposition guiding his actions is that agents' decisions to restart making a market under uncertainty turns on the revival of their collective faith in a market's integrity. Indeed, we now know (through the Freedom of Information Act) that the Federal Reserve in collaboration with the Treasury paid north of one trillion dollars for this outcome (Morgenson 2011:1).

Note that the confluence of the *real* and the *fictional* through the power of collective beliefs, as well as agents' implicit faith in the totality they have instantiated, indicates that markets have a performative aspect. They are defined by a dialectic between rites of self-objectification, large and small and most of all continuous, and the production of a financial habitus that encourages agents to have and maintain faith in a market's integrity. That, for example, agents' objectify liquidity as the normal state of the financial markets goes hand in hand with an ensemble of concepts, dispositions, and positions that normalize their collective faith in the totality or frame. Liquidity is the finance field's representation of sociality, objectified in the notion of the counterparty and the risks posed by those on the other corresponding side of a trade. Termed counterparty risk it serves to abstract and reify the financial agents whose decision-making will, slightly or greatly, now or in the near future, influence the security of securities and thus the collectivities belief in the market. An examination at what agents actually do demonstrates a constant interplay between the objectification of abstract risk through mathematical modeling (e.g., Black-Scholes) and their attempts to discern what others with the same or similar models are doing. The totality reconstructs itself out of the interplay between overlapping models and the iteration of the models that agents share and attribute to their others or counterparties that comprise the market.[10] There is thus every reason to believe that the market as a social totality lies at the intersection of specific real time trades and the imaginary community constructed out of everyone's beliefs about, and faith in, what others (counterparties) are doing with respect to similar trades and deals, such as assembling and marketing CDOs. This intersection is technically mediated by, most significantly, Bloomberg machines which everyone knows everyone else uses for price discovery. What is outstanding is how the syncopated objectification of the local and the totality performatively produces a market (e.g., for credit derivatives) as an instance of *the market*. Although the market appears as the simple aggregation of individual trades, agents' ability to consummate these individual trades presupposes and thus turns on a faith-based liquidity. Each transaction instantiates and foregrounds the market that it presupposes. This objectification leads to the self-fulfilling because collectively shared prophesy, that a universe of reliable "stranger" counterparties populate a specific market. So long as market agents share and act upon this belief their "religion" will remain intact, that market will remain liquid, and their "collective faith" will remain invisible. The magic of a market is not that it tricks its participants, but that it makes them believe. This is the essence of the *constitutive performativity* that sustains a derivative market, ultimately composed of nothing else but a circulating ensemble of contingent claims (Ayache 2010). Pricing a portfolio (of CDOs, for example) on a mark to market basis will, under these conditions, provide a reasonable assessment of a firm's balance sheet. Each successfully executed transaction reaffirms the group's collective belief in the imagined community of reliable counterparties that it presupposes. Collective belief is the operative concept insofar as it is virtually impossible in OTC markets to know or verify that the counterparties are reliable or will remain so over the term of the contract. Especially as the speculative ethos permeates these markets motivates and incentivizes risky wagers that engender continually evolving portfolios of what is (despite VAR models) unquantifiable exposure. In essence, the parties who execute a given trade, as well as those who witness it (typically as an anonymous electronic cipher), will only continue to make a market (e.g., in mortgage obligations) if they "believe" that the only possible reality is that there is enough liquidity, readily discoverable prices, and solvent counterparties such that wagers made will invariably be paid. It is the restoration of this belief through the guarantees offered by the government (i.e., the Troubled Asset Relief Program, or TARP) that Henry Paulson in collaboration with Ben Bernanke was trying desperately to restore. They were attempting to reboot the performative impulse that engenders the market as a totality by guaranteeing the efficacy of the transactions. The idea was that a string of successes would restore agents' collective faith in a/the market's integrity. Salvation thus depended on resurrecting the performative objectification of these markets as totalities. On this score, the efficient market thesis and the derivative pricing models it underwrites (Black-Scholes) are blind to this performative dimension because they reduce a/the market to individual acts of buying and selling.[11]

They cannot thus entertain the question of genesis: what are the conditions for the inculcation of similar beliefs and dispositions, which in the manner of an orchestra without a conductor, motivates the collectivities collective faith in a *real* financial market comprised of anonymous agents conditioned to function as reliable predictable counterparties. When we recognize that a market's performativity is the condition of its very existence, the analytical objective changes to illuminating the character of these beliefs and dispositions, how these inculcated beliefs and dispositions performatively objectify financial markets, and how the institutions of finance produced and reproduced them through a regime of work. Economistic definitions of the market, especially those that believe in its inherent efficiency, annul the performativity which bring markets into existence as viable entities. Against this entrenched viewpoint, I would argue that social totalities, such as the derivatives markets, are created performatively by a kind of secular ritualization that links existential events to the social imaginary that is a market. It will turn out that rituality is important because it answers the question of how does a collectivity come to believe that a conceptual object—a nation, an ethnicity, a clan, and a market—is so true, real, and constant, sufficiently permanent and transcendent that they willingly found their actions, risk their wealth, and at the point where game theoretics cease to count, predicate their very lives on the integrity of an object, which, having been created at a specific point in historical time through human agency, can also be destroyed through a collective retraction of belief? And we don't have to look farther for an example than the 2008 financial crisis. The evaporation of liquidity that ignited the system's implosion was the result of agents' collective retraction of their faith in the market just as, correlatively, the paralyzing fear of counterparty risk that gripped the market was agents' collective withdrawal of their faith in its participants. Agents can and do disinvest in the investiture of the market.

What makes rituality so important socially is that it allows practices to posit what they effectuate. In this way, rituality creates a performative impulse in which the participants presuppose the realness of the social totality that the event helps to create or effectuate, by assuming that this event—here, now—is simply a replica of previous performances. The performative aspect of the practice is so central because it shapes the illusion that the totality created socially (e.g., the market) is a naturally occurring object. The event summons the participants to believe, to have faith that the totality indexically presupposed by this specific event is as real as the existential lived event itself. There is a cognitive and dispositional obligation to assume, for example, that the efficient market is as real as the trade I have just efficiently made. By this means, the specific trade figurates what it and all of the trades (classified as) like it collectively effectuate. The capacities and dispositions of agents to collectively subscribe to the same understanding (e.g., of the market) without any collective intention does not just occur: it turns on socializing agents through their immersion in the distinctive habitus of the financial field and the hard work of its institutions in inculcating dispositions within the participants (as could be illustrated by their intensive training regimes which bear more than a passing resemblance to initiation rites). One might note that the economistic depiction of the market is an empirically robust illusion: insofar as the rituality of practices regiments a succession of events which successfully instantiate the market (e.g., the market remains liquid), its social foundations can remain below ground. As long as the rituality of practice brings about the repeated alignment of totality, type, and token, then the act of classification whereby agents typify a token derivative as part of a market totality can remain invisible. As long as this rituality motivates the syncopation of the beliefs and actions of the participants, the market can appear to be entirely formal. As long as rituality produces the collectively shared unquestioned belief that the individual trade I am making now/here is a perfect replica of a known type of trade within a specific effectively perfect market, then that market will appear to reproduce itself naturally, asocially, as a simple progression of the inevitable. Until, as we witnessed, a crisis of faith in the market ensues, at which time the constitutive power of the social seems to appear from nowhere and remain until the state of emergency subsides.[12]

We observed that the technology of the market registers trades as electronic ciphers between anonymous others. But this is only part of the story as there is also in train the circulation of information about who is actively participating, important because the players recognize that each institution (e.g., Goldman Sachs) and individual (e.g., John Paulson) is endowed with different quantities of economic and symbolic capital. There is here a kind of citational performativity in that confirmed knowledge, suspicions, hearsay that for example Goldman Sachs or Greenlight Capital (hedge fund) is a major player says much about the potential liquidity and thus the staying power of that market in that it speaks to the relative economic capitalization and longevity of the counterparties. Whether, and to what degree, Goldman Sachs and Greenlight Capital are involved may make a difference as to monetary outcomes—this is a zero sum game in which the size and power of "the whales" make a difference— but what counts in the production of agents' premise of market liquidity is the collectively shared belief in their participation as sustained by a chain of citations (based presumably on reliable evidence). This is one of the primary reasons that the participants perpetually search for, and critically evaluate, citations on who is making the market.[13] As MacKenzie following Callon points out, a source of *pragmatic performativity* is the fact that financial economics has evolved to become part of the infrastructure of the market such that derivative pricing models (exemplified by Black-Scholes Merton) do not just model prices theoretically, they are part of the process of defining them (2006:15–20). The market is also pragmatically performative in that a directional move (in a currency, for example) can and frequently does motivate an accelerating cycle of wagers which mimic and amplify that directional bet: what is called "momentum trading." These traders, armed with pools of speculative capital, aggressively take positions whose source of profit is the volatility and directional movement that they collectively create (See LiPuma and Koelble 2009). Such performativity also appears sociolinguistically in the way members of the financial field mechanically reproduce a repetitive chain of reference which attaches a specific presumably descriptive name (e.g., the merger arbitrate or credit market) to a specific socially imagined totality. And to the chain of definitive events, such as liquidity stops, which are said to characterize the history of the one and the same totality. An endless chain of micro-acts of citation, circulated through the media, are thus instrumental in iterating a market.

And finally, *retrospective narrative performativity* is an integral dimension of the derivative markets. The participants in the finance field are contually creating and solidifying a narrative about the strategic behavior of the market—a narrative in which the market as a collective agent encodes beliefs and fulfills desires based on its judgments. This includes its anticipation of the future, as when analysts remark that a market declined because it was anticipating an event that had not yet occurred during that recession in prices (e.g., the event being the failure of the European Central Bank to reach an accord on a rescue program for imperiled banks). A distinctive feature of this rear-window narrative is that it engenders a teleology by transforming correlations into causations through the application of a practical logic, which has some of the uptake of a self-fulfilling prophesy in that the circulation and acceptance of a belief may certainly motivate agents to behave in a certain way (e.g., if they collectively believe that the ECB's failure to cut rates will lead to a swoon in prices they may collectively pare their positions) thereby "proving" retrospectively that the correlation was indeed a causation. This narrative continually affirms the typification of the tokens, the totalization of the market, and the integrity of the prices through the personification of the market, including the attribution of intentionality and foresight which, in turn, bespeaks a teleological arc to its actions.

When we have put aside the objectivist account of objectification, amplified and exemplified by the mathematization of the finance market, the question of the market as a capitalist production in which the circulation of capital is the worksite of struggle among competing participants, remains. The question is whether analysis can account for derivative markets by developing an approach that considers the systemic dimension of these capitalist capital markets, the family resemblance among different markets brought about by use and adaptation of reflecting modular forms and generative schemes, and the space for the incorporation of all those things social which motivate agents to collectively reproduce the market as a totality. The genius and scandal of the Black-Scholes formula is that it is instrumental on all these levels.

Conclusion

I have expressly framed the question bracketed by both neoclassical and Marxist approaches of how are markets realized as collective agents, and how do the markets sustain themselves as such. The critical ground is that *a market enacted as a continuous set of transactions functions (remains liquid) because its agents presupposes the market as a(n imagined) totality, even as the existence of that totality depends on the continuity of those transactions.* Speaking to the relationship between collectivity and totality requires a theorization that is specifically social and that illuminates the generative structure by which financial markets accomplish this. Based on a theorization of the evidence, I argue that the objectifications of these derivative markets turn on forms of performativity that direct and harnesses the inherent rituality embodied in social practices. While rituality may seem far removed and remote from the world of finance, rituality is its modern secular form is, on our understanding, the hidden constitutive dimension of the innovation and (re)production of financial markets, including the derivatives markets. This analytical focus requires that we historize the concept of the market by illuminating the sociospecific and historically imperative character of modern derivatives markets, critically the forms of performativity these markets embody and motivate. There is too much at stake to leave the financial field to theories that bracket the social. For our aim at the present conjuncture has to be to develop theories and methods that can adequately grasp a social whose arc is moving from away the social that reigned during the salad days of production centered capitalism; a transformative social that is emerging in the context of the restructuring of the relationship between production and circulation, in ways whose dynamic lies in how new forms of detachment involve new dimensions of connectivity. Our argument is that an understanding of the relationship between performativity and objectification and of how the technical production of the spread through the wealth generating pricing mechanism of Black-Scholes open to a sociality that it must bracket if it is to maintain its internal dynamism, or dynamic replication that show the hedging strategies of rituality to lie at the heart of what was itself once bracketed as the economic is a first step in that direction.

Chapter 7

The Speculative Ethos

It is hard to make predictions, especially about the future. —YOGI BERRA

It is frequently said that derivative traders have a narrow corridor of emotions, restricted to rocking back and forth in the cradle of greed and fear. Greed and fear rehearsed as though self-evident. Self-evident because their cause is money: greed for money, fear of losing it. But there is much missing from this formula. Anyone who trades, trades on emotions. They know fear as the ghost of experience. The image: diving into a wreck promising treasure then sensing it has shifted, suddenly, the door shutting closed, so that the oxygen may expire before reaching the surface. A trader fears the recurrence of pain and loss, the memory of self-inflicted pain, a pain unto itself. This fear is not hard-wired. It is sutured to memories, reflections, streams of consciousness, experiences, and will always be inseparable from the body. —EDWARD LIPUMA 2015

Global finance and the crises it continues to generate is a deep well.[1] It will on this account reveal itself only if we're willing to fish to the bottom. As the preceding chapters underlined, this analysis entails a social reading of the structuring of the derivative and its markets. But there is also sociality on the side of the agent which entails taking on the speculative. For if anything defines the culture of financial circulation it is a collective willingness on the part of those involved to place themselves in the crosshairs of risk and uncertainty. What thus needs to be theorized is why many individual agents, who had no interpersonal knowledge of each other's ambitions and motives, were collective willing to speculate to a degree that would not have been possible, perhaps even imaginable, just a generation earlier. Collectively and repeatedly willing to speculate to the degree that they instantiate to this day a liquid market in speculative derivatives. What is happening is both historically specific and socially general to our geography, which means that theories that ignore the social and historical cannot enlighten. These accounts, which hope to explain the episodic irrationality of seemingly rational agents, are too often little more than surface-level descriptions dressed up in the vocabulary of theoretical insight.[2]

The chapter seeks to clarify the cultural ground of this mentality of speculation. The suggestion is that this willingness, deliberate and collective, stems from the matriculation of a speculative ethos: a socially circulated sensibility that has come to permeate and shape our attitude towards risk. This ethos has evolved as a concept, a disposition, a stance toward the world, a measure of self-interestedness, which motivates agents to want to wager on the uncertainties of the future. The sheer actuality of the capitalism we now experience seems to foreground a social order which is objectively infused with risk at every turn, with the opportunity to assume more in the management of our lives and in the way we play. This speculative take on the real appears to those it touches to be reasonable and useful because it reflects the actually existing state of capitalism. Not least a financial system in which the participants, the finance institutions, the media, the Federal Reserve, and most of the field's scholastic avatars valorize speculation, depicting it as a social good which arises at the intersection of creativity and courage, innovation and self-confidence. And so a dialect of speculation has been set in train, a dialectic of structure and subject which appears as a self-reflexive correspondence between our dispositions and compulsions to risk and a society increasingly objectively based on risking together.[3] The argument is that speculating with derivatives represents a new way of staging uncertainty that calls for an ethos that values and valorizes speculation. And that this ethos is the surface form of a sociostructure in which risk taking appears as an objective, necessary, and impersonal requirement of getting along in the present conjuncture.

This speculative ethos, the sense that capitalism as its best is driven by those who entrepreneurially, competitively, and often creatively face down uncertainty and take risks in pursuit of economic (and symbolic) profits. This appears on the surface as a concept of speculation (which may, for example, be given a legal definition) and as a recognized psychological impulse. This ethos, while general to financial capitalism as this historical conjuncture, attains its most advanced expressions in the play of the derivative. Here, the speculative ethos owes its logic, practicality, and coherence to the fact that the culture of financialization—with its emphasis on competitiveness, cunning, and compensation—determines the speculative character of the bets that agents willingly, often outright enthusiastically, make on behalf of improving their fortunes, literally as a capital gain and symbolically as a star among one's peers. The high-stakes derivative wager epitomizes the speculative ethos because it stages a visible head-on collusion between the deliberate and accidental, between a culture of calculation and the epistemic opacity of chance.

For derivative traders, the speculative ethos appears as an impulse that orients their immersion in and sensibility toward the market. The ethos mediates the relation between speculation as an abstract principle of the derivative market and speculation as a practical occasion for participation as a shareable sensibility. The mutually comprehensible fear and anxiety of the speculative trade is what recruits community into the market (a reality that no methodological individualism can ever entertain). Thus constituted, the speculative ethos connects the particular participants in this market, here, now to the ensemble of anonymous, similarly-sensitized others waiting on the sidelines. Its existential shape is twofold: as an awareness that is subject to reflection and remark, usually a concern for the precarity of a trade (as in "that was a speculative trade that could have gone sideways") and as an embedded disposition that unfolds in the immanence of the work of trading, trade by trade, day by day. Such speculation does not simply occur, it occurs in a social world designed for and by it. Machines, models, laws, the ladder of positions and powers within firms, that is, the socio-technical assemblage which constitutes the machine of trading, institutionally mediates the expression of traders' speculative impulses. The sociotechnical assemblage in its self-determinate function to cannel and constrain traders' speculative impulses cannot help but recognize the centrality of the ethos. And thus also the contradiction of trying to limit a disposition whose exposition is a condition of the market's reproduction. The social spatial organization of Wall Street's most iconic investment banks play out this recognition and contradiction: on the highest and most prestigious floor of the building are the traders who speculate, whereas a firm's risk managers and accountants dwell on a lower and less prestigious floor, the difference sometimes (as was formerly the case at Morgan Stanley and Goldman Sachs) given an exclamation point when the two levels are only accessible from separate elevators.

A peculiarity of the present—peculiar in that the turn toward the wager would have shocked many earlier generations—is that speculation has a fan base made up of reputable citizens. Those earlier generations cared little about the technical economic merits of speculation. For they lived at the tail end of a long Christian tradition which condemned speculation as the ungodly worship of money.[4] Konings (2015) observes: "In premodern Christianity, the critique of speculation was subsumed under the condemnation of the love of money" as reflected in the distinction between money as a *means* of supporting church and household and money as an *end* in itself (p. 254). The lustful pursuit of money led to the debasement of our human spirits. Money was a sterile inert object that could not grow and multiple by its own authority such that worshiping money challenged God's monopoly of the power of creation. As le Goff (1988) notes, the most blasphemous form of speculation was money lending because it sought to appropriate and profit from time itself, something that was a gift from god and belonged to him alone. Even with the advent of capitalism, in which money was consecrated as a critical desire of the economic order, it remained immoral to speculate. Speculation was important as a dark boundary, a border separating the mundane from the profane. And so it came to pass that speculative behavior represented an inflexion between the concrete and the abstract. Concretely, the distinction represented a line that should not be crossed while, at another more abstract level, it was a principal and contested stake in the production socially of the difference between moral and immoral. The argument appeared as a spread of historical positions whose volatility was constrained by its grounding in the sacred. Its message was that speculation cannot help but court sin and depravity because there are only two possible outcomes: either the bettor lost money and deprived his family and church of funds that God intended to nourish them or the bettor won money without the merit of work and at another's expense to their family and church. The supposition that underwrote the doctrinal argument against speculation was the existence of a use-value economy constituted as an enclosed culturally homogeneous community; a supposition that contradicted the directional dynamic of capitalism in which the treadmill like amplification of "relative surplus value" (Postone 1993:307–314) turned out to be a driver in the globalization of once national regimes of production.

One of Marx's signal contributions was his insistence that capitalism advances an approach to the world. Capitalism bespeaks not only a specific economic program, but an equally specific social epistemology. The recent evolution of this approach has been an expansion in the breadth and depth of what we count as economic. Set squarely within this expansion is the neoliberal economic celebration of the speculative ethos as a means of maintaining liquidity in the face of volatility—for only agents who are willing to go out on a precarious limb will trade a volatile market capable of huge cascading price swings that can instantaneously "blow up" a position. But the very act of market making, because it is economized as spreads whose bands are elastic, discovers and foregrounds the state of agents' uncertainty just as their act of price taking, above or below the previous calibration of the derivative, releases the hounds of volatility. The turbulence this generates appearing in the widening of spreads, thus producing an amplification in volatility and in the intensity, the foreboding, of the uncertainty. The high wire of speculation centers on the profitability of volatility so long as uncertainty does not desecrate liquidity. For presently, speculation is dampened not by a fear of God but by the absence of buyers. One of the worst mistakes associated with commentators who use greed as a one size fits all epitaph to curse the perpetrators of the crisis is that it fixates our attention on a blind desire for money and thus conceals the fact that because winning the game is the name of the game one of the most distinctive mental ticks of most traders is their hypervigilance about the risk that some unknowable risk will appear out of nowhere. The practical reality is that some risks are well-known, some are possible but hopefully manageable if I am properly hedged, while others are terrorists that blindside: that is the reality that every speculator knows and trades.

The point about many earlier generations aversion to speculation suggests that the financial institutions that speculate and the agents manning them are relatively new phenomena. Indeed, these agents occupy what are historically emergent positions in financial space, exemplified by the derivative trader for a hedge fund or for an investment bank's proprietary trading desk. Only in the 1970s did these positions even begin to take shape as up till then citizens and their representatives deemed speculation as something which needed to be prohibited legally because it was so repugnant morally. Even a benevolent god would not condone *money for nothing* (as Jackson Lear's title elegantly put it) and its not-so-implicit renunciation of work. Work meaning the jobs of a labor based production-driven national economy. However, notwithstanding these views on speculation and work, the forces of globalization were ramping up and with its ascension a host of problems that centered on managing the effects of interconnectivity. The business of globalization that disrupted fixed exchange rate regimes between nations amplified the frequency and suddenness of currency volatility making it more difficult to do business globally. The coming out party for the concept of speculation was, arguably, the document that Milton Friedman created for the Chicago Mercantile Exchange in its quest to convince Federal regulators that a derivatives market was good for the economy. The report, *The Need for a Futures Market in Currencies* (1971), argued that free efficient markets drive prosperous economies and that financial derivatives would make these markets even more so. Friedman's argument was that in a capitalist economy the market is the only worthy religion and that speculators and their willingness to assume risk is the grace that renders markets liquid.[5] Friedman remade the sinfulness of gambling into the gift of salvation in a world now beset by global currency volatilities. What is more, the world was ready for the message. The ascendant post war generation of economists, a new band of corporate executives whose strategy for enhancing profitability turned on outsourcing to emerging markets, a new class of investors whose economic philosophy fixated on shareholder value, and government regulators increasingly recruited from the new generation of economists (George Schultz, the Treasury Secretary when Milton Friedman submitted his report, had been his acolyte at the University of Chicago) all concurred with this new view about speculation and speculators.

Since that launching point, the evolving position of derivative trader (or quant or risk manager) is the result of the cumulative and volatile history of a financial space driven by derivatives. For the agents involved, the disposition to speculate seems to be inscribed structurally, in the very conditions of their employment, their advancement, and their self-realization. As interviews with traders clarify, to those in the finance of derivatives, expressions of this speculative impulse appear to be rational, coherent, and immediately intelligible. Think of an inspired composer sitting at a piano. In his head, there is the background music of the compositions he has heard recently, those he admires exerting, cumulatively and more or less subconsciously, a magnetic pull in their direction. His composition, whose aim is originality and creativity, nonetheless resembles theirs in ways compositions from an earlier generation do not. The composition is also implicitly guided by the preferences of the marketplace and invariably constrained by the inherent limits of not only the piano (e.g., the range of the keyboard) but that piano in its particularity. Even for music composers, who are the outliers and fat tails on the curve of creativity, who archetypically assemble their songs in private rooms far from anything resembling a market, there is a common, precognitive, relational sensibility which seems to implicitly steer their practice in the same direction. By contrast, that derivative traders participate in the very same markets, wagering directly against one another, and define competence and competitive success in the quantifiable and exposable measure of money, overdetermines that they will share the speculative ethos. This logos is the unconscious of finance. The speculative trade is the action that having the same sensibility for those who execute the trade as for those who observe, assess, and may respond to it, attributes no significance outside of itself. For those who risk the trade, the market is entirely understandable on its own terms, except, of course, that it is unaware of the genesis and inculcation of the speculative ethos that helps condition this self-transparency.

Somewhere in the distance this investigation ends with the observation that the speculative ethos is emerging as a critical, cutting, and capricious edge of EuroAmerican capitalism. Since the shocks of 1973, this idea—which has long been present as a strand of EuroAmerican culture—has been matriculating into something more powerful: a socially valorized ethos instrumental in structuring the design and practices of everyday life and the financial field. While others have surely joined in, the transatlantic connection between the United States and English financial communities seems to be the spearhead of the ascent and circulation of this ethos. As far removed as possible from the "depression' generation, the crisis is a symptom of the shift toward speculation as the new normal. So the techniques of speculation—borrowing, leverage, the fabrication of exotic derivatives—are mimetic of what those who have been financialized take to be the real operations of finance and asset management. A speculative life world, a central feature of financialization, is one in which each individual is condemned to decision making under uncertain levels of uncertainty, and to thus precarity and insecurity. Note that those who champion the work of speculation have, to compensate for our precarity and loss of security, gone to extraordinary didactic and theoretical lengths to convince, justify, and market a financialized vision of success. So we have commercials of couples strolling in the park or horseback riding who can retire early and on their own terms, with only bright days ahead because they have embraced the ethos that wagering on the financial markets is the key to prosperity.

The Concept of Ethos

What then is an ethos? Much less one that valorizes the act of speculation as an objective necessity. The concept of an *ethos* derives from the ancient Greek term for those dispositions and sensibilities so deeply instilled in a people, so definitive of their being and behaviors, that they were indistinguishable from their species being. In his *History of the Peloponnesian Wars*, Thucydides turns to the term ethos (and also nomos) to capture the fundamental differences between the Spartans and Athenians (between those whose souls are steeled to the earth and those that are surrounded by the sea). In his work on the relationship between capitalism and religion, Max Weber (1905) argues that "the ethos of the rational bourgeois enterprise and the rational organization of labor" is a natural fit with the ethos of Protestantism: for this ethos aligns the "profit-motive" with "the will of God" (p. 26–27). His qualification is that an ethos does not *cause* behavior nor is it a mechanistic determiner of behaviors. Rather, it is a collectively held and collectively circulated approach towards economic action that exerts a gravitational pull on agents, but which is also always subject to circumstantial influences. In contemporary social theory, Clifford Geertz (who takes his theoretical cue from Weber) maps the contours of an ethos. Geertz says that a people's ethos embodies and conveys, through their practices, "the tone, character, and quality" of their sociality (1973:126). It reflects the agents "underlying attitude toward themselves and their world" and is reciprocally constituted in respect to it (Ibid.). For those involved, the ethos appears "intellectually reasonable" because it seems to reflect the actual state of the world to which it refers. An ethos "has the air of simple realism" because it speaks to the congruence between agents' dispositions and sensibilities and those called for by the practices they participate in (Ibid.). The ethos is a culture's approved style of life, which embodied as dispositions and propensities to act in a certain way, mediates the relationship between the structures of a (financial) field and the opportunity of events. Between, for example, a derivatives market in currencies and an opportunity to profit from a fall in oil prices by speculatively shorting the ruble or going long the euro (or better yet shorting the ruble in euro terms).

An ethos thus names the cultural dimension of a people's most widely valorized approach to the world at a given point in their collective history. An ethos, such as the speculative ethos, appears in practice as a specific interest, such as augmenting my wealth by buying and selling (flipping) houses. An ethos counts because it often spurs agents to move beyond inertia and indifference, and to take an interest in, for example, the play of the real estate market or, correlatively, that of collateralized mortgage obligations. The ethos spurs those under its influence to learn and deploy the generative schemes (e.g., applying leveraging) essential to participating in these markets. It spurs agents' inclination or propensity to set aside their reservations—because what they are doing is valorized by the "fact" that others are doing precisely the same thing—and become so fixated on the rewards their speculation affords that they bracket the risks. Not least the risk of trading from the non-knowledgeable standpoint of the future's uncertainty. What is hard to appreciate from outside finance is that traders are both hypervigilant about risk and willing to chance it precisely because of the unknowability of the future. Metaphorically speaking, navigating a tightrope two inches above the ground is a meaningless act, no matter how successfully accomplished.

An ethos, as Weber sought to explain, is self-valorizing in that its collective endorsement (by, for example, those who are financially astute) proves that it is good and meritorious. An ethos exerts a gravitational pull on the subject that helps translate the relationship between a market (such as home mortgages) and the strategies generated by that market (e.g., subprime mortgages sliced into tranches) into a propensity to act (e.g., to assume outsized risks). The notion is central because it allows us to understand that an ethos, in the case at hand the speculative ethos, can embody an immanent economic logos that stands beyond, and is accordingly never reducible to, the calculus of maximizing one's utility. Though noted throughout the text, it bears repeating because it forcefully cuts against the grain of both economistic and popular accounts: what needs to be explained to explain the 2008 crisis is the genesis of acts of speculation which are anything but consciously rationally sensible (especially if one of the basic goals is the long-term financial health of the individuals and institutions), but nonetheless seem eminently reasonable to those involved. For it is hard to imagine that those homeowners who are upside down on their mortgages or those hedge fund managers that went from hero to zero, either successfully maximized anything or acted without reasons. The reason it is not easy to uncover this relationship between subjects and markets is that the relationship is transformed by its own activity into a transaction between a calculating subject and an object (i.e., the trade at a contractually determined price). The easy part is to show how prices determine agents' speculations, the hard part to show how the concatenation of things social set prices speculatively.

It is worth noting that interactionist viewpoints, weather by behavioral economics or various ethno-methodological approaches, by whittling down the social to assemblages of calculating persons interacting on a contractual basis, eliminate theoretically and in advance precisely what everyone who has been in a long term social relationship—with their parents, children, spouse, friends—knows from experience to be true. We continually make decisions under uncertainty that appear reasonable, rational, and in line with prevailing sentiments, but are hardly the mechanical result of a consciously implemented, rational maximizing utility logic. The reason is that while we sometimes monetize the "things that money can't buy" we also know that certain things are not things at all but relations. And as such, our sense of self-worth, the solidarity of friends, our commitment to those around us (think of soldiers in combat), the satisfaction of taking a risk and proving our worth by succeeding, the love of our children are singularities. We simply can't be perfectly rational because there is nothing to measure the rationality against. The ground zero of every social theory is this: can it account for the appearance of collective singularities without resorting to some extraneous typification device: such as the positing of a perfectly rational agent or quasi-omnipotent determinative structural forces.

Speculation, Time, and Risk

Speculation flourishes: appearing as a noun, verb, and adjective. But most of all speculation is a disposition, present in some form in every culture and then given an overt, specific, and highly amplified form by capitalism. More precisely, a successive set of forms tailored to, and instrumental in, the evolution of capitalism. What defines the present conjuncture is that speculation has crystallized into an ethos (in much the same way that Thucydides claimed that the asceticism of Sparta was so strong that it came to name its own ethos, i.e., Spartan). The objective form of the speculative disposition is risk, as when individuals' actions unfold across an interval, the actions themselves defined by the spread between what agents consider as compulsively prudential vs inordinately chancy. These terminals do not roam free, but appear at a specific time and place. The main arbitrage of capitalism—the generation of surplus value—always turns on the speculative disposition to invest capital, labor, and time in expectation of a forthcoming payoff. Thus chancing the tangible risks that the product in question will never see completion, or fail to reach its destination markets, or encounter an unexpected destruction of demand (as when a particular good is suddenly revealed to be particularly bad for one's health). The chanced variance across this interval that agents' anticipate through the application of the generative scheme built up from their experience and learning is its implied volatility. This generative scheme goes by the name of risk management, though what it actually manages is agents' estimation of the uncertainty generated by the production of information that can only ever become knowledge retrospectively. What the market tell us over and again is that the participants can never know certainly the actual level of speculation prospectively because, among other things, risk management is always about quoting a selectively chosen past. The fact that speculation is always about a forthcoming that traders conjure and enframe on the basis of their past experiences reveals the extent to which it is inseparable from time.

Speculation has two time signatures as risk. There is an intratemporal dimension that defines the risks consequent on making, moving, and marketing the product, and there is an intertemporal dimension that is the continuity of the systemic conditions which allow for production, logistics, and the market(s). So what defines the financial crisis is a level of speculation, actually the collective expression of the disposition to risk-take, that created the conditions for the collapse of both time signatures even though the overall economy was not imperiled. Until, of course, it was. Speculation can exist in both time registers because it corresponds to two spatial registers: risking together as constitutive of social life in all its dimensions from work to play (and also ritual), and risking competitively as constituent of derivative markets. For risk to have such a central place, there must be something like a speculative ethos whose origins go back to the inauguration of capitalism and the creation of relative surplus value, but now under the sign of the derivative matriculate to an entirely other plateau. What is clear is that speculating with derivatives based on the abstraction of risk represents a new way of staging uncertainty that calls for an ethos that values and valorizes speculation. To the point where risk taking appears as an objective, necessary, impersonal requirement of doing well financially.

The face of the present is Janus: looking toward the practice of everyday life is the financialization of the commodity relations that served as the basis of our security (most importantly, our homes, education, health, and retirement); looking toward the practice of financial markets is the ascension of derivatives and the forms of abstraction, logic, and motivation they endorse. As to where this Janus-faced sociostructure may appear, no imagination is required: the present housing crisis will suffice, with its creation of derivatives (collateralized mortgage obligations) that sliced and diced bundles or tranches of people's re-mortgaged homes. The compulsive leveraging impulse of SIVs accelerated and amplified the leveraging of houses. Houses have come to name what homes become when they become nothing more than financialized assets put into service as the underlier to the two speculative dimensions. The speculative ethos thus turned homes into a speculative asset class, as we learned that our homes could be treated as emergency bridges connecting where we are now financially with where we long to be.

The speculative ethos did not materialize from empty space. The ethos has a sociogenesis in the necessity and volatility of decision making under uncertainty when a recognized value (such as money, status, or godly reward) is at stake. It is present in the foundations of the Protestant ethic, even if that ethic was adamant in its condemnation of gambling. On this point, which speaks openly to the rituality of the social in its service as an underlier to the epistemology of capitalism, there is more to say. For now, note that the speculative ethos derives from and conjoins two narratives that have permeated American culture. The first narrative extols the virtues of taking a chance, especially the willingness to accept risk, to have the fortitude and fortune to chance the odds, in order to improve one's lot in life. This narrative implies a social and financial universe in which uncertainties rendered as probabilities matter greatly. This is a "covered wagon" narrative, ideologized in and personified by the pioneers searching westward across a vast unknown landscape laden with risk and reward. The second narrative assumes that agents can master chance and subdue probabilistic outcomes through knowledge, skill, and hard work. These character virtues allow agents to arbitrage the future, to turn a riskless profit by offsetting uncertainty with hard-won knowledge and well-honed skills so that their decision making is mercifully true. This is the "settler" narrative in which fishermen or farmer have come to understand their terrains so intuitively they can anticipate the landscape and thus offset its uncertainties (unruly weather, for example). This spread, from the culture of change to the culture of control, has always been present, always subject to the arts of mediation as the pioneers absorbed the new landscape and settlers risked planting new crops or expanding the fishing grounds. What served to further mediate and redefine the spread and conjoin the narratives was the ascension of science from the early twentieth century. This appears in pronouncements about how the application of the sciences—with their logical standards and evidentiary methods—can lead to more prudential decision making under uncertainty (underscored by game theory's development). This is a universe in which the self-disciplined agent can cultivate the technical skills to confront and profit from contingent phenomena in which chance matters. Read through the optic of Jackson Lears (2003), the derivative reveals what happens when the culture of control and the culture of chance are reassembled in a new way.

If we eavesdrop on the conversations of derivative traders it turns out that all the narratives are in play. In their narrative, traders are portrayed neither as gamblers nor as traditional bankers (who relied on lending money to long-standing, solvent, socially connected clients). Their derivative trades do not rely on the spinning wheel of blind luck or on the certainties of carefully cultivated social relationships in which the virtues of position and breeding outshine raw intelligence and gumption. For traders, their speculations lie at the intersection of a culture of hard work, mathematically calculated risk/reward ratios, their capacity to figure out the nuances of derivative pricing, and their willingness to bear the existential burden of an enormous wager. The speculative ethos draws from, and then amalgamate and amplify our native narratives in ways that make the ethos appear familiar, burnishing the concept that there is nothing unusual about the appearance of agents whose mission is to game the market volatility of abstract risk driven derivatives by leveraging enormous pools of nomadic, opportunistic, speculative capital. In this rewriting, their speculative ethos appears as a sensibility that is at once autonomous and at the same time the manufacture of the raw historical material made available in the culture of capitalism. The narratives, reshaped by a derivative logic that specializes in the art of dissembling and reassembling, seem to melt into one another in the practice of trading derivatives.

Interestingly, the speculative ethos sometimes hides behind itself. Especially the depiction of the derivative markets as rationalized, regimented, and above all calculative machines. This depiction, which is one perspective on this reality, forgets that trading is a practice in the most elemental sense of the word. As example, when caught up in the act of trading, traders cannot escape the impressions left by their most recent trades. But these memories do not appear as a series of self-subsistent pictures of their past. Rather, remembering engulfs them in a net of imbricated events such that the uptake from these experiences seems relieved of any rational calculus. The trader simply moves into the speculation or away from it based on his sensibility. Indeed the non-rationally grounded oppositional struggle between a trader's senses of greed and fear represents the financial commonsense of this uptake. The perspective of the ethos is from the interior of practice. Wherein derivative traders are craftsmen, craftsmen who inhabit the knowledge that they all funnel a complex reality down to one summary price. And then do so again in the acts of recalibration. That is their craft. This market making never apprehends the market from an analytical definition, which sees markets as founded on an unfolding of rationality or pure calculation. Though it is never thought this way in practice there is here a performative objectification of the real that defines the market as the site for the expression of the speculative ethos. The derivative is the anointed instrument for animating speculation. This speculative moment is by its evolution the incandescent point where calculation, agents' intuitions about what phenomena (e.g., Federal Reserve policy, the likelihood of margin calls) might affect the market's performance, and their gumption and willingness to challenge uncertainty are fused.

The notion of the market as a calculative engine that instantaneously digests and organizes new information is complemented by "educational processes" which inculcate the speculative ethos in respect to a view of how financial markets function. This view is encapsulated in the message circulated by financial channels, such as CNBC, which laud the desire for profit, inveigh against regulations that would limit speculation, and argue that speculation is inherently good for the markets and thus for the economy and in relay for the nation. The peculiar logic is that the speculative impulse is a character virtue that sets the entrepreneurs and the market maker apart from the normal run of humans. While anyone, anywhere can aspire to this virtue, and the media does indeed circulate model stories of immigrants (such as the founder of Interactive Brokers) who have come so that they might exercise freely their speculative spirit, it reaches its highest and most valorized form in the American character. Michele Carrara Caruso (a second-generation Cuban American), CNBC's foreign correspondent, often charge what she and the American financial media more generally define as "European socialisms" (e.g., France heads the list) with the crime of suffocating the speculative spirit necessary to drive capitalist markets. On this view, the speculative ethos is a national social good and an achievement of our character such that its endorsement is patriotic. No less important is the academe where the speculative ethos is being produced and legitimated through the reorganization of business school education and curriculum. The cornerstones of business school education have become the notions that the market is the best custodian of the American economy, that financial markets are inherently efficient, that (competitive) markets spur innovation as exemplified by the plethora of new financial instruments, and that speculation is both creative and necessary (to promote market efficiency and stimulate innovation). The redirection of business school education is also an instrumental part of the reallocation of intellectual capital away from industrial managerial sectors and toward the financial field. This reformation of the business school was part and product of a EuroAmerican shift toward the speculative; it assumes that there are agents who construct their subjectivity through arduous work regimes that center on the speculative acquisition of money. Two quick indices of this are the popularity of the financial program called appropriately enough *Fast Money* (CNBC) and the corresponding demand and availability of advanced platforms for speculative trading. Further, the recent trend is the creation of high-fee derivative wagers (e.g., binary options, the yen-dollar carry trade) that "ordinary investors" (translation: amateur, unsophisticated, small scale, home gamers) can participate in with a click of the mouse. The view is that anyone who can't speculate is at a disadvantage in today's markets because the serious money is made not from a company's progressive year over year increases in earnings, but from rapidly and repeatedly gaming volatility. The strategies proffered by the resident traders on *Fast Money* often involve extremely short-term (less than a month and sometimes less than a week), highly leveraged, convexity maximizing, speculative bets on high beta securities.

The Origins and Influence of the Ethos

The instrumentality of the speculative ethos in the creation of the crisis is itself controversial.[6] And not without merit in that an understanding of its character would almost certainly help us determine its causes, institute measures to right the markets, and forge prescriptions to prevent future crises. At issue is whether the crisis is simply an outsized speculative bubble of the kind that has punctuated capitalism since its inception, or does the crisis represent a fundamental change in the way finance and speculation interact? Is there an emergent and symbiotic relationship between the ascent of the speculative ethos and the logic of the derivative?

Opinions are divided. On the one hand, we have accounts such as Michael Lewis's memorably written descriptions (e.g., *Liar's Poker*) of the rise and demise of an era of high speculative greed and duplicity, beginning with his salad days at the now defunct investment house of Salomon Brothers in the mid-1980s and ending with his dinner with its ex-CEO, John Gutfreund, at the height of the subprime implosion. Lewis's narrative, like scores of other exposes, turn on the unbridled greed and lust for the status that money brings; the players' overweening assessment of their investing prowess, exemplified in their own metaphor of the gunslinger; and the folly that our blindness for money seems to inevitably produce, if episodically, with each new generation of players so seduced by the lure of fast money that they discarded the lessons of the past. There is a message inscribed in the titles then amplified to a scream in the subtitles of exposé such as Faber's *And Then the Roof Caved In: How Wall Street's Greed and Stupidity Brought Capitalism to Its Knees* (2009), Morgenson and Rosner's *Reckless Endangerment: How Outsized Ambition, Greed, and Corruption Led to Economic Armageddon* (2011), Madrick's *Age of Greed: The Triumph of Finance and the Decline of America* (2011), Cohan's *House of Cards: A Tale of Hubris and Wretched Excess on Wall Street* (2009), and numerous others. The message is that the feted music of caching was so intoxicating that it motivated everyone to dance until they dropped.

On the opposite end of the spectrum, there are accounts whose concern is the arcane techniques and instruments of finance. For these accounts, speculative behavior is a natural consequence of the evolution of techno-instruments. This begins with exposes, such as that featured in *Wired* magazine entitled *The Secret Formula that Destroyed Wall Street*; it lays blame for the credit crisis on a formula derived from mathematical statistics, known as the Gaussian copula, which bankers used to determine the risk and set the price of pools of collateralized mortgage obligations.[7] David Leinweber *Nerds on Wall Street* (2009) argues that there is a strain of pocket-protected, C-compatible quants who blithely engineered financial technologies whose real-world crisis effect was beyond their power of comprehension. The legendary financier George Soros has weighed in with a post-Popperian critique of the efficient market suppositions[8] of modern finance (2008), while Nassim Taleb (2008, 2012) has used fractals and the notion of the "black swan" to attack the statistical foundations of financial risk (mis)management. And what are we to make of Emmanuel Derman's work on *Models Behaving Badly* (2011), not to speak of the work in the science studies of finance, such as Donald Mackenzie's (2006) research on the social construction of arbitrage and the performativity of the Black-Scholes equation? So where speculation is concerned is there any trajectory that can unmask the connectivity between the "big swinging dicks" of Lewis's *Liars Poker* and "the masters of the universe" portrayed in *The Bonfire of the Vanities* with the quants and risk profilers of credit default swaps and the other complex derivatives? *The real question—greatly obscured by the opposition between model and behavior presupposed in nearly every account—is the construction of a spread between the cognitive model and the embodied ethos that the social practice of trading articulates and mediates. And does as a condition of its reproduction and the replication of the market's derivatives.*

Perhaps the best place to start is with context. More specifically, the social and historical context that serves as the frame and foundation for the evolution of the present financial community as part and product of what is certainly a more general societal transformation. In a quasi-historical article, appropriate entitled "The End," Michael Lewis suggests that the banking crisis and systemic risk spawned by subprime loans signals the denouement of an era of speculative reckless greed that had its origins in the 1980s, an era chronicled most notably in his *Liar's Poker*, as well as Tom Wolfe's *Bonfire of the Vanities*, Bryan Burrough and John Helyar's *Barbarians at the Gate: The Fall of RJR Nabisco*, and Oliver Stone's movie *Wall Street*. As different as these accounts are, what makes them so riveting is their portrayal of the existential implications of a *speculative ethos* so deeply embedded in the habitus of the financial community that it is transforming the character of financial work and the idea of a career trading derivatives. In these accounts there is also a palpable nostalgia for an imagined earlier time when greed, duplicity, calculativeness and speculation where not integral parts of one's work and work therefore did not cause the corruption of the person. Reflecting back over the twenty years since he wrote *Liar's Poker*, Lewis observes:

> I had no great agenda, apart from telling what I took to be a remarkable tale, but if you asked what effect I thought my book would have on the world, I might have said something like, "I hope that college students trying to figure out what to do with their lives will read it and decide that it's silly to phony it up and abandon their passions to become financiers." I hoped that some bright kid who really wanted to be an oceanographer would read my book, spurn the offer from Morgan Stanley, and set out to sea.
>
> Somehow that message failed to come across. Six months after *Liar's Poker* was published, I was knee-deep in letters from students who wanted to know if I had any other secrets to share about Wall Street. They'd read my book as a how-to manual.
>
> In the two decades since then, I had been waiting for the end of Wall Street. The outrageous bonuses, the slender returns to shareholders, the never-ending scandals, the bursting of the internet bubble, the crisis following the collapse of Long-Term Capital Management: Over and over again, the big Wall Street investment banks would be, in some narrow way, discredited. Yet they just kept on growing, along with the sums of money that they doled out to 26-year-olds to perform tasks of no obvious social utility. The rebellion by American youth against the money culture never happened. Why bother to overturn your parents' world when you can buy it, slice it up into tranches, and sell off the pieces?
>
> At some point, I gave up waiting for the end. There was no scandal or reversal, I assumed, that could sink the system.

Not only did the system not collapse under its own weight, not only was a new generation seduced by the apple of fast money, but the speculative ethos went global and percolated down through the pores of the production economy. The yesterdays of corporate pensions, state-assisted education, a citizen oriented financial system, a government whose mission was to provide the public goods necessary for our common social welfare (such as infrastructure and unemployment insurance), gave way to a present defined by its own financialization. More, a culture of financial speculation driven by ever growing amounts of speculative, nomadic, opportunistic capital ascended in New York, London,

Chicago, and Hong Kong, and collaterally in other cities like Singapore and Sydney, in the process compelling central banks across the globe to readjust their worldview to this new financial connectivity. Especially central banks in emerging market democracies needed to arm themselves with dollars to deter speculative attacks on their currencies. But the thirst for speculation was not confined to finance. From Las Vegas to Sun City to Macau, we witnessed an explosion in casinos, on-line gambling sites, and games of chance, especially poker in its live and video versions (Schull 2012). The very speed of the expansion and the ease with which this speculative impulse took hold of our reality and imagination raises the question of whether there's more a stake socially here than a financial speculative outburst.

Explaining Speculation

Most analyses of the why of the financial crisis fall back on an induction theory; namely, that greed induces blindness. Accordingly all that is required to foment a crisis is a catalyst and greedy agents willingly and collectively throwing money at a bad investment/speculative idea. Historically, the most usual choice for catalyst has been an excessive expansion of investable income, the excess unable to find a decent home. In the case of the technology bubble [2000] and housing crisis [2008] the catalyst is purportedly the Federal Reserve's overly accommodative monetary policy. Which allows our animal spirits to gnaw doggedly and voraciously on the extraordinary sums of available cash running through the economy. The insatiable hunger for more and willingness to speculate appear here as essentialist, built in dispositions thereby masking the social and economic conditions for their realization as dispositions that are specific to capitalism, and, at a more granular level, specific to the incarnation of circulatory capitalism. So the induction theory cannot imagine, let alone specify, the global dimensions of capitalism because it brackets the actually existing structures of what lies outside of political economy. Missing is the space of a capitalism instrumental in defining a planet composed of an increasingly fragmented set of increasingly interrelated parts. The induction theory is seductive because it replicates our ideology, relying as it does on the errors and sinfulness and vanity of individuals. But it doesn't drop the line very deep into the well of understanding. It reduces sociohistorical context to immediate catalysts and the collective compulsion to speculate to the inherent tendency of individuals to bow to greed. The theory projects into the minds of traders the model devised to account for their behavior. In reality, speculation taken to the borderlands of destruction depends on a collective excess of faith, on the participants' shared belief that they are on to the opportunity of a lifetime. That the reward is worth the risk and that someone else's present success speculating predicts my forthcoming success. In the age of mimicry—wherein an internet accessible by smartphone circulates strategies at the speed of sight—"if he can be successful, why can't I." Every interview with those who wagered on tranches of CMOs or speculated by flipping houses confirms that the ability to act in accordance to others served to valorize those acts. Every success is living undeniable proof of the strategy, and so though I episodically entertain the thought that the carousel of ascending prices will end abruptly, that time is somewhere ahead beyond the forthcoming of the present trade, the end that I fear continually propelled into a future whose existence has only the same abstract imaginableness as the carousel of my own inevitable death. I recognize that the playing field is not fair. There are a small cabal of investment banks—epitomized by Goldman Sachs whose suckered tentacles have become fastened around the neck of finance—who accordingly do not simply adjust to the market's volatility, but have the firepower, the inside "dope," and the rumor circulating machinery to reconfigure volatility in their own self-interests. But I am "too small" to be on their "radar screen" and there is always the chance I will be on "the right side of a market" they are surreptitiously tilting in their direction. This prayer like thought represents something like the apostle's creed of small investor/speculators, small being highly relative insofar as it encompasses everything up to "smallish" hedge funds (less than a billion dollars under management).

The speculative is about the collectivity rather than about individuals' impulses and initiatives. The subject who is willing to take large monetary risks can do so only on the condition that others are willing to do so, and that those counterparties who encircle the speculative subjects agree explicitly or tacitly on the course of action. The question the induction theory ducts is why at this particular moment in the history of capitalism has speculation gone mainstream. This ethos permeates the subjects as a disposition that is instrumental in their self-fulfillment; it represents a claim on a new means of valuing and valorizing the subject. And it moves what was once on the margin and thus outside the normative—the gambler who can both calculate the odds and has the stomach to chance the uncertain—to a station of centrality. Its secret promise is life heightened to the pitch of the perilous trade, then retrieved and made safe again thanks to the use of a careful calculus for managing risk.

The evidence suggests that the ascension and installation of a speculative ethos is precisely what induces and propels this faith. This ethos is, for traders, a source of comprehension. A relationship of immediacy and affinity attaches traders to the market. By virtue of being immersed in the financial field and being part of a market that is their space of operations, traders are from the beginning exposed to the speculative ethos as a condition of employment. Comprehension of the ethos is a regularity of the financial field and in a heightened form for those who make its markets. Agents are accordingly able to activate the generative schemes that realize the ethos even as they comprehend in a practical way the activation of these schemes by others. The speculative ethos that traders enact is thus the product of "the incorporation of the field" (Bourdieu 1977) and its markets into their trading strategies and practices. Traders presuppose the existence of the speculative ethos when they assume that everyone who trades—that is, anyone fit to be called a trader—intuitively comprehends the speculative impulse. How modern finance embeds speculation into the anatomy of practice is so important because it identifies why what would turn out to be systemically destructive behavior could seem reasonable, knowable, and necessary to those involved. That speculation inhabits the anatomy of practice also clarifies why the usual antimony of rational versus irrational has no bearing on the actual production of traders' behaviors. That is why traders frequently see deeply speculative positions, in which the principals go "all or mostly all in" on a particular wager and thus chance losing everything (Warren Buffett quips that hedge fund managers seem to forget that you only have to get rich once), as evidence of the traders' conviction and gumption not their irrationality or mental instability.[9]

Speculating about Speculation

In its everyday definition, speculation is the act of investing in assets (from houses to precious metals) in the hope of profiting from a rise or fall in their market value, with the knowledge that a loss of value is possible. Speculation involves an assumption of risk in anticipation of outsized gain while recognizing a higher than normal possibility of loss. The critical terms—terms that in finance often exist below the waterline of consciousness—are normal with its allusion to a statistical mean and risk which assumes predictable outcomes. Within the econometrics of finance both terms are deeply problematic socially, although unrecognized as such, which, functionally, imbues them with a patina of matter-of-factness which helps underwrite their credibility. The

notion of the normal, meaning moderate risk yielding moderate returns, oscil-
lates ambiguously between a statistical calculation by science, a transcendental property of species of financial instruments (e.g., derivatives as a type are
risky; AAA corporate bonds are safe), and a regularity that the participants
glean by virtue of their immersion in the market. Within finance, this spread
of possible meanings or referents is constitutive of the term and, by extension,
the term speculative (and also what counts as conservative). The basis of this
invisible spread and the ambiguity of its use stems from the reality that finance's
modus operandi exorcizes from these concepts the principles of their production, such as the influence of a speculative ethos or (as noted earlier) the
performativity involved in typifying a financial instrument.

Similarly, the notion of risk inhabits the same space. Risk appears as a statistical calculation, prominently in a financial institution's assessment of a
portfolio's value at risk. This mathematical computation is meant to define the
portfolio's level of speculation in order to predict the maximal cost of failure.
Finance also apprehends risk as a substantive property of classes of financial instruments. The idea is that risk is an essential property of certain instruments
the same way quadruped is an essential property of certain mammals, such as
horses and dogs. This essentialized risk may be offset, by hedging for example,
but such risk is a contingent property of the instrument much in the same way
color is a contingent property of mammals (i.e., a horse is still a horse irrespective of its color). This transcendent view is the flip side of the supposition that
finance can decipher and disarm risk by reference to a formal equation. The
final dimension is that actual market makers also and necessarily apprehend
risk as an immanent regularity of the practice of trading. Being in the middle of
the market, with money and everything that that entails on the line, they must
reintroduce the properties that the essentialist definition vacates in order to
gauge the actual speculation (what we might call real-world value at risk). They
cannot ignore the actual operations of the market as preconstructed data that
can be set aside in the interests of mathematizing a transcendent object. For
example and importantly so in respect to the crisis, market-makers in assessing
a position's level of speculation cannot set aside things like counterparty risk or
an impending surge in interest rates. In sum, the culture of finance constructs
a concept of speculation which implies the creation of abstract essentialized
notions of risk and normality (e.g., the mean) hovering above (in some intellocentric space) a behavioral notion of speculation as a practical inescapable
element of market-making under uncertainty. What a social perspective would
recognize is that the tools created to formally quantify speculation in no way

implies the adaptive capacities that market-makers need and acquire in order to assess risk and the level of speculation situationally in a constantly transforming market. To think that this quantitative measure captures the speculative is "to slip from the model of reality to the reality of the model" (Bourdieu 1977:29). For finance transfers the objective measure calculated by the risk model into a strategy for derivatives trading, which by its nature as a practical strategy, pays little attention to the objectivist stance that underpins the formal quantification of risk.

As the flow of events illustrate even in the long aftermath of the crisis, nothing exemplifies the speculative allocation of capital more than financial derivatives, since they represent wagers on the relative volatility of the relationship among the underlying assets. Derivatives take speculating to an even higher power when they are bets on the volatility of volatility itself (for exchange traded derivatives options on index future). Speculation as a cultural form serves as both a *model of* agents' actions insofar as it describes an identified regularity and as a *model for* behavior insofar as it guides or influences agents' actions. Derivatives are the near perfect technology of speculation; for they unite and raise to a higher calling all of the powers of convexity and leverage with the market hegemony of controlling enormous dark pools of capital. In terms of a prospective trade, speculation turns on the estimation of the position's risk, both in itself and in respect to an agent's or firm's entire portfolio. At the level of trading even the most mundane asset classes (e.g., stocks, bonds, commodities), participants tend to classify a position as speculative if, in their judgment, the prospects for the trade's success are chancy and/or that given the size of the position—that is, the value at risk—the speculator (such as a hedge fund) would collapse financially if the trade failed. Investing, speculating, and gambling differ critically, but most importantly as a spread in which the reclassification of a trade based on its outcome (what initially appeared speculative turned out to have little volatility) represents a retrospective reading, itself founded on the double performativity of classifying this token trade as an identifiable type and then reclassifying that trade retrospectively. This spectrum or spread constitutes an ideology of knowledge in the sense that one can only know retrospectively whether a specific trade was an investment, a speculation, or a gamble. Traders capture this reality in the saying that a long term investment is the name for a speculation gone south (especially one that has become illiquid). The key reason is that we are never able to know prospectively and with genuine certainty what the sources and degree of uncertainty or risk actually are. Any investment is, in other terms, a speculation on the sources and degrees of uncertainty, risk, and thus financial peril that may eventuate over the lifespan of a given investment. This observation would seem to suggest that it is best to consider all financial derivatives as spread phenomena which are tilted toward the speculative insofar as they are instruments expressly designed to discover and monetize risks they are instrumental in producing.

One way of approaching speculation is to ask what sort of wager would be non-speculative. What is the limit of speculation and how is it constituted? The answer is pure arbitrage, which are positions which profit from differences in price when the same financial instrument trades on more than one market. In such a transaction, an arbitrageur might, for example, simultaneously buy one gold contract on the New York market and sell the same contract on the Chicago exchange at a slightly higher price, thus locking in a riskless profit because at that timepoint the price of gold on the Chicago market exceeds that of New York. What pure arbitrage does is capture the market's volatility, but uses simultaneous trades to insulate the position from the risks posed by future volatility. Accordingly, when there is volatility without a temporal dimension, a position in question can be profitable while non-speculative. The other non-speculative situation is when time is elongated but there is no volatility. There are no risks involved, for example, in holding for however long either one currency or another as long as the exchange rate is fixed. Here the duration of time may be relatively long, but the absence of volatility nullifies the potential risks. This situation also presents a real opportunity for arbitrage when the price of the same good in one country is different than the other. In the archetypical case, what differs cross-nationally is the price of money itself. If the exchange rate between the US dollar and the British pound is fixed and British interest rates are higher than those in the United States, traders can turn a riskless profit by borrowing in dollars, exchanging dollars for pounds, and then lending those pounds out at the higher interest rate. What traders see as their "riskless profit" or arbitrage is, of course, the difference between interest rates in the two nations.

It is worth observing, perhaps parenthetically, that in Marx's mature account of capitalism, value is a labor power arbitrage. If arbitrage is, as indicated, taking advantage of simultaneous *and* differential pricing of the same commodity, then it follows that surplus value represents an example of a commodity that possesses two differential values. The first value is the socially necessary average, the second is the surplus created by the greater productivity of a new productive innovation. The capitalist-owner takes advantage of this difference to generate a profit, even as his actions narrows his advantage as other capitalists imitate his productivity enhancing methods. What this suggests is an underlying ontological connectivity between production and circulation-centered capitalism in that both forms take arbitrage as reference points. They are by no means the same type of arbitrage, but create and reflect a pivotal difference between production and circulation-centered economic activity. The first centers on arbitraging value as abstract labor time; the second seeks to arbitrage price as the objectification of abstract risk.

For the financial markets, speculation is the relationship between temporality and volatility. The greater the volatility over any duration of time the greater the risks incurred; similarly, the longer the duration over any projected level of volatility, the greater the risks incurred. So the management of risk thus turns on either compressing time so that financial positions are established and terminated in as close to simultaneously as possible—what is pure arbitrage—or the prospects for volatility (e.g., in the price of a currency) are minimized by hedging. Hedging is a strategy which offsets risks by assuming a position in a futures market equal and opposite to an existing position. The willing, instrumental assumption of risk or speculation is the luminous area in which markets and their players bring volatility and temporality into a calculated relation of gain and loss. Anthropologists have noticed that something like this is also true in primitive exchange, the clans' members must calculate the volatility present in their social relationships against the timing and tempo of a proposed transaction.

Speculation is thus based on an assumption of risk that turns on the creation of a relationship between an objective, such as winning the pot or consummating a successful derivative transaction, and the chances for a position's loss or gain imposed by volatility and time. Critical to all speculation (as opposed to pure chance as with a lottery) is as aspect of calculation in which participants seek to discern and manage risk. This calculus may, often simultaneously, have an overt referential dimension and an indexical dimension rooted in the participants' habituses. For example, referentially, national reserve banks and multilateral agencies such as the IMF and Bank for International Settlements presume that "fair value" predicated on nations' relative economic performance determines the exchange rate of two currencies (e.g., US dollar against Brazilian real). Indexically, speculators attempt to read sociofinancial cues (e.g., the magnitude and suddenness of real selling) so that they can wager often gargantuan amounts of capital that a cross currency rate will diverge mightily from "fair value." To understand just how this calculus is grounded it is necessary to deconstruct the semiotic hierarchy embedded in acts of speculation

Every speculative wager begins with the instance or token event. The acts are intrinsically unique at the level of the singular event in that it is always possible to identify differences. But the determining question prospectively is weather and to what extent these differences make a difference. What is interesting is that it is all but impossible to identify and therefore manage the risks posed by the singular event. People can capture singularity only meta phorically. To identify and manage risk the event or token must be typified. The agents must define the token event as an instance of a type. In order for the agents to induce the calculation, they must—to borrow the philosopher linguist Charles Peirce's term—grasp the token as an "indexical icon" of the type. The relationship of the token into the type must appear to be transparent— so transparent that the act of classification must appear as little more than a formality. Accordingly a singular derivative may be typified as a currency swap which then allows for analysis through a mathematical model tailored for such swaps. These acts of classification often appear to be preordained and hence non-negotiated because the agents involved created the token as an instance of the type—thereby prospectively bracketing differences between all the singular instances. What makes the indexical iconic function that important is that it is a template for allowing these token signs to instantiate what they self-reflexively represent themselves as typifying.

But there is more to the understanding. What is interesting and telling about the identification of a token as a transparent instance of a type is that the calculation of the risks incurred depends on the presumption of an encompassing totality. To put this from the other direction, for the calculation to go through there must be culturally and/or formally created parameters or limits to the token events that can occur. Let us provide an example form the financial markets. They offer a clear example because they seek to mathematize the pricing of their instruments, such as currency or commodity options. As noted, the method used is one or another variant of the Black-Scholes equation. All of these are variants on partial differential equations designed originally for modeling the dispersion of heat molecules within an enclosed impermeable space.[10] For the equation to meet its own internal requirements, and thus for us to have confidence in its outcome—it must occur within a self-contained and closed space, that is, totality.

For participants in the financial markets, the totality posited is that of a discrete and efficient market. The assumptions underpinning the mathematical derivation of a derivative's price embody this notion of totality. The baker's dozen of critical assumptions includes a no arbitrage clause, the bracketing of counterparty risk, the presence of a perfectly liquid market, and the absence of transaction costs or other forms of what might be called systemic[11] or exogenous friction. The positing of a secure, enclosed, and self-efficient space guarantees two key results. First, it decouples the forms of risk from their generative contexts, so that the risks fomented by a political party hostile to free market capitalism (i.e., political risk) or a nation likely to be destabilized by a citizens' revolt or a belligerent neighbor (i.e., country risk) can be treated like, and aggregated with, other market centered forms of risk, such as the risk that price volatility will affect a leveraged position's collateral requirements. This decontextualization thus allows agents to bundle and price incommensurable forms of risk, producing what we have analyzed as *abstract risk*. Second, positing a self-efficient totality allows derivative pricing models to assume that all instances are indexical icons of the type. It creates perfect transparency from a token existential instance, exemplified by a specific currency wager (e.g., dollar vs. yen), to the typified form so that the derivative can price the projected volatility of their relationship on the grounds that that derivative's future volatility will typify (i.e., fall along the curve) the past volatility of that relationship. We can now understand that if the technology of risk centers on convexity and leverage, the object of speculation is the *volatility function of abstract risk*. The critical point is that the surface form of speculation appears as fluctuations in derivative prices, the deep structure centers as the volatility of abstract risk— that is, agents' price interpretation of the variance created by the changing matrix of incommensurable risks.

We can see from this that the logic of speculation is three dimensional. In the first dimension, it must posit a social ontology in which the instance always takes place within the confines of a totality. The rupturing of this totality—that is, through systemic risk that dissembled the totality—would alter the speculative outcome dramatically. In the second dimension, the logic of speculation holds that the agents can identify the risks created by a position. The move from radical to delimited uncertainty turns on an agent's being able to accurately identify the worldly sources of risk and then aggregate these risks into a single determinable value. Nonetheless, the discernment of the risks involved and thus steps toward pricing cannot occur at the level of the instance or token. The token must be typified. Such typification is inherently speculative, although the speculative moment is veiled and misrecognized because it is so easily normalized and concealed by the very process of typification. Suppose a trader desires to price and to speculate on a specific (token) OTC derivative.[12] To do this technically, the analyst needs to calibrate the pricing model to real historical market data. This is done by using a chosen ensemble of "vanilla" (i.e., exchange traded) market instruments' prices (such as the MERC's euro-dollar contract and its T bill contract) as inputs to the model. The trader then configures the model to price all the input prices, which is then used to price the token derivative.[13] A singular derivative can thus be typified in respect to a type, which may (and in practice usually is) itself a hypostatized aggregation of several types (such as a credit derivative and a currency derivative). That this mathematized configuring is an accurate reflection of the real world is an aspect of the speculative moment. Consider also that using stochastic differential equations canonizes the typification of the token because the fitting of the token to the type is the condition of the determination of a derivative's price, without which a market would be impossible. The final dimension of this logic is that the circuitry is secure. The assumption is that because all the participants are mutually invested in the field and because the derivatives contract is a legal obligation, counterparties do not pose a risk.

The trinity token, type, and totality constitute moments of objectification created in respect to processes of circulation. They appear, however, not as provisional, perspectival instantiations—that is, moments of objectification that are temporary and organized from a socioeconomic perspective—but as pre-constituted forms that appear to exist prior to the act of circulation and to be organized from the top down. The token appears to be an instance of its type which, in turn, is part of the constellation of totalized types defined by the overarching totality. The dialectic is that agents in the financial markets, will fabricate a unique exotic derivative (e.g., linking fixed and variable interest rates) using a generative scheme derived from their knowledge of the type (e.g., credit swap) even as they simultaneously classify the singularity produced to that type. On the second level, agent's predicate their creativity in creating the indexical icon (e.g., credit swap) by presupposing the objectification of the type. The agents' presupposition serves to objectify and, in the process, totalize the type, thereby stabilizing the type in the face of circulatory process that always threatens to undermine its iteration of form. Put differently, that critical social forms have to existentially incorporate and adjust to *otherness* (other ideas, people, goods, situations, etc.) creates the necessity of stabilizing the type by presupposing its pregiven crystallization as a condition of the token's production.

The Speculative Ethos at Play

Let us begin by capitalizing on the observation articulated by a host of theorists beginning with the pioneer sociologist Max Weber that sports play and commerce while seemingly different on the surface, join hands at a deeper and more profound level. The argument is that both commerce and games that combine chance and calculation, speak to an epistemology of social life—an epistemology of the social that they capitalize on and help inculcate. Which is a form of social life in which the concrete forms of actions, objects, and practices conceal their similarities at the abstract level and thus the common mission of apparently distinct fields and forms in the construction of the social. Indeed, we can better understand the speculative ethos in respect to the ascension of the derivative and the financialization of everyday life if we tour, however briefly, the cultural politics of poker. Is it any coincidence that many hedge fund managers/derivative traders are avid to the point of compulsive poker players?[14]

There is a certain, shall we say speculative, reading of the present moment: that this moment is enfolding within a social habitus whose signature act might well be what in Texas Hold'em is known as "the flop"—the point at which the dealer turns over (or flops) three common cards for those who have survived the first round of betting. In the act, the game elevates to a typically more ferocious and intricate level of speculative intensity, a level so captivating that more people are participating and watching far more often. Incredibly, the World Series of Poker has been the fastest growing "reality" show on US television since its debut in 2004. Currently, one or another poker tournament is broadcast every day of the year, expanding to eighty-three countries and counting, making these tournaments the most widely circulated "sporting" events in the world. Trade journals on the stock and bond markets, beginning with Barron's front cover (of its February 21, 2005 edition), carry titles such as "Crazy for Poker," which feature articles about the extraordinary rise of casino and on-line gambling stocks, asking as in the Barron's case the question about where investors should hold'em for fold'em. Articles routinely appear on the front page of the *New York Times* detailing how poker had spread into teenage suburbia (2004), flourished in the ivied halls of Princeton (2005), captured larger streams of advertising revenue (2006), and developed a worldwide following to the point where most of the recent winners of the World Poker Tournament are from Europe or Asia. What is clear is that speculation has gone public and global.

Welcome to what has been called the poker nation—as its citizens only quasi-metaphorically referred to a community whose self-defining act and determination is the risk driven wager. It is perhaps reasonable to conceptualize the ascension and in the process valorization of this virtual community as a foregrounding of speculation though a new social imaginary: the poker nation. This community of players has been providing itself with an institutional grounding, but what defines it fundamentally is the circulation of a shared understanding and habitus, a mode of circulation which the presence of the internet and its plethora of "official" sites amplify. What I am suggesting is that there is the imagined community in which each poker game becomes a microcosmic instance of an encompassing poker macrocosm, much in the manner that Anderson (1983) describes acts of reading as engendering the imaginary of a national peoplehood or the way acts of buying and selling aggregate into the market. One way of grasping this new imagery is as an aspect of a post-millennial pop culture. Another way is as an advertising gambit aimed at luring people into indulging in gambling tournaments and on-line sessions—both of which are proving rather lucrative for their investment backers. But these observations, however accurate, do little to explain why at this moment gambling and speculation have come out of the back room and assumed such a visible and marketable place in the public sphere. Another, more socially attuned, way of appreciating this emergence of the poker nation is as an unveiling or auto-revelation. Namely, that tipping point at which the emergent habitus of risk taking and speculation becomes conscious of its own immanence and as an aspect of the unveiling objectifies that habitus in games that reproduce within a fixed finite event, like a poker tournament, a forum for speculating and risk-taking. The suggestion here is that the social imaginary of a poker nation reflects and reproduces at the level of entertainment a deeper transformation in the character of capitalism. Not just capitalism in the abstract, but the capitalism that sustains us as people, the economy in terms of which we define ourselves as worthwhile goal directed subjects. The suggestion is that as the speculative ethos infiltrates the various domains of life, this saturation will valorize the ethos until it becomes so deeply embedded in people's perspective and dispositions that they come to think of the ethos as an inevitable and immutable part of the way people are "naturally."

There is little new about poker as one of a succession of games of chance. For the Christian world especially, such games have long been pushed to the edge of social life, as exemplars of that sinful element of our psyche that enjoys thrills more than propriety and celebrates good luck and connivance over the more enduring and righteous virtues of hard rewarding work. But in the past quarter century especially the forces of secularization have overturned or at least diminished the force of this moral economy: instead, the habitus of speculation has become so normalized that, beyond financial circles, the risk driven wager is reemerging as a virtue, as something an economically efficient society should encourage as a condition of its continued prosperity. It is no historical accident that the Christian right's inventory of social issues places a premium on prohibiting gay marriages and abortion, but (judging from its main websites and the legislation it lobbies for) it no longer has anything important to say about two issues that have, historically, been its salvation: gambling and drinking. The virtue of speculation was the overt view of Alan Greenspan in the polices he advocated during an eighteen year reign as chair of the Federal Reserve, in speeches to key financial organizations, and in his congressional testimony. One implication of the popularity of this ethos is that speculation, once viewed negatively as symptomatic of an unseemly desire to gain profit without work, is being sanitized. And this appears to be remaining true even in the face of the outsized and disastrous risks taken by the financial sector. In the realm of public culture, it may even be that poker's popularity is advancing this sanitation process. The thinking is that as long as you don't cheat, then risk-taking and speculation are positive personal and social traits, a matter of calculating the odds, making a skillful wager, and then having the gumption to stand behind it. If there is a touchstone of speculative capital, it is its celebration of risk-taking—as measured in a derivative's *volatility* in respect to the *value at risk*. These terms mirror what in the poker universe players refer to as the *stake in the pot* (or value at risk) in respect to the *pot odds* (or volatility) of winning the hand.

But how we should ask did gambling, exemplified by the ascent of an imagined community of poker players who, judging by recent online statistics, now number several million worldwide, ever become a legitimate practice and profession on an increasingly cosmopolitan public sphere. How did gambling—traditionally impugned as illegal and reprehensible morally—ever become both legal sanctioned and moral justified. As Weber's classic implies, the notion of speculation (and thus of speculative capital) pits the basis of capitalism against the ideals of Christianity, a confrontation that has been present from the original linkage between mercantile capitalism and the reformation. How does capitalism's ambition to speculate coexist with religion's antipathy toward what its distain for worldliness considers the wanton and wasteful use of hard-earned money? It should be underlined that wagering is intrinsic to capitalism. Capital expands because producers speculate that their immediate reinvestment of surplus value in designing and creating products will meet with consumer demand. There is a measure of speculation in that given the time lag between conception and consumption of a product, consumer tastes may so change that the product realizes no surplus value. The speculative aspect of capital has also, historically, been misrecognized in that a distinction was made between wagering on production, which was referred to in a positive moral tone as investing in real economic goods, and wagering and profiting for its own sake with no ambition of amplifying production, which was known as gambling. It is worth recalling that in the 1960s and early 1970s congressmen, federal regulators, and social activists castigated and rebuffed initial attempts to develop a financial futures and options market because they viewed betting on money as nothing more than gambling, which had no positive social merit. Nevertheless, within only a few years the speculative wager had become not only a sound but "morally cleansed" practice, such that imagined communities which embody the aims and dispositions of the speculator go from marginality to the very center of the public sphere? Winner take all and no limit poker tournaments are televised on ESPN, the Disney-owned channel for games that merit the appellation, sports. Just as it is possible to win or lose a baseball game, or place in a golf tournament, so it is possible to win or lose a poker tournament or finish in a certain money position.

More than coincidentally, the ascent of poker chronologically parallels that of the derivative. In the 1971 World Series of Poker, held in a back room of a Las Vegas casino, Johnny Moss bested five professional players, each of whom had anted up $10,000. Moss's winnings were $30,000 with the rest laddered among the runner-ups. By 2008 the series counted some 6,400 players competing for a prize pool of $64,000,000, with a first prize of $9,000,000 and a bracelet, which has become the most coveted award a player can win, outstripping even the prize money. By 2015, there were a plethora of other tournaments (currently some sixty-five) in addition to the World Series, plus an official specific World Series tournament for each continent (e.g., World Series of Poker Africa), not to mention a poker academy and a real money online gaming site (Harrah's Entertainment, Annual Report 2014). The key to these tournaments arousing the popular imagination globally is that the rules of Hold'em are a variant on already known games and that, like the housing market, they offer ordinary persons with no special skills other than calculation and courage the opportunity to speculate and win large. Anyone willing to put up the entry fee (usually $10,000) can have a place at "the table," speculating on the entry fee giving one access to a world in which speculation reigns supreme to the point where one can go "all in" with the lowliest hand imaginable. *The Table* is a portal into a democratic microcosm where one's social station, accumulated riches, or previous victories are irrelevant and thus a special place of play and performance where anyone with the "right stuff" can potentially topple the professional Goliaths of the field.

As alluded to above, the poker game of choice for the expression of an expanding global speculative impulse is called Texas No-Limit Hold'em. A relatively obscure game until its recent effervescence, it draws together and heightens to a peak the speculative, individualistic, and also existential dimensions of wagering against others. Historically, it's a variant of seven-card stud: each player is dealt two cards, followed by an open ended round(s) of betting. Then three common or community cards are dealt face up (called the "flop"), with another similar round of betting. Two more cards are then turned up sequentially (called "fourth street" and the "river"), each followed by a round of folding and betting, with the best five-card hand (e.g., a full house or flush) winning. The no-limit designation refers to fact that at any time players may go "all in" and bet everything they have, compelling the other players to either match them or fold. In tournament play, like the Poker World Series, losing this all or nothing bet results in elimination. Johnny Moss, who captured the first two World Series of Poker championships, summed up the difference between Hold'em and the other, formerly more popular poker games by asserting that "Hold'em is to stud and draw what chess is to checkers." The novelist and aficionado of high-stakes poker, A. Alvarez, vividly portrays Hold'em's existential force: Hold'em is "a game of wits and psychology and position, of bluffing, thrust and counterthrust; it depends less on cards than on skill and character and courage" (Alvarez 2001:44). Essentially, in the guise of a game, sport, and entertainment the design of Texas Hold'em publicly articulates the speculative ethos by organizing the collision of the practices of calculation with the illegibility of chance. It should not surprise then that poker, especially in its speculative all-in form, dredges up existential issues so often cast in idioms that range from religious to sexual.

So embedded in this speculative framework is the possibility of pure statistical calculation, especially among the best players. Each of them calculates (and knows that the other players are calculating likewise) what poker players refer to as "pot odds"—the ratio of the amount of money presently in the pot to how much more money they need to put up to continue playing—and then compares this ratio to the implied odds (implied volatility) are of winning the hand. Note that the calculation depends on tying a token instance of a particular hand (such as two pairs) to the larger probabilities of hand distributions. At the start, no one can know with certainty that they have the winning hand (referred to as the "nuts," with its full sexual connotation), so given the underlying uncertainty of what the turn of the cards will bring, the optimal strategy is for players to position themselves in respect to other players so as to have the best prospects of winning the pot with the minimal amount of risk. Even in this measured context (there are no black swans), risk is multilayered, which includes the chances of losing the money wagered in this specific pot, the chance of having one's stake so diminished that one's betting options become more limited, and the ultimate risk of elimination altogether. For expert players, the optimal strategy turns out to be an improvised mixture of hedging and speculation, playing "tight" and bluffing. What expert players appreciate is that what makes them invest so heavily in the game is that Hold'em is not about the distribution of cards (which, because the game is a closed system, will in the long run produce an efficient market in hands) but about the speculative construction of their subjectivity. More, the logos of poker parallels that of high finance and the culture of financial circulation: a completely secular, global, and edgy lifestyle founded on executing enormous, highly leveraged wagers based on a composite of mathematics-like reasoning and intuition, and then being able to marshal the guts or fortitude to stare down the possibility of loss.

Conclusion

Crises clarify social reality, and this time around is no different. Decisive, deeply inscribed aspirations and senses of the world—what, following a rich tradition in the social sciences we can call an *ethos*—moved agents and institutions to pursue wealth, social status, an exciting life, and self-esteem by means of speculation. This speculative ethos came to define the cutting edge of finance. The ethos fed on, and was fed by, a beast of its own design: gargantuan pools of nomadic, opportunistic, mobile capital whose sole purpose was speculative. The ethos motivated, and capitalized on, the innovation of creative and increasingly complex instruments for agents' speculative wagers. The participants willingly, eagerly invested an extraordinary quantity of intelligence, training, their dearest streams of desire, and often the fullness of their beings in fabricating all manner of speculative deals. This speculative ethos has an invisibly social importance because the ethos is part of the essential clockwork of the crisis: traders' shared motivation for risk-driven transactions, the willingness of even the informed public to see speculative behavior as unremarkable, and the complicity of regulators in their celebrating speculation. Though the epicenter of speculation was finance, there is also something more broadly popular cultural, rooted in our history, about our appreciation for the art of the speculative.[15]

One of the gaping holes in financial theory is that it uses a simplistic concept of motivation that does not come close to honoring the complexity of real human motives for actions. In the rush to the mathematization of finance few have listened, but the pioneering Chicago School economist, Frank Knight, argued right from the start that its concept of motivation was too cognitive, too primitive, too individualistic to account for the collective behavior of agents such as intellectually sophisticated, mutually competitive, morally neutral derivatives traders (1999). If analysis is to apprehend the generative schemes that motivate agents to speculate, it is necessary to grasp the frame in terms of which they see and situate themselves. What this requires analytically is that we grasp the gravitational force that collectively held beliefs, values, and dispositions exert upon them. This requires, in turn, concepts explicitly designed to reveal the inclination, propensity, willingness of agents to actualize and normalize leveraged, risk driven transactions. At issue is what made these speculative deals seem reasonable, even laudatory, because they actualized a mode of work valorized across the financial field into the popular imagination. The notion of a speculative ethos has the virtue of allowing analysis to capture what has turned out to be an incendiary amalgam of collectively held sensibilities, viewpoints, aspirations, and drives.

This speculative ethos, certainly in its current incarnation, was not always so. It originates in the early 1970s—1973 being the most useful starting point—and progressively emerges as the ethos that underwrites the intercourse between pools of speculative capital, speculatively oriented institutions (e.g., hedge funds and proprietary trading desks), and the innovation of derivatives (synthetic CDOs) that would orbit further and further from the underlying reality they modeled. This ethos is an ensemble of sensibilities, viewpoints, aspirations, and drives so generative of financial practices that it appears to be an intrinsic, irremovable element of the field itself. That, at least, is how the ethos and its results are presently understood. I have argued that the ethos is articulated in agents' internalized generative schemes for financial action, inculcated through informal rites of initiation (such as helping a firm's senior partners consummate a deal), and serves as a turbine of inspiration for agents' innovative creations (e.g., creation of synthetic debt obligations). From a social theory standpoint, the speculative ethos is inherently relational. It does not have a fixed meaning: rather, its meaning is stabilized by the way it is activated and deployed practically to shape agents' behavior. And then again through the regimentation of participants' accounts of their behavior. About this space of unbridled speculation there is a rote understanding that the dominate sign is money in all its flash and power. Less understood is that the sign is money raised (and then re-raised) to its fully generative, collective symbolic and affective powers. A speculative ethic has been present since the very dawn of capitalism: but the ascension of circulatory capitalism and financialization of the economy allowed this ethic to matriculate into a consuming ethos. What to that point had been a sin worthy of the condemnation of politicians and popes had somehow become a virtue worth celebrating from ministries to monasteries (literally, see Lewis 2010). Somewhere along the line Weber's prudential German bankers morphed into masters of the universe.

The crisis clarifies another reality: while the speculative ethos no doubt reached its apotheosis in the financial field, the ethos had deeply infiltrated both popular and scientific culture. Each according to their means, formal economists, financial commentators, and government regulators valorized the ethos (i.e., risk taking) as instrumental in the vibrancy of capital markets and thus the fundamental health of an economy increasingly founded on its financialization. Long the spearheads of creative/destructive capitalism, the United States, followed by England, most deeply embraced the speculative ethos upon which circulatory capitalism rests. At the financial end of the spectrum, the speculative ethos coded in highly leveraged derivatives; at the popular cultural end in the practice of cash out mortgages and "flipping" houses and condominiums. More, in the acceptance by even those who did not speculate that speculation was how money quickly becomes wealth. For its part, the media contributed in the ethos' popular acceptance. As the shares of mortgage brokers such as Countrywide soared, it came to portray the legendary value investor, Warren Buffett (Berkshire Hathaway), as an avuncular dinosaur who once ruled the world of investing but who was too constitutionally risk averse (couldn't evolve a speculative ethos) to prosper in the new environment. That, at least, was one storyline during the gun-slinging days of securitization and leveraged buyouts, when the profits and share prices of investment banks including Lehman Brothers and Bear Stearns seemed on a perpetual upward slope toward the northeast quadrant of their charts.[16]

Historically, EuroAmerica has seen speculation as bad, then virtuous, and then ambivalently during the crisis. From the bleachers of the financial field, especially from spectator/players in the quick twitch electronic anxious to affix blame (elsewhere) for the economic carnage precipitated by the crisis, terms like speculative excess, speculative greed, insatiable speculative appetite, and speculative rampage slipped easily from their collective tongue. The castigation harkens back to what is apparently a bygone morality, a Christian backbone that condemns speculation as a flaw of failing souls, fallen from grace. But the shelf life of the condemnation had a rather short expiration date. So the market for hymns to speculation that had once filled the airwaves crashed in 2008 along with finance only to be resurrected by 2010–2011, albeit with a slightly more reserved enthusiasm about the good of speculation. As noteworthy is that the cast of the condemnation always assumed that the speculative ethos is a permanent and necessary feature of financial capitalism. Especially the view from players who officially pose as spectators is that speculation, like food, sex, other temptations, requires an inner ethic of temperance and restraint. Used in moderate dosage, government regulators and the financial press see speculation as an essential element in the wellness of capital markets and the economy.[17] And thus implicitly the ethos that motivates speculative practice.

The view from the center, that is, the view of traders themselves, is that they were participants in a real life game, a space of action which was designed to mix calculation with gumption. Here is what a few had to say:

> Looking back I have some remorse [about the housing debacle] because I was there at the center [of the CMO market]. But everything was geared to drive the deal as hard as possible. The only use of a synthetic [debt obligation] is to speculate; why else have them.

> Money was pouring into the market in torrents. Everywhere you looked, deals were being booked, and I naturally wanted my share. What the public doesn't or can't understand is that risk taking is an art: you win because you figure out what the risk factors are, but there is always the fear that something could blindside your position, blowing it up.

> Speculation is what financial markets today are about. Without the deal, unless there is real money at stake and your savvy and balls are on the line, then buying and selling bonds is like buying and selling shoes. Everything [about the economy] is about money; except trading: it's about winning, power, and not being bored.

The presence and power of a speculative ethos also shines through the many, multi-intended accounts of what happened. From talking with traders, Charles

Gasparino (2009) reports that they are driven existentially by "the ambition to make more money than" their competitors. "But to do that you have to take— and love to take—risk" to the point where speculation is "part of the trader's DNA." What everyone knows is that to win you must be entirely willing to "take more risks, borrow more money, indulge in more leverage, and make bigger bets then the guy sitting in the adjacent cubicle" (2009:84). This ethos was so dominant and collectively shared, that "nearly every firm created a system in which risk taking was rewarded to the extreme" (2009:497). Speaking of the now departed Lehman Brothers, Vicky Ward (2010) explains: the derivative traders who "forged the culture of the new Lehman Brothers could not have been more different from the polished Lehman partners of the 1970s." "They were street fighters, traders who had no time for. . . . snobbish bankers who wore fancy suits" (p. 17). Lehman's Chairman, Lawrence Fuld's "general directive was to 'do as much business as you can: take risks'" (p. 159). As importantly, the story of the great wave of speculation does not come to an end with the crisis or with the demise of once renowned institutions, such as Fuld's Lehman Brothers. These untoward events only drove speculation underground, the techno-assemblage for making risk driven derivatives was not dismantled but reinvented. It was taken apart on the margins by the passage of Dodd-Frank, but that was temporary as Dodd-Frank's teeth are being pulled out one by one in the re-legislative process.

The outcome of a speculatively driven finance was supposed to be different: more economically salutary for all involved. Knowledge, elevated through expertise and formalized through modeling, was supposed to engender a world where speculation was translated into enhanced markets, and departures from the mean tamed and contained by the precision of mathematical prediction. But what is clear, as the crisis underlined through its cascade of catastrophic consequences, is that a speculative ethos creates both a logic of action and a legitimating sensibility that made what turned out to be the leveraged, all in bets appear reasonable, familiar, and, in the context of an extremely competitive financial industry, necessary. The speculative foundation of speculation is that financial markets have the wherewithal to animate and enhance the volatility that they deem to master and profit from materially. This ascension of the speculative, based on an economy of the knowledge of the future, portends a shift in the process by which societies live their lives. A shift in social reproduction. For if we now produce speculation in such abundance that it is beyond being harnessed, absorbed, or turned to our collective ends, how might it set in crisis our habits of being together. The threat is this: what if the aggregation of speculation allows risk and uncertainty to become a force of their own beyond our controls. This excess of speculation is a mutual loss of control over the social, a mutual indebtedness from which there may be no relief. Speculation implicates each of us in the lives and works of one another, whether that is our collective intention or not. There is a crisis of speculation in markets predicted on making speculation so serviceable and available that we can join with the financial media and conceptualize it as a social benefit. Speculation is the psychosocial impulse that motivates market-makers to render the forthcoming actionable in the now. In summary, the notion of a speculative ethos allows us to apprehend the inner social movement of markets not readily detectable by economistic approaches.

Chapter 8

The Social Habitus of Financial Work

I believe that Lord God created Wall Street.

I believe he got his only son a job at Goldman Sachs.

I believe that God has a plan for all of us.

I believe my plan involves a seven-figure bonus.

I work on Wall Street. And Wall Street just believes.

—Sung by financial executives at a dinner of the Wall Street fraternity KAPPA BETA PHI, quoted in Roose 2014:211

The true mark of a theory of the crisis is not that it can explain why stupid people do stupid things; but that it can explain why intelligent and skilled people harness their intelligence and skills to do something stupid. — EDWARD LIPUMA 2015

This chapter attempts to develop an account of subjectivity that is adequate to our explaining what motivates the trading and market making of derivatives. Not least the compulsion to take on enormous speculative risks in pursuit of the endless and always insufficient accumulation of capital. The thesis is that we can understand the market and its crises tendencies only if we develop an account of the forces that generate agents' real-world motivations. Toward this end, the chapter articulates an account of the social habitus of financial work and its evolution of a *monetized subjectivity*.

One of the peculiar features of finance economics is that it resolutely avoids any description, let alone theorization, of the financial workplace or of financial practice as a sociospecific type of work. The supposition behind this omission is that the markets are composed of rational, utility maximizing, actors whose actions are, consequently, context insensitive. The economistic view adheres to this conceptual arc. Because rational agents invariably sell assets when prices, even by a modest amount, exceed fundamental value (as determined by asset pricing models that assume perfect price discovery) and, conversely, invariably buy when prices dip below fair value, there is no need to investigate the financial workplace or how the social history and design features of financial work (such as trading currency or mortgage derivatives) might inflect their decisions or their decision-making processes. And more, do so in a way that is collectively shared and general to the financial community.

But there is no empirical evidence to support the proposition that underpins finance economics. Instead, the verdict of contemporary history is that even experienced, educated, professional investors can behave in ways that confound notions of rationality and utility maximization. The skewed view that trading is rational and cognitive is the end product of a recreation that retrospectively expunges the real-world force of agents' affect and embodied dispositions from the account. As well as the constraints imposed by the socio-structures of finance, such as the speculative ethos exfoliated by a firm such as Bear Stearns. Finance economics begins by dispensing with any analysis of the difference between the theoretical standpoint and the standpoint of those traders who are invested in, and have much at stake, socially and economically, in the game. This avoidance of work is also peculiar because the financial workplace and derivative trading represents a quantum change-up from what, until rather recently (from 1973), has normally been considered what bankers do for a living. This avoidance of work and the workplace has meant that finance economics is theoretically unequipped to tell us what we need to know to grasp the dynamic relation between financial practice, agents' motivations for trading, and the reproduction of financial markets.

For its part, the financial sector contemplates work only in respect to the actions necessary to make markets function and to consummate trades. Everyone's aware they are working but there is only tangential consideration of the social and affective aspects of the workplace. Agents focus their attention, serially on a day by day basis, on the practical and immediate. Not least on what the firm announces as that day's overriding directives and imperatives (e.g., offloading certain credit instruments), what when the book closes for the day are their P&L (profit and loss), and whether those whose evaluation determines their bonus are satisfied. Precisely because the workplace, work, and the market appear as pre-existing institutions, and agents grasp the act of trading as being intuitive and instinctive because the cognitive and motivating structures which animate their practice exist as embodied stances toward the market, financial agents conceptualize what they do as doing their job. Accordingly, like finance economics but for entirely different reasons, they tend to easily naturalize the social. The performativity implicated when traders generate and then trade a derivative tends to be erased as they realize themselves in the trades that they have produced relationally, and what, as contracts beholding to our contract ideology, take on all the appearances of inert things. Similarly, power, prestige, self-esteem, and the other symbolic rewards of work tend to appear as things over which individuals struggle for and with one another. The result is that the discourse finance creates about work reveals little about the relationship between the structure of financial practices, the motivations for trading, and the reproduction of the markets.

Yet, the ethnography of finance underlines that these issues are centrally important. Thus the necessity of exploring what would be the theoretical and thematic space for construction of an account of financial work that is adequate to this object. Central to this mission—which is itself one of the findings of the investigation—is the necessity of reconnecting the financial work to the more general and encompassing phenomena that is the function of work in the production of sociality and subjectivity. And correspondingly the implications of social relations and agency for the production of the work that is trading derivatives. This redirection entails restoring the (social) value rationality that economistic accounts expunge when they whittle down agents' desires and motivations to instrumental rationality, which reduces the complex layering of desires and motivation embodied in the workplace to nothing more than rational expression of a greed-driven calculus of monetary accumulation. This narrow notion of agency reduces it to a single state, purely cognitive, mechanically unfolding, belief desire model—a far cry from what the ethnography reveals. Grasping sociality and subjectivity also entails restoring agents' second order desires and motivations, predominantly their desire for better desires and the corresponding motivation to actualize in their lives this better ordering of desires (no doubt exemplified by the oft repeated desire to spend more time with their children). In the workplace, financial agents will have another modality of second order desires: to organize and manage the varied, conflicting, complex of desires embodied in the work of derivative trading, not least the management of competition, cooperation, fear, and libido. Agents' desire to organize and manage their desires precisely because they recognize, albeit implicitly and often with little reflexivity, that crucial aspects of their lives actualized through their work, namely the creation of sociality and subjectivity, are on the line.

The notion that work can be understood exclusively in terms of making money (to purchase commodities) applies only to the most menial constricted labor (such as cleaning toilets), and even then not always. The further agents move from forced "unskilled" labor toward work which allows for the construction of subjectivities, the more they cultivate an abiding interest in *their* work as a performance of *themselves*. The blinding levels of compensation dished out by financial firms tend to obscure this reality. Nonetheless, the symbolic profits associated with finance are so real that the layoffs and retrenchments precipitated by the crisis lead many to suffer a searing psychic disfiguration. This was especially true for those who worked for firms such as Bear Stearns and Lehman that were castigated publicly. The psychic disfigurement came about not just because of the loss of compensation, but because their work had evolved to become a locus of their being and their main source of sociality. Even those at the lower end of the financial pay scale, such as secretaries, back office workers, and messengers, engulfed by the culture of the firm, often conjoin their individual labor to the identity of the house, and in so doing contribute to their relative financial exploitation. Firms foster this conjunction through their self-congratulatory allocation of year-end bonuses to all employees (however small relative to management). An analysis of work should thus embrace the proposition that the closer one gets to the alpha employees, the more what is apparently subjective and symbolic becomes the reality that an analysis must account for to account for their reality.

Work and Identity in the Present

A noted feature of modernity is that work is about much more than making a living. Work is more than what most people do most often. Work provides organizing purpose and identity to the point where charting an individual career path is an essential element of the modern life plan. Theorists suggest that especially for the professional class, work helps substitute for the fulfillment once derived from family, friends, community, and church to that degree where agents depend on their jobs to be their principle source of identity and their mainspring of self-esteem and of self-investment (Ciulla 2000; Khurana 2007; Gamst 1995). There has evolved a definite design to the valuation of the occupation-based life plan. The general rule is that the more symbolic capital (e.g., educational and intellectual training) is required for admission to a given field, the more that specific work is about the creation of a career. It follows from this that work is, and it confers, a sense of belonging to those agents who inhabit a socially acknowledged field, with those fields that receive the greatest shares of economic and/or symbolic capital endowed with the most prestige. Within this frame, it is conditioned that agents' sense of self—self-worth, self-esteem, and self-positioning in the universe of social space—can become attached to their "earned" compensation, their named position (e.g., chief financial officer, hedge fund founder, co-director) and the success experienced in improving their positioning. Work as a constitutive element of their self-construction urges agents, indeed often drives them, to compulsively invest energy and hours in their work much longer than is necessary to make a comfortable living, support a family, or gain public recognition because what is at stake transcends income, access to worldly amenities, or even status: their work has become the epicenter of who they are to themselves. Their work—understood as encompassing their knowledge, intellect, gumption, and competitive spirit in practice—has conjoined with their self-understanding of who they are. Agents come to see their work as inseparable from, because it is the ground of, the production of the self. This produces the anomaly that it finds normal, even laudable, chief executives who choose to work the same number of hours as someone who is forced to work several menial jobs just to scrap by. This choice is best characterized as quasi-obligatory in that the compulsion to work is driven by a worldview that fuses corporate production to self-production. The single-minded, high-energy corporate executive, portrayed on CNBC and Fox, is the lead sherpa of this transition in the construction of the self.

This is the prevailing logic of the social practice of work for those occupations that command high economic and symbolic capital. This description, whose signature quality is an excess of self-investment, perfectly fits the character of work in the financial field. From an instrumental and interactionist standpoint, trading derivatives resembles gambling; what sets trading apart is not only its privileged place within capitalism, which is, after all, about the pooling and allocation of capital, but the enormous degree of symbolic capital and the opportunities for personal investment that have become attached to financial speculation. If there is an outstanding contrast evident from reading accounts of financial titans of previous generations (from JP Morgan to Warren Buffett) against the memoirs and interviews of the contemporary generation of derivative traders, it is that there is a change from the notion that my work's worth (as mainly measured by the shifting value of my investments) is an index of my business acumen and commitment to doing my best, to the notion that my work's net worth is who I am.[1] Leslee Gelber, formerly with Lehman's banking unit, speaks for many when, lamenting its demise, she asserts "Lehman was who I was" (quoted in Story and Thomas 2009:7). In the bleakest moments of the credit crisis, when the investment bank Morgan Stanley was hemorrhaging money and near death, the CEO John Mack refused to surrender his firm in a takeover because Morgan was who his employees were (Sorkin 2009:469–483). As one derivative trader put it: "I trade because if I didn't, I would not know who I was." So the identification between work and the self radiates from the statements and actions of those implicated in the speculative bubble.[2] But precisely what kind of work is it socially and economically whose purpose is to accumulate and allocate speculative capital to make big leveraged bets on market volatility through the fabrication and circulation of risk driven derivatives? What kind of work product is it in which the object produced is a contractual relation about the relative volatility (price swings) of another relation, such that profits are inherently nothing more than others' losses, be they deferred or transferred? As the financial economist John Kay concludes, the work that is derivatives creation and trading turns on an ensemble of arcane "behaviours very different from the norms of either everyday business or traditional finance" (2009:12). In essence, a EuroAmerican culture of capitalism in which circulation, especially the traffic in derivatives, has emerged as a cutting edge seems to be producing a new regime of work and a new species of worker enframed within a re-formed financial field.

The ascent of a culture of financial circulation is transformative to the organization of work. For EuroAmerica, circulation is fast becoming the principal means of generating profit which, in relay, indicates that it is becoming a principal means of generating compensation. Because the total surplus value attached to direct commodity production is ebbing away, while that associated with the circulations of capital, currencies, securities, knowledge, and technologies are increasing, there is a flow of labor away from commodity production and toward the forms of work that create the structure and content of circulation. Part of this reorganization is the diverting of intellectual capital—that is, their most highly skilled workers trained at their leading universities—into the financial field. More, the amplitude of financial circulation is transforming the geography of work. Financial work moves away from stand alone, territorially attachment businesses. So each site—such as London, New York, Chicago, Hong Kong, and Frankfurt—must internalize other sites as a condition of its position and position taking in a global marketplace. Those who work financially in these sites must be connected to and intimately aware of what those in other distanced venues are doing in a way that would seldom occur for those involved in what the citation above called "everyday business or traditional finance."

On both a relative and absolute basis, more people are working in finance. And more people understand work as the new work of finance. In EuroAmerica, the world centers for derivatives markets, the financial sector can now accounts for more than 25 percent of total corporate earnings, up from 20 percent in 1990 (Morgenson 2007), and, as importantly, the sector, fueled by the creation and amplification of new financial instruments, is projected to expand in the upcoming decades despite the 2008+ crisis. The advent of financial news channels, such as CNBC, Bloomberg, and Fox, which broadcast globally to more than seventy countries, amplifies the circulation of this notion of work throughout an increasingly cosmopolitan public culture of finance. The compensation paid to those in the financial field constitutes what had, since the genesis of a derivative market in 1973 up until the systemic implosion, been a growing share of the total compensation paid workers. And so more people understand compensation based on their experience with the financial field, including media circulated stories. Financial work is very different from everyday production based business because its agents do not produce a material good or provide a service that helps circulate material goods; it is different from modes of work (e.g., law and politics) that create the framework for economic activity; it is very different from traditional finance because its operations are only tangentially related to the allocation of capital to further production and distribution of such goods and services. The socially significant result is that the work that is designing and trading derivatives, in which workers do things which are remote from the real economy, increasingly inflects what we understand work to be. It pushes the compass in the direction of a speculative, short term oriented, individually compensated, morally indifferent, economistic work regime. This is especially the case because within the global field of power, the financial field occupies a dominant position.

One of the special characteristics of a financial field that features derivatives is that traders tend to be positioned in social space in a way that departs significantly from the conventional business model. We are all familiar with business—from General Motors to General Electric—in which the firm's agents are divided into management and workers, exemplified in production-centered capitalism by the distinction between managerial class and union members.[3] The distinction reappears in investment firms, such as Morgan Stanley or Goldman Sachs, whose social space is divided into management (e.g., CEO) and salaried employees, such as secretaries and accountants. But there are also proprietary trading desks which figure centrally in their success; its members some of the most envied and highly compensated individuals in the firm. These derivatives traders do not manage others and are consonantly not part of a firm's management in any conventional sense; nor are they workers whose specific tasks are assigned by management and then compensated according to a fixed schedule of salary and/or commission. Indeed, everyone connected to trading summarily dismisses the notion that they are a part of management, the question itself seemingly alien to their instilled sense that the kind of individuals drawn to trading do not entertain bureaucratic thoughts of managing others. Their interests always lie elsewhere, to the point where the relationships between those on the trading desks and upper management are rarely fluid and occasionally boil over into overt tension. Accordingly, it would seem that the trading sector occupies a differentiated and singular space of work specific to the organization of finance. Within this frame, individuals' connection and thus also loyalty to the firm stems from internalizing its culture through their participation in practices (e.g., exercising together and swapping information) that draw upon even as they engender the networks of relations that crystallize around trading.

To grasp the work of finance it is thus necessary to recapture the sociality of the dispositions and forms of rationality that orient what agents do. And to examine how these embodied dispositions and rationalities are organized and realized in the varied markets for financial action. Critical to this aim is an analysis of work as a means of reconstituting the financial field and markets through the works of its agents even as the field and markets objectified by previous works serve to define the production of the workplace, and orient the work done. An analysis of this order is inherently grounded in the enframing concept of *the socialized habitus.* The concept is critical because it moves analysis beyond approaches, that founded on a reification of the economic, cannot begin to honor the complex socialities constitutive of financial work.

The Deeply Socialized Habitus

Because work is intrinsically social and inseparable from agency, the concept of the habitus emerges as the intellectual technology that allows analysis to ground and enframe an understanding of work. The term *habitus* was coined by Max Weber (1918), deployed by Norbert Elias (1978), and foregrounded by Pierre Bourdieu (1977; 2000). Its importance stems from the fact that it relates the objective structure of a field to the subjective agency of its participants without having to bracket or simplify the complexities of this relationship (e.g., reducing the existential thrill of speculatively going all in to execute a short squeeze on a competing hedge fund led by a rival to nothing more than a cognitive rational decision). The habitus refers to the reality that the agents who inhabit a specific field, by virtue of their participation in that field, necessarily incorporate certain dispositions, sensibilities, value hierarchies, and generative schemes for thinking and acting. Agents incorporate the field's habitus in ways defined by the simultaneity and imbrication of the cognitive and embodied (meaning that belief-desire models of behavior are far too reductive to capture what agents actually do). These incorporated and generative schemes for thinking and acting allow the participants to be complicit in their endorsement of a worldview and ethos that, short of a systemic crisis, goes unquestioned as such. Put in Bourdieu's words, "the habitus is the mediation which causes an individual agent's practices, without either explicit reason or signifying intent, to be nonetheless 'sensible' and 'reasonable'" insofar as they are both consonant with, and strategically adjusted to, other's practices (1977:79). The concept thus allows analysis to apprehend the ways in which the field's generative schemes are durable because they are quasi-automatically and non-consciously installed in the subjectivity of the participants simply by virtue of them living and working and playing inside a fixed set of financial practices. For the structure of the derivative markets is present in the cognitive schemes agents call upon to apprehend and trade them. As Ayache makes clear in his descriptions of trading (2015), this financial habitus is *pre-occupied* by the markets that it interpolates, standing in a relationship of immanence to the act of trading. The present habitus of finance represents a specific way of entering into a relationship with the markets which emboldens agents to anticipate their course—to ride, for example, the waves of volatility and persevere gaps in liquidity (most often a widening of the bid-asked spread). Thus defined, analysis can configure work as intersubjective and a site of the constitution of the person-in-action, and capture the practical mastery agents gain of the workplace, while grounding that mastery itself socially. The concept of a financial habitus invites us to theorize work and the workplace as the space of the production of the dialectic between individuals' acts of trading derivatives and a derivative market as a socially imagined totality.

The Production of the Social Space of the Habitus

Once we acknowledge that finance entails a mode of work founded on a deeply socialized habitus, analysis is then in a position to construct the social space of the habitus' production. As the worksite of financial work, this space is at once the locus, medium, and historical outcome of agents' appropriation of it and the structure that structures future acts of appropriation. This workspace—whose presence far transcends the physical institutional dimensions of a firm's trading floor—is defined by a juxtaposition and hierarchization of positions, exemplified by the dominant position of traders in respect to risk managers, salespersons, quantitative analysts, and administrative (backroom) workers. This allows the construction of a social topology that maps the positions and their relative distance from one another, the enormous gap between derivative trader and backroom worker representing its apotheosis (notwithstanding that non-combatants, such as those who clean the offices, are invisible, unratified agents). As elsewhere, the organization of social space is often roughly translated into physical space, the roughness of the translation a function of the constraints imposed by having to do business (e.g., derivative traders are compelled to deal with the salesforce much more directly than with quants to the point where they may occupy entirely different floors reachable only by separate elevators). It goes without saying that high status positions are the recipients of high economic and symbolic revenues that they presumably generate. Insofar as the financial habitus incorporates this vision and division of space, it generates behaviors, such as speech styles between those who occupy different positions, that appear to everyone involved to be a natural result of the way things are. Put theoretically, because the generative schemes animated by the financial workplace are products of the workplace in which they are animated, agents experience the workplace as natural and self-evident.

A defining (though by no means unique) features of finance is that the production of social space is one of the space's primary stakes. A firm's positions are always in a quasi-schizophrenic state of collaboration and competition, the job of executive management to orchestrate this relationship. Agents compete singly for position with those they collaborate with over the position of positions: how the institution should valorize and thus compensate the respective positions instrumental in the function of the firm. So there is an internal struggle over what constitutes the criteria of contribution, competency, and thus compensation (inscribed in traders' self-interested proposition that they make the largest contribution on the basis of their special competency that cannot be duplicated, and therefore rightly deserve the lion's share of the compensation). This quasi-schizophrenic dimension appears in the firm's unending quest to socialize agents to attach their own agency to the collective agency (i.e., culture) of the firm, even as each agent is encouraged to find in the competitive, no-holds-barred, money-at-any-cost behavior of their peers, a ratification and legitimation of their own behavior. As arcane as it may seem, it is this quasi-schizophrenic dynamic, operating beneath the surface without any explicit coordination, that allows agents of firms like Bear Stearns or Lehman to collectively push one another over an edge that they can see, precisely because they are intelligent and skilled in finance.

It is of more than passing interest that the space of the production of the financial workplace lies at the intersection of work, ritual, and play. Though this is far from the conventional view, trading is a form of work that laminates play and ritual in that the act presupposes and its collective enactment constitutes a game founded on an excess of both uncertainty and motivation. The notions of work and play are conflated in the very idea that trading is a strategic high stakes game such that the exact dispositions which allow one to succeed at competitive games of chance, such as bridge and especially poker, are the same dispositions that define the successful trader and hedge fund manager (i.e., they run their own no limit poker tournament). The conflation of work and play also appears in extramural activities, such that the members of a trading group will socialize outside the institutional boundaries of work, drinking, eating, playing sports, and attending sporting events with one another, these activities seen an extension and entrenchment of the sociality of work and workplace, especially the forms of collaboration amidst competitiveness that create a winning team. So much so that the participation of individual members is often at best only quasi-voluntary, absences eliciting no negative responses only when there is another compelling obligation (informants specifically cited weddings and bar mitzvahs). Recall the opening moments of Jillian Tett's work (2008) on JP Morgan in which she describes a carnivalesque retreat at the Breakers Luxury Resort in Palm Beach, Florida. The gathering tightropes between ritualistic quests for camaraderie and mutual belonging to a storied institution, and a violent sense of competition toward one another, other divisions of JP Morgan, and toward their competitors. The rituality of practices that commingle work and play is a foundation for the partial, provisional, and perspectival totalization of the trading group. What makes this significant is that derivatives trading presupposes the "collaborative" group that the act(s) of trading brings into existence and that the corrosive force of competition is on the verge of dissolving.

The point about the partial, provisional and perspectival character of totality is a reflection on the ideology of the market. For the integrity of a market, a hedge fund, and the financial field itself always falls far short of the objective existence attributed to it by its members, especially the media. For this attribution brackets the creation of the collective imaginary that grounds its apparently objective existence as a financial field, a market, or an institutional trading group. The tendency is to naturalize these objectification. Accordingly, books autopsying the credit crisis, models of derivatives pricing, analysis of the market's efficiency, treatises on regulation, uniformly presuppose that the space of work is a naturally occurring object. This collectively produced misrecognition that agents don't *create* the workplace is one of the signature features of the workspace they collectively create.

The Subjectivity of Financial Work

One shorthand to think about a social theory of finance is to say that the embodied sociality of the habitus takes the place of the economist's abstract invisible hand. This reorientation foregrounds the agency of the participants and the conditions of its production. Conceptualized from this perspective, the work of finance is shaped by the socially created dispositions and forms of rationality that orient what agents do. For its part, the financial workplace organizes and realizes these embodied dispositions and rationalities in the varied markets for financial action. For example, the dispositions and rationalities realized in risk management are rather different from those realized in derivative trading. This entails an understanding of work as a means of reconstituting the financial field and markets through the works of its agents even as the field and markets objectified by previous works serve to define the production of the workplace, and orient the work agents do and get done. Grasping this dynamic requires an understanding of *distributed agency* in that trading groups are founded on a mode of agency in which each member contributes a specific skill/technique/knowledge beyond the ken of the other team members. It also requires a positional analysis of the *distribution of agency*, which is the symbolic power to define the group's course of action. The practices of investment firms, exemplified by their "training" rites of initiation and intensification, are central to institutionalizing practices that seek to align agents' dispositions and rationalities with the economistic logic of the financial field and markets. This is necessary because agents in the course of their lives are also defined by other fields (e.g., religious) that are founded on alternative concepts and values and because the financial field already embodies social motivations. The implication is that a description of the financial habitus must grasp the complexity, range, and collective character of the dispositions and goals that orient agents' actions.

It is worth observing that economistic accounts, even though they elevate pecuniary interests above all others, cannot account for *money as a value* to those for whom it is supposedly the predominant motivation for work. This is critical because without a value, money does not complete itself as an object of desire. As Mr. Veblen noticed, without an account of the real values defining and driving agents' wants there is no way to adequately account for what they demand—winning trades for which money is the measure. To thus appreciate money as a value that becomes a want for those agents who traffic in derivatives requires a notion of a *monetized subjectivity*. The focus here is on the evolution of a sociospecific mode of work whose cutting edge, personified in derivative traders, lies in the creation and the valorization of a subjectivity based on a perpetual acquisitioning of money (money serving as the main unit of measure of winning wagers). The impetus to produce and valorize this mode of subjectivity above all others is specific to the relationship between the finance markets and those who are willing to play the game of betting speculatively, a derivative's game which presents itself to those caught up in the market and addicted to its rewards as imposing its own necessity and self-evidence. From the outside, this mode of subjectivity appears to be outlandish, atavistic, preoccupied with avarice, consumed by narcissism, a delusion of sorts but only to those who apprehend derivative markets from a perspective outside the arena in which the participants play the game. This concern with subjectivity underlines that what motivates financial agents to invest in the game is more complex, more social (and more interesting) than either the economistic notion of utility maximization or the popular notion of greed can possibly convey. Put another way, those theoretics that operate with a shallow concept of desire will find it next to impossible to articulate an adequate account of the motivations of agents' actions. Indeed, in a kind of confession to itself the financial field's exposes of the 2008 crisis frequently end up in that upside-down land where (presumably) perfectly rational agents acted so irrationally that it is necessary to call upon the irrationality of self-destructive greed to rationalize their actions.

Interviews with derivative deal makers and traders indicate they are motivated by corporate position-taking, self-esteem, recognition, power over others, a sense of social belonging, the psychic trophy of competitive wins against one's rivals, and other more idiosyncratic ambitions. The significant question is what are the cultural and economic conditions that generate a specific structure of desire in which money serves as a generative symbol of other ambitions? Why and how does the cipher of money, being no more than a potentiality to acquire commodities, end up as an indexical icon of a person's self-worth and esteem, or a psychic trophy of competitive wins, such that making money can become a motivation for work (as opposed for example to socializing with one's family and friends), whether or not the agent has any intention of acquiring anything. To put this in a colloquial question, why does the same Robert Cassano who earned a nine-figure sum as head of AIG's financial products unit (who, as exemplified in the quote, the media has held up as the personification of a villainous greed) reside in a modest house with a twelve year old Ford Bronco parked out front? His arrogant demeanor, his excess of investment in his work, his craving to make as much profit as possible no matter who was destroyed in the process, radiate unbridled greed, but also a greed that is not reducible in some easy way to monetary compensation.[4] It takes a particular economic culture, maturing over centuries, to produce a Robert Cassano or even his former boss and mentor at Drexel Burnham Lambert, Michael Milken. Or, for that matter, Angelo Mozillo (the inglorious indicted CEO of Countrywide Mortgage) or the principal traders in the hedge funds and proprietary trading desks. Any theorization must explicate what transforms impulses into a socially specific desire whose existence depends upon, and only makes sense in respect to, dispositions which valorize unending acts of acquisition—as symbolically represented by net worth which serves as a summation and proxy for the history and size of one's winning wagers, or concretely in the continual building up of a publicized collection (of expressionist art, antique cars, musical instruments, and so on). To paraphrase Bourdieu, the money form of greed appears as an imminently rational action because, having the same meaning for the agent who strives to accumulate money as for those who honor the quest and may envy the result, the act of acquisition "has no exterior, no excess of meaning, except that it is unaware of the social and historical conditions of this perfect self-transparency" (2000:160).

Agents' desire for money, and their belief that money is its own desire, trumping and overshadowing other motivations, appears rational because the sociohistory of finance has normalized and naturalized both the desire (greed) and its interpretation (as, for example, an animal spirit or instinct). The consequence is that for those whose dispositions embody this speculative habitus, for those for whom money has become the main unit of account in the production of the self (e.g., Joseph Cassano), there is never enough money because the enoughness of money is not what is at stake. The measure of success is successful acts of acquisition. As one derivatives trader put it, "asking me if I have enough money is like asking CC Sabathia if he has too many wins" (Sabathia is the star pitcher of the New York Yankees baseball team). Another trader, asked why he risked so much of his own money on what ultimately proved to be a losing trade, replied that "I don't think about the money [already accumulated] but about the winning" [act of acquisition]. Another trader, asked why he maintains a low profile despite extraordinary success, responded that it didn't make any difference whether other people knew of his success, because he knew and that was what counted. Another trader queried why he made substantial contributions (all total, more than eleven million) to a particular charity responded "they asked me first, and I did not have anything important to do with the money."

All these agents, each in their own way, is giving expression to the emergence of a *monetized subjectivity*. They are saying the structure of desire and motivation centers not on accumulating money or buying expensive things that index their wealth (although both are recognized values that continue from production centered capitalism and retain genuine importance), but on acts of the acquisition of money because it is the *unit of account in the creation of the self*. To paraphrase another derivatives trader: when real money enters my account it says I'm important, I'm a competitive giant because I have the brains and balls to execute a large leveraged wager that whipped the competition. If analysis peers beneath the surface what appears is agents shared deep psychological stake in repeated winning acts of monetary acquisition as a measure of personal worth. Conversely, what to most people are insanely rich men have risked jail time to conceal steep losses in their hedge fund portfolio because its revelation would result in a loss of face. What is socially fascinating about the construction is that analysis turns on illuminating a submerged, nonconscious reality, which disguises its actual character by offering itself up to journalists, economists, and its own participants in notions, such as greed and rationality, which lead to misreadings of what is ultimately going on. The central argument is not that modern finance invented this mode of subjectivity. Indeed, it has a prior existence but as a personal pathology that led some to embrace the delusion that equates money with happiness and holds that one can never, accordingly, have enough money. What the evolution into derivative finance has done is to elevate and valorize this mode of subjectivity by connecting it to the liquidity of markets and speculation as a social good. Its acquisition is part of the rite of admission to the financial workplace, where the profession sees the monetized subjectivity as the pivot and fulcrum orienting other modes, such as a desire for a familial life.

There is an institutional dimension to the creation of the subject. Specifically, that investment firms use all the resources at their disposal to mould those they hire into very particular kinds of subjects. They recognize that the fabrication of profitable groups, which presupposes a collectively held ability to manage the tension between collaboration and competition, is all the more likely to succeed if everyone has been inculcated with the same dispositions toward work and workplace. This interval of indoctrination, in which the new employees recruited mainly from Ivy League schools are imbued with the value hierarchy valorized by the field, a period in which they are removed spatially and temporally from the everyday life they once knew, a period in which everyone suffers under the same relentless competitive pressures and the same alienation from the relationships (such as siblings and friends) that were once central to the genesis of their subjectivity, a period in which they are surrounded by their seniors who often compel them to do tasks so pointless or trivial they humiliate (See Ho 2009), structurally and psychologically resembles nothing so much as an initiation rite as described anthropologically (since Van Gennep 1960) as a means of extinguishing the person's old subjectivity and replacing it with one better fitted to the initiands' new status.

Rites of Incorporation

Submission to the firm always has a patina of rock-hard force in that the firm is the conduit to real money. Traders are bought as the saying goes. Or as the Inuit Indians might rephrase it: "money makes traders like whips make dogs."[5] But agents' open and willing submission is even more the product of the way in which the institutions serve to shape their vision and sensibilities. Submission stems from the fact and act that the participants come to uphold a self-evident and pre-reflexive consensus on the meaning of the firm as an economic institution, as a player in the Markets. A collective agent in that the syncopation of the individual parts is both the touchstone of the firm's success and a moving target. Despite the celebration of individualism which, contradictorily, is often paired with collaboration and teamwork, the Street's most renowned firms are able to engender an astonishing degree of acceptance of the political order. A critical element of this is not only agents' mutual misrecognition of submission as teamwork, but that this worldview leads them to discover subjective intrinsic profits in that teamwork. The aim is to motivate agents to suspend any doubts that this financial institution, here, now, could be other than that which they are experiencing: what a firm calls and celebrates as its *culture*. Culture refers to the particular permutation of the worldview and ethos of finance endorsed by the firm's management. So Goldman Sachs is thought to have a different culture than, say, Morgan Stanley or Bank of America. The implicit program is that if the firm instills dispositions in its agents and these agents correspondingly adjust their vision and ambitions to the opportunities that the firm presents, then a firm's culture will appear as a necessity and take on the character of the self-evident. An element of Goldman Sachs' culture, for example, is that its principals should temporarily set aside the quest for monetary profits in favor of symbolic ones, such as those collected by serving as a US Treasury Secretary. Similarly, an element of Lehman Brothers' culture, which was part and product of its transition from merchant banking to speculative entrepreneur, was its self-image as a working class recruited, rolled up sleeves, rough and tumble, collective union against the world. Each firm sets out to install its culture as an ensemble of dispositions, which in a quasi-intended imitation of the military and also of professional sports (e.g., training camp), it does through the discipline and hardships that it imposes uniformly on all its agents.

The installation of the firm's culture and associated dispositions depends on the voluntary submission of the participants. But this does not limit the firm in fabricating the conditions for shaping and organizing these dispositions. Not least, and especially in an applicant's formative years with the firm, this entails appropriating agents' control over the temporal rhythms of their lives. This control over time entails, in relay, control over agents' spaces and movements. For the objectively best place to complete a report (e.g., about an upcoming bond placement) is where the information and technology reside: at the office. Similarly, the partitioning of the firm into divisions, such as traders versus risk managers, is embedded in the form of dispositions which leads to a consensus on relative worth, bonus compensation, and institutional standing. The focus on firms' cultures is important because it allows us to understand that agents' submission is neither the result of force (such as brainwashing) nor of considered consent. As one interviewee put it: "your involvement and commitment to the bank kind of sneaks up on you." In essence, a firm's culture as a lateral permutations on the culture of finance arise from the imposition on all ratified agents of "structuring structures" that owe their consistency and durability to the fact that they are, in appearance at least, coherent and systematic, and that "they are adjusted to the objectives structures" of the financial markets (Bourdieu 2000:176). A firm's culture, institutionalized, functions as a reference point and source of authority, which thus encourages its members to recognize that culture of endless accumulation.

The French anthropologist Arnold Van Gennep (1960) first described what he identified as rites of passage in 1909. Van Gennep observed that in all societies the life of individuals involves a sequence of passages or transitions from one status to another (e.g., from single to married) and from one occupation to another (e.g., from business school student to financier). Progression from one status or occupation to another involves both a canonical message which defines the rite as constitutive of the institution and a critical element in its success, and an indexical message. The indexical message is inherently Janus-faced: the first message informs the community that the initiand is matriculating from one social status (probationary employee) to another (ratified member of the team); the second message is self-reflexive in that the agents undergoing the ritual signal to themselves the message they have transmitted such that they now feel a compulsion and commitment to bring their internal processes into accord with their public position. The occurrence of the rite articulates what it itself distinguishes: that working for a financial firm is entirely different from the labor of scholastics or other professions. Focusing on kin- and community-based societies Van Gennep argued:

> Transitions from group to group and from one social situation to the next are looked on as implicit in the very fact of existence, so that a man's life comes to be made up of a succession of stages with similar ends and beginnings: birth, social puberty, marriage, fatherhood, advancement to a higher class, occupational specialization and death. For every one of these events there are ceremonies whose essential purpose it to enable the individual to pass form one defined position to another. (p. 3)

All of these rites of passage, Van Gennep argues, unfold as a progression toward an institutional objective, and are marked by three key phases: separation of the initiands from ordinary lifeways, a transition based on the incorporation of a new ensemble of ideas and dispositions, followed by the integration of the initiands on new terms (e.g., an enhanced set of privileges). Berger and Luckmann (1967) observe that the completion of the process is "conducive to feelings of security and belonging" (p. 99) and is, moreover, instrumental in amplifying the initiands' commitment to the group.

For entrants into high finance, the lure out of college is the seduction of money and excitement. Their initiation process offers, however, a world in which there is rather little excitement and although the salary is comparatively large for a graduate it is Lilliputian if calculated hourly (e.g., ten to twelve dollars an hour). The deeply seated tradition is that the firm subjects first year analysts to an abnormal and arbitrary work regime to demonstrate their uncompromising loyalty and to learn to align their individual priorities with those of the institution and their team, thus to replace an array of priorities accumulated from a life of diversified activities with the single minded focus on profits—the bank itself posited as a collective, almost transcendental, agent whose design lies outside the purview of any of its individual agents. Those agents who can accept, internalize, and then prioritize a monetized subjectivity matriculate as Wall Street material.

Separation and its reality effects are key elements of the initiation process, which, in finance, means separation from the social timespaces of ordinary lifeways. The firm accomplishes this in many complementary ways. The first is via the *monopolization* of the initiands' time by demanding work weeks which range from eighty to one hundred hours, meaning that there are few if any leisure days off or holidays with friends and family. The firm appropriates the one thing every life has in limited supply: time on earth. What this means existentially is that turning over one's lifetime to the firm constitutes a speculation on one's happiness. Or, more precisely, the bet that acts of winning the game will yield happiness. Initiands thus invest in and wager their lives on the upside of a monetized subjectivity. The second way is through *at-will scheduling*. Those who initiands work under can expropriate their time at any moment for any reason. One of the primary lessons inculcated is that unflagging and unquestioned loyalty to the firm must supersede all other claims, including those of kinship. This was clarified for one initiand in the following uncompromising example: "if you are planning to leave town because you are the best man at your brother's wedding, and we ask you to stay and complete a project, our expectation is that the firm comes first." The firm as a collective subject is imagined to stand above the normal social obligations that define one's social existence. This at-will scheduling is enforced through the issuance of a work only cell phone, which functions as an iron-link tether to the job. The canonical message is that the initiands lives no longer belong to them because they have been put in service to the rent-seeking imperatives of the firm. What this means is "that every evening activity is subject to last-minute cancellations

[and] that stress-free vacations and personal trips out of town are impossible" (Roose 2014:33).

Here is how one first year trader put it:

> After about nine months on the job, I had lost contact with my friends and with my younger brothers. Even when I did get to talk to them, the calls were frequently interrupted by someone from the office and I felt compelled to take the call. My girlfriend of two years, who had moved to New York with me, eventually left me for a musician. She said I had come to exist in just two states: absent and distant and that I blamed her for not understanding that the money was worth it (as justified by all the "stupid" things I had bought her). Almost everyone I see each day is from the firm. Occasionally, about twice a week, I hook up [have sex] for half an hour or so with a woman who works in another section. I am not even sure she likes me. *I feel I have become a different person.*

We can see here the institutionally designed funneling and formation of a monetized subjectivity—a subjectivity in which the around the clock accumulation of money for the institution and the subject subjected to this logic becomes the Rosetta stone of one's being. The estrangement of the person from their original state of being followed by their mental and physical incorporation into the involuted space of the firm turns the listened-to-world into an echo chamber. The halls and offices are sufficed with dog whistles from the firm's upper management that only unqualified commitment is enough.

The third way is by substitution. The firm replaces the ordinary spaces of action and routine with its own replicas. Instead of going to a nearby restaurant or a nearby gym, the investment bank creates an in-house restaurant and working area, which serves to isolate members of the firm in that they interact only with one another. There is no need to leave the building or interact with anyone else. These and other benefits such as on demand car service, which incentivizes the work force to work longer hours, is conceived by them as a perk or privilege. Rather than as a canalization of the geography of one's life and as a constriction of ones' worldly social relations. One's friends outside the bank fade away gradually from neglect and are replaced by friends from within the bank. There is also a kind of substitution by subtraction as almost all investment houses block social media sites, such as Facebook and LinkedIn, to curtail any communication with the outside world. The unstated message is that such communications are superfluous and extraneous to everyone's central project of accumulation. The message is that agents can only be fully committed to the monetization of their subjectivity if they excommunicate themselves from the social relations that might well impeded their work.

The fourth is competition and attrition. As the first year unfolds, the initiands are evaluated in terms of their pecuniary contribution to the firm. Periodically and progressively, all the initiands who are in the rear in respect to earning profits for the firm are summarily dismissed. The competition considers no contribution other than profits, which leads to a fixation on money as the measure of the value of one's self. The relentless focus on money normalizes and naturalizes this fixation. The only thing worth measuring, the only difference that makes a difference, is the earnings of the firms and of its individuals. The aim is to build up a self-reflexive and self-reinforcing disposition that the single minded pursuit of money at any cost should not engender existential misgivings or moral consternation. One of the first lessons I learned was: "Remember, no matter how well you appear to be doing, there is always someone making more than you."

Kevin Roose (2014) summarizes the process beautifully:

> Eventually, the changes to a first-year analyst start taking place deep in his psyche. Strange nomenclature starts becoming normalized. The id-driven testosterone-filled culture of the bank makes him a littler sharper and more direct when he's talking to his parents, roommates, and friends. Money goes from being something that is infrequently discussed to being the primary subtext to everyday life. Social relationships start to feel transactional. And the world inside the bank starts to look bigger and bigger, while the world outside it shrinks to a distraction.

The ritual leaders for the Ndembu people (southern Tanzania) say the purpose of the initiation ritual is to kill the old personality and then replace it with a new one that is more masculine, competitive, and a soldier for their clan; the chiefs at Morgan Stanley or Goldman Sachs could not have wished or said it better.

None of this should suggest that there is not a tremendous amount of push back and unease toward this reworking of the work of finance. Part of the resistance comes from mainstream public culture, which often depicts the financial community as harvesting huge compensation while contributing little to the well-being of the overall economy. Some comes from those, exemplified by Warren Buffett, who continue to vouchsafe traditional financial practices. Some comes from regulators who see a golden opportunity to rescue tarnished reputations (most notably the SEC), enhance their names for higher office, or amplify their authority. Some comes from individuals within the financial field who recognize that its fundamental design (e.g., its compensation model, its pricing models) has serious flaws that require fixing. Some comes from socially minded academics that were marginalized by the financial field and by a scholastic community dominated by the scientism of neoliberal economics. What these different sources of push back have in common is that they are responding to, and have catalyzed around, the 2008 financial crisis. This coalition or focused gathering of public, regulatory, and intellectual forces cannot help but compete against the mainstream institutions of the financial field. The struggle is over the importance and implications of the crisis, with the financial field wanting to downplay the possibility that a systemic implosion was barely averted, thus allowing for a return to the normalcy of non-transparent, leveraged, highly lucrative, derivatives trading, whereas the coalition wants to foreground the credit crisis, keeping the news that made headlines during the height of the liquidity freeze in public view as a topic for national and scholarly conversation in order to instigate both regulatory changes (e.g., limits on compensation) and a new intellectual appreciation as to how the financial field and its markets works.

The Evolution of Financial Work

Finance as an institutional space of work represents a shift away from a hierarchical paradigm in which individuals' desires and work trajectories center on climbing up a codified corporate managerial ladder and toward a paradigm founded on agents' circulation across subfields. This paradigm takes shape as pathways laid down as practical and institutional structures along which people, capital, trading strategies, sources of information, and classificatory schemes circulate. While this transformation is general, finance exemplifies the space of work as a space of circulation. This flow stems from a finance specific worldview which takes it as axiomatic that people, like all assets, are contingent and disposable. Advancement is frequently diagonal, with agents shifting from one institution into another, often an institution they are currently doing business with that offers increased responsibility and compensation. There is also a constant interchange of people between investment banks and hedge funds ("I worked at Goldman for six years before leaving to become a partner in a hedge fund"). Moreover, individuals not only circulate along fixed time horizons and institutional spaces of work, they have a flexible relation in which they are sometimes on the field's periphery, not infrequently in states of quasi-retirement trading strictly for their own personal/family account before re-joining the field by taking a new position, or spending some bracket of time in public office, a university, or charitable foundation, before returning in some capacity. There are instances in which members of the media left television to start their own hedge fund on the way to becoming an investment advisor who reappears on television as an expert witness (e.g., Ron Insana). Similarly, ideas, especially profitable investment strategies, circulate at increasing speeds through the financial community until saturation. Images and information also travel freely through the various quarters of the field, newsletters like the *Institutional Investor* circulating data on the relative compensation of compet-ing hedge fund managers. It is perhaps best then to conceptualize the financial field as a Venn diagram, composed of a set of circles of different sizes that are inherently permeable and overlap extensively. What results socially are dense networks of interrelated financial relationships. What sutures the subfields, imbuing the field with a sense of common identity and thereness, is that they share much the same habitus and ingrained sensibilities about what consti-tutes the work of finance.[6]

But the transformation of work is not only in respect to positions and strat-egies of advancement. What has evolved is a financial field composed of dis-tinctive types of social practices of work which seek to recruit, cultivate, and valorize different personality types and identities. The field foregrounds the position of the trader, meaning the agents involved in organizing and execut-ing the speculative wager. While most traders also operate individually, trading for their personal account, their influence on the market and their status in the field derives from being a part of a proprietary trading desk at an invest-ment bank (e.g., Goldman Sachs), one of the more than 7000 hedge fund that speculate (e.g., Soros Investments), or the "investment" (read trading) arm of a corporation (typified by Enron and AIG) that seek to turbocharge their other more steady-stream businesses by trading and insuring trades on deriva-tives.[7] The brokerage counterparts to traders are those agents who specialize in selling securities. These brokers have evolved to have two complementary functions. First, they organize the variegated parts of what are often complex derivatives and bring together the various agents interested in participating in a particular deal. Second, they are responsible for building a portfolio of clients that, for example, purchased the tranches of collateralized mortgage obligations. Essentially, they peddle the derivatives products that others use to speculate with. When brokers are, as is typically the case for major investment houses (e.g., Goldman Sachs and Morgan Stanley), members of the same firm as traders, this can produce a circumstance in which a firm's trading desk is shorting or betting against the same type of security that its brokers are selling to their clients.[8] The globalization of markets and their interconnectivity has promoted a third contingent of agents whose job is to assist traders and brokers: these are principally market strategists who attempt to ascertain the overall direction of increasingly interdependent global markets and research analysts who investigate specific instruments (e.g., bonds, stocks) and sectors (e.g., housing, technology). While strategists and analysis provide traders with formal trading strategies and brokers with information to pass along to their clients, they come to finance from incommensurable backgrounds—as though one aligned a gunslinger with an expert on the physics of firearms. There is, given their very different inculcated worldview, a rather distant and diffident relationship between analysts and traders and brokers ("it is as though we come from different planets" is how one derivative trader put it). Those involved in strategy and research intersect with the scholarly community of business economists and professors of finance who seek to model the markets scientifically. This has led them to focus on quantitative mathematized models about market behavior (exemplified by Black-Scholes). When mathematically oriented agents are brought in house to build trading models for a firm's traders they are called quants, which signifies not only their capacity to develop trading algorithms but their dispositional distance from the power-laden, anxiety-ridden, aggressive universe of trading. Although they putatively work together, traders exhibit distain for quants, viewing them as nerds who lack the competitive juices, gumption, and the aggression to pull the trigger on the trades their mathematical models commend. A key feature of modern finance has been the development and volatility of this relationship which personifies the tension between a mathematical model that lives in formal time with robotically rational actors and the existential time of traders which encompasses information excluded from the quantitative model (such as counterparty risk) and is hypersensitive to the intensity and magnitudes of the waves of price volatility. The quantitative analysts work in formal, homogenous, empty time where risk can be nothing other than a statistical measure, carrying no existential charge, a self-contained world where their only subjectivity on the line is doing a successful job in the modeling, whereas traders live in a financial world and volatile markets inundated with uncertainty and unknowable risks, perpetually anxious that they do not know what they don't know (e.g., there is an impending liquidity stop that will force them to maintain a deteriorating position). In their practice, the physics of finance and derivative pricing, with its pitch perfect delta hedging of risk, is an imaginary ("egg-head") reality that the transgressive forces of the real world continually eviscerate. Here is how one trader put it:

> Almost all trades are binary. Either you win or lose, though the dollar amount of the win or loss certainly counts because that is the basis of your P&L statement. At the conclusion of the trade you are either right or wrong. Once the market moves against you, you are 100 percent wrong no matter how small some quant calculated the probability of failure.

A critical aspect of the clash of personalities between quants and strategists on one side and derivative traders on the other is that the inner mechanics of the market replicates their relationship in service of its own replication. For the actual dynamics of trading depends precisely on continually closing and opening the gap between the model and real-world price setting. The process of replicating a derivative involves a back and forth between the formula constructed price and a derivative's real-world pricing.

Derivative markets as a condition of their existence seek to materially increase the dimensions and through this the downside of the risks encountered (i.e., value at risk). The institutional response has been to set up a corps of chaperones who will administer adult supervision. So overseeing traders and trading desks there has evolved risk managers who presumably calculate whether the wager's reward merits the amount of risk assumed, and bookkeepers/accountants whose job it is to keep financial score. Such managers occupy an altogether separate position in the psyche of the firm as quants view their forms of risk assessment as superfluous and traders view them as a curiously empowered impediment to profitability. If trading requires "real" men with gumption, timing, and a calculus of the real, managing risk calls only for endless timidity. Where the relationship between quants and derivative traders is distant and diffident that between traders and risk managers is openly antagonistic. There is, of course, variation from firm to firm and case to case, but this is the dominant paradigm.

Finally, outside the finance firm there has burgeoned a financial media. Once only a footnote to the general news—reports about the ups and downs of the DOW—they are now principal accompaniment to the markets. The financial media is composed of news reporters, business analysts, and media personalities, the latter typically comprised of "strong" (meaning confidently opinionated) men and attractive women (who hint at beauty and sexuality even as they take every precaution to avoid doing anything provocative) who can deliver the breaking news and conduct interviews. This media tends to function and envision itself as an unofficial spokesman and advocate for the mainstream financial community. Its members construct and repeat a set of slogans—e.g., regulation is the enemy of profits and competition, taxation undermines our incentive to invest, European states (especially France) always lags the United States economically because it is leans toward socialism—that are instrumental in circulating the dispositions of the field through the public culture of finance.[9] Traders and the media are mutually implicated in a complex semiotic process in which question and response speaks to translate a vision of the forthcoming, with the hope that the conversation will induce a higher/lower price sign for the same object, such a stock.

Because the act of trading, or strategizing, or mathematizing, or reporting presupposes dispositions and competencies that are narrowly distributed, they offer the opportunity to distinguish oneself, exemplified by the market strategist who makes a prescient call about the market's direction, the trader who shorted CMOS as they fell into the abyss, the financial mathematician who crafted a winning trading algorithm, or the reporter who broke the story of Lehman's dramatic collapse. All of these actions are social relations in that they create the divisions and distinctions that create a field of positions. Traders' identities, which relies on players' recognition of an existing yet transient set of tradable instruments, enables them to realize investing styles through this constellation of trading options (as opposed to options trading). Traders select an area of specialization (e.g., CMOS), a time horizon (from the nearly immediate to the short term), and a willingness to accept a level of risk (the value at risk), which constitutes a trading style that is also an identity. The identity of some traders—George Soros comes immediately to mind—is defined precisely by a chameleon-like ability to shift from one trading style to another. Identity is important; a now retired trader put it this way:

> When I was a Goldman [Sachs], my trading style was my identity. The trading style of our group [bond traders] was our identity. It was more of our identity then whether we were Indian, Jewish, Ivy League, or anything else. Everyone on "the street" [read: financial community] knew who we were.

Or, here is another trader discussing another attachment to trading:

> I was watching this show on cable about the whores at Hunts Point in the Bronx [*The Point* on HBO]. This girl was saying that once you're a ho you're always a ho. The lifestyle, the clothes, the walk, the sex, the way you never

knew what's going to happen—they get in your blood. You want to give it up but you know you can't. I thought to myself that trading was like that. No matter who you were with [sexually] or how many lines [of cocaine] you did over the weekend, they were not going to be as good as putting a whole lot on a trade.

Another trader, interviewed in London, put the issue thusly:

Trading derivatives, being that part of the City, is more than a job, it's a lifestyle that consumes people; it is addictive, all the money on the line. Only those who are doing it can understand what you're going through; even when you're competing against them in what is essentially a zero sum game, you share something with them, as though you were on different teams but both in premier league football.[10]

Traders' sense of self and identity, how their peers assess them, and how they believe others in finance imagine them are organically bound up with their strategies and styles. One recognized chain is that an agent repeatedly assumes a high level of risk, which over time, conveys a message both to himself and his peers that these "risk-on" speculative positions represent his trading style, which, in turn, is an aspect and an expression of his identity. The existing derivative markets and ensemble of products (e.g., CDOs) in concert with the risks assumable (i.e., leverage) serve to delimit the trading styles possible at any given point in the evolution of the field. In the crisis, the de facto and de jure deregulation of the use of leverage allowed after 2000 offered the possibility for traders to make an "all in" wager, which, by allowing them to put their financial life on the line (i.e., to "blow up" if things went badly), increased the monetary return on the wager but even more so the symbolic return.

In the economy of trading, greed and avarice refer more properly to the voracious, literally insatiable demand for status and identity realized through monetary profits, then the profits themselves. The demand is insatiable because it is not defined in respect to objective material needs, but in relation to the ongoing construction of the subject through monetary accumulation in respect to what others are making and doing. What this means is that trading involves a kind of status bloodbath, marked by wild celebration when, for example, one "takes down" a high status (collective) agent such as Goldman Sachs, Morgan Stanley, or Soros Investments. The view is that only a very smart trader with enormous guts could take the opposite side of a trade from these agents, and win. When Joseph Cassano, the former head of AIG's infamous Financial Products

Division, would find out that none other than Goldman Sachs was on the other side of a trade position, he would order his troops to redouble their research rather than close out the trade, aware that there was an amplified status reward in defeating Goldman. The high-octane trade embodies a constituted reward because professional traders have already valorized such trades as meriting status. The act of making a trade is a classifiable act, which by mapping agents' potential to accumulate symbolic capital and by creating the conditions of their positioning in the social organization of the subfield, defines trading as being about the speculative use of money to create a mode of sociality. Indeed, it enables trading to specify and realize itself as such.

Creating Subjectivity: The Temporality of Work and Workplace

There is a distinct temporality embodied in the habitus of financial work, a habitus inculcated in its agents (that infiltrates into society generally) through the institutional construction of the workplace. Nothing foregrounds this temporality more than the deal making process and the way in which it creates the existential time for the deal-makers and their squadron of assistants. The financial field generally and the workplace specifically is found institutionally on the compression of time as deals are habitually fabricated, pitched, and executed under extraordinary pressure. Ho (2009) describes in detail based on her own ethnography how investment bankers cajole their associates and analysts to assemble the financial data that they will use to engineer a deal. In only a few days, they are expected to organize the information, creating spreadsheets, flow charts, descriptive summaries, strategic recommendations, and anything else that is needed. To do this they work frenetically, often clocking seventy to a hundred hours a week (2009:chap 2). Moreover, these agents typically have to manage a small cavalcade of time horizons, as the express institutional ambition is to have multiple deals in play simultaneously. For those immersed in finance, the succession of one deadline after another, the clock and calendar appearing as enemies, exemplifies the time compression. Everyone presses to get the deal done before time expires, which ties into the allusions those in finance continually make to time constrained sporting events, especially football games. The institution programs its members to take the velocity of action done meticulously and unquestioningly as an index of the work's inherent virtues and the agents' commitment to their firm and their colleagues. What results, as our ethnography attests, is that there is little conservation or preservation of times, few deals can saturate agents' memories because there is always already another derivatives deal waiting in the wings. So as one participant put it in one of the many ubiquitous references to sports, "no one here is like a [baseball] pitcher who throws a shutout [a complete game in which the opposition is held scoreless], and then gets to savor his victory for three days before his next start" [three days being the standard rest time]. Translation: the temporal structure of the financial workplace guarantees that those doing the work have no recovery time to enjoy or contemplate their victories, no matter the quality of their performance.

Those in finance live within a narrow time band, taking directional cues solely from recently discovered information even as they remove from consideration the long term consequences of their actions. The institutional imperative is to discount the longer term and whatever lies beyond the firm's interests, and direct one's concentration and concern to the secession of present tasks. Their central focus is the exploitation of the present moment, immediately followed by the liquidation of that moment. This compressed inward directed temporality leaves little time, occasion, or calling for self-reflexivity, as those in finance are disposed by their (re)training to bracket the affects their practices *will* have on others. This socially induced asociality was underlined in the fabrication, securitization, and circulation of subprime mortgages.

One dimension of this compression is that financial agents exist within a deeply homogenized temporality, with few of the conventional variations such as play time, familial time, meal time, ritual time, and so on. Temporal archipelagos where they can go off by themselves, escaping for several days in a row free of the burdens of the job, are not only extremely rare but officially frowned upon. Taking time off is an expression of a lack of commitment. On this logic, agents' temporal commitment to work signals their position in institutional space: which is, in-group versus out-group status, those who are destined for promotion and heady compensation and those who will be left behind. This intense and repetitive schedule imparts a very sociospecific rhythm to the lives of contemporary financial workers. There is a compulsive sense of what Ancona and Chong (1996) call *entrainment* as financial agents adjust the other activities of their lives—from family vacations to ritual ceremonies to intimate relations—to the singular temporality of financial practices (e.g., institutional expectations about the length of their working hours, when the market opens and closes, when a certain deal needs to close, when the Federal Reserve is going to divulge information, and so on). Marriages, vacations, family outings, dinners with friends, are all subsumed to the temporality of finance. Karen Ho (2009) reports that her informants and confidants lamented that they broke so many dates with friends and family that they were excommunicated from the normal secular cycles of work, family, and play (p. 87–92). This institutional consumption of the sum of an individual's time leads to an intellectual cul-de-sac insofar as reduces learning to what is useful in the workplace. Moreover, as with all institutionalized phenomena, the compressed rhythms of financial institutions have become embodied in agents' habitus as expectations about the behavior of their peers. And about the behavior of others, which in turn leads to a social hierarchization in which those who work relentless long hours in competitive high-stakes finance behold their work as proof of their superiority to others: those who work normal hours in non-competitive jobs in which their compensation is small but assured. The internalization of this vision comes across in the extraordinary effort that the CEOs of financial institutions have to make to avoid sounding patronizing when they are called to congressional testimony.

There is also a temporal aspect to people's reluctance to plan ahead, and to take precautions about placing too much of their wealth in the firm's stock. Especially for those involved in the exemplary act of trading, the disposition is to focus temporally from the immediate moment out to the near future. Agents experience a preoccupation with the forthcoming, an intense looking ahead to how the outstanding trades or the deals about to be consummated will turn out. Thinking about the world fixates on a narrow window of time, a horizon so compressed, so wedded to time pressure, that some participants describe it as suffocating. There is an aiming toward the near term future inherent in trading that must constantly be adjusted to what comes forth in the market. And so agents in finance tend to experience (as opposed to being intellectually aware of) the longer term mostly when there is a sudden rupture between their career path, inscribed as an expectation of an endless future ("I didn't have any other plans than being at Bear [Stearns]"), and their immediate situation (e.g., of having lost their job, and perhaps moving into a position that re-employees them but at the expensive of their self-esteem and their sense of becoming). They experience the longer term negatively and retrospectively as a discrepancy that is sometimes a gaping hole between their expectations and the reality that they no longer have the future they subjectively but also collectively anticipated. Not surprisingly, many of those in finance were so captive and captivated by this disposition toward time that consciously contemplating a rather distant horizon simply did not readily come to mind. Asked why they did not protect their portfolio, almost all of the answers can be boiled down to two: "It just did not seem right" and "I never thought about it because I was so caught up in the action." Their inactions unified in a single perspective their disposition to fixate on the short term and their expectations about their unending employment, neither of which they posited as such. It just happened. All of this underlines that the rational calculation of risk, which for many was literally part of their job description, has nothing to do with the way people anticipate their future (and the risks it may portend). Here, as elsewhere in the financial field, once the analysis lays out the underlying socially constituted relations, the more notions such as greed and hubris appear as the surface forms of these relations.

One of the ways to understand the field and its habitus is to look at those who have "voluntarily" dropped out. They liberate themselves from this disposition toward time as the immediate future by suspending their participation, and thus their lived insertion, into the financial field. They end the endless competition—over success in trading, sports, sexual conquests, bouts of drinking, and so on. They free themselves from the fact that life on the speculative edge is similar to unskilled labor in that agents are never freed of the fear of tomorrow: that some sudden untoward, unpredictable event will crush them. An instructive example is a young couple who has purchased a farmhouse bed and breakfast on a hillside in Marche Italy with the proceeds he and his wife accumulated as a derivatives trader and an accountant for the same London investment firm. He notes that he is now free of a regime defined by compressed intimacy commingled with aggression and competitiveness, a regime in which everyone tempers their social and biological needs to the frenzied temporal rhythms of trading. He says there was a constant warfare to reconcile the interests and investments of traders with those of upper and risk management. And so he ended up recreating a social universe where most of those they encounter daily have no investments in common; they are liberated because their lifeworld is populated by a constant flow of strangers amongst whom nothing is at stake.

The Ideology of Financial Motivation

Societies have a pressing need to understand themselves; for without such self-understanding they cannot plan their futures. This quest requires self-reflexivity, and the capacity to take that reflexive understanding and translate it into a national conversation. Since the collapse of the housing linked credit markets, there has been an endless outpouring of articles, television shows (such as CNBC's *House of Cards*), and other spectacles—not least congressional hearings—seeking to determine and put a face on the extraordinary facts. There quickly crystallized a commonsense take on the character of agents' motives: a culturally clear, easy to digest folk theory whose center of gravity was our Christian ethic of deadly sins, greed, envy, pride, and sloth (all of which come before the financial fall). In its most common formulation, traders driven by greed and envy of others compensation (exemplified by their outrageous bonuses), feeding their gluttonous desires for material possessions, were aided and abetted by the hubris of the Federal Reserve and the sloth of regulators who turned a blinkered and uncaring eye to their dangerously leveraged and speculative wagers. Traders, morally bankrupt to their core, indifferent to who was hurt on the main streets across America, were armed with nuclear-like financial instruments built by mathematically fluent nerds. We did not jump to crisis mode all at once but inched toward the financial precipice by allowing our government to repeatedly, mistakenly bailout failing institutions, signaling to those in the markets that they could unleash their speculative greed without any fear of suffering the consequences of bankruptcy and dissolution that capitalist markets impose on those who fail.

This caricature of how the financial field works—which allows us to reach for an explanation which is always ready at hand—is readily intelligible and easily packaged for general consumption. There is nothing new to greed and avarice, the public has long been indoctrinated with how inefficient the government is, and it knows from experience that technology can be turned against the common interests. Add to this mix that the financial community seems to cultivate a callousness and obliviousness toward those who toil in the real economy,[11] and the stage is dressed for a theatre of villains and victims (even if on closer inspection it is not always easy to tell them apart). This is the popular narrative now in circulation. Finance columnist, Michael Daly, encapsulates the view: "In our fury over the bonuses at AIG [American International Group], we should not forget the PIGs there who pocketed millions while endangering the global economy," particularly Joseph Cassano (the head of AIG's division which fabricated the credit default swaps) who "walked away with more than 315 million," which is "three times the annual budget of his alma mater, Brooklyn College, to which he has not contributed a dime" (2009). This outburst, amplified on numerous blogs with even more unstrained anger, says that what we need are vigilant and aggressive lawmen with the legal weapons to strip thieves like Cassano of their fortunes and their freedom.

From the standpoint of social theory, however, this commonsense view—endorsed especially by the financial media in the personalities and plotlines that it finds lead story appealing—represents a public crisis of comprehension. For the commonsense formulation attains its intelligibility through a simplification that highlights only what is on the surface, presenting what is easy to understand—avarice, sloth, and hubris—as though the terms encapsulated all we need to know. Representations, especially media-circulating public representations of finance, have a view about knowledge whether or not they aspire to be scientific. And here the commonsense formulation is problematic even beyond its overt simplicity: for it replicates an underlying cause of the crisis in that it brackets the social construction of agents' practices. This ideologically infused notion—ideological because it represents a native interpretation of what motivates agents' behavior—is founded on the same social epistemology that underwrites the quantitative financial models: an epistemology that expunges the social and grasps the decontextualization of social action and practice as an analytically neutral act. Accordingly, analyses which work off of this caricature, however illuminating they may otherwise be about finance, cannot drill down socially into the institutionalization and installation in agents of the cognitive and motivating structures that underwrote the genesis, elaboration, and political legitimization of a mode of work so very different than what went on before 1973.[12]

There is also an economic version of this account that emanates from behavioral economics. The term "Animal Spirits," as appropriated from Keynes and then redirected by Akerlof and Shiller (2009), captures the view that irrational and noneconomic motives can orchestrate agents' decision-making and actions. And thereby disrupt the normal economic equilibrium of the well-functioning market. What caused the financial crisis is that agents collectively succumbed to the deep animal spirit of greed, which, in turn, led to bad faith, corruption, deception, and willful blindness in the pursuit of money. "Securitization and the exotic derivatives" became "nothing more than a new way of selling snake oil" (Akerlof and Shiller 2009:87). Maybe so, but this explanation is so problematic it barely improves on commonsense accounts. Observe that the onset of this new escalating wave of greed-driven behaviors is only known retrospectively through the foreclosures, market failures, and other outcomes of the systemic crisis. Greed itself is an interior psychodynamic state whose very existence behavioral economics extrapolates from the "seemingly" irrational behavior of the participants, which, insofar as it is shared motivation, leads to a general crisis of faith in the markets. The difficulty is real: for the practical logic that governs notions such as "animal spirits" can only attain any specificity by assuming what it purports to explain: the historical expression of a sociospecific form of greed.

We can appreciate that a notion as ambiguous as that of "animal spirits" occupies in behavioral economic accounts of the crisis only if it is understood that the notion provides a solution to the predicament that analysis is condemned by an abstract asocial account of participants' agency. It allows analysis to connect individual behavior to collective action without ever specifying the actual social structuring of the motivations or their collective installation. The theory is that the same set of animal spirits caused the savings and loan recession of 1991, the 2001 Enron-led recession, and the present financial crisis (Akerlof and Shiller 2009:30–37). This move which transforms animal spirits from an imputed (though abstract) descriptive category into an explanatory category of the objective economic fact of recession and crisis is analytically unmotivated, as is its complementary function of providing analysis with a means of connecting the economic back to the social. For in this species of explanation, collectively shared animal spirits are the organizing principal of collective action, which, in turn, causes "irrational" and unwelcome economic outcomes. The social appears, contradictorily, as an intrinsic yet exogenous variable that is meant to explain the group's formation and its collective economic behavior. In essence, the positing of a natural "animal spirits" permits analysis to avoid the questions of the social construction of a monetized subjectivity and the sociohistorical conditions that have to be realized—exemplified by the emergence of a speculative ethos—to make its expression appear as self-evident as an animal spirit. Ultimately, the notion of animal spirits is the socially unconscious simulacrum of the monetized subjectivity.

Finance economics posits as biopsychogical and thus given the full complement of dispositions that agents have acquired by virtue of their socialization. The biologization of disposition grounds the worldview that concepts such greed and avarice are ahistorical and universal. The explanatory sin, from which there is no reprieve, is that it now becomes impossible to explain culture and context. All of the social and political labor required to align agents' economic positions (such as derivatives trader) with their dispositions (notably, a compulsion to acquire money) in respect to a specific context for action (buying a CMO from Goldman Sachs) disappears. It becomes naturalized and thus invisible. Paradoxically, the concept of "animal spirits" is rooted in a worldview whose organizing principle is the unquestioned dominance of rationality. Behavior economics inscribes at the very core of its construction of its object all those expressions of "irrational" behavior whose social rational motivations are invisible because they have been expunged by economic theory. Certain behaviors appear irrational because their actual reasons have been sent offstage. Behavioral economics can circumvent this problem only by projecting into agents the model that it has concocted to account for their practices. This move is necessary because one cannot grasp how practices are infused and inflected by a social rationality simply by adding another abstract component to utility maximization. Ultimately, even in the financial field, where agents are trained to economic rationality, behavioral economics (like finance economics) cannot begin to explain the character of their investment in the field or its stakes: the reasons for their commitment to work, their willingness to speculate and place themselves in an existentially tenuous positions by wagering large (as portrayed in Lewis 2010), their singular pursuit of the acquisition of money (see Keynes's brilliant passages "on the love of money" in his *A Treatise on Money*, vol. 2, 1930) that is morphing in the present moment into a fully monetized subjectivity (as appear in our interviews with derivatives traders), lie in the socially created financial habitus, which means that, barring a crisis, agents get up every morning to trade derivatives without deliberating whether they need the money (see Bourdieu 2005:10).

A remarkable feature of the financial field is the regimentation of this asocial social epistemology across numerous, seemingly independent, social practices (from the creation of financial instruments and the determination of compensation to quantitative models and media accounts of mortgage origination schemes). The books on finance used in business school, the Black-Scholes equation used to price derivatives, the representation of market events as presented in the financial media, scholarly accounts of the credit crisis, indeed the financial sectors own definition of a market as the aggregate of potential buyers and sellers of a given security,[13] all encode this socially evacuating social epistemology. What is as important, the regimentation of this epistemology goes unrecognized, appearing as a naturalization of the financial habitus. From a social perspective, notions such as greed, competition, and their companions are surface forms that take their cue from the dispositions inculcated through exposure to the financial habitus. Moreover, in financial discourses, they often end up as fetishized forms insofar as these discourses reduce the products of the habitus to universal instincts, leading analysis to overlook the embedded, embodied, and existential dimensions of financial practices. To characterize these forms as fetishized is in no way to gainsay their importance; for the understanding circulated within finance that instincts such as greed and competitiveness are the dominant if not exclusive motives for doing the work agents do—speculative wagering—is itself a dimension of *the real relations of the production of the financial field*. It is real because this specific understanding is instrumental in producing the producers.

What is problematic about the commonly used, commonsense notion of *greed,* especially the way politicians and the media use the term—as a primitive and insatiable compulsion to singularly accumulate money—as well the "animal spirits" of behavioral economics, is that it obscures a more complex and more social reality. The real issue is the character of desire, specifically the way in which the sociospecific desires that agents acquire through their immersion in the financial field aim them toward the production of a specific ensemble of behaviors. Now it turns out that these agents embody desires bordering on compulsions—*for those things money can't buy, only index, and solely through an indexical scheme that is historically linked to the emerging culture of financial circulation.* Money's parallel function here is as a new kind of indexation in the creation of both sociality and subjectivity. This indicates that even when agents engage in utility maximizing behavior, maximizing a trade's profits does not, and cannot, explain the construction of, and agents' subscription to, the values that motivate and shape their actions (e.g., besting a formidable competitor, amplifying my self-worth, increasing my status or preventing a shameful loss of status). It is not only the case that the financial field hides this from view, it is that their concealment and misrecognition are part of the elementary structure of the production of its sociospecific form. There is more than a touch of irony in that the possibility of a derivative market, which is, a market's whose liquidity and thus existence is founded on dynamic replication, constitutes a refutation of the economistic view.[14]

Conclusion

The notion of the flesh and blood subject points to the work of finance in a real-life workplace as the site where individuals attempt to create themselves as people. The point is critical because a theory and descriptive exegesis of financial work and the workplace is necessary to explicate the embodied desires and motivations that drive the practices and existential act of derivative trading, which, in turn, is literally what makes a market as an objective realization of those acts. Even as the present state of a derivative market and the internal structure of the financial field set the objective conditions for the unfolding and exfoliations of the subjectivity of the participants. The institutions of finance seek to manage this dynamic by managing the distribution of agency; the tension between collaboration and competitiveness; the valorization of a monetized subjectivity through the definition and celebration of a mode of compensation; the creation of a temporality that segregates the participants from other socialities even as it extends the sociality of work it into the once sacrosanct temporal spaces of leisure, family, and recreation; the production of a workspace founded on a space of hierarchical positions and conventions of position-taking that are themselves stakes in the game. Financial agents at work, trading derivatives, are always presented with, and confronted by, a forthcoming that is always nothing less than a series of negotiable spreads (e.g., between the compensation they have and the one they desire as a necessity of their subjective completion) unfolding across an interval that is rife with uncertainties due to the vulnerability of all financial markets (to suffer "game changing" transgressions from without) and the actions of competing agents whose motivations always encompass the whole of the social (even when this includes bracketing a dimension of it), and though it is so imagined in the ideology of finance the real world of derivative trading never encounters abstract agents, abstracted from the real concerns and conditions of their lives, abstracted from the production of subjectivity, fixated on money and nothing more, and motivated exclusively by the rational imperative of utility maximization. The optic of the forthcoming, the spread, the progression along an interval in a context framed by the imbrications of ritual, play, and work: that is where the action is. To summarize all this in respect to the 2008 crisis. Greed did not cause the financial crisis, though there was an astounding level of avarice. Lax regulations did not cause the crisis, though the regulators generally sat on their hands. Poor science did not cause the crisis, even if finance economics endorsed a theoretic that said that market failure is impossible. Rather, an unfortunate conjuncture of events could imperil the markets and unleash great social harm because a financial habitus, whose cognitive and motivating structures were organized around capital speculation, the logos of the derivative, and a monetized subjectivity, served to confer such destructive power on those realities. The financial firm is a workshop that turns out agents inculcated with the ambition to compulsively acquire money at any cost to themselves or to society. Against this reality, the only weapon we have is an understanding that becomes a politics.

Chapter 9

The Social Dimensions of Black-Scholes

All models sweep dirt under the rug. A good model makes the absence of dirt visible. In this regard, we believe that the Black-Scholes model of options valuation . . . is a model for models: it is clear and robust. Clear because it is based on true engineering; it tells you how to manufacture an option out of stocks and bonds, and what it will cost you under ideal dirt-free circumstances that it defines. The world of markets doesn't exactly match the ideal circumstances Black-Scholes requires, but the model is robust because it allow an intelligent trader to qualitatively adjust for those mismatches. — EMANUEL DERMAN and PAUL WILMOTT, *The Financial Modellers' Manifesto*

All financial economic analyses of the pricing of derivatives take the position of the primacy of the Black-Scholes formula for options pricing. The analyses may be tweaked in numerous directions, but the centrality of Black-Scholes formula is undisputed. As the quantitative analyst Emanuel Derman (forthcoming) says "the breakthrough achievement it represents has dominated finance over the past forty years" (p. 12). This is true not only theoretically but practically. As former derivative trader Nassim Taleb observes: "no experienced trader would willingly trade Black-Scholes-Merton for another pricing tool" (1997:109).[1] Even further, resolving the BS pricing equation through the use of the finite difference method has become the standard, programmed into the computer programs and handheld calculators used by traders.[2] Finance economists as a group have argued that the discovery of the Black-Scholes options pricing formula is akin to the discovery of the structure of DNA: both discoveries spawned "new fields of immense practical importance: genetic engineering on the one hand and, on the other, financial engineering" (financial economist Zvi Bodie on the PBS documentary *Nova*, quoted in Planes 2013). A modest approximation is that yearly the face value of derivatives priced using the BS model is considerably north of global production (BIS 2012).[3] Large numbers aside, the power of derivatives to inflect economic life and the centrality of BS in the pricing of those derivatives define it as one of the primary driving technologies of the culture of financial circulation. There is again the alternative view from the standpoint of the evolution of capitalism: that the Black-Scholes formula is sociohistorically specific to the work and workings of the derivative markets and a key component of the deeper performative subject responsible for recreating a specific mode of totality.

Why is the Black-Scholes formula important socially, especially as the formula applies an abstract mathematical physics formula to the rarified and insulated world of derivatives trading? The argument for its significance is this: the Black-Scholes model necessarily posits the existence of a/the market as a totality within which it can price the derivative contracts which circulate. The model posits the existence of a specific socially imagined totality, *the market*, in which each market is an instance of the type in that each embodies the essential features of the market, the most important of which are a closed and complete marketplace populated by economically rational agents who have the capacity to instantaneously integrate any new information. BS thus posits and envisions the division of the economic from the social. It imagines that the derivative markets, their components (e.g., money), and their agents exist objectively and independently of the social. Technically this stems from the fact that to price derivatives on these terms—in this mathematical manner—it is necessary to exteriorize and reify the social. What makes this necessary is that admission of the social would destroy the conditions for the use of the mathematized model.[4] From a social perspective, the Black-Scholes method exteriorizes the social structuring of the market, setting aside both the objective structures of the financial market and the motivating structures embodied in its agents.[5]

But this is only the beginning in that BS purports to be an account of the real. So the removal of the social creates an irredeemably real conundrum. This conundrum could be glossed over if BS was a purely theoretical solution intended only for theoretical speculation (about which, as in some branches of mathematics, there would be no determined limit on abstracting from the real world). But derivative pricing is about real people and money, strategically speculating. The problem of the real is that exteriorizing the social removes a derivative market's animating force. The prices generated from within the confines of the mathematics are static, immobile, and determinative, conditions under which there is no incentive to wager on a derivative's forthcoming price. Without the social's generative uncertainty and volatility, market-making would be pointless. The market posited by the BS formula could not exist if its assumption about the social were an accurate description of financial reality. It's as if one where playing a poker game in which all of the cards were (distributed) dealt face up, rendering betting, bluffing or folding moot since every player would know the outcome in advance. The transaction only occurs when traders have divined and introduced the differences of opinion which allow for a zero-sum contestation over that derivative's forthcoming value. The clockwork of a market is predicated on the extra-model reintroduction of precisely those social aspects that were necessarily excommunicated to constitute the model. Further, the BS model in its abstract form and its practitioners tend to misrecognize what is social as confounding noise rather than information though the 2008 financial crisis has awakened some as exemplified in the recent works of Emanuel Derman (2011; 2012) formerly the chief of quantitative analysis at one of the world's preeminent investment banks, Goldman Sachs (where he worked alongside Fischer Black on the construction of exotic derivatives).[6] At its core the BS model as a condition of its own construction must exteriorize and then misrecognize precisely those social forces that are constitutive of the practical use in trade of the model. And thus its very existence and reproduction in finance economics and as a market-making technology in the circulation of derivatives. BS, like other formal models, is part and product of a specific intellectual community. To formulate this in a way that converses with another anthropology, the BS formulation is a myth of the design of the derivative markets and the origin of prices that generates contradictions in practice (i.e., trading) that are so deep they can be resolved only ritually. Or in a way that connects to the theorization of capitalism as formulated by social theorists such as Moishe Postone (1993), the BS model is an embodiment of the two performative subjects of capital: the fetishized collective agency that continually generates derivative prices in an efficient market and the more social subject generative of value and capitalism's totalizing impulse. The BS formula encapsulates these two dimensions in its mathematically induced naturalization of the social. To visualize how this works requires a deconstruction of the formulation that reveals how what is social mediates the relationship between the model's mathematics and its use in practice. The aim of an analysis that is theoretically social must thus be to peel away these layers of mediation.

What the Rise of Implied Volatility Implies

To begin the deconstruction it is useful to examine two entwined histories; the BS equation as an instrument of market pricing and the evolution, social and scientific, of the mathematics. Derivative markets and their participants are existential creatures in that P&L (financial talk for profit and loss tally) determine a trader's employment or a hedge fund's existence or an investment bank's solvency. Meaning that BS has from the start been a touchstone for the evaluation of the interrelationship between abstract formulations of how derivative markets work and the concrete real-world practice of the market in which the participants are motivated by a range of situationally specific reasons and dispositions to recalibrate prices or stop trading altogether, based on their perceptions, at once singular and collective, of an inherently uncertain forthcoming. At issue here is the practical fit or interrelationship between the abstract theoretical and the empirical. To give an example foregrounded by the crises in 2007 and then again in 2008, the abstract theoretical model assumes that the pricing of any derivative can proceed as though the counterparties to the transaction are unconditionally financially solvent, whereas those involved in a real-world transaction may and frequently do refit the price based on their practical assessment of the likelihood of this being true. In order words, the very same derivative may have radically different prices based on agents' assessment of factors and forces that are external to the formulation. As scores of interviews with derivative traders underline, these adjustments are literally the difference between financial life and financial death.

Right from the start of derivative trading in 1973, traders noticed that there was an observable difference between the prices predicted by the model and actual market prices. Generally, these variances between model and market were relatively shallow, and the larger divergences that did occasionally occur turned out to be only temporary and seemingly self-correcting. For more than a decade, the prices defined by the model and the actual prices of derivatives exhibited a sufficiently close fit that there was "enough" difference to motivate trading and "enough" convergence so as to maintain the participants' faith in the model's accuracy if not its precision. And not only was actual volatility dampened, but agents' expectations of future volatility were also curbed. As MacKenzie lays out in some detail, a dialectic was set in motion in which actual prices mimicked predicted prices even as the participants' faith in the BS model served to gravitate real prices toward predicted ones (MacKenzie 2006:256–259). From a sociofinancial perspective, there was at this time a convergence of an orderly well-behaved market that featured consistently low volatility, a regimentation of social practice that incorporated this as an expectation into agents' trading strategies, and the BS pricing model. And so for more than a decade (1983–1987) into the evolution of derivative markets (in options) there was a manageable and stable spread between model prices and market prices. What no one anticipated was that the internal logic of the derivative would motivate the invention of new trading technologies and strategies that could lead a market toward self-destruction.

And thus it came to pass that in 1987 the US stock markets went into unconditional freefall. On the single day of October 19, the S&P 500 index lost 23 percent of its value. The centripetal force driving the enormous decline was, especially by contemporary standards, a simple derivative strategy known as portfolio insurance. It employed stock index futures and options in a dynamic fashion to help institutional money managers hedge their positions in the event of a stock market decline. The strategy's purpose was to increase the temporal window so that the managers could unwind their equity positions with minimal damage. Known as dynamic hedging, the money managers would short an ever increasing numbers of futures contracts (i.e., a bet that stock prices would fall) as the equity markets declined, their short position in the futures contracts (which increased in value as stock prices declined) offsetting their stock losses.

What no one anticipated was that thanks to derivatives the market now had its own internal dynamic. Independently of what was happening in the domestic economy or in government or in global politics and economics, the markets could now encounter life threatening problems. Trading could take on a Frankenstein character in which the market's creation—the derivative called portfolio insurance—assumed a life of its own threatening a liquidity shutdown. And indeed the treadmill effect kicked in. As more and more futures contracts were executed, the buyers not only insisted on sharply reduced prices which amplified risk premiums, they, quite rationally, hedged their own long futures positions by shorting the underlying stocks. This "rational" behavior drove security prices down further, which set off a new round of dynamic hedging as institutions shorted more futures contracts, motivating buyers to initiate a new spate of sell orders. When the market had tumbled by thirteen percent, a smattering of buyers stepped in on the reasoning that the best firms had become inexpensive on a fundamental basis (e.g., a growth rate that exceeded their price to earnings), but they quickly regretted their decision to the point where most were forced to liquidate their positions before the sun set that day. The locomotive had been dialed up to derailment and the following day, October 20, ushered in the prospect of systemic collapse. The astounding fall decimated the value of institutions' collateral positions which, in response, precipitating a flood of overnight margin calls. By morning a tsunami of sell orders had accumulated, but there were no buyers. And without buyers there was no way to open the markets for trading.[7] Even the specialists whose designated job it was to make a market in specific stocks had retreated, deciding that discretion was far better than bankruptcy and unemployment. The market was no longer *liquid*, meaning that there was essentially no market. There was no way to take a reading of the stock index futures, which meant that the futures contracts at the core of institutions' dynamic hedging scheme had no discoverable value. At this point in the treadmill, it turns out that markets cease to be self-correcting. In what would become a recurring theme, the opt-out by the market's makers heralded an opt-in by taxpayers. As the crisis of 2008 would reiterate, the only way to resuscitate a market is by restoring its liquidity which requires external nonmarket state intervention. Only the US Federal Reserve has the authority and the capital to restore the collectivity's collective faith in an illiquid market. So the Federal Reserve summoned the investment banking giants (e.g., Goldman Sachs, Salomon Brothers, Morgan Stanley, and Lehman Brothers) and told them pointedly that it would backstop their stock purchases by supplying capital as needed. The CEOs then informed the specialists who made markets for the s&p 500 stocks that they would temporarily work cooperatively (rather than competitively) to finance buy offers large enough to open the frozen stocks. The firms' remedial action was successful: their financial firepower and the Fed's institutional credibility were sufficient to reanimate liquidity and restart the markets.

The alignment between the objective structure of the market and the dispositions of traders revealed itself. The crisis illustrated that what seemed to be a naturally occurring convergence was, in actually, the result of a specific conjuncture in the sociohistory of the derivative. Not only could a market be buffeted by unexpected exogenous events (e.g., a presidential assassination or terrorist attack), the market's own instrumentation could generate volatility even to the point of total systemic collapse. The crash illustrated that derivative markets could amplify volatility and risk, which, in relay, rendered volatility more volatile, thereby transforming agents' expectations about the variance that needed to be priced into derivatives. And it turns out that there exists, amplifying from 1987 to the present, a considerable, continuing, and rather unpredictable divergence between the pricing results predicted by the BS model and the empirical reality of derivative markets prices. In his excursion into the evolution of exchange traded derivatives, Donald MacKenzie (2006) comments on this divergence: "The third phase in the empirical history of options pricing is from autumn 1987 to the present, when the Black-Scholes-Merton model's *fit* has been poor, . . . in the crucial matter of the relationship between *strike price* and *implied volatility*" (p. 202, my emphasis). MacKenzie concludes what every options trader (including the author of this article) knows from experience: "no analysis now finds the Black-Scholes-Merton model to fit the observed pattern of prices of options" because there is "a volatility skew" (2006:202). This skewing was first thoroughly analyzed by Derman and Kani (1994) who referred to it as the volatility smile to denote that certain options (especially out of the money puts) trade at a substantially higher price than the model predicts. From a purely scientific theoretic, the appearance of the volatility smile and its detection should have retarded the use of the BS formula since it provided clear empirical evidence that its principal claims concerning the behavior of the derivative markets were incorrect (Derman 1994). It would indeed seem eminently logical in retrospect if finance economists and traders, assessing the evidence, concluded that derivative prices were like circus animals who had forgotten their tricks, necessitating another approach to the markets. If there was such a thing as the physics of finance, the original grail of those who pioneered quantitative analysis, the stream of counterfactuals would have doomed the theory. But as noted above both theorists and practitioners continue to rely on the BS formula. Instead of disconfirming BS and thereby motivating its demise, the crash of 1987 served to consolidate its use, albeit in an inverted fashion to calculate "implied volatility."[8] As Paul Wilmott observes, although analysis demonstrates that all of the assumptions underpinning BS "can be shown to be wrong" the "model is profoundly important in both theory and practice" (2007:140). Consonantly, the remarkable fact that needs to be explained is why so many quants continue to endorse the BS model (Hunt and Kennedy 2000; Wilmott 2007) and derivative traders (and their teams) continue to use it even though they know that the model is fundamentally flawed.

As the quotation from Derman and Wilmott underlines, the mere fact that the BS formulation is technically flawed does not mean that it is useless in social practice if the practitioners appreciate the limitations, and through a process of compensation through supplementation, draw in a practical manner on the concepts, experiences, and dispositions instilled in them through their mutual participation in contemporary financial markets, to reintegrate the social into the pricing processes. Interestingly, right from their opening paragraphs, Derman and Kani (1994 observe that "by empirically varying the Black-Scholes volatility with [an option's] strike price, traders are implicitly attributing a unique *non-lognormal* distribution" to the option (p. 1). A *unique non-lognormal distribution* is, of course, what the social would look like from inside the tent of the mathematical formulation. What I will argue, based on my experience and interviews with derivative traders, is that the abstract formula tion has a certain functional necessity in that it fixes the horizon and the space of operations, however provisionally, just as the recalibration process derives in part from the recognition, already present in Black's reflection (1986) on his own device, that the very existence of a derivative market created and re-created by market makers is possible only if volatility is a nonfinite stochastic process. This is a mathematical way of saying (with a discernible smile) that the door to the social is thrown open because what motivates the participants to use the model and recalibrate derivative prices is exterior to the model yet constitutive of the market. A BS pricing outcome provides a benchmark that allows the participants to turn the contestability of future value into a contest based on their variable apperception of what important socially deserves to be discounted. What Black appreciated, exemplified in his justly famous yet commonly misconstrued article "Noise" (1986), is that the mathematics of the BS model is the negative imprint of the social just as the sociality of the market is the positive print of the qualitative dimensions of the mathematics, that is, its founding suppositions.

The use of Black-Scholes problematizes the relationship between the model and the market. What lies in between and is constitutive of this relationship are participants' trading practices. That trading mediates the relationship between the model and the market both presupposes and begs a theorization of practice. From the standpoint of trader's practice, the model and the market do not stand in opposition to one another nor is there a directional sequencing from model to market. Their practice does not presume that there exists a contradiction between model and market or that the behavior of the market falsifies the formulation; rather, for practitioners the categories unfold as a *spread* phenomenon. A spread between technical rigor and pragmatic play that they negotiate through a reflexive series of adjustments. Traders use their immersion in the worldview of the habitus of finance to reintroduce the sociality externalized by the BS model, making what appear to them to be intuitively reasonable recalibrations. The spread names the mental device traders use to reconcile the model's externalization and removal of the social with the ensemble of social determinants presented by the market. In this space of practice, there is no opposition or contradiction between technical rigor and pragmatic play because they are both mutually imbricated aspects of derivatives pricing. The dispositions and affect of traders serve to incorporate the practice of logic into the logic of practice: the mathematized result into existential decision making under uncertainty. From the purview of the trader in the act of trading, neither the structure nor the event are apparent, only his body (rife with anxiety, pressured, and hypervigilant) serving as the interpolator of the spread between the model's abstract price and its pragmatic recalibration. To appreciate how traders can negotiate this spread, using the model's results as the horizon for reintroducing the social that the model exteriorizes, it is necessary to grasp the equation in its abstract economistic form and then deconstruct the equation so that what is social again becomes visible.

History of Brownian Motion

Now the other history. A history whose origins begin in a natural science that never envisioned a physics of finance, and to this day bats its eyes at the notion that the laws of mechanics can explain capitalism's financial apparatus or the compulsion for money that motivates its agents. But if there is a truism that marks modern markets, it is that the mathematization of finance has taken on a vitality of its own that seems impervious to the received findings of other disciplines. The interesting and social question is why critiques of economic modeling by mathematicians—even devastating critiques by the world's most renowned mathematicians—have had no uptake or effect on the discipline of economics generally or financial economics specifically.

Brownian motion has a long history. Its physical processes was first observed and formulated in 1827 by the botanist Robert Brown who was interested in understanding the diffusion of pollen particles suspended in liquid. The formula proved useful for the study of variant continuous time processes, as many physical processes take the form of lognormal random variances. For example, the atmospheric dispersion of carbon emissions follows a lognormal distribution as does the diffusion of the lava that flows from the mouth of an active volcano.[9] The formula's first foray into the realm of human action came in 1900 when Louis Bachelier used the mathematical processes of Brownian motion in an attempt to model the seemingly erratic ebbs and flows of stock prices on the Paris bourse. He proposed a simple model of equity price fluctuations based on the unfolding of a straightforward normal distribution. His work on the market garnered little attention because economics had not yet mathematized itself and economists viewed the stock market as peripheral to the overall economy. As important, the economists of his day dismissed the notion that markets were regular or rational because they had just experienced what became known as the Long Depression (1873 to 1893), a period blistered by banking failures, massive unemployment, deflationary spirals, and erratic equity prices that gyrated many sigma from any normal distribution (Rosenberg 1943).[10] Also, the mathematics of Bachelier's model was a work in progress, for it was theoretically ungrounded and the equation did not admit any tractable solution. But the mathematics evolved, motivated by its usefulness in the understanding of physical processes. In 1905, Albert Einstein gave the Brownian motion process a formal theoretical foundation, in 1911 Lewis Richardson figured out how to discretize a differential equation into a difference equation (that is the finite difference method), and in 1923 Norbert Wiener developed a process for the representation of randomness. And in 1951, Kiyosi Ito advanced the mathematics considerably by showing how a function of randomness (unlike random movement itself) is smooth and differentiable.

In the late 1960s rolling into the early 70s, the US financial environment began to undergo a quantum change. The adversity to speculation that had gripped finance since the Depression had worn off, and in its place a new sense of what was possible with financial instruments began to take shape. Not only in the financial markets, a new generation of economists, post-Keynesian in temperament, committed to the market as the essential social institution, was evolving to occupy critical positions in the academe and government. The coming out party for the concept of speculation was, arguably, the document that Milton Friedman created for the Chicago Mercantile Exchange in its quest to convince Federal regulators that a derivatives market was good for the economy. The report, *The Need for a Futures Market in Currencies* (1971), argued that free efficient markets drive prosperous economies and that financial derivatives would make them even more so. Luckily for those pressing for acceptance, George Schultz, Friedman's colleague and economic disciple at the University of Chicago, had become Treasury Secretary. Schultz vouchsafed for Friedman's analysis and the virtues of a speculative derivatives market. By the time of Friedman's 1971 report, it had become known that Black, in concert with Myron Scholes, had formulated a derivative pricing model. So at the behest of

Merton Miller, Black was invited to join the economic faulty at the University of Chicago. Mehrling comments:

> The Chicago supporters [of Fischer Black's appointment] had more than altruistic motives; they were at the center of the group that was pushing to establish an options exchange at the Chicago Board of Trade (CBOT), and so they had a special reason to appreciate the importance of the work Black was doing. As early as July 1969, the CBOT had formed an advisory committee to study the potential impact of an organized options market, and the chair of that committee was none other than James Lorie. Not only that, when the committee hired the consulting firm Robert Nathan Associates to do the study, the firm hired . . . Merton Miller to help prepare its two-volume report, "Public Policy Aspects of a Future Type Market in Options on Securities," published in November 1969. (Mehrling 2005:137)

Though he did not put it this way, Miller recognized that because options have no intrinsic value, the options market required a pricing model so that traders could get their bearings, a point that underpins Miller's euphoniously entitled treatise *Merton Miller on Derivatives* (1997). It was, in fact, their reading the Miller-inspired report in 1969 that had motivated Black and Scholes to turn their attention to derivative asset pricing, leading to an initial formulation in 1970 that was progressively refined. And so it came to pass that the refinement and publication of the Black-Scholes formula for options pricing (Black and Scholes 1973) corresponded almost to the day with the celebratory opening of the Chicago Board Options Exchange. As we will see, the BS model is a model of simplicity and elegance at the surface level that sits atop an underlying complexity generated by the countervailing forces that course through real markets.

But first, to get things rolling, an annotated version of the formulation. The Black-Scholes equation has the following form:[11]

$$\frac{\partial V}{\partial t} + \frac{1}{2}\sigma^2 S^2 \frac{\partial^2 V}{\partial S^2} + rS\frac{\partial V}{\partial S} - rV = 0$$

$\frac{\partial V}{\partial t}$ *All derivatives have expiration dates. This part of the equation models how much the option's value (v) changes over time (t) if the price of the underlying asset remains constant. In other words, its role is to determine how much the premium built into the derivative wanes as the contract moves toward expiration.*

$\frac{1}{2}\sigma^2 S^2 \frac{\partial^2 V}{\partial S^2}$ *The formula is founded on a financial argument about hedging. This part of the equation defines how much a hedged position changes when the under-*

lying asset changes. It specifies the sensitivity of delta to the underlier, thereby allowing the model to account for the volatility of the underlying asset. It is a convexity term in that it measures how changes in the underlier are reflected in the derivative. Doing this entails specifying that if the point of expiration and point of pricing are in a space of events then so are all the points on the line segment joining them.

$rS\frac{\partial V}{\partial S}$ All derivatives posit and calculate from a risk-free rate (of return). This part of the formula allows for increases in the value of the underlying asset as the risk free rate.

$-rV$ Since derivatives are valued at some time point prior to the payout which (hypothetically) takes place at the derivative's expiration, it is necessary to include a discounting term. Discounting is financial speak for valuing an asset today based on what it will be worth tomorrow.

Legend: r is the discount rate, V is the volatility, t is the length of time to the derivative's expiration, S is the asset price of the underlier.

The Black-Scholes formulation is of a specific mathematical type: a linear parabolic partial differential equation. We can simply dissect this type of equation, which figures prominently in financial mathematics. The equation is linear because it does not contain any products of the derivatives and dependent variables. Linearity imbues the equation with directionality in that the sum of the discrete solutions (the +s) is itself a solution. Practically, this allows an analyst to solve for or price a portfolio of derivatives by solving each contract individually and then adding them up. The equation is parabolic in that it has the bell shaped curve characteristic of heat or diffusion equations in mechanics. This results because the first variable time has a first derivative term while the second variable, asset price, has a second derivative term. It is a partial rather than ordinary differential equation because there are two independent variables: asset price and time. Accordingly, the equation contains the partial derivatives of a function of the two variables.

The equation basically tells us that analysis can construct a portfolio that mimics the derivative's value above the risk-free rate of return as time dwindles down and the contract approaches expiration. Plugging in the values and solving the equation numerically tells us precisely how much of x we need to buy or sell at what price to create a perfectly hedged portfolio (theoretically at least). This hedging part of the formula is founded on two linked assumptions: (1) the market is closed, complete, and efficient, which then allows for the construction of a group of assets that replicate the derivative, and (2) the replication of the derivative can be done continuously. Now the assumption that we can hedge risk and do so continuously is significant because once the analysis exorcises risk it is unproblematic to calculate the value/returns on a portfolio. This hedging method is known theoretically as *delta hedging*. Delta is the sensitivity of a derivative's price to fluctuations in the price of the underlying asset; hedging refers to monitoring and adjusting the portfolio so that the two instruments (however constructed) are maintained in amounts inversely proportional to their calculated deltas. As we will see, those who trade in the derivative markets know from experience there is no such thing as genuine delta hedging and thus risk neutrality, but nonetheless integrate the concept practically into their generative schemes for assessing a portfolio's risk and then rehedging it discretely (i.e., from time to time) according to their sensibilities about a given market. The risk free interest rate part of the BS formula is unproblematic so long as one assumes that the state (i.e., the United States and the European Union) guarantees its securities' principal and interest, price discovery, and the time value of the currencies (i.e., there is no inflation that would cause the value of interest and principle to degenerate). The assumption which appears quite straightforward because treasury rates are extremely liquid and thus easily discernible is in fact quite problematic, especially in the aftermath of crises. Finally, the $-rV$, or the discounting part of the equation, is a technique for summarizing all of the forces that create volatility. Observe that the perceived power and versatility of the equation stem from the (social) fact that it brackets the social so that a manageable ensemble of parameters can capture a wide constellation of outcomes. This is ultimately what makes the BS formula a wonderful ideational tool for socially imagining the market (as a totality) as well as a practical tool that allows agents to add on all of the uncertainties present in the real world (i.e., in real world markets both the sensitivity of a derivative to the underliers [delta] and the sensitivity of delta [gamma] to changes in the underliers are moving targets).

If the BS equation is flawed then it stands to reason—especially given the money involved—that quants and the financial firms they work for, would attempt to improve the equation's efficiency. And, indeed, there has been a continuing stream of attempts to tweak, modify, and otherwise improve its performance (e.g., Gatheral 2006 attempts to model the volatility of volatility). With small success, however. As Paul Wilmott observes with his characteristically wry humor: "there have been many extensions to [BS], some people call them 'improvements'; . . . but these extensions are all *trivial* when compared . . . with the original equation" (Wilmott 2009:129, my emphasis). It is easy to observe that these various "extensions" of BS, attempts to improve the precision of the model usually by adding complexity, end up making little difference either theoretically or practically. Theoretically because the problems that compromise its real-world application are not mathematical and practically because derivative traders don't expect the equation to render anything like exact predications. One would think that this would be a topic of analysis. But it turns out that financial economists are in a particularly poor position to detect the distinction between the official version of BS as a mathematization of the derivative and its practical version as a template for agents' trading strategies. Everything in their training—interrupted but only temporarily by the 2008 financial crisis (Mirowski 2010)—disposes the economist and the quantitative analyst to take at face value the field's official conception of BS as a pure mathematical representation of a market. By contrast, traders who are subjected to a brutal calculus in which their firms and their pocketbooks compel them to tally up their profits and losses precisely (many traders are compensated on the basis of what the street refers to as risk adjusted return on capital) have every reason to apprehend that the calculation of implied volatility simply sets the stage for the trading that follows.

Finance Economics and the Official Position

Technically, the orthodox position that dominates finance economics is that mathematized models based on Brownian motion are tractable and accurate for pricing derivatives. The understanding is that analysts can price derivatives using a diffusion type equation that is solved numerically. To develop such an analysis it is standard to posit the existence of (1) an explicitly defined probability space in respect to (2) a continuous set of functions within that abstract space of events. The probability space is treated as explicitly defined on the founding premise that the two parameters, the risk-free interest rate and asset volatility, can be unconditionally specified. Thus defined, derivative prices will follow a continuous process rather than experience discontinuous jumps or ruptures, such as those motivated by seven- or eight-sigma "black swan" events or, more often, by the dynamic degeneration of a market. From this perspective, the market is simply a way of staging probabilistic risk.

Once these conditions are set, the mechanics of derivative-pricing can engage. Tractability determines that the model start with a derivative pricing process in a closed and technically perfect space. The supposition is that the market is so technically efficient in processing information, discovering prices, and executing transactions that it is possible to discount any exogenous transgressions and endogenous disruptions. Another feature of this technically perfect space is that the returns are normally distributed. In a most common derivation, the analyst specifies the derivative pricing process by means of a stochastic differential equation embedded in a real-world probability measure P—"real world" in that P represents the volatility of the derivative being modeled, such as the volatility of a given collateralized mortgage obligation. The analyst selects a numeraire N (typically the most representative traded contracts) and then changes the probability measure to an equivalent martingale measure N, under which all N-rebased derivatives are martingales (note that the martingale is a sequence of non-determined prices in which variability is confined to that derivative's price history and where the best estimate of any recalibrated price is the previous price). Accordingly, expectations in the value of N determine the derivative's price. The interpretation is straightforward: the price of a derivative is the net present value of the expectations in the value of N under a risk-neutral random walk. In the case of an "exotic" derivative, the analyst simply adds together the prices of the various component parts. In the language of finance, "vanilla" contracts are added together to price a more exotic one.[12]

From an abstract mathematical standpoint all is well and good. Both the basic mathematics (differential equations and probability theory) and the numerics are rather well understood. It should then come as no surprise that Brownian motion models can reliably capture the variability in the stream of values (e.g., emission of carbon or heat conduction) generated by all sorts of natural phenomena. But there is a telling problem in the math's application to derivatives and their markets. Both in respect to a market's structure and its participants' agency. Specifically, the social space in which a market is embedded and its derivatives priced is never an explicitly defined probability space and its agent driven transactions are not a martingale measure. Right from the start, the mathematician Benoit Mandelbrot (1971 and 1997) called into question the validity of using a random walk and martingale model. Mandelbrot's analysis, although mathematically beyond reproach, was dismissed by finance economics.[13] Speaking of financial models, Emanuel Derman observes (2012) a curious conflation between *a model* that aims to describe a regularity and *a theory* that purports to explain that regularity. It is worth noting that the parameters in the original mathematical formulation have no ontological reality nor do they claim any (beyond their mathematical uses). Because equations do not contain instructions on how and under what circumstances to apply them in the real world, even in the most natural of sciences (that is physics) human intentionality grounds the *declaration* that *this* mathematical representation is the explanatory theory for *that* phenomenon (keeping in mind that the declaration is a performative collectively ratified by members of the field).

When this mathematics is deployed to price derivatives problems accrue immediately because the BS formula does not account for the modus operandi of the equation, instead reducing the generative schemes that agents use to instantiate the equation to a mechanical operation. More precisely, the formal economic suppositions about the use of the equation expunge the generative schemes without which the equation would be nothing more than a lifeless artifact. The power of the equation to price derivatives in no way implies the performative power that is required to make use of the equation in constantly changing situations. Finance economics fades this problem by overlooking the slippage between the abstract model and the open-ended agent driven process of selecting and inserting specific numerical data into the model. But the model does not come with instructions on the incorporation of data. This compels the analyst to assume (1) all the token derivative contracts are actually indexical icons or exact replicas of a derivative type (while straightforward with vanillas this can be quite problematic when it comes to exotics); (2) an intuitive judgment, inscribed as an act of classification, regarding which data to fit to what version of the BS formulae (so where does the pricing history come from given the many derivatives in circulation?); and (3) an intuitive estimation as to what constitutes a sufficiently robust time series (important because there are no mathematically based criteria for what constitutes an adequate time series for any particular real-world derivative). This intuitive fitting process, clearly a crucial component of pricing in that selection can and frequently does determines the outcome, can be used to enhance speculation, obfuscate losses in a portfolio, or disguise a position's vulnerability to volatility (all of which are especially true in respect to exotic OTC derivatives).[14] What is so telling about the process is that it is inherently performative in that the analyst must sweep various tokens up into a type and set the temporal boundaries of the probability space. Furthermore, the appearance of a derivative-pricing equation as a finished product, tends to expunge the performative events on which it is based. Contrary to the neoliberal economistic theoretic, the pricing of a real-world (especially OTC) derivative lies at the intersection of the dispositions collectively inculcated in the market's participants and their uses of the mathematization of finance. Let us underline that there is nothing amiss in the equation's mathematics or its numerics (diffusion type equations and martingales have an honorable history). It is just that relying on a primitive finite difference model with reality bracketing assumptions can provide only a hypostatized but reasonable starting point for price (re)calibration under *normal*, thus presupposed, market conditions. That is, and this is the meaning of the normal that is presupposed in the (re)calibration, as long as that market remains liquid because its participants maintain their collective faith in the efficacy of the government, the capital markets, a market price discovery mechanism, and their specific counterparties. Normal is thus a particular social state of the world founded on a regime of volatility that conforms to agents' expectations such that they collectively believe that forthcoming volatilities will mimic existing ones, which, in turn, allows for market creating liquidity. *What this says is that the final pricing of any real-world derivative is intrinsically extrinsic to the derivative pricing model.*

The Social Entailments of the Formula

To understand what the use of the derivative pricing model entails it is necessary to deconstruct the Black-Scholes formula in a way that allows us to indicate the various social entailments built into it. This is critical because the formula makes an ensemble of social ontological claims about the relative influence of the social on the determination of derivative prices. This encompasses, on the side of objectification, the organization, reproduction, and temporality of the (any) market, and on the side of the subject, agents' positions and dispositions, cognitive and motivating structures, and decision making under uncertainty. Put another way, the Black-Scholes equation embodies, even as it disavows, a theory of financial practice.

Let us begin by enumerating some of the characteristics of the Black-Scholes formula. I do not intend the roster of characteristics to be exhaustive as the principal objective is to illuminate what assumptions it needs to make about the social to satisfy the conditions for its execution. What will become clear is that many of the suppositions that underwrite the BS formulation make overlapping and reiterative claims about the asocial character of the market. What is so critical about what the model exteriorizes is that this constitutes the contestable knowledge that defines the limits of the spread between the technical price and the recalibrated one.

Simple Diffusion Equation

Black-Scholes and all of its offspring are essentially diffusion equations (i.e., Brownian motion). Diffusion equations work with and on *natural types:* that is to say semiotically, phenomena in which every token is a perfect indexical icon of the type. Such equations unconditionally rule out the existence of differences among tokens that require agentive acts of classification and the possibility of singular, one of a kind, phenomena. Accordingly, the difference between types and tokens that stands at the core of the social, the relation between objective classifications and the practical practice of classifying an event, an object, or a financial instrument, etc. cannot be represented in such equations. There may be forces that regiment these processes and their distribution, thus imbuing them with a real measure of regularity—including the institutionalization of the use of the BS equation and the field's inculcation of a shared speculative ethos in its agents—but these social forces elude the formulation's powers of representation and analysis. What this means is that the Black-Scholes pricing model will variably capture some dimensions of the regularities (such as expected volatility) when the participants, in the manner akin to a trained and experienced orchestra without a conductor, collectively apprehend the state of the market as normal and therefore productive of an expected range of values. BS can do no more, no less, having exteriorized the social. Conversely, when unexpected events occur, traders assume that an unexpected range of values is in the offing, this rising *risk of uncertainty* reflected in the widening of the spread (beyond anything calculable by the model). Interview after interview with derivative traders—meaning those who survive its brutal calculus—reveals that they intuitively grasp this. In sum, by expunging the relation between classificatory systems and agents' practical acts of classification the BS equation exteriorizes a foundational semiotic dimension of the social.

Randomness

The Black-Scholes equation posits what is referred to as an Ito process (after the Japanese mathematician Kiyosi Ito). What this means is that the generation of values must be independent of one another and the values must be distributed identically across the space of financial events. This is important because derivative pricing starts with the lognormal stochastic differential equation for the trajectory of an asset. Ito's lemma, as his discovery is called, allows analysis to determine the stochastic differential equation for the value of a derivative of that asset. Without randomness, there is no way to make the jump from the stochastic differential equation for an independent variable (the price of the asset) to the stochastic equation for a function of that variable (the derivative). The notion, or better principle, of randomness lies at the very foundation of the equation and is, accordingly, indispensable to its solution.

This principle is significant because two founding principles of the social are the suppression of randomness and the creation of memory as embodied in institutions and the habitus of agents. The social world is replete with imagined totalities that institute modes of organization (e.g., the market) designed to minimize randomness and generate the kind of regularities in human behavior that allow us to apprehend the actions of a stranger or an anonymous other (trades on an electronic screen) as intentional and meaningful. More, the derivative markets create products that destroy randomness in that the very creation of the derivative materially influences the price of the underlier (as we saw earlier in the case of portfolio insurance). The notion of randomness presupposes that financial acts, such as executing a trade, are not collectively generated, and that there is no social memory in the minimal sense that previous trades have absolutely no bearing on forthcoming ones. This is ethnographically untrue for institutional traders who calculate their P&L (profit and loss) cumulatively on a daily basis and frequently make trading decisions based on building a relationship with a given client or counterparty. In an Ito process, there is no such thing as collectively instilled ideas and dispositions and there's no such thing as memory, collective or otherwise. The existence and persistence of the "volatility smile" represents the market's collective memory that unpredictable, potentially devastating, price distortions are always possible. Particularly when agents, in their quest to maximize short-term returns in order to best their peers, a competition that determines compensation, *put on* leveraged positions with borrowed funds. This is one reason why attempts to explain real-world deviations from predicted prices almost always bring the social back in, albeit in a rather subterranean fashion (exemplified by explanations for "out of the money" puts, which are consistently more expensive than the BS model predicts).[15]

Linearity and Homogenity

The BS equation relies on two parameters: time and volatility. In mathematics, a parameter is an unanalyzed and constant variable. The equation treats the parameter as an external and immobile aspect of the phenomena under consideration (such as y in the partial derivative—f{x,y}). Mathematically, the linearity of BS means there is a combination of derivatives of order less than some finite n. This linearity entails that not only is the time derivative known and certain, the volatility is also known and certain. This provision thus guarantees that all future events (price points) will be iterations of past events (nothing blasts past the finite n). The reason for this is that linearity works only when there is a normal distribution, symmetrical around the mean. Analysis can then measure volatility as a standard deviation, which logically holds if and only if only randomness has a known probability distribution. The quality, homogeneity, says that the value (in prices) of a portfolio of derivative contracts is the direct sum of the individual contracts. And correlatively that an individual "exotic" contract is the direct sum of the portfolio of "vanilla" exchange traded contracts that it embodies (based, as shown earlier, on the performative act of classification undertaken by the exotic derivative's creator).

These two provisions rule out the possibility of decision making under uncertainty, replacing it with decision making under a known probability distribution. As in the act of throwing a die, the outcomes are predetermined (i.e., one through six) though any specific outcome is not (throwing a one rather than a four). Given the value of the underlier, the derivative pricing model specifies which outcomes are consistent with an efficient market, manned by economically rational actors, in a certain environment. This is where critics like Ayache and Taleb enter the fray. They note that if the agents all know the outcome (for a derivative's price) they will, by virtue of this accessible and shared knowledge, have no motivation to enter into a zero-sum wager on that derivative, thus recalibrating the price and making a market, unless the future is uncertain, the market has inefficiencies that can be exploited, and numerous forms of rationality as well as embodied dispositions drive the participants. From a social perspective, the assumption built into the model is that agents' projections and common consensus about the forthcoming direction of interest rates, their projections about changes in a derivative's volatility (due to a perception of escalating speculation) or any of the other real life sources of recalibration will not have any effect on derivative prices. To put this socially, the model in its pure form (as it is often used by quantitative theorists and finance economists) does not have any room for a sociospecific concept of agency, for markets in which agents act under conditions of variable epistemic opacity, or for markets having a nonlinear history (of the kind that would occur, and historically has occurred, from liquidity stops). The model thus removes some of the critical variables that traders price into derivative transactions.

Another way to think about this is that these provisions mean the BS formulation endorses a finalism. This is a theoretical approach that says that the eventual result is predetermined in the genesis of the phenomena. Applied to natural types, this approach is productive and predictive as when a specific amount of a gas diffuses through a particular medium under certain conditions (think of the real-world example of anesthesia in which the anesthetist ideally calculates the diffusion of a certain volume of a gas through a patient's bloodstream based on a coefficient).[16] In the derivative market, this finalism means that the interval between the initiation of a contract and its expiration occurs in a noneventful and homogeneous space. The space is noneventful in that the menu of possible events is known exhaustively, with certainty, in advance. Every market is thus like a concert in which the performers randomly lip synch songs from their recent albums with nary a hitch. It is homogeneous because the model precludes internal differentiation based on the social institutional positions and pricing power of the agents. What this says is that there is no possibility prices will be inflected by the exercise of power by financial institutions such as Goldman Sachs, Morgan Stanley, or omnivorous hedge funds endowed with giant pools of opportunistic and nomadic speculative capital. In the flat homogeneous space created by backwardation, there are no moments of agency in which a market's participants respond to financial events (another firm's impending collapse), their own subjective dispositions, the information that a powerful institution is taking a particular side of a trade, or unpredictable exogenous forces (such as an attack on a financial center or the disruption in the flow of an essential commodity particularly oil). Actual traders are, of course, acutely aware and compulsively hypervigilant about such interventions.

Replication and Singularity

As observed above, the BS pricing model contains an argument about hedging. The argument posits a nonmathematical parameter that guarantees that the interior space of a derivatives market is immune from social differentiations that would alter the pricing of a derivative. Replication and singularity are the analytical mechanisms that drive the hedging argument. Replication means that pricing a derivative is based on assembling a set of assets guaranteed to universally yield an amount identical to the derivative. This is presumably possible because an analyst can fabricate and model a complex derivative out of more basic instruments (e.g., a bond and a FOREX contract). This means that the analyst can hedge the derivative with the underliers to generate a perfectly risk free instrument. For this artificial instrument to accurately reflect the derivative the market must be complete in that prices are singularities. As Roy Bailey (2001) explains in *The Economics of Financial Markets,* this determines that there is a linear pricing rule because there are the same number of linearly independent securities as there are future states of the market (p. 173). The result is that no derivative or portfolio of assets can have more than one price (called *the law of one price* in financial economics); this *law* is secured through the axiom that markets by virtue of their constitutive principles eschew arbitrage such that the existence of singular or state prices precludes arbitrage. The supposition, dressed as a natural law, is that for a market to be sufficiently efficient to allow such hedging, arbitrage must be impossible. So one of the foundational suppositions of BS is that the very possibility of a market depends on the non-existence of arbitrage, complemented by the secondary supposition that should arbitrage opportunities materialize (due to market anomalies) the spread between prices would be instantaneously closed.

Note the peculiar logic of the argument. The presentation and closure of the arbitrage presupposes the failure, the end, of the market within which the opportunity arose in the first place. The occasion of arbitrage can occur only within a market that cannot exist as such because a market's existence is inseparable from the null set of arbitrage possibilities. The notion that closure occurs instantaneously, whether ever empirically true which it is not, is irrelevant since the disavowal has already removed the (healing) power of time. The relative length of an interval that cannot exist is a meaningless measure. Nevertheless, for the BS formula the nonexistence of what exists is critical to the formation of the state prices that underwrite the analysis. Ironically, this move is an archetype of the economic tradition that Fischer Black took pains to distance himself from. For it consists in recognizing that the possibility of arbitrage is always present, that the non-arbitrage clause needs to be a critical supposition only on the condition that arbitrage is an ever-present possibility in the financial markets. But in the name of a tractable mathematics it inserts an idealized perfectly homogeneous space that banishes arbitrage to a timeless exteriority that can no longer influence prices. Thus conceived, analysis can now no longer interrogate how arbitrage influences the structuration of the markets. The model thus excludes what it recognizes as a possibility for every market transaction by valorizing an immediate simultaneity—the instantaneous eradication of two prices for the identical security—that lies exterior to the concept of the market that it posits. To put this another way, the fact that the real world is saturated with arbitrage opportunities reveals why spreads are so ubiquitous.[17]

Now it turns out that the notion of a complete market contains three claims or propositions about the social. Finance economics endorses the idea of a complete market because this reinforces the notion of a perfectly efficient market that can be rendered mathematically; quantitative analysts like the idea because in complete markets they can replicate exotic derivatives with simpler instruments or, conversely, fabricate a risk-free instrument by hedging the derivative with the sale or purchase of the underlier. The first proposition or claim about the social is that space of a derivatives market is perfectly homogeneous. The market is flat insofar as there are no internal forms of differentiation and motivation (such as those based on race, class, gender, status and position, institutional affiliations, nationality, generation, and so on) which the social history of the present tells us permeate capitalist societies and imbue them with a historical dynamic or aiming (toward the evolution of derivative markets for example). The foundational claim is that for a market's participants the social forces of the real world have no effect on their thoughts, desires, or practices. In this respect, the axiom of homogeneity is a socially flattening abstraction that displaces an ethnographic analysis of how things actually work. The second social claim or proposition is that agents and markets can and do forecast the future always perfectly (i.e., forthcoming volatility is transparent to the agents), meaning that decision making under uncertainty, a critical feature of how agents conceptualize their own social practice, does not exist. The final claim is that there exists a liquid market on which to hedge all outcome influencing phenomena. What this indicates is that capitalist markets are systemically self-reflexive in that these markets contain all of the necessary elements for their mutual self-construction. Note additionally, this final proposition encompasses the reverse claim that phenomena that cannot be successfully hedged—such as a terrorist attack but also more significantly the systemic collapse created by the complete cessation of liquidity—never influence derivative pricing processes. Collectively, these claims preclude the existence of unpredictable "Black Swan" events (Talib 2005). More importantly, these three factors are critical inputs in determining the spread that forms the foundation of traders' real-world replication schemes.

Risk-Free Interest Rate and Asset Volatility

Solving the BS equation requires two equation external social fictions: the risk free interest rate and the asset's volatility. The first assumes that there exists a natural risk free interest rate, which, in relay, assumes that the state can guarantee a risk free rate of return because the national state presents no counterparty risk due to the fact that it is perpetually solvent, that the price of money remains constant (there is neither currency inflation nor deflation), and that the interest rate for government bonds can serve as proxy for the risk free return. These conditions are not natural, but represent a point in an historical process for metropolitan capitalist nations. (As far as we know no one has suggested that Argentine government bonds could just as well serve as a measure of the risk free rate of return). The significant point is that what BS considers the natural risk free interest rate is actually a historical outcome subject and subjected to political considerations. Theoretically, the calculation of the risk free interest rate assumes a perfect market in which the state does not intervene to influence rates. But this is of course precisely what the US Fed did from 2008 through 2014, exemplified by its purchase of trillions of US Treasuries and mortgage backed securities. The Fed's aim is to revive the liquidity that the risk free rate presupposes as a condition of its utility.

The second supposition involves the fiction that the volatility assigned to the asset is ontologically real. In reality, analysts can only ever infer a derivative's volatility. Either volatility that is implied from historical data or volatility inferred backward from the present market price (i.e., implied volatility). What is inferred is critical because the model's predictions are very sensitive to initial conditions. Indeed, traders treat the volatility suggested by the model as an initial condition that will be subject to revision on the road to generating a pricing structure, that is, wagerable spread.

Supply and Demand

Earlier analysis indicated that if the BS model was the final word on the pricing of derivatives, a market would not exist as such insofar as a derivatives market depends on its participants' willingness to wager on price. The reason for this is that there is no place in the Black-Scholes formula for the market itself; that is a trading platform composed of competing agents who create bid and asked prices for securities. This pricing spread already indicating a difference in the valuing of the securities. There is consonantly nothing in the equation that deals with supply and demand, and more precisely imbalances in supply and demand. The underlying social assumptions are that markets are virtually perpetually in equilibrium and that all participants are term indifferent speculators who will equally and opportunistically assume long or short positions. Several counterpoints: (1) this is empirically inaccurate as supply/demand ratios are congenitally skewed to the point that the social reproduction of the market counts on this skewing; (2) the world as a whole is long stocks as cultural values seem to place a premium on investing in well-known national companies by investing in their stocks; (3) the economistic ideology that posits the existence of an "indifferent speculator" (willing to go short as easily as long) has become part of the derivative pricing model. Contrast the premise of BS with the reality that the directional positions responsible for generating a market in the first place are bets that either demand will exceed supply or vice versa.

Since supply and demand form no part of the analysis, and demand is often a direct function of social forces, the BS equation cannot account for any instrument whose price is heavily inflected by a social demand function. Finance economists have noted that the BS formula has a difficult time in accurately pricing what are called "out of the money" puts. Examination of the empirical data reveals that often the real-world market prices for these contracts are, at least from the theorization of the BS efficient market model, seemingly impossible because they violate the tenets of rationality, symmetry, and the no arbitrage provision. What this underlines is that the extent to which supply and demand drives a derivative's price, the model's forecast of its future volatility will likely miss the mark. Accordingly, accounts of options pricing archetypically begin with the call option as the paradigmatic contract, thus marginalizing out of the money puts or dealing with them parenthetically by observing that they have fat tails. The following presumably impossible scenario occurs over and again in the options market, particularly at the end of quarters for equities that have outperformed the broader indexes by more than 10 percent.

The scenario:

a) the underlying stock is trading at a given price, say, $100 per share.
b) the price of the 95 put is significantly more than that of the 105 call, in some instances by a factor of two or even more (the model predicts the prices will be symmetrical and identical since both contracts have equal probability that variance in the underlier's price will put them "in the money"). There is thus an extraordinary and heavily skewed volatil-

ity smile in which the out of the money puts are very expensive both on historical grounds and as calculated through implied volatility.

c) with the stock still at $100 per share and the options contracts grinding toward expiration, the price of the 95 put barely recedes even as the contract inches towards worthlessness. The model predicts a much steeper decline in price; for why, on earth, would a rational investor pay nearly the same amount for an already overpriced asset dwindling in value.

The answer to this spate of seeming irrationality, usually by mutual fund managers whose MBA education has inculcated them to be the most rational investors who have ever walked the face of the earth, is the outcome of social forces and can accordingly only be explained socially. The reality is that the demand for the puts on these advancing stocks is significantly greater than for the calls, even as the price for the underlier has little chance of declining because demand remains strong as fund managers add such winning stocks to their portfolio (what the trade calls "window dressing"). The mutual fund managers are willing to purchase the puts en masse, even though they are acutely aware that they are overpaying on technical grounds, because no one wants to underperform their peers if the stock happens to crater in the days leading up till the end of the quarter when they present their results to shareholders and/or institutional bosses. To put this another way, that the puts are more expensive than the calls simply reveals that what is socially rational often trumps what is economically transparently so.[18] Parallel examples where social rationalities push aside the supposedly hegemonic economic rationality can also be found in the debt and currency markets (see LiPuma and Koelble 2009).

A Left-Handed Equation

Solving the BS equation involves what mathematicians refer to as backwardation. For the equation, this means that it is necessary to specify the payoff at expiration and then work backward in time to determine present values. This backward regression from the future to the present derives from the fact that Black-Scholes, like a percentage of people, is left handed (i.e., there is a zero to the right of the equal sign). For equations at least, this is important in that when applied to the things social such as trading derivatives, left handed equations have specific consequences. In the critical sense that their satisfaction entails exteriorizing the social practices and circumstances of the circulation of derivatives in the real world. To begin with, the equation's calculus works if and only if the terminal payoff is foreordained; that is, the payoff must be a riskless event in several senses. First, the value of money must be constant in that inflation or deflation would change the calculation. In real-world trading, either this is insignificant because the temporal interval is relatively short or, in the case of longer-term contracts, traders take this possibility into consideration in respect to their overall price calculation. In other words, the future price of money is an enshadowed variable in which traders use their understanding of the world's political economy (e.g., Federal Reserve and ECB monetary policies) to assess inflationary trends. Second, the payoff must adhere to a finalism in which the initiation of a contract determines its final outcome. There cannot, accordingly, be any possibility whatsoever that a counterparty (e.g., Lehman Brothers) will default on the payoff. The formula assumes that the participants' evaluation of their counterparties will never influence the pricing process. In practice, these can be very critical determinations especially when evaluating OTC derivatives, Traders take into consideration the fact that a solvent counterparty may rapidly become insolvent, and they use their sense of the market and knowledge (or lack thereof) of the counterparty in question to price this uncertainty into what they are willing to pay for a derivative. Again, we see that the theoretical model that allows backwardation is eminently different from the prospective character of practice.

BS Viewed Theoretically and as Social Practice

The godfather of modern mathematical statistics, Andrei Kolmogorov,[19] laid out the architecture for constructing an abstract space of events where the action, such as pricing derivatives, would occur. Now, as alluded to earlier, analysts could deal with the flaws and failings of BS by adding missing variables to enrich the space. That said, including other plausibly variables, like whipsaws in volatility, oscillations in market liquidity, the effects of (changing) supply and demand, distortions to the risk-free rate, the solvency of the counterparties, the persistence of arbitrage opportunities, and more would soon render the BS equation far too complex to be tractable or useful in practice.[20] Given traders' mathematical limitations—they are after all recruited and rewarded because they excel at trading not computation—and the fact that the realities of the market usually mock the model and occasionally explode its usefulness, real world finance has opted for a BS model with the smallest number of variables or unknowns. The ethnography of trading indicates that, for traders, their trading practices are coherent and meaningful not only because they lead to the creation of repeatedly profitable strategies but because they are readily mastered and manageable. So what appears socially is that practice leans toward an economy of practice whose aims are its own not those of finance math. What is more, traders have from their experience every reason to subscribe to the virtues of their economy. There is an important distinction between precision and accuracy: such that greater precision does not inherently produce greater accuracy. Adding "improvements" to BS presumably results in greater theoretical precision at the cost of increasing complexity. But, and here is the double-sided conundrum, not only do these improvements make the BS formula more difficult to master and manage practically, they do not result in greater accuracy if the new inputs don't do what they mathematically cannot do: encompass the social and its strictly sociological modes of regimenting practice. This is why attempts to tweak BS to make it consistent with the socially induced "mispricings" of volatility that characterize and thus *make* a derivative market add several coats of complexity but fail to improve the model's accuracy.[21] And why traders gravitate toward the simplest model possible.

Approximating a Conclusion

The Black-Scholes formula exists in a polychromatic space, a space that agents interpolate from the four cardinal directions of its (re)production and use. These various interpolations, which are all in their own way constitutive of the production of a derivative market, depend on what the users of the formula believe it does, and more foundationally and critically, on what is happening socially beneath transactions whose appearance is that of pure calculation. This deep sociality is important because the reproduction of the market and the success of the formula depend on a sociality that is so exteriorized that it is unrecognized as such.

The first interpolation of BS is as a scientific mathematized theory of how derivatives work and can be priced. As noted, this account is unsound theoretically because parameters constitutive of the object—from supply and demand to the market itself—are bracketed as a condition of the production of the mathematized account. And it is unsound empirically in that real market transactions almost invariably violate some of the founding principles: for example, two derivatives with the same underlier having different volatilities. Notwithstanding these serious problems—which in physics would lead to the abandonment of the paradigm—finance economists feel compelled to affirm and uphold the scientific truthfulness of this account because any recognition of its theoretical and empirical failings would undermine the suppositions that undergird the discipline. That is, they are socially motivated, and understandably so given the awards and rewards that have become attached to this position, to cling to an objectivist account of objectification in which mathematical axioms give rise to financial theorems. This interpolation is also social in its construction of the object of knowledge. Specifically, it constitutes a financial market as a homogeneous structure populated by agents whose forms of rationality are purely cognitive, singular, and identical to the mathematized (asocial) rationality by which the economist constructs that space as an object of contemplation staged from an Archimedean view from nowhere. The deep social moment is that finance economists transplant into the market the principles of their relation to it, leading them to conceive the market as a pregiven totality intended for cognition alone, in which all transactions are reduced to axiom driven utility maximization. Unfortunately, this bears no relationship whatsoever to the real world of derivative pricing and therefore to the reproduction of these markets. Which explains why neoclassical economics cannot begin to explain the 2008 financial crisis.[22]

The second moment of BS is that it allows for the objectification of the market as a totality. No matter for what purpose it is used or how the equation is solved, its construction posits, as pregiven and inalienable fact, a closed and complete market. That is essentially a self-referential totality. But the objectification is more than theoretical. The BS model is an award winning representation—circulated globally via the EuroAmerican financial media—that the economy is separate from other forms of social life, and that the market is its own independent collective agent. The social ontology is that the model's representation of the market is the totality which, subjected to real-world forces, becomes deformed. Nonetheless, to believe in the market is to believe in the ontology of the model's suppositions in that collective participation in any market in which the counterparties are anonymous makes sense only if the agents believe that there is price discovery, only unusual counterparty defaults, continuing liquidity in that there is a quorum of players and enough sufficiently speculative capital, regulatory tolerance toward that market (here, now, for the foreseeable future). In other words, the BS formulation does two thing socially: it is a mathematical representation of the market as a natural perduring type, and it is part of the solution to the construction of a social form which circulates excess capital via the financialization of life. Central to the project of capitalism is to make all markets, even derivative markets which are not only the most contemporary of financial inventions but also synthetic, appear natural to those who encounter them. That these markets can be modeled mathematically—using the tools we use for nature—helps them to assume the aura of self-evident facticity. What is so interesting about BS is less that it is an essentialist reading of the present, but that it is a central ideological cog in the real relations of the (re)production of the conflation between economic categories of practice and analytical categories.

The third direction of BS is as a communal tool. Where the model assumes every token is a perfect exemplar of the type, traders know better. And so they operate on a different model, on the implicit understanding that markets have a protean character. Every derivative market and every trade is irredeemably particular, yet they are also general and discursive. Accordingly, traders think of BS as a modular form. Essentially, the doubled idea that BS is universally applicable though invariably in need of contextual refinement. In this respect, it mirrors the doubled character of the market as simultaneously universal yet granular in its capacity to price even the most exotic singular abstract risk-driven derivative. The ethnography underlines that traders have an inherently sophisticated grasp of markets, although their contexts of practice never call on them to use this understanding more than as the implicitly, unspoken ground of practice. For them, each derivatives market is a multiform and differentiated axis of circulation to which certain generative schemes, such as BS, may apply. Each market is an arena of monetary but also symbolic struggle in that grasping all of those things that lie beyond the BS formula is simultaneously the source of profit and a public commentary about oneself. And more, all markets are interfunctionally dependent in that pricing in one market may well be radically interdependent with other markets. On the ground, traders can use BS as a modular form integrated in a more general generative schemes for pricing. That is, BS intersects with the generative schemes for the inclusion of the social, allowing for the creation of a spread that serves as the ground of the speculative wager. It thus comes to serve as a departure point because there has evolved a deeply inculcated consensus on the utility of BS, meaning that the founding concepts are easy to understand, the model's faults which reside mostly in its underlying assumptions (e.g., no counterparty risk, perfect price discovery) are common knowledge (e.g., discovering a derivative's price often requires a combination of economic insights and social maneuvering), and traders have learned how to discount what the model dismisses or omits. At the molecular level, traders know every derivative is different in some respect (especially volatility), so they don't organize their calculation to each feature of the contract. Rather, they assume that while no two derivatives or combinations thereof are ever entirely alike in all possible respects, they are sufficiently alike in key respects to allow an approximation of price. Based on their practical knowledge traders take account of and incorporate into their generative schemes for pricing an expectation of volatility which while inconsistent with the theoretical mathematization of the market is consistent with their more practical calculus of their reality.

The final and most critical dimension is the social practice of pricing and trading derivatives. In contrast to the usual scholastic portrait, which arises from an only implicit conceptually mushy notion of practice, the pricing of derivatives flows from the habitus of the market's participants, a habitus that encompasses the collective supposition of a derivative market's totality, the notion that the mathematization of the BS formula imbues it with legitimacy, and the shared belief that BS is a communal or collective tool that creates the common ground for pricing. The economy of pricing takes place at the intersection of the objective structure of a market at a specific point in time—the players, the participating institutions, the derivative instruments, the BS model—and the embodied dispositions and generative schemes of traders. It is these incorporated dispositions and schemes, visibly articulated as players' sense of the game, which allows them to begin with the BS pricing formula as a launching point to recalibrate a derivative's price founded on the common understanding that there is always an element of contingency and indeterminacy yet also a recognizable necessity in that traders can use their knowledge and intuitions to decipher that derivative's "correct" price, its forthcoming value at expiration, thus moving them to jointly "pull the trigger" and consummate the bet.[23] To fathom why traders continue to use the BS formulation—despite its well documented theoretical flaws and empirical failings—it is necessary to appreciate that a mathematical logic unfolding in a perfect world (the complete market) is, for traders, only a first approximation of a practical logic unfolding in a social universe. Because agents' habitus is the product of a confrontation with a market defined by irregular regularities, it can produce through reasonable adjustments a wager adapted to the probable volatility of the market. At an existential level, the price of a derivative stems from agents recognition of conditional cues to which they are predisposed to react owing to their indoctrination in, and experience of, that specific market. The basis of these reactions may encompass, but also extend far beyond and sometimes owe little to, rational calculation. The market as a social fact owes its practical coherence and continuity in the face of volatility, illiquidity, counterparty failures to the reality that it is the product of practices that are coherent practically in that the participants can recalibrate them to the objective state of the market (e.g., a terrorist attack or a hedge fund collapse) and are manageable because they are parsimonious. On these grounds, it is easy to see how useful the BS formula is practically: adaptable, economical, mutually shared, and robust.

When analysis has put aside the objectivist account of objectification, amplified and exemplified by the mathematization of the finance market, the question of the market as a capitalist production in which the circulation of capital is the worksite of struggle among competing participants remains. The question is whether analysis can account for derivative markets by developing an approach that considers the systemic dimension of these capitalist capital markets, the family resemblance among different markets brought about by the use and adaptation of reflecting modular forms and generative schemes, and the space for the incorporation of all those things social that motivate agents to collectively reproduce the market as a totality. The genius and scandal of the Black-Scholes formula is that it is instrumental on all these levels.

Chapter 10

Derivatives and Wealth

when we speak we are afraid

our words will not be heard

or welcomed

but when we are silent

we are still afraid

so it is better to speak

remembering

that we were never meant to survive

—AUDRE LORDE, *Litany for Survival*

What follows seeks to re-find and to refine the points I have made by inserting conclusions about derivatives into a politics of wealth and a moral purpose that cares about justice. In the beginning there was the wealth of nations. Specifically the beginnings of capitalism as imagined by Adam Smith. The end terms of his equation, wealth and nations, conceptualized the existence of a surplus, what was created beyond the provision of pure necessity, and collectively so by those nations summoned into being by their notions of peoplehood. The molecular structure of his analysis was that the generation of wealth was founded on how a united people drew the terms and conditions of their division of labor and vision of wealth. The wealth of a nation was thus accordingly a collective enterprise and a collective reward. Smith's voicing was echoed in that constitutive American vision that all citizens have an unbreakable and mutual obligation to share with their fellow citizens the prosperity wrought by our common capitalism. But like river against rock, the flows and counterflows of money defining our present are eroding this vision.

Sure Smith is more complicated and normative ideals are just that, normative, so sometimes remote from how history happened. But this does not change the fact that the covenant has been broken. And with it a new trajectory that is leading down a road named escalating inequality. The track derivatives are on does not reward pit stops for enhancing morality or solidarity. So a corrosive insecurity is burrowing deeper and deeper into our peoplehood and our selves, fomented by changes now outrunning their authors' capacity to comprehend or adjust to. And thus there are cries for change to the changes that have been occurring. Although all too often they sound the way a silenced gunshot sounds, diffuse, seemingly distant, and suggesting something else.

There is a reason for this. Increasingly the wealth capitalism creates appears in the derivative form, governed by a logic that seems possessed by an absurd logic that worships fictitious capital that produces nothing but the expression of our basest desires and the acceleration of social disequilibrium. One response is to survey the destruction caused by derivatives, people's dispossession of their jobs, homes, life savings, retirements, and their hopeful vision of their future, and to call for a temperance movement that will lead to their abolition. Or at least intern them under maximum security banking where they can only do damage to themselves. The idea that we could erect an internment camp for derivatives is unrealistic because political and economic power have never more kept the same bed. Over the last four US presidencies, investment banks like Goldman Sachs have furnished our economic advisors and together with hedge funds are major financial donors to both parties. More importantly, the call to abolish derivatives fails to appreciate that the culture of financial circulation and its logics has already seeped into the pores of everyday life such that the distinction between finance and the *real* economy is no longer (if it ever was) an accurate portrayal of the present. The response sometimes contains a prayer: that commonsense will delete our derivative trading gene when we realize just how destructive the crisis has been economically and beyond. Unfortunately, politics put politically as raw intention is too estranged from the concrete to point us in the right direction.

A second alternative response is to recalibrate what we collectively take as the worthwhile measure of our common worth. The idea is to redeem our tarnished notion of peoplehood so that we, the people, can take the wealth that we produce and use it to shape a world in which we flourish. Open the manifesto of this second response and there begins a chapter that asks what economic and political turns need to be made in order to harness and redirect the wealth that derivatives create for socially productive purposes. If we orient our investigation with a realist notion of reason and possibility, and we don't see any genuine alternative, the question becomes whether we can animate a discussion that allows us to collectively rethink how the form of finance now ascendant adds a radically new logic to capitalism. How do we rethink derivatives and their markets in ways that open the way to conceptualizing how the general social good may be enhanced? Through this aperture, the critical question is not how can we duct tape a fragmented social together—which leads inevitably to nostalgia—but whether we can create and nurture a politics that reshapes an existing sociality so that we, collectively, may sentence derivatives to work for our mutual advantage. As the poet, Audre Lorde, has reminded us, silence will not silence our fears, only political action, here to redirect the wealth of society to our common interests, will suffice to redeem beings who are only ever mortal.

One does not need a statistical review to see that those in EuroAmerica live amid unprecedented riches. But material wealth is too much a good thing and poverty especially disabling, when they are tethered to insecurity. And thus perverse as it is, the paradox of the present is that for poor and prosperous alike the horizon of true wealth seems to be forever receding no matter how rapidly we approach. Our cultural DNA seems to have all but extinguished, through its own process of unnatural selection, any sense of satisfaction and contentment with our material wellbeing. Although not the heartbeat of the analysis, the compulsion for more that is always not enough suggests that we need to imagine wealth differently. At the very least, imagining wealth more socially as a kind of human societal security; wealth as not only money and things but emancipation from the deep fear that our student loans are call options on our future that may expire worthless, that we'll outlive a retirement savings that depends on financial markets and investments beyond our ken to comprehend, that harrowing financial forces we know nothing about may annihilate our communities and home values (for almost all Americans their main store of wealth accumulation), and that there are dark forces that can terminate our employment no matter the quality of our work. Where once we could expect a lifetime of labor to end joyfully in an emancipation from work, now retirement is a bridge to self-employment in finance.

Wealth presents the following paradox. Only socially can wealth be defined and accomplished, yet when tallied up individual by individual it appears to be the antithesis of peoplehood and our collective life. It is through the social that we forge a consensus, an approximation subject to historical revision, as to what amount exceeds subsistence and only through collaboration can we generate the great carnival of goods, services, and accumulated assets valorized as each individual's measure of wealth. What wealth is, and the way it is crafted, states what the social is. Wealth as cleaved from the social points to the prevailing sociostructures of capitalism, now transforming owing to the inflection of derivatives, and concomitantly, what those now in power desire wealth to be, exemplified by the chieftains of finance from banking executives to neoliberal economists and hedge fund managers and their constant shuttling back and forth between the towers of corporate finance and the state's governance of the economy.

Economies seem to evolve like transparencies one laid over another. This is a simplification to be sure, but more than a century of investigation into the vast ensemble of economies exhibits certain telltale lines. For the unbridled accumulation of wealth, the commonplace sense of capitalism, is not the only way people have joined in their mutual reproduction. Before the kingdom of the commodity subsumed almost all of our economic breath, there were societies in which the circulations of gifts was the honored repository of wealth. Across these societies, sociality imparted significance to labor such that gifts were enchanted because they were inscriptions of the sociality of their producers. And with the instrumentation of the gift, kinship and community mediated social relations and society's directional dynamic was more often than not tilted toward the cyclicality of seasonal and genealogical time. With the ascension of capitalism, the commodity became the source and measure of wealth. Labor came to mediate social relations but in an abstract manner that misrecognizes the participation of labor in the production of wealth—reducing labor to a technical activity to be steered instrumentally. Nowadays, the commodity and the social it engenders is bowing before another denomination of wealth, that of the derivative and the sociality it rests upon. Commodities can generate wealth because labor adds value in that interval between the investment (exemplified by production capital used to buy plant and equipment) and the money earned from the sale of the finished product. This form of wealth creation is possible because (in contrast to kinship-based economies) labor-power itself has become a commodity. Such labor-power was the bedrock of nation-state based, production-centered capitalism.

Derivatives portend a new kind of wealth, manifest in the ascension of the self-expanding quantities of borderless credit money. A wealth whose mode of generation is not beholden to the gift, and only circumstantially so to the commodity. The newness poses a quandary, as much for the academe as for the public and republic. The wealth present by derivatives appears inaccessible. Both because it seems to inhabit a restricted domain answerable only to those who make a proprietary claim on it and because it dares the uninitiated to entangle themselves in complexities too technical and arcane for any ordinary person to digest. And thus the point of the analysis is, however provisionally, to suggest a starting point and to theorize an intellectual compass. My view is that a sociologic of the derivative should be our north star, the financial crisis our starting point. This is important because derivative-driven capitalism, exemplified by the logos of the financial markets, is reproduced in and through a transformed form of the social life that it is instrumental in producing. Focusing on the derivative markets foregrounds the financial crisis as a reference point, particularly given its blazing empirical data points and a violence that permeates all communities, wrapped in a politics of wealth. A system foundering in crisis can no longer condone or tolerate the intellectual austerity of business as usual and the standard operating procedure. It must pass through its own answerlessness to reveal what it otherwise would not. Here, that finance is grounded in a sociologic that it denies yet eventually, inevitably loops back to the sociologic question of what we, collectively, will become. One point is clear from the outcome of the Occupy Movement: where the financial markets reign, the soft-core political activism of demonstration will not suffice. What is required is a hard-core activism that harnesses derivatives for the good of all.

Because capitalist economics is mainly about the production and increasingly the circulation of the things and relations that generate wealth, and because the collective organization and circulation of wealth and scarcity are intrinsically political, the production, circulation, and public acceptance of what counts as knowledge lie at the epicenter of the economy. And therefore any economics that attempts to apprehend that economy. Nothing exemplifies this reality more than the derivative, and the way that we the people have collectively chosen based on our common understanding to allow its logos—via our elected political representatives and central bank—to inflect the governance and circulation of *our* societal wealth. In the most critical sense, knowledge and its production constitutes the connective tissue tying the economic to the political. The prevailing economistic thesis that the economy lies outside of politics and governance, that most of the economy lies outside of finance, and that most of finance lies outside the derivative and its markets represents an historically specific and financially self-interested production of knowledge.[1]

Derivatives as a Way of Life

There is a point of view that concludes this account: the financial crisis is not a contingent or temporary disturbance in the field. The alternative view is that the present financial crisis is endemic to the way in which EuroAmerican capitalism has evolved the circulation of capital. This view organized the analysis. It recognizes that circulation is necessarily social and historical. It recognizes that derivatives are at the center of their own hurricane. Changes in the economic guard, the arrival of government officials schooled to a neoliberal view of how economies work, capped by a report from Milton Freedman and the ascension of speculative capital, cleared derivatives for take off. Thus the serial post-1973 financial crises; the saving and loan crisis brought about by the sprouting of the *junk bond* market, the stock market crash of 1987 driven by failure of portfolio insurance, the crisis engendered by the implosion of internet technology stocks, and, more recently, the credit and housing crisis are culminations of a transformative process still in motion. The welding of the financial world has come loose. And it is hard to envision how repairing the weld and the wealth being transferred can be accomplished without an understanding of derivative markets, not as they present themselves but as social. For many reasons, as detailed, this is far from easy. Moreover, we have not vanquished the root causes of the crisis, for derivatives by design are infinitely generative and shape shifting (as the securitization of subprime auto loans has illustrated). So as late as April 2016, Neel Kashkari, President of the Minneapolis Branch of the Federal Reserve, told CNBC that dismantling the too-big-to-fail banks remains the key to preventing another crisis. Let me underline the point because it runs counter-clockwise to our normal way of thinking about the world. Derivatives are not things with easily discernable thingly properties (like cars that come in different styles, colors, amenities); if they were they would be a lot easier to understand. Derivatives are multivariate generative schemes for amalgamating and pricing the volatility of abstract risk.

New regimes of work arise in response to, and as an instrumental part of, a transformation of the structure of an economy. Presently, in the opening decade of the new millennium, there is an unmistakable and widely reported transformation in the character of capitalism (Postone 2012). This is leading to the emergence of this new regime of work enframed in a context of the globalization of capitalism and in that process its fundamental reorganization. This basic reorganization is at once sociogeographic (Harvey 2000) and sociostructural, exemplified by the ascension of the cultures of circulation (Lee and LiPuma 2004), not least the ascent of a culture of financial circulation. What this underlines is the socioeconomic genesis and political importance of the rise of financial derivatives and the speculative ethos that accompanies it. These are bound up with a difference signaled by the special character of the present financial crisis; the presence of a deep contradiction in that the continued dominance of US and European capitalism depends enormously on their dominance of a system of financial circuitry whose speculative foundations portend the possibility that the entire system may fail.

There is a growing and conclusive literature that China, India, Brazil, and Russia are coming to dominate commodity production in the immediate years, and in the out-years consumption as well due to the gargantuan size of their population, some two thirds of the planet's inhabitants. What this means is that a prosperous culture of financial circulation represents one of the best opportunities for the continued dominance for US and European capitalism. More precisely, from a EuroAmerican perspective, it seems that a speculative financial field must flourish if transatlantic capitalism is to sustain its dominance given the ongoing geographic reorganization of the structure of production. And with that strength the affluent lifestyle, the global influence militarily and culturally, and the sense of national accomplishment that accompanies it. There are a powerful set of cultural and national logics, coupled to great incentives and fear of a diminution of global standing (usually articulated politically as a desire to remain strong), that motivates the United States and Europe to risk the consequences of liberated speculative capital. The real threat is that financial crises that periodically erupt and damage the real economy are intrinsic to the operation of unregulated speculatively-driven capital markets.

The contradiction is that for the EuroAmerican sphere to maintain itself given that its proportion of global product is continuing to decline (OECD 2012), it must indulge in a dangerous species of capitalism based on speculative capital. This sphere must develop capital markets and a habitus of speculation without allowing the risk to become so systemic and cataclysmic that it literally implodes the capital markets, thereby shutting EuroAmerican capitalism down—as nearly occurred in the credit crisis ignited in 2008 before massive intervention by the US Federal Reserve and the European Central Bank. In *Too Big to Fail* (2009) Sorkin explains in unmistakable detail that it was all too easy for US and European monetary authorities to envision and fear the chain reaction of bank failures that would essentially obliterate the capital markets driving capitalism. As Ben Bernanke said on the occasion of the rescue program, if others could see what he sees—that is, the toxic assets on the balance sheets of the troubled banks that are hidden from view—they would immediately understand that the impending collapse is much more systemic than the periodic secular downturns that have historically been animated by recessions in the business cycle. For EuroAmerica, the unspoken objective is to remain dominant by developing speculatively-based capital markets that are too sophisticated and innovative in the fabrication of financial instruments to be easily replicated, and a corps of financial agents endowed with the special dispositions and the mindset needed to profitably circulate such instruments. And to do this without provoking recurring rounds of crisis.[2]

Embodied in the rise of modern finance is an enormous problem that only became apparent when it became real. The problem is *systemic risk*: the chance that a market will structurally fail to the point where circulation ceases to exist. And since the markets are interconnected, institutionally and globally, that the failure of one market might become so contagious that it precipitates global systemic failure. Although a number of theorists have broached the issue, neither their analyses nor warnings were taken seriously as long as the derivatives markets were literally printing money and mainstream economists asserted that systemic risk was impossible because their models had shown that capitalist markets are inherently self-correcting. That the credit crisis pushed capital markets to the very brink of systemic failure demonstrated that this species of risk is real indeed. And, that there is correspondingly a necessity to disarm systemic risk.

But this is easier said than done. What makes this difficult is that its defining characteristic is that it is the one kind of risk that cannot be hedged against, and that it is intrinsically social because the risk is that the participants lose their collective faith in the integrity of the system. It is also difficult because the speculative history of the derivatives markets have become embodied in the most symbolically capitalized agents of finance—epitomized by celebrated hedge fund managers—who increasingly have come to define themselves subjectively through their work of speculating. Accordingly, the only antidote to systemically-based crises is the intervention of an external force, an agency with enough financial firepower to restore liquidity and faith in the system. The problematic is how to continually align and then realign a regulatory regime and a regime of work founded on speculation with constantly evolving, intimidatingly complex, markets in such a way as to discern and disarm systemic risks before they strike again, next time with perhaps greater magnitude. What renders this mitigation even more challenging and persistent is that the derivative markets engender volatility as a condition of their reproduction, such that they are constantly slouching toward collapse. As with nuclear reactors, a systemic meltdown is not inevitable nor is the problem overdrawn no matter how much the captains of the derivatives business talk-down its potential danger. For the United States and Europe the use of wealth-seeking derivative markets is so pressing that the gears of forgetting have been set in train to make it appear as if the extraordinary dangers so recently avoided were less grave and far more manageable than it first appeared, and that, on this account, reforming the financial system requires only that we update our regulatory structure by, for example, lifting reserve requirements and giving it a more cosmopolitan complexion as signaled by the expansion of nations invited to the table from G7 to G20. In May 2015, the former CEO of Lehman Brothers, Richard Fuld, gave a talk in which despite the enduring economic havoc he had helped precipitate, despite the fact that he had remained enormously wealth in the wake of what for numerous households was a financial nightmare, he assigned no blame to himself or to the financial industry, positioning himself as a hapless victim of economic circumstances and government overreach. Dick Fuld and others seem to have no idea what the nation meant when they told him to repent. The problem with this interested interpretation and the regulatory adjustments it suggests is that the next derivative induced systemic crisis may be of such magnitude that the external agencies, notable the US Federal Reserve and ECB, do not have enough financial firepower or the political leverage to right things.[3] Again we reach the conclusion that it is hard to envision how we can transcend the ideology of the markets and create a platform for the production of knowledge without an understanding of derivative markets, not as they present themselves but as social. For many reasons this is far from easy.

Not least, the space of derivatives is rather intimidating, with its overabundance of complicated terms, euphemisms, financial instruments couched in three letter acronyms, and academic texts filled with periodic puddles of mathematical equations. These instruments are complex and gravitate toward even greater complexity, the terminology equally complex and removed from everyday discourse. This opacity derives from the necessity to capture descriptively far from ordinary financial arrangements (i.e., securitization), and, in another register, from the effects produced by a specialized language that regulatory bodies, such as Congress' finance committees, are uncomfortable with. In *Language and Symbolic Power* (1991), Bourdieu notes that the "specialized languages that specialists produce . . . through the systematic alteration of the common language are . . . a compromise between the expressive interest and a censorship constituted by the structure of the field in which the discourse circulates" (1991:137).

And so I have noted in the political asides that especially for derivatives and their markets the finance community has evolved and embraced an argot that allows insiders to communicate with one another, even as it impedes those unfamiliar with this specialized language from appreciating what is happening to their world. Moreover, the opacity seems to animate a certain anxiety in the uninitiated which, in turn, leads those outside the financial community to bracket the very possibility of coming to grips with a culture of financial circulation that is instrumental in shaping their economic well-being and governance. The financial field gravitates toward what Bourdieu calls "strategies of euphemization" (1991:137) because financial instruments coded in acronyms such as credit default swap (CDS) and collateralized debt obligation (CDO), strategically defined by terms such as delta hedging, implied volatility, and the greeks, in concert with dark OTC markets that have very little transparency, help to shield the markets from the public scrutiny that invites governmental regulation. Complex, insider terms, distilled into acronyms, also drive home the self-understanding that dealmakers and traders on the frontlines of finance stand far above the ordinary citizenry in the production of the economy on which we all mutually depend (Ho 2009:104).[4] Thus the ground of our politics: that in order for citizens to appreciate what is happening to them, in order to get the truth to speak we need a theory of the sociality of the derivative.

Those who inhabit finance take a certain joy in speaking this language, in becoming proficient in its nuances, in conjugating the different terms. But it is not simply that the production of opacity services their economic interests: it gives a stamp of uniqueness and intelligence to the ownmost space of their work life, even as its mastery confirms their individuality. There is a lesson here that runs throughout the analyses: the public effect of an individual's action—such as a financier speaking in a jargon that shields him from public scrutiny—is not the same as that action's subjective causes which often embrace aims like engendering self-esteem and solidarity. As to what motivates people, the default setting is money and power, when for sophisticated and intelligent moderns, such as those who inhabit finance, much more is going on beneath the surface. Understanding this has been key to understanding what compels traders to take on huge risks again and again in the face of uncertainty. Indeed, it turns out that actions this dangerous, that compel people to confront extraordinary, existentially unnerving losses of money and face, require a more complex and compelling set of motives. As in real lifeways, where agents inhabit multiple fields, from familial to financial, where their ideas of identity scale from the intensely personal up to nationality, their inventory of motives habitually compete and conflict. More accurately, the motives orienting derivative traders unfold practically as a spread, as a confluence of psychological-somatic rapids that they navigate mostly intuitively as they face down the challenges of executing a zero-sum trade. As noted theoretically and even more so in my ethnography of finance, the present has led to the celebration and foregrounding of what was always latent but overlain by other values (especially family and community): namely, a *monetized subjectivity* that welds self-worth, self-esteem, and social status, to unending acts of capital accumulation.

Derivatives and Finance

The depth and persistence of the crisis says that something is amiss in our financial system and in our methods of apprehending it. My view is that apprehension entails an intellectual commitment to constructing an approach that can grasp the concealed and constitutive sociality that founds and inflects the creation and circulation of derivatives. Why financial derivatives especially? What god do they pray to that they should merit so much attention? When a match is struck the risen flame burns blue closest to the source of combustion; in the financial universe, derivatives are the burning blue flame nearest its incendiary center. The great recession brought about by the near collapse and very costly government rescue of the US financial system underline that an analysis of derivatives is necessary if we are to grasp the financial forces that, since the 1970s, have increasingly determined our reality—a reality in which, at least for the time being, the EuroAmerican economy remains the primary force in determining the redirection of the global political economy. Derivative markets driven by speculative capital are not all of capital markets, certainly not all of finance, and even less the overall economy: but they are the active and volatile core that drives the ascent of circulatory capital. They always seem to be imposing themselves on a world that is reacting to them, unprepared and visibly flustered, the reaction itself always it seems aimed at derivative instruments, institutional arrangements, and OTC markets that, owing to their accelerated dynamic, have already materially transformed into an unpredictable something else.

Analyzing the crisis on these terms is a formidable task because finance not only conceals its sociality, the concealment of all that is social is a necessary element of its self-construction. In this way, a social dimension of modern highwire finance is that it does not appear social at all. The redaction of the social—its translation into a pure economic individualism encased in a rational and free market—pervades the field's every pore. The alternative are accounts that not only expose the powers of the social in the creation of derivatives and their markets but how the social is made to disappear. In analyzing that dimension of finance wed to the derivative I have focused on the particular assemblage of financial institutions, ongoing markets, agent-networks, government agencies, scholarly disciplines, and media enterprises that collectively embody and perform a socially specific financial ethos and an ensemble of economic practices based on the speculative, risk-driven allocation of capital. These institutions and agent-networks encompass investment banks (particularly securitization and proprietary trading desks), private equity firms, hedge funds, governmental offices (e.g., US Federal Reserve), transnational agencies [e.g., Bank for International Settlements (BIS)], the finance economics industry, and the financial media (e.g., CNBC). The argument that this analysis first presupposed and then confirmed is that an understanding of derivatives requires the emancipation of financial circulation from an economistic viewpoint. So the objective throughout has not been to remove, bracket, or downplay the economic, but to understand that the financial field and its markets—not least derivative markets—derive from the ineluctable imbrication of the economic with the other spheres of social life and the reproduction of the social. The aim has been an analysis of circulation that can grasp the very concept of a separable economic as the perspectival and provisional result of the application of a historically specific social logic of practice. This theoretic would allow us to apprehend finance's most iconic, economistic, most apparently rationally pure action—the risk driven, wager based trade—as a product of an underlying sociality.

The thesis of the account, at once social and historical, can be stated as follows. Economics has grasped finance by banishing the social from the project of analysis. It has accomplished this removal of the social by fashioning an analytical object that is abstract, individuated, perfectly rational, and therefore reducible to a mathematized rendition of the financial universe. From my perspective, however, the theory that dominates finance fails precisely because it removes or externalizes all that is social. The theory's inability to conceptualize let alone analyze the 2008 crisis was a collect call from the economy telling anyone who will listen that an account of financial markets adequate to its object must encompass what is social. The social is not a dimension of finance, rather finance is its contemporary incarnation is a historically and sociospecific instantiation of the social. The excursions into performativity and objectification were part of an attempt to fabricate a framework for restoring the social to financial analysis. There's a point that bears repeating because it presses hard on the nerve of theoretical reflection. The social we have sought to restore is not the same social that held sway during the pre-derivative days of production capitalism; it is the social that has and is emerging in the context of the restructuring of the relationship of production to circulation, in ways that implicate both decoupling and new imbrication. Less me emphasis that on every level, theoretic, thematic, and expository, my theorization is a work in progress. The entire complement of crises are still in motion, still evolving, still seeking real resolution. The work is thus, and can be, no more than a first installment on why and how an analysis of derivatives might reincorporate a social whose transformed form is one of the primary results of financialization and, more globally, the recalibration of the spread between circulation and production.

There exists a general sociological critique of neoclassical economics. The critique maintains, beyond reasonable doubt, that a vast array of legal, technological, and political processes shape the foundation on which markets rest (Fligstein 2001). Without the legal protection of property rights and commercial claims, for example, the allocations of scarce resources for efficient uses would be a chimera. Similarly, without the consent of state regulatory authorities, a broad amalgam of financial practices from short selling to bankers' bonuses to speculation might receive unfavorable treatment (as indeed they once did historically). It is also clear that the growing independence of the financial field is part and product of the processes of social differentiation that has characterized the trajectory of capitalism. The principle of this analysis agrees with but goes beyond the idea that social processes undergird finance: the argument is that the financial field and its markets are determinatively social at their very core. And that this sociality is intrinsic, operative, and decisive from the existential act of buying or selling this security, here, now, under these conditions to the abstraction of *the market* itself as a foundational category of the social epistemology of capitalism. In this view I am not alone. And increasingly so, as Martin exemplifies when he says that "the social" names "the missing third term that is otherwise suppressed in current conceptions of possessive individualism realized through market participation" (Martin 2013:93).

Indeed, the scientific and technical products created via the application of "scientific economics" to the financial markets not only promulgates the invisibility of the social they conceal the character of the concealment by presenting and representing their data sets as socially unmediated empirical measurements of naturally occurring phenomena. Which then, imitating physics, allows for the generation of testable hypotheses that may be solved mathematically. However, it turns out that transmuting what is humanly social into purely natural phenomena requires more than a little intellectual surgery, and it is here that finance economics operationalizes four methodological tropes. First, concrete social relations are transformed into abstract objects which are then imputed to have a life of their own. Accordingly, liquidity goes from being the outcome of faith-based relations within a social community of real agents to a freely floating, impersonal, abstract category. Second, the methodology eliminates the specific qualities of the agents. This is done by positing that the abstract objects (like liquidity) interact with abstract general agents. This move entails bracketing the specific social and economic characteristics that make the concrete agents precisely who they are. For example in *Liquidity and Crisis* (2012) a volume whose stated mission is to address the "massive illiquidity" that fostered the crisis, the abstract agent, "financial intermediaries," encompasses institutions that are fundamentally dissimilar and had extraordinary different roles in the market's cessation of liquidity. Thus the abstract agent, "financial intermediary," encompasses the derivative creating and market making of the proprietary trading desks at Morgan Stanley and Goldman Sachs, non-bank banks like GE Capital, hedge funds such as Soros Investment, Vanguard Mutual Funds, the Baton Rouge Community Savings Bank, and the California State Pension Fund. A notable result of the abstraction is that the institutional behaviors and power of Goldman Sachs, AIG, Morgan Stanley, Lehman Brothers, and Bear Stearns are made invisible in that not one of them is mentioned, even one, over some twenty-six separate articles by more than forty finance economists. The third trope fixates on regimenting and decontextualizing the actions of the abstract agents. To do this, the different concrete agents that comprise the abstract agent are posited as behaving uniformly in respect to the abstract objects, because they all behave as economically rational, utility maximizing, entities in a hypostatized economy (such as an economy that maintains perfect equilibrium). This allows, in turn, for the production of an imaginary ethnography in which an author will declare, for example, that any financial intermediary faced with a certain circumstance (e.g., increased risk) will invariably behave in a certain manner (e.g., implement hedging strategies). Historically speaking, sometimes so, sometimes not, a fact underlined by the crisis which "naturally" begs the question of what actually determines their behavior. What, rather ironically, helps the concealment of the conceal-ment to pass undetected is that "finance economics" is socially endowed (by, for example, the great social capital gleaned from the awarding of Nobel prizes to finance economists). This capital endows it with the authority to certify the objectivity of its own objectifications, critically the realness of the efficient market and its foundational set of categories, such as especially agent's rational expectations.[5] At the end of the day, finance economics ends up being rather agnostic about the crisis because it never gets around to interrogating the con-struction of its objects of investigation: what in the real world of the derivative are relational objects that agents produce and use practically, according to the cognitive and dispositional structures instilled within them by virtue of their immersion in the sociality of the world that produces them. Standing afar and safely, social scientists all too frequently visualize the fate of the working class as though it is a train crash in slow motion, which, in turn, authorizes their fantasy of witnessing and debating.

These mechanisms of invisibility suggest that a true understanding the fi-nancial field requires an understanding of the ideology of the market. This ideology is central because it legitimizes the economistic suppositions that underpin many of the analyses of the financial crisis. These suppositions about rational actors, the uniformity of agent's information, and the closure and completeness of the market are the cornerstones of what I have called the *illusio*. More than passing mistakes or theoretical inconsistencies, the illusio refers to the forms of misrecognition (of the social) that are components of *real relations of the production of the structure of financial circulation*. Adherence to the illusio is and remains an imperative of financial analysis, talk of the social automatically redacted from discussion (at least by the ratified members of the analytical community) until the crisis opened a crack in its defense mechanism (business school textbooks, economic publications, and government reports that represent the efficient-market formulation as settled science). Initially it seemed that the evidence would erode support for the efficient-market para-digm. But this has not come to pass despite the facts, admonitions and amend-ments to the doctrine from the neo-Keynesian camp, and even the award of the Nobel Prize in 2014 to a French economist specializing in market imper-fections. Still, within finance economics it remains a hegemonic position [as a 2012 interview with Eugene Fama underscores, as does Lawrence Summers's 2013 course on the financial crisis]. Indeed, years into the crisis, interviews with business school deans and professors (less so their students) indicate an unwavering allegiance to the efficient market thesis. Numerous journals, especially those that are mathematically inclined, invariably presuppose an efficient-market to ground their calculations. Some conclusions follow. The character and power of this illusio reside in its capacity to fabricate depictions of reality that redirect that reality, exemplified by US Federal Reserve policy under Alan Greenspan, the decision that publicly funding the financial system is necessary and sufficient to restart a deleveraging economy, and the fact that an inherently efficient market which requires no regulatory oversight fits perfectly with the interests of the financial sector in general and speculative capital in particular. A further conclusion is that unveiling the sociality that lies beneath an economy oriented around the derivative and its markets requires a collective enterprise that openly eschews any disciplinary concerns. At its best, social sciences' relationship to the social world exists with at least one arm and one foot beyond the veil of ideology.

Asked why he had rendered a landscape so impressionistically, Matisse replied that "precision is not truth" (l'exactitude ce n'est pas le verite). He reminds us that no sum of precision can guarantee accuracy, though the charisma of exactitude with its suggestion of the most realistic account of the real possible gains its own reality when it dampens our critical judgment. A social movement toward an accuracy of the social does not require that science need begin anew. It does require that we reopen the bottle that has been stoppered since the second world war, and let out a deeply social science that is not siloed into disciplines, mesmerized by math, or sheepish in its politics (as though a commitment to fairness automatically renders one's analysis "unfair"). One of the points hammered home by my colleagues Randy Martin and Robert Meister is that committing to this social movement is less a career choice then the only way there is of remaining unbroken on the wheel of financial derivatives. Scholars in the United States too often demure as if they are guests in their own society, as though the university should be the site of political neutrality and intellectual disarmament, its civic purpose to turn out the most well-trained, well-mannered, discrete, gentlest thinkers this side of Wall and Broad. The politics of science turns on seeing things, especially invisible things, that we are not supposed to see. Social theory can either be an escape from reality—a portal into a land of unlimited abstraction from the real, an analysis of analytical objects that exist only inside their analytic containers, or the imprisonment of an open-ended economy on the false charge of disorderly conduct—or better a means of apprehending the real with an intensity that derives from honoring its complexities. Social theory at its best stages a raid on the invisible and inarticulate. The point is not to have faith in theory but in the work it can do. One alternative (see Meister 2016) is a politics and economy defined by optionality in which claims, injustices, and repairs to our sense of people-hood are, through reforms that distribute the wealth of society to all those who create it even if their contributions are not easily visible, by rolling over the claims, reparations, and repairs from one generation to the next generation and then next through laws and programs that begin by recognizing and accom-modating the sociality that underlies our individual successes.

The false distinction between an economy of choices and a politics of op-tionality represents the prevailing ideological formulation. Given the political culture of the United States, it is usually coded differently: as the difference be-tween the free market and state intervention. Between the methods of market-based distribution (i.e., the quasi-gravitational physics of trickle down) and laws for distributing wealth mandated by government fiat. This formulation is ideology precisely because an economy of market choices is inseparable from a politics of wealth—not to mention the wealth of societies that allow capitalist markets to function. By the same token, a genuine politics of optionality goes beyond not only redistribution (for which, under the ethos of "free-market" capitalism, there is never the right time or circumstance), it implicates the work of economics in the life of the collectivity.

Despite the celebration and canonization of the free market as the singular path to prosperity, the reality is that an economy of choices has failed us, espe-cially when it has to be preserved through austerity measures. This economy of trickle down is marginalizing half the population, whose incomes have been stagnant for forty years and whose life prospects for themselves and children seem to be diminishing. And just what kind of choice is it among numerous variants of commodified medical insurance all of which are expensive, too labor and knowledge intensive for most consumer and many medical profes-sionals, and frequently only marginally effective. Variety is no substitute for coverage, quality, and ultimately our human security. Similarly, an economics of choice closes down the possibility of considering reparations for those who have suffered from socioeconomic injustices. For the calculus of choice is a prisoner of the present that effaces and closes off the possibility of the intergen-erational solution for injustices that were, by their social and political design, intergenerational. More, this calculus foregrounds the individual, mistaking our ideology of personhood for all there is politically, which thereby serves to hide and misrecognize the collectivity that actually grounds that reality. The virtue of optionality is that it restores the collectivity and intergenerational temporality that is always, already the time at hand for that collectivity. It sweeps from the table the easy excuse that the time for justice, for the fair allocation of the wealth of society, was in a past that, being past, we can never now reclaim (no matter how honorable our intentions) and that the people of the present should not be held responsible for social injustices and misallocations of wealth that they, as individuals of the molecular present, can only look at through the inverted telescope of history. Any wealth that the individual I may have accumulated through the mediations of past injustices—such as the appropriation of AmerIndian lands—was an accident to my existence. On this vision of the social which denies the social that it must presuppose, culpability and responsibility are synonymous with the presentist market for individual choices. A political of optionality would redefine the relationship between the social and the market for derivatives. The objective would be to go beyond the present uses of derivatives, which create and redistribute wealth to the financial sector, and use derivatives to enhance the wealth of society taken critically as an intergenerational collectivity.

Science at its best amplifies our level of ignorance in that, through its findings and advances, we more clearly know the expanse of what we do not know. And in that process orient ourselves toward the production of knowledge anew. This aim joins with another mission: to alter, however slightly, the ideological coordinates of public understanding. The political mission must be to interrogate, denaturalize, reframe, perhaps even water-board the language of the public sphere until it agrees to tell people the truth about the drip by drip renunciation of their original covenant to help one another. In its place a falsely liberating nationalism predicted on the suspension, attenuation, and rendition of the moral and ethical scriptures that once defined who we were. It is not just that those in public office decided to award public monies to the banks because they were too-big-to-fail; it is that they withheld monies from homeowners because they seemed too small to matter. These homeowners were disappeared owing to our apparent collective renunciation of the covenant that we all have an Americanness in common and will, accordingly, come to one another's aid. And no more so than in time of one crisis built on a preceding one. The question of who we are requires a national inclusive conversation, although it turns out that our ability of convene such as conversation is itself a principal stake in the game. So far, out of our cynicism and despair perhaps, we have been all too eager to vaporize concepts into sound bites and to reduce arguments to gestures. The emergence of the alt-right and its luminary, Donald

Trump, only perpetuate and legitimize this flight from the real—our tweeter-in-chief (as he's been called) filling the airwaves with alternative facts. The key question, still struggling for recognition, is how can we re-find and refine the political voice and the understanding of the social that we never so badly needed until the derivative showed up on our doorstep.

Notes

▰▰▰▰▰▰▰▰▰▰

Prefacing a Theory of the Derivative

1. See, for example, the claim by Anastasia Nesvetailova (2010) that the notion that derivatives can create either money or wealth is nothing short of an "illusion" (p. 17–23). Or the claim by Maurizio Lazzarato in *The Making of Indebted Man* (2011) that it is necessary to organize a critique from the standpoint of production owing to the "speculative, parasitic, usurious character of financial capital" (p. 61). Or, the claim by Steve Keen (2011; 2013) that derivatives only appear real because the fictitious world they create is so hegemonic and encompassing that it escapes our powers of comprehension. The headline is that traditional Marxisms do not have the theoretical tools to deal with the derivative and the ascension of circulatory capitalism. That said, there are other social theorists, exemplified by Dick Bryan (Bryan and Rafferty 2013) and Randy Martin (2013; 2015), who are forging a path that analyzes the financial markets without dissolving the critique of capitalism emanating from the Marxist traditions. Given the political importance of derivatives, I remain astounded about how many Marxists take a certain pride in the fact that they know nothing about how markets operate.

2. Because for so many middle-class families in the United States their house is the embodiment of wealth accumulation and of self-investment, the onset of a deflationary housing spiral opened a continent of hardship that went far beyond their economic distress. A minister in a black Baptist church in South Florida put it thusly: "foreclosure not only takes the houses of my parishioners, it breaks their families and their spirits." What this means is that the effects of the crisis will ripple through generations, especially in poor communities. Most subprime foreclosures in African American communities in South Florida were on homes these families had lived in for decades. A report by HUD and the Treasury revealed that more than 80 percent of subprime mortgages were refinancing, that in 60 percent of the cases the borrower pulled out cash, and that rarely did the borrower understand what they were paying for the refinancing or what the subsequent debt burden would be in respect to their incomes. Socially economically, the unregulated securitization of mortgages in collaboration with predatory mortgage lending was the centerpiece of a great transfer of wealth from those poor in income, education, and life chances to those already well endowed. Remember this is a zero-sum game. Hedge funds and other financial actors can only extract differentially higher returns because, especially those with low incomes, pay for these returns with comparably poorer or even negative returns on what, for them, is the investment of the only kind of capital they possess: human capital.

3. From the poem "Under One Small Star," in *The Collected Poems of Wislawa Szymborska*.

4. On the desk of a principal in a derivative trading firm was a plaque that laid out its corporate philosophy. The engraving said: Principle number one is to make as much money as possible; principle number two is that if you suffer any doubts about the ethics of your behavior consult principle one.

5. The crisis also reverberated through the Marxist community; for it undermined their view that it was possible to bracket or dismiss the derivative markets, and the culture of financial circulation more generally, because they were external to the *"real"* economy. The crisis clarified that the derivatives market could extract painfully high rents from the productive sector, and inflect monetary and fiscal policies in ways that reshaped the trajectory of the political economy on many scales from national to global.

6. In more than a few instances, Alan Greenspan being a case in point, an individual circulates among and is mutually involved with academic economics, financial institutions (e.g., being a board member or consultant), and federal regulatory agencies. The same is true of Larry Summers. Or consider R. Glenn Hubbard. He is a neoclassical economist who was dean of the Columbia Business School. At the same time he continued to receive a salary from Goldman Sachs and JP Morgan Chase, coauthoring a paper in 2004 with William Dudley, the chief economist at Goldman, that sung the praises of CMOs in offsetting housing risk. During the presidential campaign of 2012 he agreed to be Mitt Romney's go-to economist in exchange for the position of Treasury Secretary if Romney was elected with the further intention of imposing his economic vision on the world by becoming the head of the IMF (Segal 2012:4).

7. There were dissenters, important economists who argued that markets can be inefficient and that economies could enter into disequilibrium. Nonetheless, the heterodox position coexists with the orthodoxy owing to the character of heterodoxy in economics, which is viewed less as an alternative theorization and more as a diagnostic of those phenomena the orthodox positions still needs to shore up.

8. The rise of Donald Trump as a presidential candidate is unthinkable without the financial crisis. His base of support is essentially those who have been crippled first by the crisis of labor, which led to diminishing job prospects and incomes, and the jeopardy that the crisis placed on their primary asset, their house. Trump's message which is virulently anti-immigration and anti-establishment capitalism touches both of these themes for this audience, which is precisely why they support him irrespective of whatever else he does.

9. Interview with Brian Sullivan on "Power Lunch" segment, CNBC, March 19, 2015.

10. Think of the relational forces of buying and selling that take place within a market that buyers and sellers have socially imagined, such *capitalist capital markets* only coming into existence through their imagination in sixteenth century Protestant Europe followed by centuries of development and institutionalization. The streamlined idea of a financial field composed of markets is a kind of conceptual shorthand for this process.

11. It turns out that those who witnessed the extraordinary suffering of the Great Depression and Nazi Germany's attempt to exterminate one of the most educated and entrepreneurial segments of its own populace could not conceivably contemplate the notion that economies are efficient or that economic agents are rational.

12. It is also worth noting that Emanuel Derman, a quant who formerly was a managing partner at Goldman Sachs, has, in his attempt to grasp financial behavior, come upon a similar concept through his invocation of Spinoza's notion of intuition, which was one of the earliest accounts of action as combining mental and dispositional elements (Derman 2011).

13. Taken to its limit, this concept of the social means that the inscription of the social is agent's presence at that moment when truth, things, values are constituted for them because they are collectively constituted; that the social reverberates with a nascent logos that teaches agents, apart from all dogmas and intellocentric views, the true conditions of objectivity itself; a social that summons them to all of the tasks of knowledge and action done in the name of subjectivity.

Chapter 1: Originating the Derivative

1. Financial commentators and analysts implicitly acknowledge the difficulty of giving a definition or a definite description of the derivative when they sidestep the issue. The most common trope is to simply introduce *the derivative* as though anyone attuned to the media would know from experience what it is (e.g., Morgenson and Rosner 2011; Geithner 2014; El-Erian 2008; Evanoff, Kaufman, and Malliaris 2011; Das 2011). Or, to introduce the derivative through reference to straightforward stock options: puts and calls.

2. The Russian case is instructive about the transformation underway. By the end of December 2014, the ruble had fallen disproportionately greater than oil prices, and continued to fade even as oil prices stabilized. Most nations that experience a currency crisis—think of Argentina in 2002 or earlier Indonesia in 1998—do so by running a trade deficit, the public and private sectors borrowing money in dollars and euros to pay for imported goods. However, this scenario does not fit the Russian situation. Russian manufacturing produces many of the products that its citizens consume and Russia has run up a significant trade surplus. In other words, from the standpoint of production and trading in commodities, the ruble should have remained strong. Indeed, many standard foreign exchange models developed for production centered capital were forecasting an upper limit of 30 rubles to the dollar when in fact there were more than twice that amount. But the new reality is that the price of money is no longer tethered to the production system, but is determined by the flow of speculative capital which profits not from stability but from volatility. By mid-January 2015, the Russian Central Bank had already purchased some eighty billion dollars' worth of borrowed rubles from hedge funds, the vast majority of purchases at 35 to 45 rubles to the dollar, resulting in an enormous transfer of wealth from the Russian Central Bank to these speculative investment vehicles.

3. Expressed in Marxian terms, the derivative gives expression to a form of relative surplus value that was always present in capitalism but was dormant because immaterial until the 1970s with the advent of globalization. For circulatory capital, relative surplus value represents the difference between what is the ever-diminishing cost of producing connectivity and the value produced from it. In this sphere, increasing speculation reduces the cost of discerning and disarming risk by amplifying market liquidity and thus bolstering the general productivity of the derivative in respect to its meta-use value of regulating global connectivity. The intellectual labor invested in dissembling and reassembling capital to manage the risks engendered by the uncertainty that surrounds global connectivities, amplified by the practical labor of making a market in derivatives, generates a surplus of value which reduces the amount of effort necessary to keep the circulatory process in train. This will generate a striving for expansion, which, as is evident from their exponential growth, characterizes derivative markets. For a powerful dialectic has been set up between the growth of global circulation and the growth of this emergent form of relative surplus value. The contradiction that lies *within* the mode of circulation is that the creation and regulation of connectivity is predicated on markets whose very existence is predicated on its destabilization, which may lead to their outright systemic destruction.

4. Mathematically, Jensen's inequality informs us that if $f(*)$ is a convex function and x is a random variable, then $E[f(x)] > f(E[x])$. What this says is that same operation will produce proportionately different results depending on where they are on the curve. Think of a dice game market in which the return is based not on the number rolled, but on the square of that number. Note that $f(x) = x$ squared is a convex function. Thus if you roll a four, you get more than twice as much money than if you rolled a two ($16 versus $4). Options are convex when there is (a) volatility and (b) that volatility is limited. Both conditions are almost always met, except of course when there is a systemic meltdown.

5. Also for this reason in non-publicly traded companies (e.g., in 2015, Uber or Airbnb), which can be typified as belonging to that sector should they come public.

6. The financial system is built on credit whose derivation come from the Latin word for believe.

7. The functions of the derivative also suggests an alternative account of money. Namely that money represents a triangulated measure (most often a quantification) of the relationship between a cultural object (such as a given derivative or a football franchise), a collectively engineered value (what the market's participants think the derivative or football franchise is worth), and the functional which is to say performative value of that money (their willing to mutually accept a specific kind of credit money—dollars or euros for example—in payment). Under this account, it is irrelevant whether "the money" is a commodity, gold, metallic coins, fiat paper, credit money, or anything else. The critical questions become under precisely what circumstances do the participants

mutually understand something to be money and precisely what functions and to what degree can this money performatively objectify.

8. Economistic accounts conflate the question of why derivative trade with why trade derivatives. Without an appreciation of the social, they are naturally indifferent to the social production of difference. They thus have no account of how the sociostructures which underwrite why derivatives trade become imbricated with the agency animating derivative trading. Such that these sociostructures and the forms of subjectivity valorized by the derivative mutually reproduce one another.

9. An example of a tradable difference across social space is the fact that, given the same economic data (e.g., on consumer prices and wages), the German central bank will invariably pursue a more conservative policy than its US counterpart because the nation is hyper-mindful of the history that the economic turmoil created by runaway inflation helped the ascension of the Third Reich. This has motivated the German central bank to develop a culture that endorses tighter monetary policies and higher short term interest rates than the economic data would conventionally warrant.

10. The crisis of work further exposes the darkening illusion at the heartland of the American dream: that with hard work and stout intentions anyone can elevate themselves to create their own Norman Rockwell–like family and community.

11. For an illustration of such hedging works, see LiPuma and Lee 2004:39–41.

12. Though her focus is different than our own, in that she does not focus on speculative capital or derivatives, the anthropologist Karen Ho (2009:chap.3) provides a discussion of shareholder value that is mandatory reading for anyone interested in the sociology of the concept.

13. This appears in the practice that whenever a corporation contributes to the public interest, its participation is increasingly publicly announced and the product in question festooned with its logo. One has only to look as the historical relationship between not-for-profit public broadcasting (PBS) and its corporate sponsors to witness this transformation. Corporations that once accepted simple acknowledgement for underwriting a program, such as *Wall Street Week*, now demand nothing less than toned down versions of the commercials that they run on for profit stations. The express goal is amplify shareholder value by touting the product or service, but not so blatantly that it undermines the value added conferred on a product when consumers believe its producer is a good corporate citizen.

14. The financial media plays a key role in disseminating and valorizing the importance of the dominant notion of shareholder value favored by speculative capital. Here is one example that could be multiplied many times over. Speaking about Yahoo, the comment prompted by a noticeable decline in its share price, CNBC analyst Herb Greenberg (August 13, 2012) reported that the actions of the new CEO indicate that she thinks that "*building the business* is part of shareholder value" (my emphasis). Greenberg added that "the Street [meaning Wall Street collectively] is disappointed by the news" resulting in a

downgrade of the stock "because this [attempt to build the business] will hurt short term results." Note that what is happening is that institutional advisory services are concluding that the stock should be sold because the CEO is trying to build the business, thus reneging on her obligation to maximize short term profits; CNBC is circulating the view that, contrary to the contention of the new Yahoo CEO, building the business is not a part of shareholder value; due to its global reach, this view is being disseminated worldwide, educating viewers from South America to Asia to Africa about how capitalist markets evaluate stocks (i.e., according to this dominant notion of shareholder value). At the same time, its report of the downdraft in Yahoo's share price affirms the validity of the dominant notion and the consequences of pursing an alternative longer-term strategy. The bottom line is that there is a hegemonic notion of shareholder value that is articulated by advisory services, enforced by fast money, and propagated by the media. Interestingly enough, the financial media habitually denies its real and newsworthy economic impacts on the organization of capital in the interests of legimating itself as a source of real news.

15. Its use to pay union wages in Anytown America a mistake if the same commodity could be produced for less elsewhere. Similarly, the use of capital to bolster a pension account a mistake if simply deploying more optimistic projections about the fund's future returns would allow the corporation to distribute more capital to shareholders.

16. To give some idea of the transformation, in 1973 JP Morgan earned almost all of its revenues from making commercial loans. Twenty years later, nearly 75 percent of its profits derived from derivatives, bank executives telling Fortune magazine that they now considered them part of the "basic business of banking" (quoted in McLean and Nocera 2010:53–54).

17. The sovereign wealth funds of Saudi Arabia, the Arab Emirates, Kuwait, and Qatar, which exist in a variety of permutations including subsidiary investment vehicles, control somewhere in the neighborhood of eight trillion dollars, although given the absence of transparency and reporting requirements for other structured investments, and the political angst they occasion in Europe and the United States, the total sum may well be higher (see Xu Yi-chong and G. Bahgat 2011).

18. This in no way suggests that institutes of speculative capital do not compete with one another or that regulation is not itself a site of such struggles. One internal slug fest between the participants turns on attempts by one participant (e.g., Fannie Mae) to secure unregulated access to the home mortgages market even as that market's regulations serve to exclude or handicap its rivals (e.g., Goldman Sachs). See McLean and Nocera (2010) for an account of these struggles.

Chapter 2: Social Theory and the Market for the Production of Financial Knowledge

1. Martijn Konings (2011) reminds us that accounts that theorize the globalization of finance "as a process through which financial markets autonomize themselves from the institutional frameworks that organize the economy's more basic productive functions"

fail to see that derivative finance uses and transforms existing institutions even as it necessitates new ones often to its own design (p. 110).

2. The conventional economic view is that "market liquidity varies with the state of the economy. . . . liquidity crisis being released by economic downturns" (Allen, Carletti et al. 2011:4). In an article on the nature of banking crises, Smith (2002) extrapolates from the standard economistic theory to show that a low inflation rate coupled with low interest rates, such as those that prevailed in the period leading up to the 2007 crash, preclude the possibility of a banking crisis because the system is flush with liquidity. There is little doubt that within the framework of the neoclassical equilibrium model, it is a titanic struggle to imagine how a liquidity crisis could occur when there are a plethora of liquid assets or that contractions in liquidity can have harmful implications for the real economy. The reason for this is that in a hypostatized equilibrium economy composed of purely rational actors, liquidity is indistinguishable from liquid assets. According to the theory, we can empirically calculate the state of liquidity by tallying up the liquid assets held by financial institutions (e.g., mortgage obligations). In the real economy, to the contrary, formerly liquid assets can become extremely illiquid, touching off a credit crisis in which even good assets cannot be bought or sold. The crisis demonstrates that, contrary to standard economic theory, *liquidity is not a property of an asset (or asset class), but of agents' willingness to trade that asset*. This disposition, agents' willingness to trade with one another, depends on their collective faith in the solvency of their counterparties and the price discovery mechanism, both of which are extrinsic to the asset. The liquidity of an asset is analogous to the propensity of wood to burn: the wood may never burn and can do so only with the addition of two external agents, oxygen and heat.

3. As Geithner notes, "Greenspan did have an almost theological belief that markets are rational and efficient, as well as skepticism that government supervision and regulation could make them safer" (2014:85).

4. The greatest account of the relationship between appearance and essence in commodity capitalism is the work of Moishe Postone, most importantly *Time, Labor, and Social Domination* (1993). Especially but not only chapter 4, entitled simply "Abstract Labor," theoretically grounds, in the most incisive and powerful fashion imaginable, the necessity of the relationship between capitalism's sociostructures and forms of appearance.

5. Even those theoretical approaches that focus on financialization as a critical element of capitalism's history, exemplified by Giovanni Arrighi's *The Long Twentieth Century* (1994), tend to become unglued when they try to theorize the current financial system. Arrighi, for example, thematizes capitalism's evolution in terms of systemic cycles, each cycle characterized by phases that begin and end with financial expansion. Financialization is thus inseparable from capitalism's transformational path. Nonetheless, when Arrighi get to the ascension of circulatory capitalism in the early 1970s, his accounts seems to assume something of a random walk as he turns to simply enumerating an

anomalous slew of economic phenomena, such as increasing global connectivity and competition. Though descriptively accurate, his account is woefully incomplete and does not approach a coherent picture of the ongoing transformation.

6. This is no doubt a bit technical, but it is worth point out that a determination of the conditions of systemic risk would require an analysis of the space of spaces. This means the field within which the markets have a certain autonomy based on their internal features (e.g., they trade stocks versus credit instruments), yet are also intrinsically imbricated in specific ways such that, for example, a disruption in liquidity in one market bleeds into each of the others markets in ways specific to those relationships between markets.

7. Many of these accounts read like extended magazine articles, and seem to be beset by an unnoticed contradiction. Peering into the psyche of the hedge fund manager or embattled CEO, they exude an odd admixture of barely concealed admiration for the street smarts, guile, and extravagant wealth of the financiers alongside righteous indignation over their insatiable greed. The language is tuned to blunt facticity, occasionally then tempered by a subordinate clause of outrage.

8. Whereas Paulson presents himself as the knowledgeable insider and Greenspan presents himself as an outside objective economist who has an Archimedean view of the markets, Geithner wants us to believe that he is a man who rarely ventured from his forty acres until he was commandeered by the Treasury Department only to be drawn into the maelstrom.

9. Reading the work of Greenspan, Geithner, and Larry Summers one is reminded of the comments by the social theorist Pierre Bourdieu. Speaking of them he writes that "Trusting in models that they have never subjected to experimental verification, tending to look down from on high on the conclusions of the other historical sciences, recognizing only the purity and crystalline transparency of their mathematical games whose real necessity and deep complexity they are most often unable to comprehend, they participate and collaborate in an enormous economic and social transformation which, even if some its consequences horrify them, cannot entirely displease them, since, with a few 'blips,' mainly attributable to which they call 'speculative fevers,' it tends to give reality to the ultra-consistent utopia to which they have devoted their lives" (1998:101, my translation).

10. The godfather of the free market, Milton Friedman, summed up this perspective in his oft repeated statement that economic agents, most of all in finance, are driven by "the single-minded pursuit of pecuniary self-interest" (reference). In his class, he would repeat in various phrasings that against monetary self-interest, all other interests paled (though he did allow at a dinner at which his wife was present that love was sometimes an exception).

11. The sociality (or non-sociality) of the financial market is a critical stake in a complex struggle. It helps define which disciplines have the authority to represent the economic;

it suggests which government agencies should be included in any regulatory regime; it determines whether markets are responsible only to themselves (as exemplified by the creation of clearinghouses) or whether they bear a responsibility toward the nation as a whole; it might influence a president to place a non-economist (e.g., consumer advocate) on the Federal Reserve's Open Market Committee.

12. The most celebrated answer to this question is Marx's account of objectification and reification, especially as presented in volume I of *Capital*. But Marx was nothing if not historically specific and sensitive to the changes unfolding before his eyes. So he lashes that account to the development of the money form and value as they serve to structure the emergent sphere of capitalist production. The organization of the allocation of capital was, at that time, parasitic to production. And thus required less attention. However, the ascension of finance-driven, circulation-centered capitalism leads to its own specific form of objectification. Accordingly, it would hardly be surprising if, taking account of this historical transformation, Marx argued that this new form of objectification combines a financial worldview with a speculative ethos in ways that echo the past and present structure of production, yet are also new.

13. Philip Mirowski (2002) has crafted a carefully constructed and deep critique of the operation of economic models. While Mirowski's analysis does not restore the social, it does reveal the gapping theoretical and empirical holes generated by its exclusion. The economic community has done its best to shun Mirowski's work (also 1989), lest recognition of his heresy would undermine their faith in the efficiency of markets.

14. Having read hundreds of these technical market analyses, it is clear that they do not understand themselves as having any conception of the market, let alone one that is asocial. Moreover, those who consume these analyses think of them as assembling data sets into more or less useful formats, not as embodying any view of the market qua market.

15. At one point in the mid 1970s economists began to scan the ethnographic literature much like an invading army learns the terrain of the region it seeks to occupy. The idea was that since all humans are innately utility maximizers, formal model should be universally applicable. They were, however, turned away by economic anthropologists, led by Marshall Sahlins, Stanley Tambiah, Terrance Turner, and Clifford Geertz who illustrated that an economistic model could not capture kin and community based societies whose economics centered on gift exchange and competition for social status.

16. A series on heterodox approaches to derivative finance, provisionally approved by the editors of Columbia University Press (2014), was torpedoed by the leading lights of Columbia's economic department on the grounds that publishing alternative approaches would only deflect from its scientific mission. They are indeed right as to their assessment as some of the younger members of that department, especially those with genuine mathematical sophistication, confessed in my conversations with them that they were aware that "market efficient" "equilibrium models" are misguided empirically and mathematically.

17. Jeremy Grantham, an institutional money manager, framed the issues as follows: "The incredibly inaccurate efficient market theory, believed in totality by many of our financial leaders, and believed in part by all . . . left our economic and government establishment sitting by confidently, even as a lethally dangerous combination of asset bubbles, lax controls, pernicious incentives, and wickedly complicated instruments led to our current plight" (2009 letter to clients entitled "The Story So Far: Greed + Incompetence + A Belief in Market Efficiency = Disaster"). Grantham's brief against the efficient market theory is its claim that there is no connection between the price of assets such as houses and financial instability. Precisely the connection created by derivatives, or, more sociologically, what the inventors of the derivatives that securitized mortgages were precisely trying to do. See the Evanoff, Kaufman, and Malliaris (2012) edited collection *New Perspectives on Asset Price Bubbles*, which, in tune with our "rational expectations," entertains only old perspectives in the sense that there are no real challenges to the conventional wisdom.

Chapter 3: Outline of a Social Theory of Finance

1. One is reminded here of the view, arguably apocryphal, attributed to the New York Yankee baseball catcher Yogi Berra about the "science" of catching. Berra observed that "in theory, there is no difference between theory and practice; but in practice, there is quite a difference." Had Berra turned to his eye to economics, he might have observed that while financial crises are possible in practice, the scholastic question is whether they are possible in theory.

2. No one who witnessed the extraordinary suffering of the Great Depression or Nazi Germany's attempt to exterminate the most educated and entrepreneurial segment of its own populace could conceivably contemplate the notions that economies where efficient or economic agents rational.

3. The habitus refers to the way that agents who occupy a specific field incorporate schemes of perception, appreciation, and action. These schemes enable them to perform actions based on this practical knowledge. These actions arise from agents' recognition of conditional, conventional cues to which they are predisposed to react due to their indoctrination in that field. The basis of these reactions may encompass, but extend far beyond, rational calculation. These schemes allow agents to produce and invent generative schemes for action, but always within the limits of the structural constraints imposed by the field. It is also worth noting that Emanuel Derman, a quant who formerly was a managing partner at Goldman Sachs, has, in his attempt to grasp financial behavior, come upon a similar concept through his invocation of Spinoza's notion of intuition, which was one of the earliest accounts of action as combining mental and dispositional elements (Derman 2011). See also Bourdieu 2000:138–163 for a comprehensive introduction to the habitus.

4. Taken to its limit, this concept of the social means that the inscription of the social is agent's presence at that moment when truth, things, values are constituted for them

because they are collectively constituted; that the social reverberates with a nascent logos that teaches agents, apart from all dogmas and intellocentric views, the true conditions of objectivity itself; that summons them to all of the tasks of knowledge and action done in the name of subjectivity.

5. The universalistic project of imagining a *rational economic man* cannot help but bracket the question that is the condition of the production of the concept. Namely, the social creation of a universe in which a universal can be posited as such. The positing of such universals is historically inseparable from, and intrinsic to, the rise of the epistemology of capitalism, which posits an abstract category of value that transcends and subsumes all particular concrete realizations of value (see Postone 1993:chapter 4). One of the paradoxes of the notion that the derivative markets represent the height of free market capitalism is that those who hold this notion decline any invitation to analyze the meaning of the adjective "free," or the genesis and character of "the market" and "capitalism" as social forms.

6. For the financial community, liquidity refers to the relative amount of friction that attends the exchange of assets. Agents' degree of willingness to circulate assets is the most important source of friction. A liquid market is one in which exchanges occur often, easily, and inexpensively; whereas an illiquid market one in which exchanges are infrequent, difficult, and/or expensive to consummate. When markets are liquid, asset holders can convert that asset to cash (or cash equivalents) expediently and at full present value. Expediency, however, is not absolute, it represents the amount of time that the participants in a specific market deem consistent with a well-functioning marketplace; full present value means that the participants suffer only expected transaction fees and encounter what they believe is a reasonable spread between the bid and asked price for an asset. A market fails systemically when the participants tender no bids for the assets for sale because they believe that the absence of liquidity, which their withdrawal only serves to reinforce, precludes proper price discovery (what the fundamental value of the asset is) and, correlatively, an outlet to resell the asset if necessary. What constitutes an expedient transaction and a reasonable spread varies across markets, and is the product of an informal group consensus orchestrated by the field's circulation of cultural views and values. In addition to belief in the solvency of the counterparties, assessments as to the liquidity of a derivatives market turns on the collectively judgment of the participants. This collective judgment is not intrinsic to the market or to the instrument, meaning that it is always necessarily a social product whose genesis and reproduction can only be grasped analytically by examining the circulation of those views and values.

7. Interestingly, in his scholarly publications on price volatility, Bernanke explicitly ruled out the possibility of liquidity problems. In the now famous analysis of *Monetary Policy and Asset Price Volatility* (Bernanke and Gertler 1999:40), the authors note in their conclusion that "although our framework omits the microecomomic details of episodes of stress (for example, reduced liquidity of financial markets) . . . we believe these omissions are unlike to affect our general conclusions about aggregate stabilization

policy" [economic speak for policies that create a stable real economy]. Bernanke and Gertler feel free to make these assertions because in their neoclassically based model *reduced financial liquidity* is a microeconomic *detail* that can exert only a fleeting and minor effect on the real economy. To their surprise, the real economy called their bluff and raised them a crisis.

8. Though it is beyond the scope of this analysis to explore the issue further, it is worth underlining that market mediated circulation is inseparable from the very existence of derivatives, whereas a market mediated mode of circulation is not inseparable from production centered capitalism because its constitutive mission is ever-increasing levels of use value (as measured by price). Consonantly, many enormously successful capitalist societies, those of Scandinavia stand out, bypass the market when it comes to the distribution of public goods such as health care, education, retirement incomes, and national defense. The abstract question of whether the capitalist market or the capitalist state is better at distributing these goods is rather meaningless: for the real question is the nationally historically specific incarnations of the market and the state that are doing the distributing.

9. Liquidity in the derivatives markets has an entirely different functionality than in commodity based markets, because commodities, such as a house or a car, has a use value. Even if I cannot sell my house, I can live in it or let others do so. Derivatives contracts have no use value, meaning that *derivatives are their liquidity.*

10. One technical sign of the problems was that even nations in Asia that had strong economic and financial fundamentals, suffered precipitous falls in equity indexes coupled with a sharp spike in credit default swap spreads, indicating a potential liquidity crisis as investors sought to deleverage en mass (for commentary see Filardo 2011 and Kim, Loretan, and Remolona 2010).

11. In recognition for his labors, in 2004, *Business Week* (November 29 issue) ranked Lewis Renieri as one of the greatest innovators of the past seventy-five years.

12. Essentially, the longer the maturity, the lower the credit score, the higher the risk and thus the higher the interest rate paid on the certificate.

13. One of the most common mistakes, embodied in what the financial sector refers to as technical analysis but commonplace in other forms, is to read backwards from the present to the past in such a way that an outcome appears determined and inevitable. And to then identify one or more factors in that past which are designated as having determined that inevitable outcome. This (mis)reading of history dismisses the work of history. Prospectively, the willingness to accept securitization was historically dependent: those born after World War II were buyers, whereas those who had experienced the great depression exhibited reluctance. Ranieri encountered a *generation gap*, which scientifically is a way of saying that the dispositions inculcated in those who had experienced and endured the banking failures of the depression were far different from those whose primary experience was the postwar boom years. A friend, a banker who special-

ized in wealth management, now in his nineties but still sentient, reflected on financial change in this very human way: "I know the two are not connected and that there is nothing rational about this; but sitting across the dinner table from my father after we had lost our savings [in 1931], he his job managing the bank, looking into my mother's eyes as she set a lone bowl of black grapes and water on the table for supper for all seven of us, left me too fearful to buy the new securitized instruments because I didn't really understand them." The point of this vignette is that for securitization to have arisen the history embodied in institutions and that embodied in agents' dispositions had to have been transformed, tilting toward innovation and speculation.

14. Note that one of the findings of the Financial Crisis Inquiry Commission (2011) was that no one, not even the Federal Reserve or the Treasury, knows with any certainty the exact amount of subprime loans that were executed, or all of the default provision or interest rate escalation clauses that were incorporated into the contracts.

Chapter 4: Temporality and the Financial Markets

1. The ability to anticipate that a market will snap back results from agents immersion in that market, and as such differs from the kind of knowing that agents can summon by consulting technical analyses or retrieve from their memories. As Bourdieu notes: "It is only manifest in concrete situations and is linked as if by a relation of *mutual prompting* to the occasion which calls it forth and which it causes to exist as an opportunity to be seized" (2000:211, italics in original). Though conventionally expressed in terms of the rational calculation of chances—risk/reward ratios—what defines the great hedge fund managers is their practical anticipation of how markets work.

2. Derman summarizes the problem in the uncensored language of the physicist: "the invisible worm of finance economics is its dark secret love of mathematical elegance regardless of its efficacy, and its belief that rigor can replace fact and intuition" (2011:144).

3. The concept that any derivatives portfolio can be valued on a "mark to market basis" (i.e., marked in terms of existing posted prices) assumes that the market resides in a permanent state of equilibrium and has no temporal directional dynamic of the kind we have described here. To put this another way, the concept works only for a hypostasized market quite remote from a real market approaching systemic failure.

4. The technical definition of accuracy is as follows: (1) the facts must correspond to the world, meaning that the information must be a true account of the real (e.g., the seller of the CDS is leveraged at no more than 4 to 1 and maintains a substantial cash position); (2) the conclusion drawn from the facts must follow a logical chain, meaning that there exists an internally cohesive relationship between the facts and conclusion (e.g., given my counterparty's leverage and substantial cash position they can pay off in the event the insured credit obligation defaults); and (3) the data synthesized must be comprehensive in that nothing pertinent has been omitted (e.g., they are under SEC investigation for falsifying their books).

5. Here is how one hedge fund manager, when placed under oath, described the process of borrowing securities. "I view stock loan as a sort of Mafia" [an organization whose reputation for fair market pricing is apparently less then stellar]. The manager goes on to say: "It's a black box where you don't know people's inputs and costs," leading to a situation in which prices are so opaque that firms like Goldman Sachs can say, "Here is the rate; if you want to borrow it, this is the rate. And it is what it is" (quoted in Morgenson 2012:B6).

6. This means that the notes would have a negative yield even if the inflation rate was zero over their duration. Negative yields are an impossibility according to the neoclassical account of the market, not least because it would assume that there are agents who do not seek utility maximization. The idea that these agents might be seeking to immunize themselves against the uncertainties of the future can never enter the economistic account because the hypostatized agents of financial theory presumably know the future with certainty.

Chapter 5: Theorizing the Financial Markets Socially

1. At this conjuncture in his journey between the mathematical model and the trading floor, Ayache has reached something of an impasse. He notes that the market is the medium in which the pricing of contingent claims—their recalibration—can take place in a reality that is between the present and future. He then invokes the notion of "absolute contingency" and says that to be in the market and to trade contingent claims via a pricing tool that recognizes recalibration is to be at the epicenter of the absolutely contingent event. The impasse come about because Ayache—in concert with Talib— does not have a conceptual means to distinguish between the processes of recalibration that imbue a market with liquidity and contingent black swans that can destroy that liquidity and thus the market itself. It is at this juncture that an account of the social is telling, for it reveals that contingency is itself contingent on the state of the market in respect to the habitus of its participants. This is illustrated by the fact that what counts as a black swan, that is what counts as a devastating market event is not an attribute of the event itself (e.g., a terrorist attack, a money center bank failure, a presidential impeachment, etc.); rather, it depends on the state of a derivative markets at a particular moment in its evolution (e.g., the degree of leverage and risk) in respect to the dispositions of those involved.

2. Think here of the tennis play of someone like Roger Federer. He is playing a point in which he has hit three consecutive cross court top spin backhands. Though he cannot measure the speed or the spin on the ball, he "knows" the weight of his shot: in tennis terms the "impression" he is making on his opponent. He senses that his last backhand has produced the cumulative result of his opponent being slightly off-balance, his weight on his left outside foot in anticipation of another Federer cross court shot. As the third shot is struck, Federer moves one step in from the baseline to cut off the angle. As his opponent's shot arrives, Federer senses its diminished speed and spin, and stepping further into the court closes his right shoulder, changes his grip on the racket, bends

his knees further to hit the ball on the rise, accelerates the speed of his racket head, and strikes a flat shot down the line for a winner. Federer has played a carefully constructed, thoughtful point that, of course, could not involve any careful thinking in that his opponent's shots are reaching him in less than a second.

3. The term of art here is "choppy trading," which means that buyers have provisionally decided that it is more prudent to be on the "sidelines" such that the market becomes less liquid, prices more opaque, and arbitrage opportunities more plentiful. The economic notion of market equilibrium assumes that speculators will step into the breach, seize these opportunities, and in so doing restore regularity. Recent history tells us that they do this until market conditions continue to deteriorate, after which they don't. Nothing underlines the power of finance more than the fact that the Federal Reserve feels compelled to use taxpayer money to fund and organize the deleveraging process instigated by the crisis.

4. Let it be said immediately that, as Benjamin Lee explains in *Talking Heads* (1997), even object categories have a relational dimension in that, for example, members of American linguistic community always grasp football fields in respect to soccer fields and baseballs fields and lacrosse fields and so on.

5. The account by Callon and those who follow in his footsteps falls short of grasping what is certainly a well considered and important target—the market—because they have yet to devise an account that motivates the sociostructure which generates a frame. And so, by assuming the totality into existence without ever attempting to explain it, they mistake the market's surface performativity, which they correctly identify and explore in often interesting ways, with its foundational dynamic. Theoretical issues must be addressed theoretically, and there is accordingly no way to bridge, through description alone, the gap between an empirical accounting of a market's network of relations [as in his review of the strawberry market in France's Sologne region (1998:19–21)] with its structural incarnation. Indeed, the former presupposes the latter.

6. Algorithmic trading is the recursive procedure by which agents (hedge funds especially) program a computer(s) attached to an electronic trading platform to identify financial moves (e.g., buying or shorting a given security and for what duration) based on a finite number of mechanical steps.

7. Anyone who thinks that magic and divination are confined to primitive societies should take a look at the epistemology of technical analysis. Like some forms of divination, its logic of trend lines, head and shoulders formations, and similar veiled patterns is founded on a magical vault from correlation to causation. The famous fundamentalist investor Warren Buffett opines somewhere that he presumes fortune tellers invented technical analysis to make their predictions about the future look good by comparison.

8. Mackenzie (2012) conceptualizes the conflation of derivative instruments as a problem in the sociology of knowledge. But this sociology is only a provisional description and partial explanation because it brackets the construction of interests and dispositions.

And thus the way in which their interaction contributes to the creation and routinization of this specific type/token performative act. The irony is that it is only through the presence and expression of a certain scientific habitus, which valorizes the act of turning relational categories into concrete categories, that the classification of the derivative can be subsumed under a regime of rationality. That is, the performative act of classifying *this* conflation as a problem that can be answered by reference to the sociology of knowledge turns on the existence and force of a habitus whose presence the regime of rationality excludes as a condition of its valorization.

9. Those pursuing this approach were naturally attracted to natural metaphors. In his instantly famous textbook, *Economics* (1948), Paul Samuelson, a pioneer in the mathematization of economics, submitted that markets were like "the surface of the ocean" because both exist in a state of "equilibrium that is constantly being disturbed but is always in the process of re-forming itself" (p. 570).

10. Technically, a market is complete when the trajectory of each security is linear, independent of the movement of other securities, and when future states of the market have the same number of such securities. Which means that there exist unique martingale measures, which has the virtue of making the mathematics tidy, even elegant. The idea of a complete market creates an interesting paradox in that it presupposes that analysts can predict what about the future is unpredictable. This leads to the common assumption that nothing about the future is unpredictable—which is true, of course, until something foreseen happens.

11. As philosophy has pointed out since its inception, humans are social and self-reflexive, meaning that the knowledge that they generate about the market can be injected back into the object of their understanding, such that the "moves" motivated by his knowledge can (and do) motivate a collective response. The notion indigenous to the financial field that money managers (mutual and hedge funds) congenitally copycat one other implicitly recognizes this self-reflexivity.

12. A term such as *market imperfections* is a curious intellectual concept. For it is actually nothing more than a label posing as a description of the deviations from what is a hypostatized perfect market, this description, in turn, poses as an explanation for what is going on. From a social perspective, market imperfections are the result of that portion of the investing population whose dispositions move them to actualize trades that depart from the mainstream. The entire investing philosophy of men like Warren Buffett is to identify and capitalize on market imperfections.

13. Rituals such as Sunday church services foreground faith, though they are one of the most lucrative markets in the United States judging by the many billions of dollars that church-goers contribute annually in exchange for improving their odds of salvation.

14. This formulation intends no metaphysics. Only that the market cannot be real the way concrete categories such as earth, salt, and water are real. Rather, the market is "real" the way the nation-state is real, brought into existence in the late 18th century by

virtue of a particular historically specific imagination of peoplehood configured in respect to territorial sovereignty and governance. There was once a world without nation-states, and there may so be again in the future, but for us nothing is as ontologically real as the nation we live in, that collects and pools our taxes, that replaces and elevates citizenship over kinship, that defends our borders, and that on occasion asks some of us to put our life on the line for a totality composed of persons the vast majority of who's very existence we will never know of, other than abstractly.

Chapter 6: Rituality and the Production of Financial Markets

1. This duality ultimately rests on a contrast and comparison between *the surface forms of capitalism and what primitive exchange would look like from the perspective of those forms.* The italics are important because the surface forms of capitalism, exemplified by production-centered commodity production, impart an objective, law like, and thus apparently economically rational character to commodity circulation, primitive exchange with its overt reliance on kinship and community appears to be guided by subjectively guided subjects that have no allegiance to assessments of risk, calculations of value and return, or strategies of how to use the interval between the giving of a gift and its future requital. A deeper reading of the ethnography would show that "primitive" subjects act in interested ways, a point Pierre Bourdieu stressed right from the beginning (e.g., 1972). It is also a misreading of the ethnography to think that primitive societies do not have markets, commodities, and wealth accumulation and that these surface categories constitute adequate grounds for differentiating them from capitalism. The real comparison must be between the deep sociostructures of capitalism and the real ethnographic character of social economies that feature ritualized gift exchange: for even the apparently purely descriptive idea that there is the singularity called *the gift* is misleading. For it attributes a totalization to the gift which is actually read off of the appearance of the commodity, whose underlying form is a striving toward a totality which can never be completed due to the dissembling effects of circulatory forces, such as the rise of derivatives (see LiPuma and Postone, unpublished manuscript, for a more comprehensive version of this argument). Primitive societies have markets, commodities, and wealth accumulation; they just constitute them differently in respect to the social.

2. At one point in the mid 1970s economists began to scan the ethnographic literature much like an invading army learns the terrain of the region it seeks to occupy. The idea was that since all humans are innately utility maximizers, formal model should be universally applicable. They were, however, turned away by economic anthropologists, led by Marshall Sahlins, Stanley Tambiah, Terrance Turner, and Clifford Geertz who illustrated that an economistic model could not capture kin and community based societies whose economics centered on gift exchange and competition for social status.

3. From this perspective, the intervention of social forces to redirect and inflect the reproduction of the market do not appear social at all. They are thus characterized as "noise," "herd-like behavior," "animal spirits," "primal fear," "contagion," and the like. All of these terms re-introduce the social by way of metaphors that point away from it,

thereby preserving the ideology of systemically natural reproduction through systemically natural replication.

4. Dividuality is a term derived from the Indian and Melanesian anthropological traditions to help explicate societies where persons' relationships to others is the primary constituent of their identity across most socially meaningful situations. Dividuality is not a kind of personhood; it is the functionality of being in the world that represents the collectivity's creation of a person's singularity. As such, dividuality and individuality are the twin inseparable dimensions of personhood. The critical question becomes, given the society in question, what are the socially constructed situations/conditions in which the partible aspects of persons become attached to others to create a collectively created singular person. What characterizes capitalism is that even those social situations redolent with dividuality are, on the model of the world read off of the commodity, cast as instances of individuality.

5. This observation becomes a kind of theory in the hands of behavioral economists, culminating in the notion that financial crises occur when our deeply Puritan animal spirits of avarice, envy, and lust emerge from hibernation, casting us into a diabolical world in which what we think is rational, following the crowd on its pilgrimage toward financial success, is actually the epitome of irrationality and folly. Note that in behavioral economics the notions of *following* and *the crowd* are surrogates for an account of the social. For these irredeemably ambiguous notions lie almightily at the intersection where the objective outcomes of a market (houses that have soared in value and been flipped for huge gains) inflect agents' collective forthcoming actions. The language of behavioral economics constitutes an admission of the power of the social, which it is powerless to understand so long as it lives in the netherland between the rational and irrational.

6. Rituals such as Sunday church services foreground faith, though they are one of the most lucrative markets in the United States judging by the many billions of dollars that church-goers contribute annually in exchange for improving their odds of salvation. In her account of the relationship between *Faith and Money* (2011), Lisa Keister shows just how inseparable religion and economy are.

7. Inscribed in our characterization of these theorists is a critique. Its central point is that in order to go beyond the appearance of ritual as operating in respect to already finalized totalities, it is necessary to construct an account of the performativity of practices. Only through such an account is it possible to grasp the dialectic of incorporation and objectification that shapes the reproduction of these totalities. Despite their ethnographic insights, what limits these and other theorists of ritual is that by beginning their analysis at the moment of the already constituted totality they are prone to look at the effects of a totality's practices and to overlook how the practices produce that totality. It is agreed and indeed proven that sound research requires an objectivist dimension. This is necessary in order to get beyond and to contextualize agents' experiences inasmuch as the participants' "native points of view" tend to fixate on the local, to natu-

ralize social conventions, to be almost exclusively referential, and to emanate from specific positions and perspectives within the social. But there is here a critical however, for having overcome the limits of agents' primary experience, it is mistaken to declare the analysis complete by turning immediately to how the structure functions (e.g., what a clan or a market does). To the contrary, analysis must transcend and supplement this objectivism by generating an account of how agents' generative schemes are instrumental in reproducing that structure in respect to itself in relation to others. The reason so many analyses are condemned to focusing only on pragmatic performativity is that they have implicitly transmuted the system of objective relations into finished totalities, a move which serves to underwrite the illusion that they are already constituted outside the dynamics of circulation and thus history.

8. This progressive fitting of platform and practice has been referred to as "Barnesian performativity" (MacKenzie 2006:33) in the sense that platform and practice are self-referential because they mutually confirm and sustain one another.

9. This formulation intends no metaphysics. Only that the market cannot be real the way concrete categories such as earth and water are real. Rather, the market is "real" the way the nation-state is real, brought into existence in the late eighteenth century by virtue of a particular historically specific imagination of peoplehood configured in respect to territorial sovereignty and governance. There was once a world without nation-states, and there may so be again in the future, but for us nothing is as ontologically real as the nation we live in, that collects and pools our taxes, that replaces and elevates citizenship over kinship, that defends our borders, and that on occasion asks some of us to put our life on the line for a totality composed of persons the vast majority of who's very existence we will never know of, other than abstractly.

10. Since risk is a relation that objectifies itself in other relations, most notably the wager internal to financial derivatives, its function in defining and stimulating liquidity is inseparable from the moment of objectification. Thus the production of derivatives, by amalgamating numerous context specific risks in order to model and price them, objectifies risk in an abstract form. Even the notion of counterparty risk is inherently plural and social, inasmuch as it may encompasses an open ended ensemble of otherwise incommensurable risks, from a run of the mill bankruptcy to a government's seizure of counterparty's assets to a terrorist attack.

11. It is worth point out that the efficient market theory is actually not a theory of the market. It is a theory of circulation—i.e., trades that define prices—that presupposes a process of production that it cannot account for. For example, that a market is self-correcting (whether true or not) presupposes that that market is closed and complete, but cannot possibly account for the production of that closure or completeness.

12. Those in the financial field find it next to impossible to think or frame problems socially. Their disposition is to frame problems technically, in an object language organized around common oppositions. For example, in arguing against a proposed ban on OTC derivatives, they submit that it is important to distinguish between the tool and

its user. In this case, between derivative instruments and the ruthless speculators who pushed the system to the brink. However reasonable sounding, this is a false opposition socially. For what we know about agents is that they adjust their strategies to the potentialities of a given instrument just as they seek out and create instruments that allow them to execute their speculative strategies. The strategies of the users and the use of the instruments are symbiotic, each adjusted and readjusted to the conditions present in the financial field at any point in time. Derivative instruments cannot but inscribe the history of the use that speculators have made of them, which is, leveraging speculative capital. This incapacity to think socially also underlies the celebrated "moral hazard" argument. Commentators have argued that the reason traders speculated so recklessly is be*cause* they knew the government bailout would spare them the consequences of their actions. Note the argument's asocial design: it quasi-automatically transmutes an effect of the crisis—the bailout of some impaired firms—into *the* cause of *all* firms' actions. The switch eliminates having to explain the social production of knowledge: How "did" "could" "would" agents come to the certain conclusion that the government would bail them out? How did this knowledge become so widely institutionalized that, when the music stopped, many investment houses ended up with worthless and illiquid tranches of CDOs? Under what mental formula would agents reach this conclusion given that, historically, not everyone was bailed out—exemplified by Lehman Brothers, but also by firms such as Bear Stearns, which essentially disappeared. Could we, for example, imagine Bear's senior management issuing a memo that said, "Speculate to the hilt, the worst that can happen is that our personal stock becomes worthless and we're devoured by our hated rival JP Morgan Chase?" So the question of the production and circulation of knowledge remains, especially as many investment firms "acted" as though they would be bailed out. One might refer here to the theory that "belief in the action of demons is found at the roots of our concept of causality." Here the shape of the argument excludes the social by identifying a demon—the US government's bailout policy—that caused agents to make insanely speculative trades. One might also refer here to the poet who cautioned that "you have been in full command of every plan you've wrecked; but don't take a coward's explanation and hid behind the cause and the effect" (from Leonard Cohen's song *Alexandra Leaving*).

13. This information is critical in that it can cut both ways: it can assure the players that the market is liquid and that they can exit their positions, but also that a large player may have so much financial ammunition that it can afford to wait, sustaining or doubling down on a position in the hope that its prospects may change. This was precisely the situation in the recent debacle at JP Morgan.

Chapter 7: The Speculative Ethos

1. This chapter is defined and inspired by my conversations, over many years and across many venues, with my colleague and friend, Benjamin Lee. Ben has always had an extraordinary amount of insight about many areas of derivatives, especially speculation. I am particularly indebted in the section on poker, a game close to both our sensibilities.

2. A characteristic explanation is some variant of what is called "herd behavior" (e.g., Kim and Kim 2000 and Kindleberger 2005). The naturalistic metaphor allows the descriptor of agents acting in concert to pose as an explanation of that very behavior. The metaphor of herding suggests the expression of a deeply entrenched instinct as that which compels cows, sheep and other animals to act collectively and without forethought, as when they are led to the slaughter. The notion of herd, like that of mania and panic, is meant to impart the impression that these are not learned behaviors: no one refers to the European use of a fork or the Chinese use of chopsticks as examples of herd behavior. This "explanation" ignores one of the central insights of anthropology: namely, that culture is human's overriding biological adaptation precisely because it freed them from instinctually-driven behavior. The notion of herding behavior is an off-the-shelf substitute for a real analysis of the formation of vectors of social force and compulsion.

3. Many aspects of our ordinary existence, from riding a bike and driving a car to undergoing anesthesia for a surgical procedure, will involve uncertainty and risk. But not speculation. We conceptualize these activities, such as driving to work or flying to visit our siblings, as imbued with a certain basic necessity. Safety is a mandated aim of the airline and automotive industries, such that the risks incurred are literally an accidental rather than an essential property of the activity. The contrast here with the derivative is stark: for risk is an intrinsic property of the derivative and speculation is a voluntary and volitional acceptance of risk, and sometimes an avowed pursuit of it.

4. As long ago as 1202, the Italian mathematician Fibonacci gave an exposition of the inherently speculative relationship between the repayment of a debt over time in respect to the present value of money. Reading his masterwork, *Liber Abaci*, some eight hundred years later, it is hard not to be impressed by how easily he develops a notion of uncertainty and the realities that attend decision making under uncertainty (1202:45–67). Luckily for Fibonacci, the Church fathers seemed to have no idea what the book was about.

5. In class, Friedman once even jested that speculators were providing the economy with a *micvah*—Yiddish for a meritorious deed that God will look favorably on. And on another occasion remarking that "where there is true capitalism, market makers are the only chosen people."

6. This section of the chapter was written in conjunction with, and inspired by, my friend and colleague Benjamin Lee. The section especially but also the chapter in its entirety is the product of several decades of conversation, and owes much to his creative brilliance.

7. The first derivation of this formula was by David Li, a quant at JP Morgan. His paper "On Default Correlation: A Copula Function Approach," which appeared in the *Journal of Fixed Income* (December 2000), was widely circulated through the quant floor of investment houses. The model allowed analysts to correlate tranches of collateralized debt/mortgage obligations based on how the credit default swap (CDS) market priced

the various underlying securities. Though its adherents did not, of course, conceptualize it this way, the real underlying thesis is that the best way to avoid a crisis is to assume that crises can't happen.

8. The two basic presuppositions are that market forces drive markets toward equilibrium and that, accordingly, deviations from this equilibrium are random events that arbitrage quickly and efficiently corrects.

9. See Lewis's *The Big Short* (2012) for some telling examples.

10. In their book *Financial Derivatives in Theory and Practice* (which was published in a series on probability and statistics), Hunt and Kennedy (2000) note that "models based on Brownian motion have turned out to be high tractable and usable" for the pricing of financial derivatives. As they and others have noted, to develop a Brownian analysis it is necessary to posit the existence of "an explicitly defined probability space" (i.e., a totality) in respect to a continuous set of functions within this space (p. 20).

11. It is assumed, in any model that follows a Brownian motion, that derivative prices follow a continuous process rather than undergoing discontinuous jumps. The reason for this and the other assumptions is that the model starts with a derivative price process in a complete economy—that is, a closed and technically perfectly efficient economy. This is specified by means of a stochastic differential equation embedded in a real-world probability measure P (such as the history of the price of that derivative). The analyst then selects a numeraire N and changes the probability measure to an equivalent martingale measure N under which all N-rebased derivatives are martingales. Accordingly, expectations in the value of N than determine the price of the derivative. The problem is, of course, that the real world is not a martingale measure, with the only correction between an analysts' intuitive assessment of what market data to calibrate to the model selected. Sociologically, analysts need draw upon their inculcated concepts and dispositions of the market—that is, their financial habitus which is itself a permutation of a more encompassing grasp of what the economic is—to determine which data to fit to the model. This fitting process is an aspect of pricing that is itself derived from the culture of speculation.

12. OTC stands for "over the counter," which means that the derivative in question is not traded on an established and regulated exchange, such as the Chicago Mercantile Exchange (MERC), but is rather specifically crafted for one or more of the counterparties to the contract. Importantly, most derivatives are created, marketed, and traded OTC.

13. Mathematically, a simple formula can be used. The analyst calibrates a series of data points (x_i, y_i), $i = 1, \ldots n$ to the equation $y_i = f(x_i)$ with the goal of finding $f(x)$ for some given value x. Analysts can then either postulate a functional form for f and perform a least squares fit to the points, or they can fit the function f using the prices close to the given x. One rather counterintuitive result, which reveals the subterranean relationship of fitting a token to a type, is that if the analyst fits too many prices exactly

it becomes impossible to price the derivative because the equation admits no reasonable or approximate solution.

14. It is no surprise that gambling and high finance go hand in hand. *Liar's Poker* begins with a legendary story about two titans of finance, John Gutfreund, then chairman of Salomon Brothers, and John Meriweather, a member of Salomon's board and its leading bond trader. In an atmosphere radiant with tension and suspense, Gutfreund challenges Meriweather to a single hand of liar's poker for a million dollars. Meriweather replies that if we're going to play, let's play for real money and raises the stakes to ten million dollars. Speaking about Meriweather's speculative impulse, Gutfreund replied, "you're crazy," and so a legend was born about Meriweather's appetite for risk. What is interesting is that the speculative ethos seems to require outsized stories as an essential part of how people create their identities in a sea of speculations (of all sorts). Later on Meriweather would take the risk-taking environment of the Salomon Brothers' Arbitrage Group to Long-term Capital Management, which he founded in 1993. Joined by Nobel Prize winners Myron Scholes and Robert Merton Jr., an avid poker player, Long-term Capital Management became the leading hedge fund of its time. Its collapse in 1998 would become a symbol of arrogance and speculative excess. Given the gambling backgrounds of its founders, the strategies that it used resembled the combination of statistical brilliance and risk-taking possessed by the best poker players. A good portion of Long-term Capital's trades consisted of discovering arbitrage opportunities, that is, historical mispricing of assets, and placing highly leveraged and statistically refined bets that the market would correct these mispricings. The discovery phase would require the statistical manipulation of large data sets; the construction of the appropriate derivative instrument would be akin to calculating the odds and making the bet; then there would be the moment of radical uncertainty before the flop would fall and the future would become the present and then history and hopefully the speculator a winner. The thrill of the win was said to be indescribable, better than sex, better than anything. And then the hands would be redealt and positions restaked, and another round of trading would begin.

15. The explosive increase in popular margin debt was an index of speculation. It indicated that speculation had become acceptable, the assumption of risk no longer frightened investors, but was viewed as the thoroughfare to profits beyond what they could achieve with safer investments (such as US treasury bonds). All the retail brokerages created special trading platforms so that the average investor could speculate on stocks, bonds, currencies, etc. Schwab, Fidelity, Trade Station, Ameritrade, TD Waterhouse, have all installed technical analysis programs to assist and encourage speculation. From any terminal, anywhere, traders with as little as a few thousand dollars can run stochastic models to determine buy and sell points on their speculative bets.

16. The panel on the CNBC show *Fast Money*, along with various money and hedge fund managers interviewed daily suggested (with all due respect, of course) that Buffett's methodology represented yesterday's way of investing, as exemplified by the stagnation in Berkshire Hathaway's stock price during the heyday of CDO promotion.

17. This stance has been called into question, most recently and explicitly by Freedman (2010). He submits that the costs of allocating capital in this manner are too expensive for the results obtained.

Chapter 8: The Social Habitus of Financial Work

1. The titans from the previous generation, such as Charles Munger (Buffett's partner at Berkshire Hathaway) and Hank Greenberg from AIG, have expressed anger and frustration at what they see as the recklessness, insatiable greed, and hubris of many of the traders that broke the credit markets. It is clear that many of the CEOs and financial officers not only didn't understand the complex structured instruments being traded, they did not understand the motivations that drove the traders to take such speculative positions.

2. Based on their interviews with ex-Lehmanites, Louise Story and Landon Thomas Jr. (2009) note that "bound by the financial promise of their company stock, as well as a shared sense of professional purpose," the "Lehman crew drank together, exercised together, dated one another, and kept constantly in touch as they traded market information" (p. 7). There was a solidarity created by being a member of a team confronting a treacherous and hostile environment, which included other investment firms, state and federal regulators, and sometimes even members of upper management. It is no accident that to this day the members of now defunct firms, such as Lehman Brothers, Merrill Lynch, and Bear Stearns, blame this trio of regulators, upper management, and other too predatory firms for their demise. It is clear that for many, the deep sense of belonging, solidarity, and self-esteem led to a suspension of their rational, monetary maximizing, calculative self in favor of a collective, for some even quasi-charismatic, faith in their common project. From a Weberian standpoint, there is a deep and understandable sociality in the claim that my work is who I am, when there is a deep-seated identification between the work, the worker, and his co-workers. And descriptions of the interrelationships among co-workers are infused with their investment in a work-centered sociality—however much agents relegated this sociality to the un-thought of background, however much this sociality was cloaked by an ideology which foregrounded money as the bedrock issue. The interviews also reveal that many people felt that having an unyielding commitment to the company stock was a demonstration of their faith in themselves and their coworkers.

3. Bertrand Russell (1935:11) famously pointed that there were only two kinds of work: altering the position and composition of matter relative to other matter, and telling other people to do so. Had he met derivative traders he might have had to add a third category: speculating on the volatility of that relation.

4. See Michael Lewis's scathing portrait of Cassano in the high-brow publication *Vanity Fair* in 2011.

5. The original saying, which reflects their gift as opposed to commodity based economy, is that "gifts make [discipline] people like whips make dogs."

6. An instructive aspect of media interviews with powerful men and firms, such as Lloyd Blankfein the CEO of Goldman Sachs, is the overestimation of his firm's ability to control the market through sheer monetary force, even as the media underestimates his, and his firm's, ability to shape financial markets by shaping the conditions of their reproduction. There is a substantialist bias which accords a greater reality to that which is countable, the dollar amount of compensation for example, than to the social relations that define the reproduction of the instilled dispositions of the field. Goldman alumni (former Treasury Secretaries R. Rubin and H. Paulson) have shaped the markets' reproduction at the point where the dispositions inculcated within them by virtue of their long term immersion in the financial field intersects with the Goldman creed of providing public service. The issue is not the one the media usually poses: whether they did or did not use their position to enrich their own; but rather the connectivity between financial dispositions that have been inculcated within them over decades, the inflective power exercised through high government office, and their desire to actualize what they perceive as the economic interests of their country. Whether posing as a democratic or republican, they were predisposed to believe that a free and unregulated market in derivatives was *objectively* both necessary and good.

7. Betting is alluring. Gambling thrills because it slices into our sense that life involves decision making under uncertainty when a value is at stake. But there is also a companion reason, or at least it seems so. Trading is a profession in which the clarity of the result rebalances the uncertainty of the wager. Across much of the corporate landscape there is the tyranny of the bottom line: the notion that good performance guarantees bottom line results. But in an increasingly service oriented economy in which what agents produce has only a fleeting social connection to customers founded on their own transient relationship with their employer, the only external standard of job performance are management evaluations, which are an object of intense employee distrust because they seem to activate unconscious biases. In these work contexts, process becomes more important than results, because the process is more visible. By contrast, for traders, trading produces clear visible results. There is complete clarity in either making money or losing money. When in 2012, the Goldman's proprietary trading desk made extraordinary returns on capital, their performance was crystal without the need of a management evaluation. Trading transcends one of the contradictions of a modern service oriented economy which features a bottom line mentality but only a seemingly amorphous, ambiguous, and subjective evaluative methodology. Anyone who doubts this need only visit a bookstore and thumb through any of the innumerable titles on management, most of which have sections cast in psychological jargon about overcoming this contradiction. It is beyond this scope, but part of an understanding of the ongoing transformation of capitalism would entail a comparative theory of work.

8. The firm is betting that the products its brokers are selling will fall in price because the security is overvalued. Selling short is simply the process of selling a security that a firm does not own on the prospects that the firm can acquire the security at a lower price later on.

9. The power of the media to advocate these dispositions resides in its creations of a space of information in which it can impose the terms of the presentation of evidence. This appears in instances in which a media outlet presents several panelists all of whom draw on the same dispositions to endorse the same counterfactual statement. For example, on October 30, 2009, Erin Burnett (CNBC) hosted several panelists all of whom emphatically agreed that there was a direct causal relationship between job creation and marginal tax rates at the top end: thus the unanimous conclusion that the higher the tax rates the less job creation. Anyone watching the show would have come away thinking that this was settled science, even as they would have been subliminally exposed to the dispositions that produced those statements. The show aligned a set of dispositions with a specific objectification of the real. This serves to reinforce and circulate both the dispositions and an interested construction of the real. In this media context, it is only coincidental that scientifically, there exists no correlation, much less causative chain, between marginal tax rates for the wealth and job growth. Recall just for an empirical moment that both tax rates and job growth were substantially higher during the two terms of the Clinton Administration than during a similar period of his successor, George W. Bush.

10. Within English soccer, the Premier League is the highest and most revered; playing for a team such as Manchester United is equivalent in the United States to playing baseball for the New York Yankees.

11. There is perhaps no better illustration than Mitt Romney, a founder of Bain Capital, a formidable leveraged buyout firm, who ran for president in the 2012 election. Even as he tried to connect with real economy working class voters, a series of callous, disparaging, off the cuff remarks seeped out inadvertently, wounding his candidacy even as they illuminated the worldview common to finance.

12. In our previous work, *Financial Derivatives and the Globalization of Risk* we identified 1973 as the turning point in the genesis of a culture of financial circulation. Chapter 3 defines the terms of this argument.

13. For a definition from an economistic view of markets, see Fama's (1976) classic on the foundations of finance, which presupposes a market that is so efficient that the agents involved disappear. From an alternative social theory perspective, a financial market is a socially imaginary form (See Taylor 2004: especially chapter 5), produced from the continuous objectification of the aggregation of the actions of those agents who create and circulate securities with those agents who have the dispositions and the requisite social and economic capital to buy and sell them. Adding the social complicates the problem, complicates the math, and complicates the methods of investigation; expunging it, however, leads to a failure of understanding, which, because it is a "financial" market after all, can be very costly for all involved.

14. We cannot grasp the success of the rational market thesis unless we appreciate that it provides a solution to the contradictions to which an account of finance is condemned by an inchoate—or what amounts to the same thing—an implicit theory of financial

practice. The thesis permits its users to account for the sociality of finance by seeing that sociality as nothing more than a reflection of the market—as though agents' socio-historically grounded interactions require no explanation at all. The rational market thesis allows its users to forget all that is lost when the product, such as a CMO deriva-tive transaction, is divorced from the conditions and contexts of its production [e.g., the competitive expression of a speculative ethos in a period (2002–2007) of historically high liquidity and inflating home prices]. Speaking of the crisis, the economist, Paul Krugman (2009) argues that his fellow economists went astray when they "mistook beauty, clad in impressive looking mathematics, for truth" and that the remedy is to jet-tison their utopian view of "a perfect, frictionless market system" and realize that mar-kets are "shot through with flaws and frictions" (p. 42). The sociologist Pierre Bourdieu is more caustic in his assessment of these economists. "Cut off by their whole existence and above all by their generally purely abstract and theoretical intellectual training from the real social and economic world, they are inclined to take the things of logic for the logic of things. Trusting in models that they have never had the occasion to subject to empirical verification, recognizing only the purity and crystalline transparency of their mathematical games, they tend to look down from on high on the conclusions of the other historical sciences, and whose real necessity and deep complexity they are most often unable to comprehend. . . ." (1998:101). One might think Bourdieu too harsh if Krugman did not verify Bourdieu's argument. About how remote these econo-mists are from the real world when Krugman points out that Edward Prescott (a Nobel prize winner in 2004) and Casey Mulligan maintain that unemployment can best be understood as "a deliberate decision by workers to take time off" (p. 40). Krugman also observes that Alan Greenspan's assurances about the soundness of the housing market "weren't based on evidence—they were based on the a priori assumption that there simply can't be a housing bubble" (p. 41). Krugman also testifies on Bourdieu's behalf when he reports that these same economists "mocked" as hopelessly "misguided" those social scientists who warned of systemic risk.

Chapter 9: The Social Dimensions of Black-Scholes

1. Fischer Black and Myron Scholes developed the derivative pricing model named after them, abbreviated in the literature and here as BS. At the same time, Robert Merton was developing a similar model, such that his name is sometimes appended to BS, ab-breviated as BSM. More than a decade later, Scholes and Merton were awarded the Nobel Prize in Economics on the basis of the equation (Fischer Black had died and was therefore ineligible). The irony is that, of the three authors, only Fischer Black seems to have appreciated the deeper issues implicated in the equation.

2. The Black-Scholes equation is generally solved with the finite difference method. Quantitative theorists recognize that there are alternative means of solving the pricing equation (e.g., Monte Carlo method), though in the practice of pricing the alterna-tives disappear. So much so that the traders who rely on the BS pricing model have, it turns out, frequently never even heard of alternative mathematical methods. The finite

difference method is a way of solving a differential equation by turning it into a difference equation. This technique turns continuous variables into discrete variables so that the equation may be solved numerically. Nonetheless, the overall importance of the BS equation is infinitely greater than the manner in which it happens to be solved.

3. This paper draws off of, and is very indebted to, the work of our colleagues Robert Meister and Randy Martin. Equally the work on derivatives modeling by Nassim Taleb, in particular Dynamic Hedging (1997), Paul Wilmott's introduction to quantitative finance (2007), and Perry Mehrling book on Fischer Black (2005). The account also draws on extensive, longitudinal interviews with derivative traders, focusing especially on OTC derivatives, as well as our own derivative trading experience mostly in exchange traded stock option, currency (FOREX), and credit derivatives.

4. For anthropology and social theory generally, *the social* has a specific reference. It constitutes the unmarked term that encompasses all of the ways in which concrete human actions enacted with sociospecific practices (such as executing a derivative trade) are the product of the organization (both institutionally and through the habitus) of deeply imbricated social, economic, political, moral/ethic dimensions of contemporary life.

5. This could theoretically portend a mathematics that could encompass the social dimensions of finance and correlatively mathematize as a probabilistic spread the risk of internal systemic devolution (e.g., based on levels of outstanding leverage), the risk posed by the intervention of unforeseeable forces (i.e., black swans), and the risks engendered by the government's securitization of financial markets through the massive (but extremely secret) collection of data on those markets.

6. As Derman notes in his autobiography, coming from physics, he began with the assumption that he and his colleagues were going to construct a physics of finance only to reach the conclusion that this objective was illusory because of the constant intervention of other forces, the conceptualization of which eventually led him to invoke Spinoza's notion of intuition (2011:81–106). There is a kind of intellectual circle here in that the systemic moment in Spinoza's notion was picked up by Weber who imbued it with a more social grounding through his concept of habitus, which was then brought to prominence in the works of Norbert Elias and Pierre Bourdieu.

7. The chain reaction is as follows: if there are no buyers than there is no way to price securities; if there is no price for these securities, then they are worth nothing; if the securities are worth nothing then they no longer have value as collateral; if they no longer have value as collateral then the institutions who collateralized their trades with these securities are in default; if these institutions are becoming insolvent en masse, then the banks which loaned these institutions the money to establish their positions have impaired capital structures; if these banks have impaired capital structures and are approaching insolvency then the banks these banks borrowed money from are also approaching insolvency.

8. The BS formula calls for the specification of volatility: this with time are the two parameters. But how then can one assign a volatility measure when crisis events have driven historical or past volatilities literally off the charts. The answer was to invert the polarity of the relationship between the derivative and its volatility. The analyst looks at the price at which the derivative is trading and then calculates the volatility that would produce the equation-correct market price. So *implied volatility* specifies the movement of the underlier, which when inserted into the BS equation, generates a theoretical price identical to the market price. The theoretically generated prices can then be used to substitute for the unreliable, because crisis torn, historical prices. The contradiction is that the use of implied volatility measures assumes that crises are one off events that do not make a difference even as these measures necessarily incorporate agents' expectations of future possible crises.

9. *Log*normal abbreviates logarithmic normal. This is the distribution of a random variable, *x*, when log *x* is a random variable with a normal distribution. A normal (or Gaussian) distribution is a distribution that is continuous and symmetrical. A well-known example is the results of repeatedly rolling two dice: seven will appear more often than six or eight, both which will appear equally more often than five and nine, and so on. The graph of a probability density function of a normal distribution is a normal (bell-shaped) curve. What this means is that while any given outcome (a roll of a six versus a seven) is random, the possible outcomes are known (from two through twelve) as is their distribution. Lognormal distributions (thanks to the central limit theorem) approximate many distributions of natural kinds; they do preclude, however, the kinds of uncertainties that have defined the social history of societies and capitalist finance.

10. The Paris Bourse crashed entirely in 1882, prices plummeting some 30 percent in just a few days, leading to the wholesale destruction of the French financial sector.

11. This section of the paper owes much to the work of Paul Wilmont, who, like Emanuel Derman his coauthor on the manifesto, intuitively grasps that there is a social dimension to trading that cannot be reduced to mathematical formulas.

12. Derman gives as an example adding together the price of ten efficiency apartments to determine the price of a ten-room apartment that, owing to its rarity, has no market pricing mechanism.

13. Interestingly, Mandelbrot's analysis was rejected on the grounds that if it was correct, it would invalidate the statistical methods used in finance economics. To which Mandelbrot replies precisely so because "they've made assumptions which were not valid" (quoted in Patterson 2010:297).

14. Investment banks fabricate exotic (non-exchange traded) derivatives for prospective clients and for their own proprietary trading desks. The banks then value these derivatives by selecting some ensemble of "vanilla" (i.e., standardized exchange traded) derivatives and combining them, often fractionally and in varying proportions, to generate a pricing model.

15. A common explanation is that investors overvalue "out of the money puts" (a put with a strike price of 60 on a security trading above that price) due to their collective fears and anxiety about the future price movement of that security. Left unanswered is why the most economically rational investors the world has even known should act irrationally out of fear and anxiety, or why this irrational behavior should be collectively pursued, or how the institutions they work for influence their behavior, or the implications of such persistent presumably behavioral anomalies on the structure of financial capitalism, and so on right down to the sociologic of the derivative itself.

16. It is interesting that even the anesthetist knows that this is only an ideal calculation which must be adjusted, sometimes radically so, based on the medical history of the patient, such as whether they have had certain classes of diseases, have a lifestyle that accelerates enzyme induction, or an occupation in which they are likely to take anabolic steroids, and so on.

17. In practice, certain arbitrage spreads, motivated by social forces, can remain open for years at a time. This is especially true in the credit markets. A salient example. In the United States, AAA rated municipal bonds and US Treasuries have a common history in this respect: for both instruments, the default rate for the previous century is zero. Nonetheless, the AAA muni has paid a higher interest rate—sometimes by as much as 250 basis points—over comparable treasuries with an identical coupon and maturity date. Moreover, the AAA municipal bond is free of federal income tax. Accordingly, an extremely profitable arbitrage from 2008 to the present has been to short US Treasuries and to use the money gleaned from the sale to buy comparable municipal bonds, thus capturing the difference or spread in interest rates. One reason for the persistent arbitrage spread is that it does not pay foreign governments to hold municipal bonds as opposed to the infinitely more liquid US Treasuries which can be sold instantaneously in the event that a nation's currency is under attack from speculators.

18. I have put on such trades some sixty-three times, a number that is instructive though too small to be statistically reliable. Of those sixty-three trades, in all but one instance the puts expired worthless. The one exception was a bet on the now infamous Enron, whose stock cratered after it was discovered that it had falsified its accounting records. Enron also illustrates why fund managers are willing to buy what they know is overpriced insurance. Thankfully, I only work for myself and already have a day job.

19. In 1933, Kolmogorov set out in remarkable fashion the set theoretic foundations of modern probability theory. Note that the Black-Scholes equation for implied volatility is really only a permutation of the *backward Kolmogorov equation*, which sets out a means for determining the transition probability density function for a stochastic process. The permutation is that BS substitutes the discount rate r for the drift rate u. The basis for the substitution is that inasmuch as we can always perfectly hedge a portfolio we should not be rewarded for taking unnecessary risks.

20. For example, Hull and White (1987) argue that adding a stochastic volatility measure would improve the accuracy of the equation. But this improvement would require determination of two more parameters, the volatility of volatility and the correlation between the volatility and an indicator of the underliers price. Both of which are well neigh impossible.

21. When I sat down with two active derivative traders and went through how a deterministic volatility model works, they looked at us with a mixture of bemusement, puzzlement, and a dash of incredulity that anyone would think this was an accurate reflection of the real practice of trading. Traders as a group tend to know very little, nor do they care to know, anything about finance economics.

22. One thinks here of books such as *Liquidity and Crisis* (edited by Allen, Carletti, Krahman, and Tyrell 2011), whose purpose is to address the fact that an "important reason for the global impact of the 2007 financial crisis is massive illiquidity in combination with an extreme exposure of economically and politically relevant parties to liquidity needs and market conditions" ("Introduction," p. 3). This gesture toward the real world notwithstanding, the articles cannot escape their intellectual heritage. They pivot around formulations such as a "decline in the supply of liquidity" (Allen and Gale 2011:112), "aggregate liquidity risk" (Bhattacharya and Gale 2011), the misbehavior of the value of money [as in "the value of money is not well behaved" (Allen, Carletti, et al. 2011:11)], and a plethora of other terms and noun phrases that treat concrete social relations as though they were abstract objects. From a social standpoint, four methodological tropes lie at the heart of finance economics. (1) Concrete social relations are transformed into abstract objects (e.g., liquidity) which are imputed to have a life of their own. (2) These abstract objects then interact with abstract general agents constructed by bracketing the specific social and economic characteristics of the concrete agents. In *Liquidity and Crisis*, the abstract agent, "financial intermediaries," encompasses institutions that are fundamentally dissimilar and had extraordinary different relations to the market's construction of liquidity. The abstract agent, financial intermediary, encompasses institutions as dissimilar as investment banks like Goldman Sachs, non-bank banks like GE Capital, hedge funds such as Soros Investment, Vanguard Mutual Funds, the Baton Rouge Community Savings Bank, and the California State Pension Fund. (3) The concrete agents that comprise the abstract agent are posited as behaving uniformly in respect to the abstract objects, because they all behave as economically rational, utility maximizing entities in a hypostatized economy. (4) This allows for the production of imaginary ethnography in which an author will declare, for example, that a financial intermediary faced with a certain circumstance (e.g., increased risk) will invariably behave in a certain manner (e.g., implement hedging strategies). Historically speaking, sometimes so, sometimes not, which begs the question of what actually determines their behavior. Twenty-six articles and seven hundred pages later, the reader of *Liquidity and Crisis* is not one bit closer to understanding what about liquidity was instrumental in creating a real world crisis. Not once in all 707 pages is Goldman Sachs, Bear Stearns, AIG, Morgan Stanley, Lehman Brothers, or Fannie Mae even given so much as a mention.

There is no mention of agents speculatively-driven trading in CMOs and CDSs. Also absent is any mention of the political power of the financial sector to influence regulatory regimes and government responses to the crisis.

23. A real, albeit somewhat complex, example: A trader recognizes that due to a large stake in a security held by Berkshire Hathaway (Warren Buffett), his huge cash hoard and his intention to augment that stake if the price of the security falls, and that any number of well-endowed hedge funds mimic Buffett's trades, that that security will in all likelihood have a very smooth ride—mathematically appearing as a smooth curve—in the upcoming months. This price tranquility means that the manufacturing costs of a derivative through gamma rebalancing will be relatively inordinately low, producing an improved risk reward ratio. At the time of writing, this is the case for IBM. Note socially that the foundation of the trade is the trader's understanding of Buffett and even more so of how investors' respect for him inflects their investing behavior.

Chapter 10: Derivatives and Wealth

1. In response to the financial crisis, the economist Steve Keen has analyzed his own profession as follows. "It may astonish non-economists to learn that conventionally trained economists ignore the role of credit and private debt in the economy." And even those that do "do so from the perspective of an economic theory in which money and debt play no intrinsic role. An economic theory that ignores the role of money and debt cannot possible make sense of the complex, monetary credit-based economy in which we live. Yet that is the theory that has dominated economics or the last half century" (Keen 2011:6).

2. The political battle waged over the implementation of the Volcker rule exemplifies the struggle and difficulties of crafting a systemically safe derivatives market. Named after the former Federal Reserve chairman, the (Paul) Volcker rule would inhibit banks from making speculative wagers with shareholder monies. The financial sector sees the rule as too costly and constrictive. The Center for Capital Markets Competitiveness (actually, a lobbying arm of the US Chamber of Commerce) contends that the rule is a threat to the health of the financial industry, the overall stability of the economy, and American competitiveness on global capital markets (Protess and Eavis 2012:B4). The struggle for EuroAmerican regulators is to strike a balance between keeping the financial money machine in gear and preventing another systemic crisis.

3. Woody Allen tells a joke about going to his psychiatrist and complaining about a dream-like hallucination in which he lays golden eggs. When Woody says he fears what he is becoming, the psychiatrist asks if he might prescribe a medicine to contain the hallucinations. Woody replies that he would like that if only he didn't need the eggs so badly. The United States and Britain are in this same boat; they would like to regulate and corral derivatives, especially the most wildly speculative uses, but they need the financial eggs. The intrinsic problem, for which there is perhaps no solution, is that instituting just the right amount of regulation for a complex,

cloistered, and changing market is arguably the ultimate example of decision making under uncertainty.

4. Because these strategies of euphemization are so deeply embedded in the financial community, they can create a problem when its members need to communicate with the public and their congressional representatives. During the congressional hearings (2008) on an emergency rescue plan for the imperiled credit markets, neither Henry Paulson nor Ben Bernanke could explain what was happening without resorting to a language that was unintelligible to the uninitiated. Clarifications such as "CDO delinquencies impede liquidity flows in commercial paper operations" and "balance sheet capital contractions disincentives lending," which were meaningless to those outside finance and thus failed to convey to the electorate the gravity of the crisis.

5. The notion of rational expectations gains much of its explanatory power from the fact that it subscribes simultaneously to two competing explanations of human action. Adherents unknowingly commingle these explanations in the same account. In the first scheme, agents act volitionally based on their complete and well delineated knowledge of the market. In the second scheme, objective market mechanisms that lie outside the participants' purview (e.g., are discernible only through statistical analyses) cause them to consummate rational economic acts. In the first scheme, agents are the source of their own causation based on their rational calculation of known alternatives (e.g., probabilities); whereas in the second, causation occurs, as it were, behind the backs of the participants. All of this involves a theoretical sleight of hand. For the rational expectations paradigm presents post festum, an abstract account of what the participants would do in the market if they were driven exclusively by economic rationality as though this were an accurate concrete description of what agents actually do when, for example, they trade derivatives. (As the state has yet to demand a license), finance economists freely perform operations in which they transplant their logo-centric reasoning processes into the minds and bodies of traders. Because finance economics has attached itself to a narrow notion of rationality, scheme two becomes the logical fallback position when scheme one fails.

References

Akerlof, George, and Robert Shiller. (2009). *Animal Spirits*. New York: John Wiley & Sons.

Allen, F., E. Carlotti, et al. (2011). *Liquidity and Crisis*. Oxford: Oxford University Press.

Allen, Franklin, and Douglas Gale. (2011). "Financial Intermediaries and the Market." In *Liquidity and Crisis*, edited by F. Allen, E. Carlotti, et al., 78–110. Oxford: Oxford University Press.

Ancona, Deborah, and C. L. Chong. (1996). "Entrainment: Pace, Cycle, and Rhythm in Organizational Behavior." *Research in Organizational Behavior* 18:251–284.

Anderson, Benedict. (1983). *Imagined Communities*. London: Verso.

Arrighi, Giovanni. (1994). *The Long Twentieth Century*. London: Verso.

Austin, John. (1962). *How to Do Things with Words*. Cambridge: Cambridge University Press.

Ayache, Elie. (2010). *The Blank Swan: The End of Probability*. New York: John Wiley & Sons.

Bachelier, L. (1995 [1900]). *Theorie de la Speculation*. Paris: Jacques Gabay.

Bailey, Roy. (2001). *The Economics of Financial Markets*. Cambridge: Cambridge University Press.

Bamber, Bill, and Andrew Spencer. (2008). *Bear Trap: The Fall of Bear Stearns*. New York: Brick Tower Press.

Barth, James. (2009). *The Rise and Fall of the U.S. Mortgage and Credit Markets*. New York: John Wiley and Sons.

Berger, Peter, and Thomas Luckmann. (1967). *The Social Construction of Reality*. New York: First Anchor Books.

Bernanke, Ben, and Mark Gertler. (1999). "Monetary Policy and Asset Price Volatility." *Economic Review of the Federal Reserve Bank of Kansas City* (fourth quarter), 19–51.

Bernstein, Peter. (1992). *Capital Ideas: The Improbable Origins of Modern Wall Street*. New York: Free Press.

Bernstein, Peter. (1996). *Against the Gods: The Remarkable Story of Risk*. New York: John Wiley & Sons.

Bernstein, Peter. (2007). *Capital Ideas Evolving*. New York: John Wiley and Sons.

Bhattacharya, Sudipto, and Douglas Gale. (2011). "Preference Shocks, Liquidity, and Central Bank Policy." In *Liquidity and Crisis*, edited by F. Allen, E. Carlotti, et al., 33–50. Oxford: Oxford University Press.

Bjerg, Ole. (2014). *Making Money: The Philosophy of Crisis Capitalism*. Brooklyn, NY: Verso.

Black, Fischer. (1973). "Yes, Virginia There Is Hope: Tests of the Value Line Ranking System." *Financial Analysts Journal* 29:10–14.

Black, Fischer. (1975). "Fact and Fantasy in the Use of Options." *Financial Analysis Journal* 31:61–72.

Black, Fischer. (1986). "Noise." *Journal of Finance* 41:529–543.

Black, Fischer, and M. Scholes. (1973). "The Pricing of Options and Corporate Liabilities." *Journal of Political Economy* 81:637–659.

Bodansky, Jossef. (2005). *The Secret History of the Iraq War*. New York: Harper Collins.

Boltanski, Luc, and Eve Chiapello. (2005). *The New Spirit of Capitalism*. London: Verso.

Bookstaber, Richard. (2007). *A Demon of Their Own Design*. Hoboken, NJ: John Wiley & Sons.

Born, Brooksley. (1998). "Regulatory Responses to Risk in the OTC Derivatives Market." Speech given to the American Bar Association Section of Business Law. Washington, D.C., November 13.

Bourdieu, Pierre. (1977). *An Outline of a Theory of Practice*. Cambridge: Cambridge University Press.

Bourdieu, Pierre. (1991). *Language and Symbolic Power*. Cambridge, MA: Harvard University Press.

Bourdieu, Pierre. (1998). *Acts of Resistance: Against the Tyranny of the Market*. New York: The New Press.

Bourdieu, Pierre. (2000). *Pascalian Meditations*. Stanford, CA: Stanford University Press.

Bourdieu, Pierre (2005). *The Social Structures of the Economy*. London: Polity Press.

Boutang, Yann Moulier. (2011). *Cognitive Capitalism*. London: Polity Press.

Brooks, John. (1987). *The Takeover Game*. New York: Truman Talley Books.

Bryan, Dick, and M. Rafferty. (2006). *Capitalism with Derivatives. A Political Economy of Financial Derivatives, Capital and Class*. New York: Palgrave Macmillan.

Bryan, Dick, and M. Rafferty. (2013). "Fundamental Value: A Category in Transformation." *Economy and Society* 42:130–153.

Bryan, Dick, and M. Rafferty. (2015). "Decomposing Money: Ontological Options and Spreads." *Journal of Cultural Economy* 9:27–42.

Bryan, Dick, M. Rafferty, and C. Jefferis. (2015). "Risk and Value: Finance, Labor, and Production." *The South Atlantic Quarterly* 114:307–329.

Calhoun, Craig. (2011). "From the Current Crisis to Possible Futures." In *Business as Usual*, edited by Craig Calhoun and Georgi Derluguian, 1–27. New York: Social Science Research Institute.

Callon, Michel. (1998). *The Laws of the Market*. London: Blackwell Publishers.

Callon, Michel. (2007). "What Does It Mean to Say That Economics Is Performative?" In *Do Economists Make Markets?*, edited by Donald MacKenzie, F. Muniesa, and L. Siu, 311–357. Princeton, NJ: Princeton University Press.

Calvo, Guillermo, A. Izquierdo, and L. F. Mjia. (2004). *On the Empirics of Sudden Stops: The Relevance of Balance Sheet Effects*. Cambridge: National Bureau of Economic Research.

Caputo, Philip. (2006). *A Rumor of War*. New York: Henry Holt and Company.

Carruthers, Bruce, and Arthur Stinchcombe. (1999). "The Social Structure of Liquidity: Flexibility, Markets, and States." *Theory and Society* 28:353–382.

Cassidy, John. (2009). *How Markets Fail: The Logic of Economic Calamities*. New York: Farrar, Straus and Giroux.

Ciulla, Joanne. (2000). *The Working Life: The Promise and Betrayal of Modern Work*. New York: Three Rivers Press.

Cohan, William. (2009). *House of Cards: A Tale of Hubris and Wretched Excess on Wall Street*. New York: Doubleday.

Daly, Michael. (2009). "Pin AIG Woes on Brooklyn Boy: Joseph Cassano Walked away with $315 Million while Company Staggered." *New York Daily News*, March 17.

Das, Satyajit. (2011). *Extreme Money: Masters of the Universe and the Cult of Risk*. New York: FT Press.

Davis, Gerald. (2009). *Managed by the Markets*. Oxford: Oxford University Press.

Derman, Emanuel. (2004). *My Life as a Quant: Reflections on Physics and Finance*. New York: John Wiley & Sons.

Derman, Emanuel. (2012). *Models, Behaving Badly*. New York: Free Press.

Derman, Emanuel. (2016). "Remarks on Financial Models." In *Derivatives and the Wealth of Societies*, edited by Benjamin Lee and Randy Martin, 199–239. Chicago: University of Chicago Press.

Derman, Emanuel, and I. Kani. (1994). "Riding on a Smile." *Risk* 7:32–39.

Derman, Emanuel, and I. Kani. (1994). "The Volatility Smile and Its Implied Tree." *Quantitative Strategies and Research Notes*. New York: Goldman Sachs.

Dominus, Susan. (2012). "Exile on Park Avenue: How the JP Morgan Chase Trading Fiasco Took Down the Most Powerful Woman on Wall Street." *New York Times Magazine*, October 7, p. 33–39, 54–55.

Dosse, Francois. (1997). *History of Structuralism*. 2 vols. Minneapolis: University of Minnesota Press.

El-Erian. Mohamed. (2008). *When Markets Collide*. New York: McGraw Hill.

Elias, Norbert. (1978). *The Civilizing Process*. Oxford: Oxford University Press.

Evanoff, Douglas, G. Kaufman, and A. Malliaris, eds. (2012). *New Perspectives on Asset Price Bubbles*. Oxford: Oxford University Press.

Faber, David (2009). *And Then the Roof Caved In*. Hoboken, NJ: John Wiley & Sons.

Fama, Eugene. (1976). *Foundations of Finance*. New York: Basic Books.

Fama, Eugene. (1991). "The Cross Section of Expected Stock Returns." Working paper no. 333. Chicago: Center for Research in Security Prices.

Filardo, Andrew. (2012). "The Impact of the International Financial Crisis on Asia and the Pacific." In *New Perspectives on Asset Price Bubbles*, edited by D. Evanoff, G. Kaufman, and A. G. Malliaris, 138–169. Oxford: Oxford University Press.

Fisher, Irving. (1928). *The Money Illusion*. New York: Adelphi.

Fleckenstein, William. (2008). *Greenspan's Bubbles: The Age of Ignorance at the Federal Reserve*. New York: McGraw Hill.

Fligstein, Neil. (2001). *The Architecture of Markets*. Princeton, NJ: Princeton University Press.

Fox, Justin. (2009). *The Myth of the Rational Market*. New York: Harper Collins.

Fraser, Steve. (2004). *Every Man a Speculator: A History of Wall Street in American Life*. New York: Harper Collins.

Freedman, Seth. (2009). *Binge Trading*. New York: Penguin Books.

Friedman, Milton (1971). "The Need for a Futures Market in Currencies." *Cato Journal* 31 (3): 635–641.

Gamst, Frederick. (1995). *Meanings of Work*. Albany: State University of New York Press.

Gass, S., and A. Assad. (2005). *An Annotated Timeline of Operational Research: An Informal History*. New York: Kluwer Academic Pub.

Gatheral, J. (2006). *The Volatility Surface*. New York: John Wiley & Sons.

Geanakoplos, John. (2011). "Leverage and Bubbles: The Need to Manage the Liquidity Cycle." Reprinted in *New Perspectives on Asset Price Bubbles*, edited by D. Evanoff, G. Kaufman, and A. Malliaris, 387–406. Oxford: Oxford University Press.

Geertz, Clifford. (1973). *The Interpretation of Cultures*. New York: Basic Books.

Geertz, Clifford. (1995). *After the Fact*. Cambridge, MA: Harvard University Press.

Geithner, Timothy. (2014). *Stress Test: Reflections on the Financial Crisis*. New York: Crown Publishers.

Granovetter, Mark (1985). "Economic Action and Social Structure: The Problem of Embeddedness." *American Journal of Sociology* 91:485–510.

Gray, John. (2009). "We Simply Don't Know!" *London Review of Books* 31 (21): 13–14.

Greenspan, Alan. (2007). *The Age of Turbulence: Adventures in a New World*. New York: Penguin.

Greider, William. (1987). *The Secrets of the Temple: How the Federal Reserve Runs the Country*. New York: Simon and Schuster.

Harvey, David. (1989). *The Conditions of Postmodernity*. Oxford: Basil Blackwell.

Harvey, David. (2000). *Spaces of Hope*. Berkeley: University of California Press.

Harvey, David. (2010). *A Companion to Marx's Capital*. London: Verso.

Ho, Karen. (2010). *Liquidated*. Chicago: University of Chicago Press.

Hudson, Michael. (2013). *The Bubble and Beyond: Fictitious Capital, Debt Deflation and Global Crisis*. Dresden: ISLET.

Hunt, P. J., and J. E. Kennedy. (2000). *Financial Derivatives in Theory and Practice*. New York: John Wiley & Sons.

Irwin, Neil. (2014). "Economic Expansion for Everyone? Not Anyone." *The New York Times*, September 27, B1, 5.

Jameson, Fredric. (1991). *Postmodernism: The Cultural Logic of Late Capitalism*. Durham, NC: Duke University Press.

Josse, Jeremy. (2015). *Dinosaur Derivatives and Other Trades*. New York: John Wiley & Sons.

Karpik, Lucian. (2010). *Valuing the Unique: The Economics of Singularities*. Princeton, NJ: Princeton University Press.

Kay, John. (2009). "What a Carve Up." *Financial Times*, August 1–2, 12.

Keen, Steve. (2011). *Debunking Economics*. London: Zed Books.

Keynes, John Maynard. (1930). *A Treatise on Money*. 2 vols.

Khurana, Rakesh. (2002). *Searching for a Corporate Savior*. Princeton, NJ: Princeton University Press.

Khurana, Rakesh. (2007). *From Hirer Aims to Hired Hands: The Social Transformation of the American Business School and the Unfulfilled Promise of Management as a Profession*. Princeton, NJ: Princeton University Press.

Kim, D., M. Loretan, and E. Remolona. (2010). "Contagion and Risk Premia in the Amplification of Crisis: Evidence from Asian names in the Global CDS Market." BIS paper 52:318–339.

Kim, S., and S. Kim. (2000). "Financial Panic and Exchange Rate Overhooting during a Financial Crisis." Retrieved from http://www.tufts.edu~skim20/paper/ero.pdf.

Kindleberger, C. (2005). *Manias, Panics, and Crashes: A History of Financial Crisis*. New York: Wiley.

Knight, Frank. (1921). *Risk, Uncertainty, and Profit*. New York: Houghton Mifflin Co.

Knight, Frank. (1956). *On the History and Method of Economics*. Chicago: University of Chicago Press.

Knight, Frank. (1999). *What Is Truth in Economics?* Chicago: University of Chicago Press.

Knorr Cetina, Karin, and U. Bruegger. (2002). "Global Microstructures: The Virtual Societies of Financial Markets." *American Journal of Sociology* 107:905–951.

Knorr Cetina, Karin, and A. Preda, eds. (2001). *The Sociology of Financial Markets*. Oxford: Oxford University Press.

Konings, Martijn. (2011). *The Development of American Finance*. Cambridge: Cambridge University Press.

Kripke, Saul. (1972). "Naming and Necessity." In *Semantics of Natural Language*, edited by D. Davidson and Gilbert Harman, 253–355. Boston, MA: D. Reidel.

Krugman, Paul. (2014). "The Dismal Science. Review of *Seven Bad Ideas: How Mainstream Economists Have Damaged America and the World*." *New York Times Book Review*, September 28, 1, 26.

Latour, Bruno. (2005). *Resembling the Social: An Introduction to Actor-Network Theory*. Oxford: Oxford University Press.

Lazzarato, Maurizio. (2011). *The Making of Indebted Man*. Los Angles: Semiotext(e).

Le Goff, Jacques. (1980). *Time, Work, and Culture in the Middle Ages*. Chicago: University of Chicago Press.

Leinweber, David. (2009). *Nerds on Wall Street: Math, Machines and Wired Markets*. New York: John Wiley & Sons.

Levi-Strauss, Claude. (1969). *The Elementary Structures of Kinship*. New York: Beacon Press.

Lewis, Michael (1989). *Liar's Poker: Rising through the Wreckage of Wall Street*. New York: W. W. Norton and Co.

Lewis, Michael. (1999). "How the Eggheads Cracked." *New York Times Magazine*, January 24.

Lewis, Michael. (2009). *Panic: The Story of Modern Financial Insanity*. New York: Norton and Company.

Lewis, Michael. (2010). *The Big Short*. New York: W. W. Norton and Co.

Li, David. (2000). "On Default Correlation: A Copula Function Approach." *Journal of Fixed Income* (March): 43–54.

LiPuma, Edward. (1998). "Modernity and Forms of Personhood in Melanesia." In *Bodies and Persons: Comparative Perspectives from Africa and Melanesia*, edited by Michael Lambek and Andrew Strathern, 53–79. Cambridge: Cambridge University Press.

LiPuma, Edward. (2000). *Encompassing Others: The Magic of Modernity in Melanesia*. Ann Arbor: University of Michigan.

LiPuma, Edward. (2015). *Burnt Offerings: Observations on the Financial Crisis*. Unpublished manuscript.

LiPuma, Edward. (2016). "Ritual in Financial Life." In *Derivatives and the Wealth of Society*, edited by Benjamin Lee and Randy Martin, 37–81. Chicago: University of Chicago Press.

LiPuma, Edward, and Thomas Koelbl. (2009). "Currency Devaluations and Consolidating Democracy: The Example of the South African Rand." *Economy and Society* 38:203–229.

LiPuma, Edward, and Benjamin Lee. (2004). *Financial Derivatives and the Globalization of Risk*. Durham, NC: Duke University Press.

LiPuma, Edward, and Benjamin Lee. (2005). "Financial Derivatives and the Rise of Circulation." *Economy and Society* 34:404–427.

LiPuma, Edward, and Benjamin Lee. (2012). "A Social Approach to the Financial Derivatives Markets." *The South Atlantic Quarterly* 111:289–316.

Lopez, Linette. (2015). "How Wall Street Bonuses Have Exploded since 1986." *Business Insider*, March 11.

Lowenstein, Roger. (2004). *Origins of the Crash: The Great Bubble and Its Undoing*. New York: Penguin Press.

MacKenzie, Donald. (2006). *An Engine, Not a Camera: How Financial Models Shape Markets*. Cambridge: MIT Press.

MacKenzie, Donald. (2011). "The Credit Crisis as a Problem in the Sociology of Knowledge." *American Journal of Sociology* 116:1778–1841.

MacKenzie, Donald, F. Muniesa, and L. Siu. (2007), eds. *Do Economists Make Markets?* Princeton, NJ: Princeton University Press.

Madrick, Jeff. (2011). *Age of Greed: The Triumph of Finance and the Decline of America, 1970 to the Present*. New York: Alfred Knopf.

Mandelbrot, Benoit. (1991). "When Can Price Be Arbitrated Efficiently: A Limit to the Validity of the Random Walk and Martingale Model." *Review of Economics and Statistics* 53:225–236.

Mandelbrot, Benoit. (1997). *Fractals and Scaling in Finance: Discontinuity, Concentration, Risk*. New York: Springer.

Marazzi, Christian. (2011). *The Violence of Financial Capitalism*. Los Angeles: Semiotext(e).

Markowitz, Harry. (1959). *Portfolio Selection: Efficient Diversification of Investments.* New Haven, CT: Yale University Press.

Martin, Frank. (2006). *Speculative Contagion.* Bloomington, IN: Author House.

Martin, Randy. (2002). *Financialization of Daily Life.* Philadelphia: Temple University Press.

Martin, Randy. (2013). "After Economy? Social Logis of the Derivative." *Social Text* 31:83–106.

Martin, Randy. (2015a). *Knowledge LTD: Toward a Social Logic of the Derivative.* Philadelphia: Temple University Press.

Martin, Randy. (2015b). "Money after Decolonization." *South Atlantic Quarterly* 114:377–393.

McDonald, Lawrence. (2009). *A Colossal Failure of Common Sense: The Inside Story of the Collapse of Lehman Brothers.* New York: Random House.

McLean, Bethany, and Joe Nocera (2010). *All the Devils Are Here: The Hidden History of the Financial Crisis.* New York: Penguin.

Mehrling, Perry. (2000). "Minsky and Modern Finance: The Case of Long-Term Capital Management." *Journal of Portfolio Management* (winter): 81–88.

Mehrling, Perry. (2005). *Fischer Black and the Revolutionary Idea of Finance.* New York: John Wiley & Sons.

Meister, Robert. (2016). "Liquidity." In *Derivatives and the Wealth of Societies*, edited by Benjamin Lee and Randy Martin, 143–173. Chicago: University of Chicago Press.

Merton, Robert. (1992). *Continuous Time Stochastic Models.* London: MacMillan Press.

Miller, Merton. (1997). *Merton Miller on Derivatives.* New York: John Wiley & Sons.

Milken, Michael. (2000). "The Vision: How Access to Capital Has Fueled the New Economy." *California Lawyer* (July): 5–59, 90.

Minsky, Hyman. (2008). *Stabilizing an Unstable Economy.* New Haven, CT: Yale University Press.

Mirowski, Philip. (1989). *More Heat than Light.* Cambridge: Cambridge University Press.

Mirowski, Philip. (2010). *Never Let a Serious Crisis Go to Waste: How Neoliberalism Survived the Financial Meltdown.* London: Verso.

Morgenson, Gretchen. (2007). "There's No Superhero Waiting in the Wings." *New York Times*, November 11.

Morgenson, Gretchen. (2012). "Anger at Goldman Still Simmers." *New York Times*, March 26.

Morgenson, Gretchen, and Joshua Rosner. (2011). *Reckless Endangerment: How Outsized Ambition, Greed, and Corruption Led to Economic Armageddon.* New York: Times Books.

Morris, Charles. (2008). *The Trillion Dollar Meltdown: Easy Money, High Rollers, and the Great Credit Crash.* New York: Public Affairs.

Mullins, David. (1982). "Does the Capital Asset Pricing Model Work?" *Harvard Business Review* (January-February): 105–113.

Nesvetailova, Anastasia. (2010). *Financial Alchemy in Crisis: The Great Liquidity Illusion.* London: Pluto Press.

North, Douglas. (1977). "Economic Growth: What Have We Learned from the Past?" *Carnegie-Rochester Conference Series on Public Policy* 6: 1–14.

Offit, Michael. (2009). The Root of the Recession. *Vanity Fair* (October).

O'Sullivan, Arthur, and Steven Sheffrin. (2003). *Economics: Principles and Tools*, 3rd ed. Upper Saddle River, NJ: Prentice Hall.

Panitch, Leo, and Sam Gindin. (2012). *The Making of Global Capitalism*. London: Verso.

Partnoy, Frank. (2003). *Infectious Greed: How Deceit and Risk Corrupted the Financial Markets*. New York: Profile.

Patterson, Scott. (2010). *The Quants*. New York: Crown Business.

Piketty, Thomas. (2014). *Capital in the Twenty-First Century*. Cambridge, MA: Harvard University Press.

Planes, Alex. (2013). "The Most Valuable Formula Ever Created." www.fool.com /investing/ genera12013.

Paulson, Henry. (2009). *On the Brink: Inside the Race to Stop the Collapse of the Global Financial System*. New York: Business Plus.

Poole, D., and A. Mackworth (2010). *Artificial Intelligence*. Cambridge: Cambridge University Press.

Postone, Moishe. (2003). *Time, Labor, and Social Domination: A Reinterpretation of Marx's Critical Theory*. Cambridge: Cambridge University Press.

Postone, Moishe. (2012). "Thinking the Global Crisis." *North Atlantic Quarterly* 18:227–249.

Postone, Moishe (2014). "The Task of Critical Theory Today: Rethinking the Critique of Capitalism and its Futures." In *Globalization, Critique and Social Theory: Diagnoses and Challenges* (Current Perspectives in Social Theory, vol. 33), edited by Harry F. Dahms, 3–28. Bingley, UK: Emerald Group.

Ranieri, Lewis. (1996). "The Origins of Securitization, Sources of Its Growth, and Its Future Potential." In *A Primer on Securitization*, edited by Leon Kendall and M. Fishman, 31–43. Cambridge: MIT Press.

Rappaport, Roy. (1979). *Ecology, Meaning, and Religion*. Richmond, VA: North Atlantic Books.

Rappaport, Roy. (1999). *Ritual and Religion in the Making of Humanity*. Cambridge: Cambridge University Press.

Ridley, Matt. (2007). "Letter to the Editor." *Economist*, September 29.

Rodrik, Dani. (2007). *One Economics, Many Recipes: Globalization, Institutions, and Economic Growth*. Princeton: Princeton University Press.

Roose, Kevin. (2014). *Young Money: Inside the Hidden World of Wall Street's Post-Crash Recruits*. New York: Grand Central Publishing.

Rosenberg, Hans. (1943). "Political and Social Consequences of the Great Depression of 1873–1896 in Central Europe." *The Economic History Review* 13:58–73.

Rubinstein, Mark. (2006). *A History of the Theory of Investments*. Hoboken. NJ: John Wiley & Sons.

Sahlins, Marshall. (1972). *Stone Age Economics*. Chicago: Aldine-Atherson.

Sahlins, Marshall. (1976). *Culture and Practical Reason*. Chicago: University of Chicago Press.

Samuelson, Paul. (1948). *Economics: An Introduction*. New York: McGraw-Hill.

Sandor, Richard. (2012). *Good Derivatives*. New York: John Wiley & Sons.

Schama, Simon. (1988). *An Embarrassment of Riches: An Interpretation of Dutch Culture in the Golden Age*. Berkeley: University of California Press.

Scheinkman, Jose, and Wei Xiong. (2012). "Overconfidence and Asset Price Bubbles." In *New Perspectives on Asset Price Bubbles*, edited by Douglas Evanoff, G. Kaufman, and A. Malliaris, 283–317. Oxford: Oxford University Press.

Schull, Natasha. (2012). *Addiction by Design*. Princeton, NJ: Princeton University Press.

Segal, David. (2012). "Romney's Go-To Economist." *New York Times*, October 14, BU1, 4.

Sahlins, Marshall. (1985). *Culture and Practical Reason*. Chicago: University of Chicago Press.

Sewell, William. (2005). *Logics of History*. Chicago: University of Chicago Press.

Sorkin, Andrew Ross. (2009). *Too Big to Fail: The Inside Story of How Wall Street and Washington Fought to Save the Financial System—and Themselves*. New York: Viking.

Soros, George. (2008). *The New Paradigm for Financial Markets*. New York: Public Affairs.

Story, Louise, and Landon Thomas J. (2009). "Tales from Lehman's Crypt." *New York Times*, September 13, BU1, 7.

Strathern, Marilyn. (1988). *The Gender of the Gift*. Cambridge: Cambridge University Press.

Taleb, Nassim. (1997). *Dynamic Hedging: Managing Vanilla and Exotic Options*. New York: John Wiley & Sons.

Taleb, Nassim. (2005). *Fooled by Randomness*. New York: Random House.

Taleb, Nassim. (2007). *The Black Swan: The Impact of the Highly Improbable*. New York: Random House.

Taleb, Nassim. (2008). "Infinite Variance and the Problems of Practice." *Complexity* 14: 7–9

Taleb, Nassim. (2012). *Antifragile: Things That Gain from Disorder*. New York: Random House.

Tambiah, Stanley. (1985). "A Performative Approach to Ritual." *Proceedings of the British Academy* 65:113–169.

Tavakoli, Janet. (2003). *Collateralized Debt Obligations & Structured Finance: New Developments in Cash & Synthetic Securitization*. Hoboken, NJ: John Wiley & Sons.

Taylor, Charles. (1989). *Sources of the Self*. Cambridge, MA: Harvard University Press.

Taylor, Charles. (2002). "Modern Social Imaginaries." *Public Culture* 14:91–124.

Taylor, Charles. (2004). *Social Imaginaries*. Durham, NC: Duke University Press.

Tett, Gillian. (2009). *Fool's Gold*. New York: Free Press.

Triana, Pablo. (2009). *Lecturing Birds on Flying*. New York: John Wiley & Sons.

Turner, Victor. (1967). *Forest of Symbols: Aspects of Ndembu Ritual*. Ithaca, NY: Cornell University Press.

Turner, Victor. (1969). *The Ritual Process*. Chicago: Aldine.

Udland, Myles (2015). The Market Is Getting Nervous about Something Experts Are Struggling to Define. *Business Insider*, April 26.

Vogel, Harold. (2010). *Financial Market Bubbles and Crashes*. Cambridge: Cambridge University Press.

Van Gannep, Arnold. (1960 [1909]). *The Rites of Passage*. Chicago: Chicago University Press.

Wagner, Roy. (1972). *Habu: The Invention of Meaning in Daribi Religion*. Chicago: University of Chicago Press.

Wagner, Roy. (1974). "Are There Social Groups in the New Guinea Highlands?" In *Frontiers of Anthropology*, edited by Murray Leaf, 95–122. New York: Van Nostrand Company.

Wagner, Roy. (1988). "Visible Sociality: The Daribi Community." In *Mountain Paupans*, edited by J. Weiner, 39–72. Ann Arbor: University of Michigan Press.

Wallerstein, Emmanuel. (1974). *The Modern World System*. New York: Academic Press.

Weber, Max. (1958 [1904]). *The Protestant Ethic and the Spirit of Capitalism*. Translated by Talcott Parsons New York: Charles Scribner's Sons.

Weber, Max. (1978 [1918]). *Economy and Society*. Berkeley: University of California Press.

Wessel, David. (2009). *In Fed We Trust: Ben Bernanke's War on the Great Panic*. New York: Random House.

Wilmott, Paul. (2007). *Paul Wilmott Introduces Quantitative Finance*. New York: John Wiley & Sons.

Zaloom, Caitlin. (2003). "Ambiguous Numbers, Trading Technologies, and Interpretation in the Financial Markets." *American Ethnologist* 30:258–72.

Zandi, Mark. (2009). *Financial Shock: Global Panic and Government Bailouts*. Upper Saddle River, NJ: FT Press.

Index

abstract risk, 30, 34, 49, 58–63, 74, 144, 254, 373n10; compared to abstract labor, 61, 252; versus concrete risk, 59–60; as a social mediation, 60; and time, 157; volatility function of, 254

accuracy: definition of, 367n4

Akerlof, George, and Robert Schiller, 112, 299, 300

American International Group, 3, 132

animal spirits, 112; critique of, 299–301

anthropology, 17–18; and economics, 200–207, 363n15; and ethnography, 100; Melanesian example of performativity, 217–19

arbitrage, 56, 238, 251; Black-Scholes, 314–16; in economistic theories, 325–26

Arrighi, Giovanni, 361–62n5

Ayache, Eli, 56–57, 171–73, 175, 203, 275; on contingency, 171–72, 368n1

Bailey, Roy, 325

Bank for International Settlements, 83

Bernanke, Benjamin, 123, 342, 365–66n7

Bjerg, Ole, 39, 51–52

Black, Fischer, 192, 311, 381n1

Black-Scholes formula, 41, 55, 193, 253, 315; and complete markets, 326; equation, 314–15; and implied volatility, 307–12; importance of, 304–5; and the market, 327–28; as a modular form, 333–34; and risk free interest rates, 327; social entailments of, 320–30; in social practice, 330–31; underlying assumptions, 315–17

Bourdieu, Pierre, 20, 116, 202, 248, 250, 275, 280, 301, 367n1; economistic theories, 362n9; concept of habitus 283–84, 364n3; on language and power, 344–45

Bretton Woods System, 68

Bryan, Dick, and R. Rafferty, 32, 36, 51

Buffett, Warren, 248, 263, 369n7

Callon, Michael, 181, 369n5

capital, 6, 240, 345–49; global expansion of, 36; and labor, 29, 270–74; its reorganization, 69, 89–90; and speculation, 21, 46. See also speculative capital

capitalism, 20, 29, 137; contradictions of, 66; and finance, 1; globalized, 65, 67–68; and the lure of gambling, 379n7; and nation-state based production, 32–33; and primitive economies, 199–200, 371n6; production-centric, 92; as a sociohistorically specific form, 11–12

Cassano, Joseph, 298

circulation, 3, real relations of 104; in respect to production 29, 66, 109, 119

contagion, 33, 126, 336

convexity, 37, 51

counterparty, 124; character of, 123; and risk, 222, 307

culture of financial circulation, 1, 63; duplex structure of, 90–91 derivatives, 1, 6; attempts to define, 31, 357n1; basic design, 28–29, 33, 36; versus bonds, 40; classification of, 190; versus commodities, 36–37, 39–40, 47–48; contract, 29–30; and crisis, 1–2, 50–57; driven capitalism, 1, 2, 42–44; and everyday life, 341–44; exchange value of, 49; genesis of, 64–70; influence on production, 29, 90; key principles, 29, 31, 35, 125; and leverage, 136, 154; and money, 51–53, 358–59n7; motivation for, 56; over-the-counter (OTC) 164; and politics, 2, 55; pricing of, 44, 162, 191–192, 320; productions of knowledge of, 102–3; as promissory note, 30; recursive aspect, 149–50; as a refutation of the economistic view, 302; securitization, 127–28, 131; social epistemology of, 46; as social relations, 74, 99–101; and speculation, 250–51; and speculative capital, 54; symbiosis of tool and user, 196; systemic character of, 187–88; temporality of, 144–69; value 5, 54; and volatility, 37, 57; as wagers on volatility, 37; and wealth, 53, 339–40; and work, 271–72

Derman, Emanuel, 18, 147, 203, 304, 306, 310, 318, 357n12, 367n2, 382n6

Division of Scientific Labor, 105, 114

Dodd, Frank, 76

economistic financial theory, 82, 83, 95, 100, 109–10, 208; account of motivation, 267–68, 279; annulment of performativity, 224; and behavioral economics, 372n5; belief-desire model of agency, 269–70; and derivatives, 103–4, 115, 172, 190–91, 319–20; efficient market thesis, 18, 104, 189, 223, 350–51; emancipation from, 347; genesis of, 193–94; methodological

tropes, 349–50; models of the market, 117–18, 137–39, 160, 162; notion of complete market, 326; and social practice, 380–81n14; as a robust illusion, 225; and utility maximization, 122

El-Erian, Mohammad, 135

European Central Bank (ECB), 149

Federal Reserve Bank, 82, 87, 111, 149

Federer, Roger, 368–69n2

Financial Crisis Inquiry Report, 96, 148

financial crisis of 2008, 3, 4, 6, 13; and Barack Obama, 86; and belief, 224; centrality of, 6; deleveraging cycles, 125–26; dimensions of, 84–88; explanations of, 95–98, 137, 246–48, 279, 298–302; forerunner of, 150; importance of, 288; innovation of, 127–32; and liquidity, 122–27; mechanics of the crisis, 132–38; and production, 84–85; scholarship of, 108–14; systemic failure, 136; types of crisis, 8–11; use of leverage, 135

financial field, 15, 49–51; character of, 14–15; contagion, 33; and the creation of subjectivities, 294–97; design of 289–90, 301; dimensions of temporality, 146–48; and mathematization, 56; opting out, 297; play of risk and uncertainty, 44; privatization of risk, 68; self-understanding, 12; and trading styles, 293

financial habitus, 92, 101, 176, 274, 364n3; asociality of, 295; compression of time, 294–95; of derivative traders, 334–35; production of, 121, 276–78; of risk taking, 257–58; socialized habitus, 274–75; and solidarity, 378n2; and work, 121; and the workplace, 268

financial ideology, 41, 44, 46–47, 50, 75, 147; bases of, 194; illusio, 103–5, 149, 178, 194, 350; mathematization, 93,

193; misrecognition of, 186–87, 249, 254, 259; motivation of and practice, 122, 250, 331

financial institutions: conversion of partnerships into corporations, 35–36; control over time, 283–84; and corporations, 77; creation of subjectivities, 279–80; culture of, 283; hierarchy of positions within, 276; initiation process, 284–85; relation of traders to quants, 290; relation of traders to risk managers, 291–92; rites of incorporation, 282–88

financial media, 23, 242, 273; composition of, 291–92; explanations of the 2008 crisis, 299–300, and shareholder value, 359–60n14

Foley, Duncan, 114

forthcoming, 38–39, 42, 145, 202; notions of, 159–60; and traders, 296

Freedman, Benjamin, 161

Gasparino, Charles, 265

Geanakoplos, John, 153–54

Geertz, Clifford, 236

Geithner, Timothy, 88, 361n3, 362n8

generative schemes, 31, 233–36, 276

globalization, 54–64

global markets, 34, 232

Goldman Sachs, 7, 35, 231, 337

governance, 29, 158, 339, 340, 362–63n11, 386n2

Grantham, Jeremy, 364n 17

Greenspan, Alan, 88, 123, 134, 136, 189, 356n6; and the efficient market, 194, 351, 361n3; and speculation, 258

Gross, William, 179

Harvey, David, 75

hedge funds, 35, 145, 151–52

hedging, 41–42, 233, 252, 314

Ho, Karen, 148, 184, 294, 295, 359n12

houses, 236; as financial assets, 75, 239

International Monetary Fund, 55

Kay, John, 272

Keynes, John Maynard, 13, 118, 163, 179, 192

Knight, Frank, 163, 192

Konings, Martin, 31, 232, 360–61n1

Lears, Jackson, 240

Lee, Benjamin, 23, 120, 374n1

Lewis, Michael, 134, 204, 243–45

liquidity, 9, 123, 132–33, 146, 179, 222, 366n9; definition of, 365n6; excess liquidity, 69; faith based, 223, 361n2; and volatility, 42, 168–69

Mackenzie, Donald, 45, 218, 226, 307, 310, 369–70n8

Mandelbrot, Benoit, 318–19, 383n13

market(s), 42, 43, 119, 172, 185, 197; and anonymous sociality, 183–84; appearance of, 180–86; asocial view of, 104, 138; belief in, 197–98; in the Black-Scholes equation, 327; complete market, 370n10; contagion process, 382n7; directional dynamic, 182; efficient market thesis, 104, 111; essentialist notion of, 171–72; and herd behavior, 375n2; irrationality of, 328–29; performative production of, 222–23; and performativity, 220–27; primitive versus capitalist, 201–2; productions of knowledge about, 101–8, 174; 173–76; recognition of, 186–91; as a relational category, 178; as the site of a speculative ethos, 241; theorization of, 170; as a totality, 174–75, 180–86, 197–98; and traders' practices, 174–75; viewed as a problematic, inherent rituality, 43, 197

marriage: performativity of, 214–19; ritualized exchange, 217, 219

Martin, Randy, 11, 26, 32, 55, 64, 81, 211, 248

Marx, Karl, 251–252; and derivatives, 363n12

Marxism, 15, 90; its concept of capitalism, 201–2; and crisis, 1, 3; and derivatives, 113, 358n3; and value, 54

Mehrling, Perry, 314

Meister, Robert, 352

Mirowski, Phillip, 363n13

money, 52, 54, 73–74, 130

monetized subjectivity, 107, 121, 267, 279–80, 293–94

Morgan Stanley, 35, 231; process driven trading, 164

neoclassical economics, 4, 7; and analysis, 20, 94; and censorship of heterodox views, 363n16; concept of capitalism, 201, 232; and crisis, 1, 11, 88, 91, 95; and the market, 171; view of money supply, 52–53

non-knowledge, 102–3

objectivist account of objectification, 83, 94, 211, 332

optionality, 351–53

Panitch, Leo and S. Grindin, 67

Pasani, Robert, 124, 205

Patterson, Scott, 145, 149, 165

performativity, 191; citational performativity, 217–18, 226; constitutive, 216–17, 223; and language, 209; and markets, 220–27; and objectification, 372–73n7; pragmatic performativity, 218; retrospective narrative performativity, 219–20, 226; and ritual, 207–14; and scientific models, 319; type-token performativity, 215–16, 220–21, 253, 319

Piketty, Thomas, 84

politics of misrecognition, 86, 192

Postone, Moishe, 27, 89, 109, 113, 173, 185, 232, 306, 361n4, 365n5

power: first law of, 88; second law of, 103; third law of, 111

production of knowledge, 82, 196; competing sources, 83; game within the game, 83

Ranieri, Louis, 128–30, 366n11

Rappaport, Roy, 210, 217

regulation, 78–79, 340–42

risk, 33, 54, 87; 90; management of, 238–39; modeling of, 290–91; objectification of, 46; versus uncertainty, 43, 45

Roose, Kevin, 287

Sandor, Richard, 126

shareholder value, 70–72, 128, 359n13

Smith, Adam, 336–37

social, the, 13–15, 89, 98; and agency, 357n13; and Black-Scholes formula, 305; and collective action, 118; concealment of, 92–94, removal and return, 192–97; structuring events, 208; theory of, 105, 118–19

social approach: concept of montage, 5; principles of, 141–43; theoretical turns, 15–17

social science, 4, 17; and crisis, 19; and modernity, 180; moral obligation of, 4; transformation of, 18

social theory, 2, 4, 14, 21, 114–15; conceptual basis, 15–17; defining speculation, 254; ground zero of, 238; and interactionist viewpoints, 237–38; and practice, 118–19; principles of, 141–42; production of markets, 120; theses, 2, 8, 24–25, 32, 65, 66, 91, 92, 130, 144, 146, 163–64, 167, 180, 203, 302; veiled expressions of, 123, 192; visualizing sociality, 99–101

speculation, 256; logic of 254; traders' accounts of, 265
speculative capital, 58, 64, 70, 152; in corporate America, 70–74; and derivatives, 54; institutionalization of, 75–79; relation of risk and uncertainty, 45; and risk, 46
speculative ethos, 30, 160, 166; and abstract risk, 254; and Christianity, 232–33; collusion between calculation and chance, 231; concept of ethos, 235–38; as a disposition, 234–35; dual narratives, 239–40; in respect to time and risk, 238–43; and play, 256–61; sociogenesis, 243; speculative investment vehicle (SIV), 70, 76, 159
spread phenomena, 15–17, 41; 45; as a basis of derivatives, 251; and derivative pricing, 311–12; and risk, 238; and speculative ethos, 244–46; transgressions of, 47; ubiquity of, 326
strategic intelligibility, 81, 82
systemic risk, 21, 32, 36, 65, 144, 155–56; leading to market failure, 167, 177, 254, 343–44, 358n3; and liquidity, 362n6; mediation of connectivity, 62

Taleb, Nassim, 172, 326
temporality, 37, 145, compression of time, 152–53; and contingency, 158–69; and credit money, 52; practical use of, 145–46; of risk, 156–58; and uncertainty, 42

Tett, Julian, 277
trading, 41, 42, 47, 176; motivations for 56; phenomenology of 174–75
totality, 254; and the Black-Scholes formula, 316; defined, 211; misrecognition of, 278; socially imagined, 119, 278, 370–71n14
treadmill effect, 135, 137, 145–52, 154–55, 182, 308–9; 1987 example, 150–51

uncertainty, 64, 126, 177, 229, 241; and the cash premium, 166; and certainty, 368n6; in Fibonacci, 375n4; and liquidity, 167; and nonknowledge, 236; production and management of, 160–66
underliers, 28–29, 31, 37–38

value, 114; self-valorizing, 74
Van Gennep, Arnold, 284
violence, 4, 25, 86
volatility, 37, 41, 68, 131, 147–48, 309; historical versus implied, 57; implied, 238; and liquidity, 42; and risk, 46; and uncertainly, 164; and wealth, 37, 50

wealth: and crisis, 7–8; and financial markets, 68; paradox of, 338–39; of society, 7, 113
Weber, Max, 202
Wilmott, Paul, 304, 310, 316–17, 383n11
work, 16, 270–74
World Bank, 55